Lecture Notes in Computer Science 6579

Commenced Publication in 1973
Founding and Former Series Editors:
Gerhard Goos, Juris Hartmanis, and Jan van Leeuwen

W0235105

Neil Spring   George F. Riley (Eds.)

Passive and Active Measurement

12th International Conference, PAM 2011
Atlanta, GA, USA, March 20-22, 2011
Proceedings

 Springer

Volume Editors

Neil Spring
University of Maryland, Department of Computer Science
College Park, MD 20742, USA
E-mail: nspring@cs.umd.edu

George F. Riley
Georgia Institute of Technology, School of Electrical and Computer Engineering
777 Atlantic Drive NW, Atlanta, GA 30332-0250, USA
E-mail: riley@ece.gatech.edu

ISSN 0302-9743   e-ISSN 1611-3349
ISBN 978-3-642-19259-3   ISBN 978-3-642-19260-9 (eBook)
DOI 10.1007/978-3-642-19260-9
Springer Heidelberg Dordrecht London New York

Library of Congress Control Number: 2011922045

CR Subject Classification (1998): C.2, H.4, K.6.5, D.2, D.4.6, E.3

LNCS Sublibrary: SL 5 – Computer Communication Networks and Telecommunications

Typesetting: Camera-ready by author, data conversion by Scientific Publishing Services, Chennai, India

Printed on acid-free paper

Springer is part of Springer Science+Business Media (www.springer.com)

Preface

The 2011 edition of the Passive and Active Measurement Conference was the 12th of a series of successful events. Since 2000, the Passive and Active Measurement (PAM) conference has provided a forum for presenting innovative, early work in Internet measurement. The event focuses on new research, measurement tools, large network data sets and analysis techniques. The conference's goal is to provide a forum for current work in its early stages. This year's conference was held at the Georgia Institute of Technology in Atlanta, Georgia.

PAM 2011 attracted 56 submissions. Each paper was reviewed by at least four members of the Technical Program Committee. After review, competitive papers were discussed online to reach consensus. The reviewing process led to the acceptance of 24 papers. The papers were arranged into seven sessions covering passive measurement, wireless models, bandwidth, automated bots, route avoidance, interdomain protocols, timing, and diagnosis.

We would like to thank the members of the Technical Program Committee for their thorough and timely reviews and for shepherding accepted papers as needed.

March 2010

Neil Spring
George Riley

Organization

Organizing Committee

General Chair — George Riley (Georgia Institute of Technology)
Program Chair — Neil Spring (University of Maryland)

Program Committee

Nevil Brownlee	University of Auckland, New Zealand
K.C. Claffy	CAIDA, USA
Amogh Dhamdhere	CAIDA, USA
Benoit Donnet	Université Catholique de Louvain, Belgium
Constantine Dovrolis	Georgia Institute of Technology, USA
Mehmet Gunes	University of Nevada, Reno, USA
Gianluca Iannaccone	Intel Research, USA
Arvind Krisnamurthy	University of Washington, USA
Aleksandar Kuzmanovic	Northwestern University, USA
Sridhar Machiraju	Google, USA
Alan Mislove	Northeastern University, USA
Ricardo Oliveira	Thousandeyes, USA
Dina Papagiannaki	Intel Research, USA
George Riley	Georgia Institute of Technology, USA
Eve Schooler	Intel Research, USA
Rob Sherwood	Deutsche Telekom Inc. R&D Lab, USA
Fernando Silveira	Technicolor, France
Joel Sommers	Colgate University, USA
Oliver Spatschek	AT&T Labs – Research, USA
Neil Spring	University of Maryland, USA
Nina Taft	Intel Research, USA
Arun Venkataramani	University of Massachusetts, USA
Walter Willinger	AT&T Labs – Research, USA

Steering Committee

Nevil Brownlee	University of Auckland, New Zealand
Ian Graham	Endace, New Zealand
Arvind Krishnamurthy	University of Washington, USA
Sue Moon	KAIST, Korea
Bernhard Plattner	ETH Zurich, Switzerland

George Riley   Georgia Institute of Technology, USA
Neil Spring   University of Maryland, USA
Renata Teixeira   LIP6, France

Additional Reviewers

Randolph Baden   University of Maryland, USA
Rob Beverly   Naval Postgraduate School, USA
Matthew Luckie   University of Waikato, New Zealand
Cristian Lumezanu   Georgia Institute of Technology, USA
Olaf Maennel   Loughborough University, UK
Kishore Ramachandran   NEC Labs, USA
Lixia Zhang   University of California, Los Angeles, USA

Table of Contents

Operating a Network Link at 100%

Changhyun Lee[1], DK Lee[1], Yung Yi[2], and Sue Moon[1]

[1] Department of Computer Science, KAIST, South Korea
[2] Department of Electrical Engineering, KAIST, South Korea

Abstract. Internet speed at the edge is increasing fast with the spread of fiber-based broadband technology. The appearance of bandwidth-consuming applications, such as peer-to-peer file sharing and video streaming, has made traffic growth a serious concern like never before. Network operators fear congestion at their links and try to keep them underutilized while no concrete report exists about performance degradation at highly utilized links until today. In this paper, we reveal the degree of performance degradation at a 100% utilized link using the packet-level traces collected at our campus network link. The link has been fully utilized during the peak hours for more than three years. We have found that per-flow loss rate at our border router is surprisingly low, but 30 ~ 50 msec delay is added. The increase in delay results in overall RTT increase and degrades user satisfaction for domestic web flows. Comparison of two busy traces shows that the same 100% utilization can result in different amount of performance loss according to the traffic conditions. This paper stands as a good reference to the network administrators facing future congestion in their networks.

1 Introduction

Video-driven emerging services, such as YouTube, IPTV, and other streaming media, are driving traffic growth in the Internet today. Explosive market expansion of smart phones is also adding much strain not only on the cellular network infrastructure but increasingly on the IP backbone networks. Such growth represents insatiable demand for bandwidth and some forecast IP traffic to grow four-fold from 2009 to 2014 [1]. Network service providers provision their networks and plan for future capacity based on such forecasts, but they cannot always succeed in avoiding occasional hot spots in their networks. However, traffic patterns in a network are usually confidential and few reports on hot spots are available to general public. Beheshti *et al.* report that one of the links in Level 3 Communications' operational backbone network was once utilized up to 96% [5]. A trans-Pacific link in Japan was fully utilized until 2006[1]. Choi *et al.* have reported on a link on the Sprint backbone operating above 80% and likely causing a few moments of congestion [8].

Korea Advanced Institute of Science and Technology connects its internal network to the Internet via multiple 1 Gbps links. One of them is to SK Broadband, one of the top three ISPs in Korea, and its link is the most utilized of all. The link to SK Broadband has experienced *persistent* congestion in the past few years. The measurement on

---

[1] The packet traces at Samplepoint-B from 2003/04 to 2004/10 and from 2005/09 to 2006/06 in the MAWI working group traffic archive at http://mawi.wide.ad.jp/mawi show full utilization.

N. Spring and G. Riley (Eds.): PAM 2011, LNCS 6579, pp. 1–10, 2011.

our campus network tells us that the link has experienced 100% utilization during the peak hours for more than *three years*! To the best of our knowledge, our work is the first to investigate a 100% utilized link. Even at 100% utilization the link has no rate limiting or filtering turned on. However, the operational cost of a 1 Gbps dedicated link is typically in the order of thousands of US dollars a month and a capacity upgrade is not always easy. Also the empirical evidence demonstrates that persistent congestion, although itself pathological, does not always incur pathological performance–we still get by daily web chores over the congested link!

In this paper we report on the persistent congestion in our network and analyze its impact on end-to-end performance. The questions we raise are: (i) *how much perfor-mance degradation does the fully-utilized link bring?*; (ii) *how badly does it affect the end-to-end performance?*; and (iii) *how tolerable is the degraded performance?* Based on the passive measurements on our campus network link we present quantitative an-swers to the above three questions. Per-flow loss rate at our border router is surprisingly low, mostly under 0.1% even at 100% utilization, but 30 ∼ 50 ms delay is added. The increase in delay results in overall RTT increase and degrades user satisfaction for do-mestic web flows. Flows destined to countries outside China, Japan, and Korea suffer less for both web surfing and bulk file transfer, but they account for less than 5% of total traffic. Comparison of two busy traces shows that the same 100% utilization can result in different performance degradation according to the traffic conditions.

The remainder of this paper is structured as follows. Section 2 describes the mea-surement setup and Section 3 the traffic mix. In Section 4 we quantify the performance degradation in terms of loss and delay. In Section 5 we study the impact of increased delay and loss on the throughtput of web flows and bulk transfers. We present related work in Section 6 and conclude with future work in Section 7.

2   When and Where Do We See 100% Utilization?

Our campus network is connected to SK Broadband ISP with a 1 Gbps link, over which most daily traffic passes through to reach hosts outside KAIST. Figure 1 illustrates the campus network topology and the two packet capturing points, *Core* and *Border*. We have installed four Endace GIGEMONs equipped with DAG 4.3GE network mon-itoring cards [2] to capture packet-level traces to and from our campus network; each GIGEMON's clock is synchronized to the GPS signal.

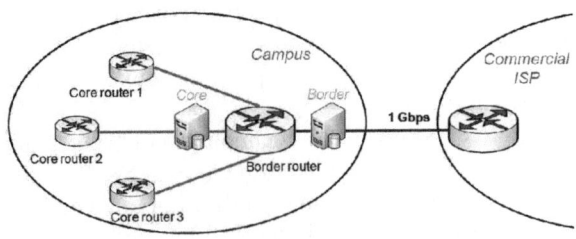

Fig. 1. Network topology on campus

The main observation, key to this work, is that the outgoing 1 Gbps link between the campus and the commercial ISP has been fully utilized during the peak hours for more than three years. The link utilization plotted by Multi Router Traffic Grapher (MRTG) on one day of July from 2007 to 2010 are in Figure 2. The solid lines and the colored region represent the utilizations of the uplink and the downlink, respectively. We see that the uplink lines stay at 100% most of the time. To the best of our knowledge, such long-lasting *persistent* congestion has never been reported in the literature.

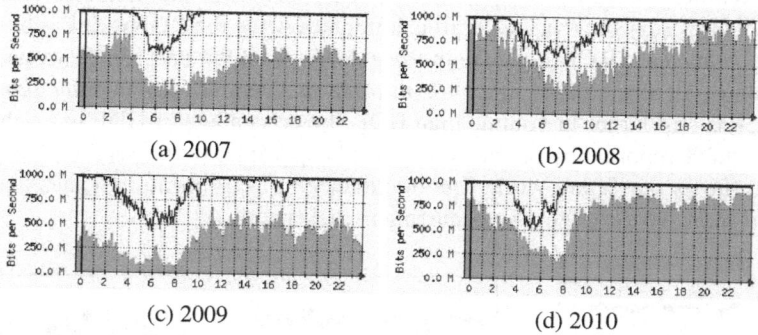

(a) 2007   (b) 2008

(c) 2009   (d) 2010

Fig. 2. Link utilization of one day in July from 2007 to 2010; solid line is for uplink and colored region is for downlink. The time on x-axis is local time.

We have collected packet headers for one hour during the 100% utilized period from 2pm on March 24th (*trace-full1*) and September 8th in 2010 (*trace-full2*). We have also collected a one-hour long packet trace from 6am on August 31st in 2010 (*trace-dawn*) for comparison. As we see in Figure 2 the link utilization drops from 100% to around 60% during the few hours in the early morning. *Trace-dawn* has 65.6% of utilization and the number of flows is only half of those from full utilization. We summarize the trace-related details in Table 1.

Table 1. Details of packet traces

Trace name	Time of collection	Duration	Utilization	# of flows
trace-full1	2010/03/24 14:00	1 hour	100.0%	9,387,474
trace-full2	2010/09/08 14:00	1 hour	100.0%	9,687,043
trace-dawn	2010/08/31 06:00	1 hour	65.6%	4,391,860

The capturing point *Core* has generated two traces for each direction, and the point *Border* does the same; we have four packet traces in total for each collection period. In the following sections, we use different pairs of the four traces to analyze different performance metrics. For example, we exploit uplink traces from *Core* and *Border* to calculate the single-hop queueing delay and the single-hop packet loss rate. The uplink and downlink traces from *Core* are used to calculate flows' round trip times (RTTs).

We monitored only one out of three core routers on campus, and thus only a part of the packets collected at *Border* are from *Core*. We note that, although incomplete, about 30% of traffic at *Border* comes from *Core*, and this is a significantly high sampling rate sufficient to represent the overall performance at *Border*.

3 Traffic Mix

We first examine the traffic composition by the protocol in the collected traces. As shown in Figures 3(a) and (b), TCP traffic dominates when the 1 Gbps link is busy. The average percentages of TCP and UDP in *trace-full1* are 83.9% and 15.7%, respectively. The portion of UDP increases to 27.7% in *trace-full2* and 33.7% in *trace-dawn*. Although TCP is still larger in volume than UDP, the percentage of UDP is much larger than $2.0 \sim 8.5\%$ reported by previous work [7] [11]. We leave the detailed breakdown of UDP traffic as our future work. The dominance of TCP traffic indicates that most flows are responsive to congestion occurring in their paths.

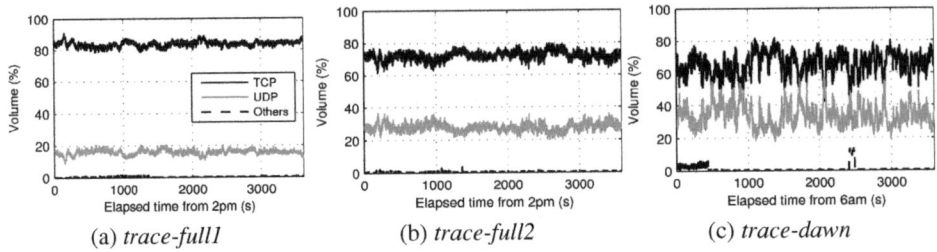

(a) *trace-full1*   (b) *trace-full2*   (c) *trace-dawn*

Fig. 3. Protocol breakdown of the collected traces

In order to examine user-level performance later, we now group TCP packets into flows. Figure 4(a) shows the cumulative volume of flows. Flows larger than 100 KBytes take up 95.3% of the total volume in *trace-full1*, 95.8% in *trace-full2* and 97.2% in *trace-dawn*. We call those flows *elephant* flows and those smaller than 100 KBytes *mice* flows. In Figure 4(b) we plot the total volume in *trace-full1* contributed by elephant and mice flows in one second intervals and confirm that mice flows are evenly distributed over time. The other two traces exhibit the same pattern and we omit the graphs from them.

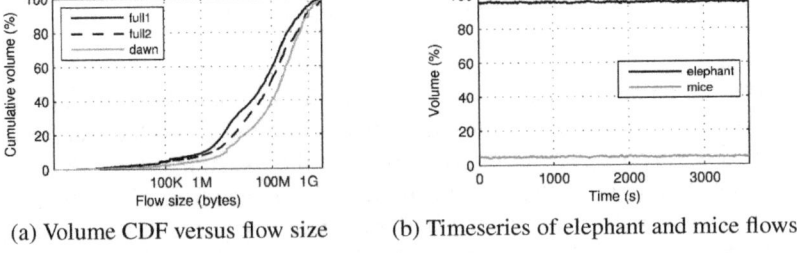

(a) Volume CDF versus flow size   (b) Timeseries of elephant and mice flows

Fig. 4. Traffic volume by the flow size

4 Impact of Congestion on Packet Loss and Delay

In this section we explore the degree of degradation in single-hop and end-to-end performance brought on during the full utilization hours in comparison to the low utilization period. We begin with the analysis on loss and delay. In Section 3 we have observed that TCP flows, more specifically those larger than 100 KBytes, consume most of bandwidth. We thus focus on the delay and loss of elephant TCP flows in the remainder of this paper.

4.1 Packet Loss

We examine the single-hop loss rate of the elephant TCP flows at our congested link. From the flows appearing both at *Core* and *Border*, we pick elephant TCP flows with SYN and FIN packets within the collection period. Existence of SYN packets improves the accuracy of RTT estimation, as we use the three-way handshake for our RTT estimation. For those flows we use IP and TCP headers of each packet collected at the capturing points *Core* and *Border* and detect loss, if any, through the border router as in [13].

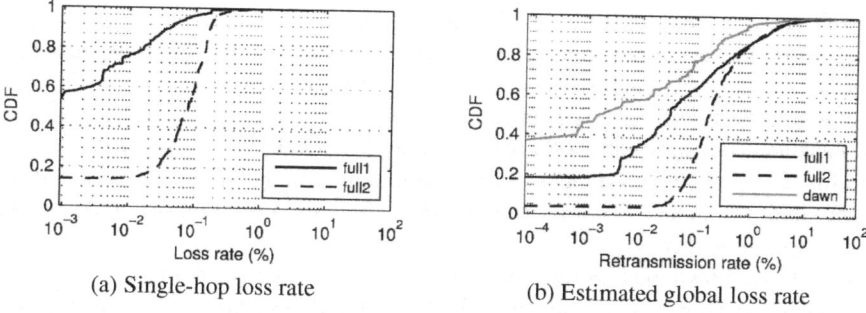

(a) Single-hop loss rate   (b) Estimated global loss rate

Fig. 5. Single-hop loss rate and estimated global loss rate (volume-weighted CDF)

Figure 5(a) shows the cumulative distribution of loss rates *weighted by the flow's size*: the cumulative distribution function on the y-axis represents the proportion in the total traffic volume as in Figure 4. Throughout this paper, we use this weighted CDF for most of the analysis so that we can capture the performance of elephant flows.

Because no loss is observed in *trace-dawn*, we do not show the loss rates in Figure 5(a). The maximum loss rate of flows reaches 5.77% for *trace-full1* and 5.71% for *trace-full2*. Flows taking up 53.1% of the total TCP traffic have experienced no loss during the collection period in *trace-full1*, whereas a much lower ratio of 13.8% in *trace-full2*. The performance degradation even at the same 100% utilization varies. *Trace-full1* and *trace-full2* differ mostly in the region between no loss and 1% loss. In the former 3.6% of traffic has loss rate greater than 0.1%, while in the latter the percentage rises to 39.5%. Apparently flows in *trace-full2* suffer higher loss. Here the utilization level alone is the sole indicator of performance degradation. In the future, we plan to identify the main cause for such performance difference between the two fully utilized traces. Yet still 99.3% of *trace-full1* and 95.4% of *trace-full2* experience a loss rate less than 0.2%.

The full loss rate a flow experiences end-to-end is equal to or higher than what we measure at the border router. The loss rate in Figure 5(a) is the lower bound. It is not straightforward to measure the end-to-end loss rate for a TCP flow without direct access to both the source and the destination. Consider the following example. Let us consider a bundle of packets in flight en route to the destination. The first packet in the bundle is dropped at a hop and the second packet at a later hop. The sender may retransmit the entire bundle based on the detection of the first packet loss without the knowledge about the second packet loss. By monitoring the entire bundle being retransmitted at the hop of the first loss, one may not be able to tell if the second packet was dropped or not.

For us to examine the end-to-end loss performance we analyze the retransmission rate seen at the capturing point *Core*. A retransmission rate is calculated based on the number of duplicate TCP sequence numbers. There could be loss between the source and the border router, and the retransmission rate we observe is equal to or lower than what the source sees. However we expect the loss in the campus local area network to be extremely small and refer to the retransmission rate at the border router as end-to-end. We plot the retransmission rates for the three traces in Figure 5(b). We use logscale in the x-axis and cannot plot the case of 0% retransmitted packets. In case of *trace-dawn* 28.9% of traffic has no retransmission. In case of *trace-full1* and *trace-full2*, 18.3% and 3.8% of traffic has no retransmission, respectively. As in the case of single-hop loss, *trace-full2* has worse retransmission rates than *trace-full1*.

We count those flows that experience no loss at our border router, but have retransmitted packets. They account for 34.9% in *trace-full1* and 9.4% in *trace-full2* of total TCP traffic. For them the bottleneck exists at some other points in the network and our link is not their bottleneck. That is, even at 100% utilization our link is not always the bottleneck for all the flows.

Here we have shown the loss rates of only TCP flows, and we note that UDP flows in our traces can have higher loss rates than elephant TCP flows since the TCP congestion control algorithm reduces loss rates by throttling packet sending rates.

4.2 Delay

We now study delay, where we aim at examining the impact of the local delay added by our fully utilized link on the RTT of the whole path. To calculate the single-hop delay, we subtract the timestamp of each packet at the capturing point *Core* from the timestamp of the same packet captured at *Border*. We calculate the single-hop delay for each packet in the flows from each of the three traces and plot the distributions in Figure 6(a). *Trace-dawn* has almost no queueing delay at our border router. Note that the median queueing delay of *trace-full1* and *trace-full2* is 38.3 msec and 44.6 msec, respectively, and the delay variation is strong as most delays oscillate from 20 msec to 60 msec. Such high queueing delay badly affects user experience, which we will show in the next section.

To infer RTT of each flow from bi-directional packet traces collected in the middle of path, we adopt techniques by Jaiswal *et al.* [10]. Their tool keeps track of the TCP

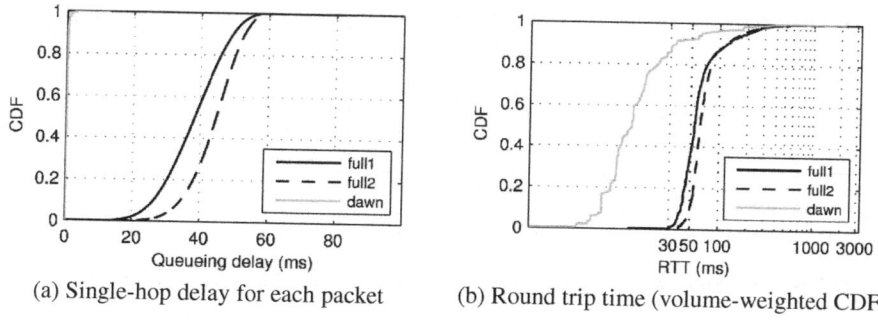

(a) Single-hop delay for each packet   (b) Round trip time (volume-weighted CDF)

Fig. 6. Single-hop delay and round trip time

congestion window and gives RTT samples for each ack and data packet pair. Figure 6(b) shows the average per-flow RTT distribution weighted by the flow size. We note that the large queueing delay at the router adds significant delay to RTT for both *trace-full1* and *trace-full2*.

5 Impact of Congestion on Application Performance

We have so far investigated the impact of the network congestion measured on our campus on the performance degradation in terms of per-flow end-to-end delays and packet losses. We now turn our attention to an application-specific view and examine the impact of the fully-utilized link on the user-perceived performance.

5.1 Web Flows

In this subsection, we consider web flows and examine the variation in their RTTs caused by the 100% utilized link. As port-based classification of web traffic is known to be fairly accurate [12], we pick the flows whose TCP source port number is 80 and assume all the resulting flows are web flows. We then divide those flows into three geographic regional cases, domestic, China and Japan, and other countries. Each case includes the flows that have destination addresses located in the region. Our mapping of an IP address to a country is based on MaxMind's GeoIP [3].

In Figure 7, we plot RTT distributions of web flows for different network conditions. For all three regional cases, we observe that *trace-full1* and *trace-full2* have larger RTTs than *trace-dawn*. In section 4, we have observed that the median of the border router's single-hop delay at the border router is 38.3 msec in *trace-full1* (44.6 msec in *trace-full2*) when its link is fully utilized, and our observations in Figure 7 conform to such queuing delay increase.

In the domestic case, 92.2% of web flows experience RTTs less than 50 msec in the dawn, while only 36.2% (9.8% in *trace-full2*) have delays less than 50 msec during the fully utilized period. We observe similar trend in the case of China and Japan, but the delay increase becomes less severe for the case of other countries. Most flows have RTTs larger than 100 msec regardless of the network condition.

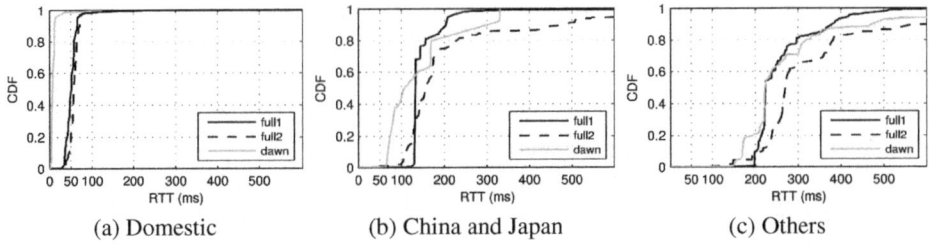

Fig. 7. RTT of domestic and foreign web flows for each trace (volume-weighted CDF)

Khirman *et al.*, have studied the effect of HTTP response time on users' cancelation decision of HTTP requests. They have reported that any additional improvement of response time in the $50 \sim 500$ msec range does not make much difference in user experience as the cancelation rate remains almost the same in that range; they have also found that additional delay improvement below 50 msec brings better user experience. According to these findings, our measurement shows that users in *trace-dawn* are more satisfied than those in the fully utilized traces when they connect to domestic Internet hosts. On the other hand, user experience for foreign flows stays similar for all the three traces because most RTTs fall between 50 msec and 500 msec regardless of the link utilization level.

5.2 Bulk Transfer Flows

We now examine the performance change of bulk transfer flows under full utilization. Bulk transfer flows may deliver high-definition pictures, videos, executables, etc. Different from the case of web flows for where we analyze the degradation in RTTs, we examine per-flow throughput that is a primary performance metric for the download completion time. We first identify bulk transfer flows as the flows larger than 1 MB from each trace and classify them into three geographic regional cases used in the web flow analysis. We summarize the results in Figure 8.

In the domestic case, 85.0% of bulk transfer flows have throughputs larger than 1 MByte/sec in *trace-dawn*. When the network is fully utilized, the performance degrades greatly, and only 36.6% (9.6% in *trace-full2*) of total volume have throughput larger than 1 MByte/sec in Figure 8(a). In Figure 8(c), the previous observation that

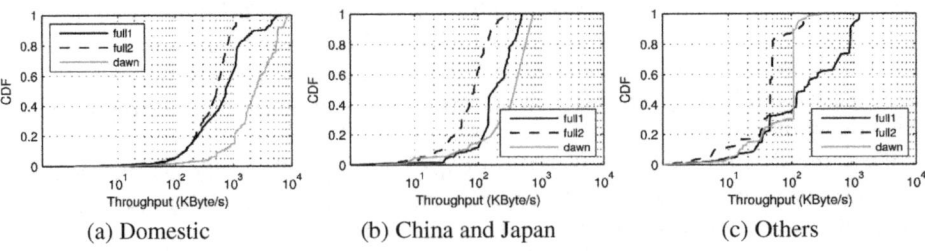

Fig. 8. Throughput of domestic and foreign bulk transfers for each trace (volume-weighted CDF)

trace-dawn has better throughput than the others disappears. We conjecture that our fully-loaded link has minor effect on the throughput of the overseas bulk transfers. There are other possible causes that limit a TCP flow's throughput (e.g, sender/receiver window, network congestion on other side) [16], and we plan to have the flows categorized according to each throughput-limiting factor in the future.

We are aware that comparing RTTs and throughputs from different traces may not be fair since source and destination hosts of flows can differ in each trace. We expect that the effect of the variation of hosts on campus should not be too serious because most hosts on campus are Windows-based and have the same 100 Mbps wired connection to the Internet.

6   Related Work

A few references exist that report on heavily utilized links in operational networks [5,6,8]. Link performance of varying utilization up to 100% has been studied in context of finding proper buffer size at routers. Most studies, however, have relied on simulation and testbed experiment results [4] [9] [14] [15]. Such experiments have limitations that the network scale and the generated traffic condition cannot be as same as the operational network. In our work, we report measurement results of 100% utilization at a real world network link with collected packet-level traces, so more detailed and accurate analysis are possible.

7   Conclusions

In this paper, we have revealed the degree of performance degradation at a 100% utilized link using the packet-level traces; Our link has been fully utilized during the peak hours for more than three years, and this paper is the first report on such *persistent* congestion. We have observed that 100% utilization at 1 Gbps link can make more than half of TCP volume in the link suffer from packet loss, but the loss rate is not as high as expected; 95% of total TCP volume have single-hop loss rate less than 0.2%. The median single-hop queueing delay has also increased to about 40 msec when the link is busy. Comparing *trace-full1* and *trace-full2*, we confirm that even the same 100% utilization can have quite different amount of performance degradation according to traffic conditions. We plan to explore the main cause of this difference in the future. On the other hand, fully utilized link significantly worsens user satisfaction with increased RTT for domestic web flows while foreign flows suffer less. Bulk file transfers also experience severe throughput degradation. This paper stands as a good reference to the network administrators facing future congestion in their networks.

We have two future research directions from the measurement results in this paper. First, we plan to apply the small buffer schemes [4] [9] [14] to our network link to see whether it still works on a 100% utilized link in the real world. Second, we plan to develop a method to estimate bandwidth demand in a congested link. When network operators want to upgrade the capacity of their links, predicting the exact potential bandwidth of the current traffic is important to make an informed decision.

Acknowledgements. This work was supported by the IT R&D program of MKE/KEIT [KI001878, "CASFI : High-Precision Measurement and Analysis Research"] and Korea Research Council of Fundamental Science and Technology.

References

1. Cisco Visual Networking Index: Forecast and Methodology 2009-2014 (White paper), `http://www.cisco.com/en/US/solutions/collateral/ns341/ns525/ns537/ns705/ns827/white_paper_c11-481360.pdf`
2. Endace, `http://www.endace.com`
3. Maxmind's geoip country database, `http://www.maxmind.com/app/country`
4. Appenzeller, G., Keslassy, I., McKeown, N.: Sizing Router Buffers. In: Proc. ACM SIGCOMM (2004)
5. Beheshti, N., Ganjali, Y., Ghobadi, M., McKeown, N., Salmon, G.: Experimental Study of Router Buffer Sizing. In: Proc. ACM SIGCOMM IMC (2008)
6. Borgnat, P., Dewaele, G., Fukuda, K., Abry, P., Cho, K.: Seven Years and One Day: Sketching the Evolution of Internet Traffic. In: Proc. IEEE INFOCOM (2009)
7. Cho, K., Fukuda, K., Esaki, H., Kato, A.: Observing Slow Crustal Movement in Residential User Traffic. In: Proc. ACM CoNEXT (2008)
8. Choi, B., Moon, S., Zhang, Z., Papagiannaki, K., Diot, C.: Analysis of Point-to-Point Packet Delay in an Operational Network. Comput. Netw. 51, 3812–3827 (2007)
9. Dhamdhere, A., Jiang, H., Dovrolis, C.: Buffer Sizing for Congested Internet Links. In: Proc. IEEE INFOCOM (2005)
10. Jaiswal, S., Iannaccone, G., Diot, C., Kurose, J., Towsley, D.: Inferring TCP Connection Characteristics Through Passive Measurements. In: Proc. IEEE INFOCOM (2004)
11. John, W., Tafvelin, S.: Analysis of Internet Backbone Traffic and Header Anomalies Observed. In: Proc. ACM SIGCOMM IMC (2007)
12. Kim, H., Claffy, K., Fomenkov, M., Barman, D., Faloutsos, M., Lee, K.: Internet Traffic Classification Demystified: Myths, Caveats, and the Best Practices. In: Proc. ACM CoNEXT (2008)
13. Papagiannaki, K., Moon, S., Fraleigh, C., Thiran, P., Tobagi, F., Diot, C.: Analysis of Measured Single-Hop Delay from an Operational Backbone Network. In: Proc. IEEE INFOCOM (2002)
14. Prasad, R., Dovrolis, C., Thottan, M.: Router Buffer Sizing Revisited: the Role of the Output/Input Capacity Ratio. In: Proc. ACM CoNEXT (2007)
15. Sommers, J., Barford, P., Greenberg, A., Willinger, W.: An SLA Perspective on the Router Buffer Sizing Problem. SIGMETRICS Perform. Eval. Rev. 35, 40–51 (2008)
16. Zhang, Y., Breslau, L., Paxson, V., Shenker, S.: On the Characteristics and Origins of Internet Flow Rates. In: Proc. ACM SIGCOMM (2002)

Dynamics of Prefix Usage at an Edge Router

Kaustubh Gadkari, Daniel Massey, and Christos Papadopoulos

Computer Science Department, Colorado State University, USA
{kaustubh,massey,christos}@cs.colostate.edu

Abstract. We investigate prefix activity on peering links between a regional Internet aggregation point and two tier-1 ISPs by analyzing a 24 hour packet trace from our regional ISP. Our data shows that a small number of prefixes carry the bulk of the packets, which corroborates previous work. However, unlike previous work, which focused on traffic from backbone routers, we look at edge traffic. In addition, we look at prefix activity at fine timescales, in the order of minutes, instead of just the aggregate view, which allows us to better understand the dynamics of prefix behavior. We define two metrics to capture the dynamic behavior of prefixes: the *duty cycle* captures a prefix's activity, while the *mean rank difference* captures how busy a prefix is. This allows us to estimate not only how much traffic a prefix carries, but also how that traffic is distributed throughout the day. We expect that our work will inform new route caching strategies (to alleviate the strain from an ever expanding global routing table) and evaluation of the performance of new routing architectures such as virtual aggregation and map-n-encap.

1   Introduction

According to a recent IAB report [1], Internet routing, specifically the Forwarding Information Base (FIB), faces scalability issues due to the ever expanding size of the global routing table. This size increase is fueled, among others, by the injection of prefixes into the routing table due to multihoming, as well as the need for traffic engineering. Large FIBs affect lookup speed as well as the price of routers, which now become more expensive due to the need for increased memory. Moreover, this increase threatens to push existing routers over their current limits, pushing ISPs into forced upgrades.

Several approaches have been suggested to overcome the routing scalability problem [2, 3]. Many of these approaches call for routers to route packets while storing less than the full FIB. This impacts the way the packets are routed to their destination in the following way: the packets that are destined to prefixes stored in the reduced FIB on the router can be delivered to the next hop directly as before. However, packets that are destined for prefixes not stored in the reduced FIB are routed via a default route. Such packets incur a performance penalty, which can be in the form of path stretch, loss etc. There is thus a tradeoff between the number of prefixes stored on the router and the number of packets that can be delivered directly to their destinations.

N. Spring and G. Riley (Eds.): PAM 2011, LNCS 6579, pp. 11–20, 2011.

With a reduced FIB size, it is important to carefully choose the prefixes that are stored in the FIB. Currently, most proposals call for the most popular prefixes (prefixes that receive the most packets) during the course of a day to be stored in the FIB [2]. However, this is a tradeoff that favors ease of selection, as there is no consideration for the dynamic behavior of the prefixes. Prefixes that are popular over the entire day may not always be popular *during* the entire day; it is conceivable that prefixes receive a large number of packets in only a few hours, resulting in a high daily rank, but receive very few packets during other time periods in the day. This opens the possibility to employ some sort of a dynamic cache.

Optimum prefix selection for a reduced FIB cache is a hard problem, because there are many dimensions that must be taken into account: traffic load, percentage of the time the prefix is active and activity patterns, and most importantly, the interplay of prefix dynamics at any given time. We note that traditional caching approaches such as LRU do not work due to the *cache hiding problem* (described in section 3.2).

We believe that this complex problem must be addressed by first understanding the data. In this paper, we use two metrics, the *duty cycle* and what we call the *mean rank difference* to capture the prefix dynamics. The duty cycle is a standard metric that captures a prefix's activity. The mean rank difference is a new metric that captures how busy a prefix is. We study packet traces captured at a regional ISP to investigate, among others, the current assumption that dominant prefixes (those with the most number of packets) are always active and busy.

Our primary contributions in this paper are twofold. First, we study traffic at finer timescales, in the order of minutes, rather than assume an aggregate view of traffic as in previous work. Second, since we study traffic between a regional ISP and its tier-1 providers, our measurement is closer to the network edge than previous work that looked at core routers. The growing FIB size at routers near the edge is arguably a more pressing problem than the core since the former tend to be less powerful than routers in the core, tend to stay in service longer and infrastructure cost is more critical to smaller operators.

2   Related Work

In [4], the authors studied traffic patterns between autonomous systems, based on traces collected at research institutions as well as commercial networks. The paper looks at flows with different end-point granularities (applications, end hosts, networks, ASes etc.) and found that traffic is not distributed uniformly on the flows; at any end point granularity, a small number of flows carry a disproportionately high volume of traffic.

This result is corroborated by [5]. The authors study the volume of load originating from an ingress link on a backbone router, and destined to a set of egress links. They find that a small number of *heavy hitters* account for nearly 80% of all bytes.

In [6], the authors study packet data collected at a *point of presence* (POP) in a commercial Tier 1 IP backbone network. They find that a few POPs account for a large portion of the traffic entering the backbone at all times. They also find the existence of a few very high-volume traffic streams (*elephants*) and many low-volume traffic streams (*mice*). This is further corroborated by [7, 8], in which the authors report that a majority of the traffic travels to a small fraction of destination prefixes; the rest of the prefixes received little or no traffic. A recent study [9] shows that 150 autonomous systems are responsible for more than 50% of all inter-domain traffic, while the remainder of the traffic is originated across a heavy-tailed distribution of the other 30,000 autonomous systems.

Unlike our work, the papers cited above capture *incoming* traffic in the Internet backbone. We measure *outgoing* traffic at an edge ISP and at a finer granularity than other work. Moreover, our results are based on packet (not flow) data, which enables us to capture prefix hit ratios better for small measurement intervals. Our results are more useful to research looking into new route caching strategies and evaluation of new routing architectures.

3 Data Description

In this section we describe our data collection and provide descriptive statistics from our datasets.

3.1 Data Sources and Trace Statistics

Our data was collected at two 1 Gbps links between our regional ISP and two of its tier-1 providers. We captured a 24 hour packet trace on each of these links. For each trace we isolated the out-bound packets, and determined their prefixes from the routing table using a trie-based longest-prefix match algorithm. We used a routing table obtained from our regional ISP. At the time of this study, the routing table had 292851 entries. Table 1 shows some trace statistics. The

Table 1. Trace Statistics

	Tier-1 ISP 1	Tier-1 ISP 2
Date	8/3/2010	8/3/2010
Number of outgoing packets	2,084,398,007	2,050,990,835
Number of prefixes hit (% of global routing table)	80,654 (28%)	66,639 (23%)

numbers in parentheses indicate the number of prefixes hit in terms of the total routing table size. At most 51% of the global routing table was hit on both links combined during those daily traces. The trace was captured on a weekday

(Monday), and we believe that the trace is representative of the traffic through our regional ISP. Although we present results for only one 24 hour trace for the sake of brevity, we note that the results are similar to another trace we captured a few months earlier at the same regional ISP.

3.2 Traffic Distribution

Figure 1 shows the distribution of the outgoing traffic for both tier-1 ISPs monitored. In this figure the X-axis plots prefixes after they have been ranked based on total daily traffic. In other words, prefix one is the prefix that sent the most traffic during the day, prefix two the second prefix in terms of total daily traffic, etc. The figure shows that a large majority of traffic is destined to a very small

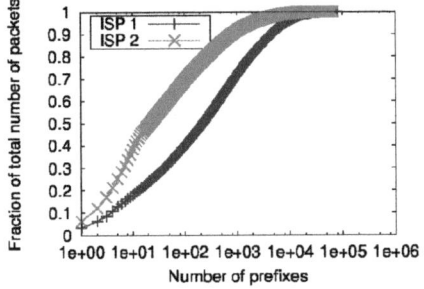

Fig. 1. Distribution of outgoing traffic

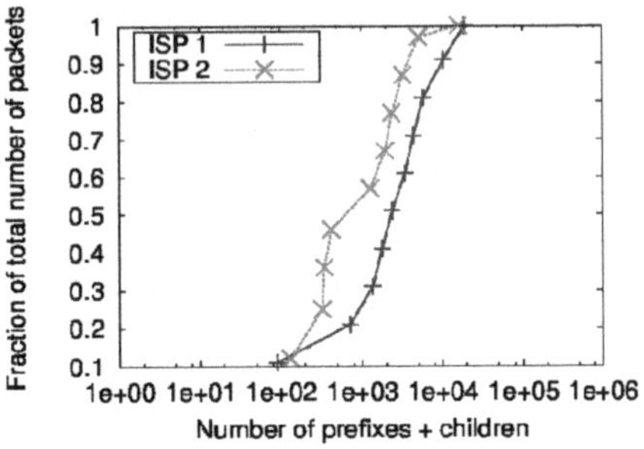

Fig. 2. Distribution of outgoing traffic, counting children

fraction of prefixes. This is in line with past studies [4, 5, 6, 7]. For example, looking at the graph, we see that approximately 1850 prefixes carry 80% of all packets at ISP 1. For ISP 2, the phenomenon is even more dramatic: approximately 250 prefixes carry 80% of all packets.

A naive design for a reduced FIB would be to store these popular prefixes, in order to route 80% of the packets. However, this approach does not take into account the hierarchical relationships between prefixes and therefore ignores the *cache hiding problem*. This problem arises when routes are cached rather than loading the full routing table in memory. If a less specific prefix already exists in the cache and a packet arrives for a more specific prefix that has a different outgoing interface than the less specific prefix, then the packet will be forwarded on the wrong interface. This happens because the packet destined for the more specific prefix will not result in a cache miss due to the existence of the less specific prefix in the cache.

A simple solution to the cache hiding problem is to bring all children of a given prefix in the cache. Figure 2 shows the same graph as before, except that now all children of a prefix are included in the count. The number of prefixes and their children required to cover 80% of the traffic is approximately 8500 for ISP 1 and 5100 for ISP 2. This shows that this solution to the cache hiding problem substantially increases the required cache without covering significantly more traffic. While using the number of cached prefixes assumes a linear cost for the cache and is probably an oversimplification, it does provide an intuitive metric to estimating the cost of caching prefixes. We also note that these costs may vary with different routers.

Another solution to the cache hiding problem is presented in [8], in which the authors eliminate the cache hiding problem by storing only /24 prefixes in the cache. Another scheme of prefix caching is to pull only those prefixes that have a different interface than their parent. While this evaluation is part of our future work, other work [10] has evaluated similar schemes for FIB aggregation. They did not evaluate a caching strategy that employs this scheme.

4   Results

In this section we show results according to two metrics, the prefix duty cycle and its mean rank difference. We define these metrics below. For the results in this section we move beyond global ranking based on total daily traffic. To capture prefix dynamics better we divide the trace into intervals of duration i, and perform our analysis on packets within that interval. We measured prefix dynamics at 5min and 1min intervals. We found that prefixes have similar duty cycles and mean rank differences irrespective of the interval duration. Since the results for both intervals are similar, for brevity we present results for the 5min interval only.

4.1   Duty Cycle

The duty cycle metric captures a prefix's level of activity. This metric is designed to determine whether a prefix receives packets continuously or in bursts. Prefixes that continuously receive packets will have a high duty cycle, while those that receive packets in bursts will have a low duty cycle.

To calculate the duty cycle of a prefix we first subdivide the trace as described above and then determine the number of intervals in which the prefix receives at least one packet. If the prefix has at least one packet in a given interval then we consider the prefix active for that interval.

Given the total number of intervals T and the number of intervals in which the prefix was active (i.e. had at least one packet destined to it) N, the duty cycle D is calculated as follows: $D = \left(\frac{N}{T}\right) * 100$.

Figures 3 and 4 show the duty cycles of all prefixes observed on the links to ISP 1 and ISP 2. We again plot prefixes according to their global rank on the x-axis and their duty cycle on the Y-axis. We can see from the figures that popular prefixes tend to have very high duty cycles. This shows that the popular

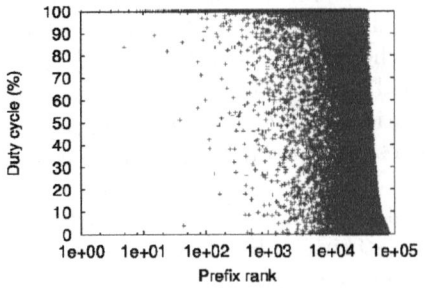

Fig. 3. Duty cycles of prefixes, ISP 1

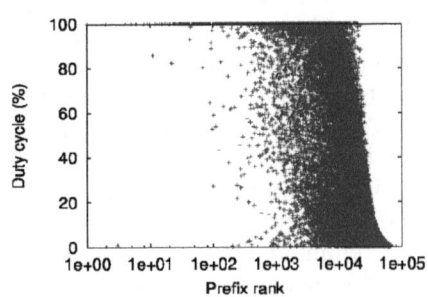

Fig. 4. Duty cycles of prefixes, ISP 2

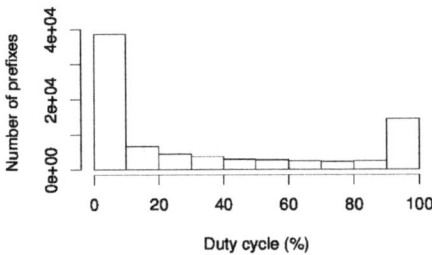

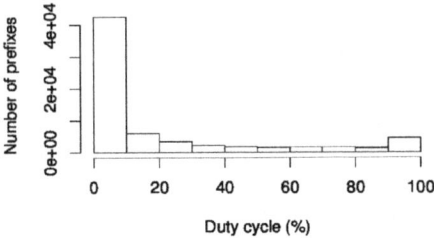

Fig. 5. Histogram of duty cycles of pre-fixes, ISP 1

Fig. 6. Histogram of duty cycles of pre-fixes, ISP 2

prefixes are always active i.e. receive packets. Unpopular prefixes have low duty cycles.

Figure 5 and Fig. 6 show histograms of the duty cycles of all prefixes. From the figures it is clear that the vast majority of prefixes have a duty cycle in the range 0-10%. On the other end of the histogram, we see a significant bump in the 90-100% range, with 9070 prefixes on ISP 1 and 2485 prefixes on the ISP 2 link have a duty cycle of exactly 100%.

Since we do not consider the number of packets a prefix receives in the duty cycle calculation, it is possible that a prefix is busy (high duty cycle) but does not send a significant amount of traffic overall. The pathological case is a prefix that sends one packet per interval, which would give that prefix a duty cycle of 100% but with only a few hundred packets. We therefore counted the number of prefixes that had duty cycles greater than 50% and also were a part of the list of prefixes that contributed to 50% of the traffic (which we know from Figure 1). The results for ISP 1 and 2 are shown in Tab. 2 and Tab. 3, respectively. The numbers in parentheses indicate what percentage of the total number of prefixes hit on the link is in each category.

As the results show, the majority of the prefixes have a duty cycle of less than 50% and are not of the top 50% based on traffic. The next big group are pre-fixes that have a duty cycle greater than 50%, yet they are not part of the prefix

Table 2. Prefix categorization, ISP 1

	Duty cycle >= 50%	Duty cycle < 50%
Contributes to 50% of traffic	210 (0.2%)	7 (0.009%)
Does not contribute to 50% of traffic	24188 (30%)	56249 (70%)

Table 3. Prefix categorization, ISP 2

	Duty cycle >= 50%	Duty cycle < 50%
Contributes to 50% of traffic	20 (0.03%)	1 (0.002%)
Does not contribute to 50% of traffic	10671 (16%)	55947 (84%)

group that contributes 50% of traffic. Only 7 prefixes in ISP 1 and one prefix in ISP 2 had a duty cycle of less than 50%, yet were part of the high-traffic group.

Since most of the low ranked prefixes have low duty cycles, they show up in the 0-10% bin in the histogram. For clarity, Figure 7 shows the duty cycles for the top 10,000 prefixes, where we see that these prefixes tend to have high duty cycles.

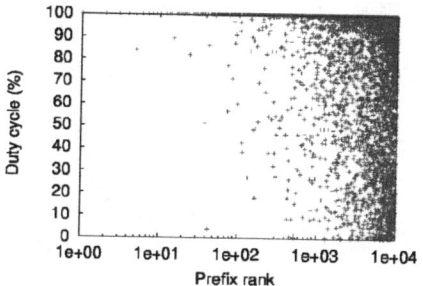

Fig. 7. Duty cycles of top 10000 prefixes, ISP 1

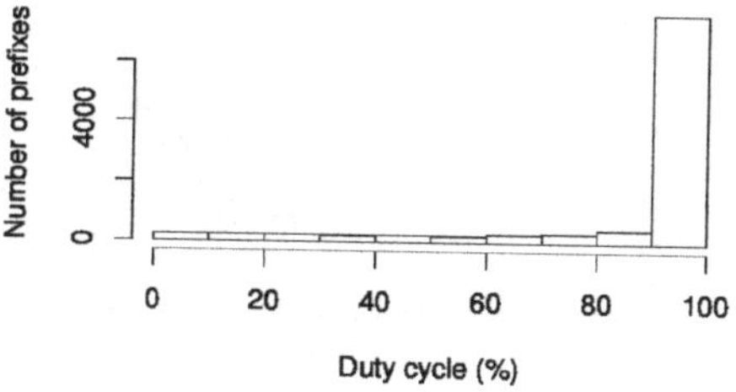

Fig. 8. Histogram of duty cycles of top 10000 prefixes, ISP 1

For further clarity, Figure 8 shows the histogram of the top 10,000 prefixes. It can be seen that approximately 4000 out of the top 10,000 prefixes have a duty cycle in the 90-100% range, with 2264 prefixes having a duty cycle of exactly 100%. Note that Figures 7 and 8 show data for only ISP 1; data for ISP 2 is similar, which we could not include due to space constraints.

The duty cycle will affect the performance of any reduced FIB design that employs a caching strategy. While a complete discussion of the effect of the duty cycle on caching is outside the scope of this paper, it is clear that the 4000 prefixes with duty cycle between 90-100% will almost never be ejected from the cache. This is advantageous, since these prefixes also account for a significant fraction of the daily traffic load (88%). We expect that this will allow reduced FIB designs that employ a relatively small cache, yet still achieve high hit rates.

4.2   Mean Rank Difference

In the figures in the previous section, each prefix observed in the trace was ranked according to daily load. To calculate duty cycles, we split the traces into intervals. Next, we take our traces that have been split into intervals and rank the prefixes according to packet load *in that interval*, thus creating a new rank called the *interval rank*. In contrast, the rank based on daily load is called the *global rank*.

Our new metric, *mean rank difference*, is calculated as follows. First, for a given prefix we create a time series by calculating the difference between its global rank and each interval rank, but only for the intervals in which the prefix receives at least one packet. The mean rank difference is the mean of the values in the timeseries.

More formally, given the global rank G, the interval rank R_i for the ith interval and the number of intervals during which the prefix receives at least one packet N, the mean rank difference M of the prefix is given by $M = \frac{\sum_{i=1}^{N}(G-R_i)}{N}$.

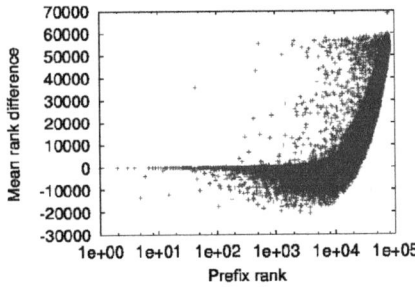

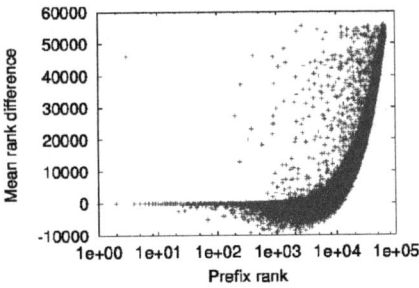

Fig. 9. Mean Rank Differences, ISP 1   **Fig. 10.** Mean Rank Differences, ISP 2

Figures 9 and 10 show the calculated mean rank differences for all prefixes observed on the links to ISP 1 and 2, respectively. By visual inspection, we define the following classes of prefixes. We note that the boundaries we define for each class may not hold for other studies.

Stable: Stable prefixes are prefixes having a mean rank difference between $+10,000$ and $-10,000$. These prefixes maintain their rank throughout the day. The most popular prefixes over the day fall into this category. These prefixes therefore are not only popular over the 24 hour trace period, but also in each interval. Also, the prefix ranked 1 stays at rank 1 in all intervals, prefix rank 2 stays at rank 2 and so on. Approximately 0.12% prefixes in ISP 1 and 0.15% prefixes in ISP 2 fall into this category and account for 40% and 70% of the traffic respectively.

Generally Popular: Generally popular prefixes have a negative mean rank difference, between $-10,000$ and $-20,000$. These prefixes, on average were ranked lower in many intervals compared to their global ranks. This could be because they received very few packets during those intervals or because other prefixes overtook them in the number of packets received. The mean rank difference can also become negative if the prefix becomes less busy often. Approximately 5% of the prefixes in ISP 1 and 1% in ISP 2 fall into this category and account for approximately 55% and 29% of the traffic respectively.

Generally Unpopular: Generally unpopular prefixes have positive mean rank differences greater than +10,000. This implies that although these prefixes generally do not account for much traffic, there were intervals in which these prefixes were busy enough to overtake the generally popular prefixes. Approximately 60% of the prefixes in ISP 1 and 72% of the prefixes in ISP 2 were generally unpopular and account for 5% and 1% of the traffic respectively.

Note that the more positive the mean rank difference becomes the more bursty the prefix is. Lower globally ranked prefixes achieve more positive values simply because the difference is much higher from their daily rank. The magnitude of the difference also shows how many other prefixes they were able to "beat" when they became active. A negative rank means the prefix tends to "fall behind" in general, compared to its global rank.

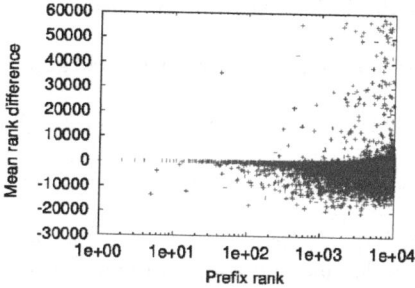
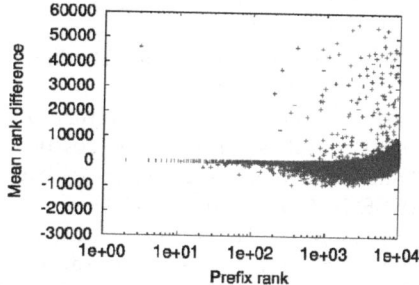

Fig. 11. Mean Rank Difference of top 10000 prefixes, ISP 1

Fig. 12. Mean Rank Difference of top 10000 prefixes, ISP 2

Figures 11 and 12 show zoomed in versions of Figures 9 and 10. It can be seen that the rank differences of the top 10000 prefixes are a lot more stable than the lower ranked prefixes.

5   Conclusion and Future Work

In this paper, we investigated the dynamic behavior of prefixes at two near-edge routers at a regional ISP. We defined two metrics, the *duty cycle* and the *mean rank difference* to capture the prefix's activity and their "busy-ness".

Our results show that there are very few dominant prefixes, which carry the bulk of the traffic during a 24 hour period. This corroborates previous work [4, 5, 6, 7]. Going further, our results show that these prefixes are almost always active, with almost all the prefixes maintaining 100% activity during our observation intervals, as well as being busy. The majority of the prefixes are either not used, or have a very low activity. We believe that these results are encouraging in terms of developing feasible strategies employing reduced FIBs at routers. In future work, we plan to extend the work in the following directions. Instead of looking at just one regional ISP, we plan to look at other near-edge ISPs. We also plan to investigate the dynamics of the prefixes at other measurement intervals, both shorter and longer than 5min and 1min. Finally, we want to leverage our study of prefix dynamics to design and evaluate reduced FIB designs.

We realize that our study has some limitations: we focus on one regional ISP serving mostly academic networks; other user populations may behave differently. We look at traffic for only one day, although this is sufficient to capture diurnal patterns. We use just two metrics to capture traffic dynamics; and we only look at a few measurement intervals (5 and 1mins). However, while more analysis should be done, we believe that our work captures many prevalent patterns of prefix dynamics when examined at a fine scale.

References

1. Meyer, D., Zhang, L., Fall, K.: Report from the IAB workshop on routing and addressing (2007)
2. Ballani, H., Francis, P., Cao, T., Wang, J.: Making routers last longer with ViAggre. In: NSDI 2009 (2009)
3. Farinacci, D., Fuller, V., Meyer, D., Lewis, D.: Locator/id separation protocol (LISP), draft-ietf-lisp-08.txt (2010)
4. Fang, W., Peterson, L.: Inter-AS traffic patterns and their implications. In: Proc. IEEE GLOBECOM (1999)
5. Feldmann, A., Greenberg, A., Lund, C., Reingold, N., Rexford, J., True, F.: Deriving traffic demands for operational IP networks: methodology and experience. SIGCOMM Comput. Commun. Rev. (2000)
6. Taft, N., Bhattacharyya, S., Jetcheva, J., Diot, C.: Understanding traffic dynamics at a backbone POP. Scalability and Traffic Control in IP Networks 4526(1), 150–156 (2001)
7. Rexford, J., Wang, J., Xiao, Z., Zhang, Y.: BGP routing stability of popular destinations. In: Proc. Internet Measurement Workshop (2002)
8. Kim, C., Caesar, M., Gerber, A., Rexford, J.: Revisiting route caching: The world should be flat. In: Moon, S.B., Teixeira, R., Uhlig, S. (eds.) PAM 2009. LNCS, vol. 5448, pp. 3–12. Springer, Heidelberg (2009)
9. Labovitz, C., Iekel-Johnson, S., McPherson, D., Oberheide, J., Jahanian, F.: Internet inter-domain traffic. In: Proceedings of the ACM SIGCOMM 2010 Conference (2010)
10. Zhao, X., Liu, Y., Wang, L., Zhang, B.: On the aggregatability of router forwarding tables. In: Proceedings of the IEEE INFOCOM 2010 Conference (2010)

Evolution of Cache Replacement Policies to Track Heavy-Hitter Flows

Martin Zadnik[1] and Marco Canini[2]

[1] Brno University of Technology, Czech Republic
izadnik@fit.vutbr.cz
[2] EPFL, Switzerland
marco.canini@epfl.ch

Abstract. Several important network applications cannot easily scale to higher data rates without requiring focusing just on the large traffic flows. Recent works have discussed algorithmic solutions that trade-off accuracy to gain efficiency for filtering and tracking the so-called "heavy-hitters". However, a major limit is that flows must initially go through a filtering process, making it impossible to track state associated with the first few packets of the flow.

In this paper, we propose a different paradigm in tracking the large flows which overcomes this limit. We view the problem as that of managing a small flow cache with a finely tuned replacement policy that strives to avoid evicting the heavy-hitters. Our scheme starts from recorded traffic traces and uses Genetic Algorithms to evolve a replacement policy tailored for supporting seamless, stateful traffic-processing. We evaluate our scheme in terms of missed heavy-hitters: it performs close to the optimal, oracle-based policy, and when compared to other standard policies, it consistently outperforms them, even by a factor of two in most cases.

Keywords: Network traffic measurement, scalability, tracking heavy-hitter flows, replacement policy, genetic algorithms.

1 Introduction

Flow-based network traffic processing, that is, processing packets based on some state information associated to the flows to which the packets belong, is a key enabler for a variety of network services and applications. For example, this form of stateful traffic processing is used in modern switches and routers that contain flow tables to implement firewalls, NAT, QoS, and collect statistics.

Flow-based traffic processing faces scaling challenges in that it potentially requires tracking and managing the state of millions of concurrent flows while keeping up with ever increasing data rates. In a number of cases, it is not necessary to track the state of each individual flow. Based on the generally known observation that a small number of flows account for a large amount of network traffic (e.g., see [1]), it has been suggested that scalable traffic measurement and accounting can be done by accurately measuring only the few large flows [2]. This can be generalized to other applications where the application goals can be

N. Spring and G. Riley (Eds.): PAM 2011, LNCS 6579, pp. 21–31, 2011.

met well enough by just focusing on the so called "heavy-hitters". For example, a traffic shaping system may focus on rate-limiting the large flows while the low-rate flows can utilize a small share of bandwidth at their will.

In [2], a memory-efficient structure called the Multistage filter has been introduced to define a scalable and efficient algorithm for *identifying* heavy-hitters. The limit of this approach is that a flow will only be accounted for once its traffic volume has passed the filter and until this time no state can be assigned to that flow. As this limit is intrinsic to the filtering approach, the works that have extended the method above (e.g., [3,4]) have inherited this limit.

However, associating flow state since a flow's first packet is critical for certain applications. For example, classifying traffic based on application identification (e.g., [5]) require statistics or payload data collected from the first few packets of a flow. In addition, network security schemes implement stateful processing for the initial packets of each flow. Further, OpenFlow switches [6] are managed by a controller that acts upon the first packet of each flow and installs flow-specific rules into the switch flow table. Therefore, filtering approaches are not always applicable and other approaches must be utilized despite their higher costs.

In this paper, we treat the problem of *identifying and tracking* heavy-hitters as that of finding a cache replacement policy that strives to avoid evicting the heavy-hitters from the flow table (from now flow cache). The intuition is that, if in the presence of a full cache and a new flow starting (causing a cache miss) the policy only chooses to evict flows that are not heavy-hitters (or unlikely), then the state of heavy-hitters is definitely preserved in the cache since their first packet. Effectively, compared to filtering, we trade-off the absence of false negatives and, partially, memory efficiency to support *tracking with state* the heavy-hitters from their initial packets.

In order to find such a replacement policy we utilize Genetic Algorithms (GA). GA explore the space of possible solutions in a search for a solution that exploits characteristics learned from recorded traffic traces and tailor the replacement policy to traffic patterns which could hardly be considered when manually designing a policy. We compare the evolved policies with other standard replacement policies. In our trace-driven evaluation, our scheme performs the best, even by a factor of two in most cases. The results demonstrate that our approach is promising in supporting stateful traffic processing focused on the heavy-hitters.

2   Background

Genetic Algorithms. GA are widely used in various areas of science and engineering to find solutions to optimization and search problems [7]. The main idea is to evolve a set (a population) of candidate solutions to find better replacement policy. A candidate solution is encoded as a genome which is an abstract representation (e.g., a binary string) that can be modified with standard genetic operators such as mutation and crossover. Starting from a population of randomly generated candidate solutions the evolution happens in generations. In each generation, some highly-scored solutions are selected to produce offspring. The offspring are evaluated in terms of their fitness to the problem and form a new generation. The evolution stops once a maximum number of generations has been produced or a satisfactory fitness level has been reached.

In their recent work [8], Kaufmann *et al.* described the usage of GA to minimize data collisions in a CPU cache line by tuning the address mapping in an application-specific way. We regard this work as orthogonal to ours in that they optimize the selection of a cache line to avoid collisions, but maintain the original replacement policy while we are concerned with the optimization of the cache replacement policy within a single cache line.

Cache Replacement Policies. Least Recently Used (LRU) is a widely used replacement policy for managing caches. However, LRU caches are susceptible to the eviction of frequently used items during burst of new items. Many efforts have been made to address the inability to cope with access patterns with weak locality. For example, Segmented LRU (SLRU) [9] seeks to combine both locality and frequency to achieve better hit ratios. An SLRU cache is divided into two segments: a probationary segment and a protected segment. When the cache is full and a miss occurs, the new item is added to the probationary segment and the least recently used item of this segment is removed. If a cache hit corresponds to an item in the probationary segment, the item is moved to the protected segment taking the place of the least recently used item in that segment.

We proposed a minor variation of SLRU for tracking large flows called Single-Step SLRU (S^3-LRU) [10]. Compared to SLRU, S^3-LRU does not order the items within each segment by their last access, but on each cache hit it advances the hit item of a single step toward the front of the cache (protected segment) by swapping its position with that of the adjacent item. However, S^3-LRU is only marginally better than SLRU in certain cases as our evaluation demonstrates.

Molina [11] proposed an algorithm for evicting small flows from the flow table using forecasts of the future flow volume based on the current volume and recent flow growth rate. Statically partitioning the flow cache in several subsets makes the approach efficient for identifying heavy-hitters. However, in this approach heavy-hitters can be evicted before having a chance to significantly increase their growth rate. For example, in our datasets we found that with this strategy 80% of the heavy-hitters witness a cache miss.

Filtering. Estan and Varghese [2] suggested a scalable traffic accounting scheme which focuses upon the identification and monitoring of heavy-hitter flows. In this scheme, only the packets which belong to flows identified as heavy-hitters are recorded by the flow table. The identification algorithm takes advantage of a memory-efficient data structure called Multistage filter. However, the limit of this approach is that a flow will only be accounted for once its volume has passed the identification stage, and no state in the flow table can be assigned to this flow until that time. We consider their approach as complementary to our scheme (also it would not be straight-forward to compare fairly).

Table 1. Mawi dataset. (1 hour, 155 Mbps link, avg/min/max active flows: 67.3K/ 56.5K/250.1K) Equinix dataset. (15 min, 10 Gbps link, avg/min/max active flows: 1.7M/179K/1.8M, only 160 instances of very large flows)

	Mawi				Equinix			
	v.large	large	medium	Total	v.large	large	medium	Total
Flows	0.23%	0.93%	9.43%	4.0M	0.00%	0.02%	0.35%	21.8M
Packets	31.97%	18.92%	20.71%	53.0M	0.36%	10.15%	17.07%	344.1M
Bytes	68.35%	17.13%	9.22%	33.5G	0.85%	24.01%	36.48%	207.7G

3 Datasets

The definition of a flow changes based on the application. One that is commonly used identifies a flow based on the 5-tuple composed of its IP addresses, port numbers and protocol. In our work, a flow is a unidirectional stream of packets sharing the same 5-tuple, but our approach can be easily generalized to allow the flow identifier to be a function of the header field values. A flow ends based on an inactivity timeout of 60 s or based on the TCP connection tear down.

We define a *heavy-hitter* to be a flow that utilizes more than a certain percentage of a link bandwidth during its lifetime. Also, we only consider a flow as heavy-hitter if it exceeds the threshold utilization for at least 5 s. Therefore, we compute a flow's link utilization as $\frac{bytes}{\max(5, lifetime)}$. This excludes short-lived flows with intensive bursts of packets that do not carry a significant amount of traffic overall. Lowering the 5 s interval significantly increases the number of heavy-hitters which potentially causes the GA to focus on short-lived flows at the expenses of long-lived heavy-hitters, although the traffic volume due to these short-lived flows is just a small fraction (e.g., with 1 s interval the number of heavy-hitters increases by 50% while the number of additional bytes due to heavy-hitters increases by less than 1%).

We group flows into three reference categories based on their link utilization: very large flows ($> 0.1\%$ of the link capacity), large flows (between 0.1% and 0.01%), medium flows (between 0.01% and 0.001%). We then report how well our approach performs for each category.

We use two traces of Internet backbone traffic: a 1-hour trace from the Mawi archive collected at the 155 Mbps WIDE backbone link (samplepoint-F on March 20th 2008 at 14:00)[1], and an anonymized, unidirectional 15-min trace from the Caida archive collected at the 10 Gbps Equinix San Jose link (dirA on July 17th 2008 at 13:00 UTC) [12]. Table 1 summarizes the working dimensions of our traces and shows a breakdown of the composition of the three flow categories.

4 Approach

Definitions. We regard the flow cache of size N as a list of up to N flow states (or simply flows) F. This allows us to treat the cache management problem as

---

[1] http://mawi.wide.ad.jp/mawi

keeping the list of flows ordered by their probability of being evicted (highest goes last). Then, the role of a replacement policy (RP) is to reorder flow states based on their access pattern. Each packet causes one cache access and one execution of the RP. If the current packet causes a cache miss (i.e., a new flow arrives) and the cache is full, the flow at the end of the list is evicted.

Formally, we can express a RP that is based solely on the access pattern as a pair $\langle s, U \rangle$ where s is a scalar representing the zero-based position for inserting new flow states and U is a vector $(u_1, u_2, \ldots, u_N)$ which defines how the flows are reordered. Specifically, when a flow F stored at position $pos_t(F)$ is accessed at time t, its new position is chosen as $pos_{t+1}(F) = u_{pos_t(F)}$, while all flows stored in between $pos_{t+1}(F)$ and $pos_t(F)$ see their position increased by one. For example, the LRU policy for a cache of size 4 is expressed with $LRU = \langle 0, (0, 0, 0, 0) \rangle$.

Evolution of Replacement Policies. Our goal is to find a RP that has the least number of evicted heavy-hitters or, using caching terminology, minimizes the miss rate for heavy-hitters. We use the number of heavy-hitters that witness a cache miss as a metric to capture the effectiveness of a RP—the objective is to reduce this number. Finding such a RP is difficult due to a large number of factors including flow size distribution, flow rate, and other traffic dynamics. We propose using GA to explore the space of possible RPs to identify the most effective. We chose GA for its ability to infer useful discriminators from traffic characteristics and to be easily customized to accommodate changes in the problem specification, e.g., different flow definitions, different traffic subpopulations of interest [4], etc.

The vector-based definition of a RP is a good fit to encode the candidate solution. It supports the standard genetic operators for mutation and crossover. Mutation modifies a particular value in the vector with given probability p_{mut} while crossover swaps parts of the vector between two solutions with probability p_{cross}. The RP evolution is performed offline using network traces. The following pseudo-code illustrates the evolution process:

```
population = GenerateRandomPopulation();
Evaluate(population); best = SelectBestIndividual(population)
while (not endcondition):
    newpopulation = SelectNewPopulation(population + best, fitness);
    CrossoverIndividuals(newpopulation, p_cross);
    MutateIndividuals(newpopulation, p_mut);
    FixInviableIndividuals(newpopulation);
    Evaluate(newpopulation);
    best = SelectBestIndividual(newpopulation + best);
    population = newpopulation;
result = best;
```

We start with a population of $C = 5$ candidates generated at random. The population size is a trade-off between evolution progress and population diversity. A large population means having a long time between replacements of generations due to lengthy evaluation of all candidate solutions. On the other hand, a small population cannot afford preserving currently low-scored solutions which could become good solutions. We use a relatively small population so the

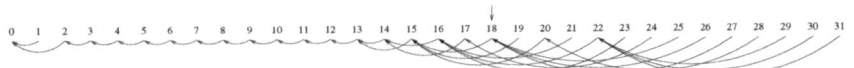

Fig. 1. An example of a RP produced by GA using the Mawi dataset. The arrows represent where to move a flow state when it is accessed. $RP = \langle 18,$ $(0, 0, 0, 2, 3, 4, 5, 6, 7, 8, 9, 10, 11, 12, 13, 13, 14, 14, 15, 15, 15, 16, 16, 16, 17, 18, 18, 18, 20, 22, 22, 22)\rangle$.

evolution process can progress faster allowing the RP to be adapted to ongoing traffic. We will study adaptation mechanisms in future work. During each step of evolution, 5 candidates are selected using tournament selection from a parent population and the best individual so far. Then, crossover and, subsequently, mutation operators are applied and the resulting offspring are evaluated with a fitness function. The fitness function is the sum of cache misses for the flows in the three reference groups weighted by the link utilization thresholds: 0.1% for the first group, 0.01% for the second and 0.001% for the third[2]. Effectively, the fitness function simulates the cache behavior with a candidate RP. To lower the evolution time, we evaluate the fitness using only a small part of a traffic trace, namely 5 min for Mawi and 1 min for Equinix. This has negligible impact on the results because we use a small cache size which becomes full within few seconds of simulation time. In each generation, the candidates are replaced by the offspring and the best candidate so far is preserved (so called elitism).

Search Optimizations. Without imposing any constraint on the vector-based definition of RP, we allow undesired candidate solutions: those that (i) do not utilize the entire list due to unreachable positions in the update vector U, or (ii) worsen the position of a flow despite it being accessed. Excluding these solutions reduces the search space, which helps GA to perform better and faster. Using simple heuristics we ensure the reachability of all positions and that any access improves the position of a flow. In our experiments, we observe that the GA converges to a promising solution faster if we split the run of GA into two consecutive phases, each with a different setup. The first phase is intended to search through the space to quickly find various viable solutions. Therefore, mutation changes the values in the vector to new, randomly-generated values. While experimenting with GA, we found that $p_{mut} = 0.3$ works well during this phase but close values work well too. The probability of one-point crossover is set to $p_{cross} = 0.3$ which allows to exchange information (parts of vector) between the selected parents. If there is no significant fitness improvement in the population, we enter the second phase which focuses on optimization. The crossover operator is no longer utilized as the possible solutions either differ significantly (crossover would produce a hybrid that would quickly be discarded) or are very similar. We modify the mutation operator to increase/decrease each vector value by one with probability $p_{mut} = 0.5$. In total, we produce 50 generations and we make 10 independent runs of GA, from which we select the best solution. Figure 1 presents

---

[2] This assigns higher importance to track true heavy-hitters.

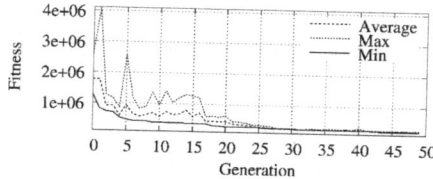
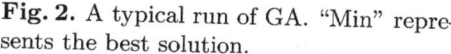

Fig. 2. A typical run of GA. "Min" represents the best solution.

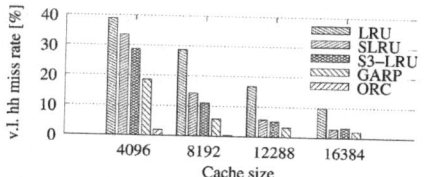

Fig. 3. Missed very large heavy-hitters vs. cache size (Mawi trace).

an example of a GA-produced RP while Figure 2 shows the fitness evolution in a typical run of GA.

Discussion. So far we have considered a flow cache as an ordered list of flow states. In such a simplistic model, the complexity of our scheme is $O(n)$ in the case of a hit and $O(2 \cdot n)$ in the case of a miss where n is the cache size. However, the applications we target typically already have a certain hardware support for stateful traffic processing at wire speed. Our scheme is meant to be implemented in hardware and integrated with the existing support for stateful processing. A practical hardware implementation usually divides the cache into a number of equally-sized lines which are managed independently. Each line is able to accommodate multiple flow states and the lookup of a flow state is performed in parallel by a set of comparators. Thus, the scheme runs with complexity $O(1)$. An hash value of the flow identifier is used to address a line in the cache. In such a basic scheme called Naïve Hash Table (NHT), each line in the cache executes the same RP. We evaluate our approach with these realistic settings. Our previous work in [10] shows that a line size with up to 64 items can be implemented in an FPGA (Field Programmable Gate Array). We choose to evolve RPs for a line size of 32 items as we consider it a good trade-off between what can be easily implemented in hardware and accuracy performance.

Finally, as our scheme operates online, the question arises how to maintain low false negatives (cache misses for heavy-hitters) despite changing traffic conditions. A plausible solution is to run our scheme in parallel with a Multistage filter to estimate the number of flows evicted from the cache which are identified as heavy-hitters by the filter. If this count exceeds a given threshold, we could trigger the creation of a new RP based on recently recorded traffic traces. Due to space limitations, we do not further discuss a complete solution and leave a thorough study for future work.

5   Evaluation

In this section, we present the results of our evaluation with a software implementation of the flow cache which allows us to easily report on the cache misses.

We compare the performance of a genetically evolved RP (referred to as GARP) with that of LRU, SLRU [9], S³-LRU [10] and the best possible policy, which is based on an oracle (ORC). ORC uses the knowledge about active

Table 2. Comparison of cache misses for heavy-hitters between GARP and other RPs. Cross-evaluation of GARP trained on different datasets. (Mawi – cache size: 8K, line size: 32; Equinix – cache size: 128K, line size: 32)

RP	Mawi			Equinix		
	v.large	large	medium	v.large	large	medium
LRU	19%	30%	10%	5%	25%	28%
SLRU	9%	19%	7%	3%	19%	18%
S^3-LRU	7%	21%	11%	2%	16%	22%
GARP	3%	8%	6%	2%	9%	10%
ORC	0.3%	1%	9%	0%	0%	0%
GARP-Eq.	5%	9%	8%			
GARP-Ma.				2%	11%	12%

heavy-hitters and their remaining duration to evict a flow that is not a heavy-hitter if possible, otherwise the heavy-hitter that will end soonest. For SLRU and S^3-LRU, we select the insert position that performs the best across our datasets. The values are 21 and 7 for SLRU and S^3-LRU, respectively.

We experiment with cache size of 64K, 96K, 128K, 160K flow states for Equinix, and 4K, 8K, 12K and 16K flow states for Mawi. We use line size of 32 states. In our experiments, the flow cache is approximately one order of magnitude smaller than the number of concurrently active flows.

Table 2 presents the number of heavy-hitters that experience a cache miss, normalized by the total number of heavy-hitters in each category obtained on the Mawi and Equinix datasets. In the case of Equinix dataset, the cache size is large enough to accommodate all heavy-hitters and so ORC does not cause any cache miss. However, using smaller cache sizes quickly deteriorates the cache misses for any real RP because of the large number of non heavy-hitters (99%) present in the Equinix dataset.

The results show that GARP consistently outperforms LRU and in most instances performs at least two times better than the other RPs which already have an ability to cope with access patterns with weak locality. Most of the heavy-hitters witness just one cache miss. We note that when experimenting with larger caches (see Figure 3) the difference in performance between policies decreases as the cache itself can store a significant share of all concurrent flows. However, it is often prohibitively expensive to have a large cache.

We perform a cross-evaluation to assess whether a GARP produced for one network link is applicable to another or whether the performance are unsatisfactory due to GA over-fitting for a particular training dataset. Second part of Table 2 demonstrates that the difference between two GARPs evolved on different datasets is quite modest. The suffixes -*Equinix* and -*Mawi* indicate the dataset the GARP was evolved on. These results indicate that our approach is promising and might find more general applicability, e.g., with different definitions of flows of interest [4]. Finally, to gain insight on the temporal stability of GARP, we test the performance of RPs evolved on our datasets and applied to traffic traces collected one year later than the training datasets (at the same links). We find that the performance does not significantly decay (on average less than 1.5% for Mawi and 2% for Equinix). Moreover, we evolve RPs on these newer traces and we find that, for both Mawi and Equinix, the newly obtained GARP is very similar to the GARP produced from the corresponding older dataset: quantitatively, the differences between the RPs' update vectors expressed as mean squared error are 0.42 for Mawi and 0.57 for Equinix.

6   Replacement Policy Extension

We now extend the RP with the ability to exploit information from the header fields of the packet that causes a cache hit. We consider two fields: packet size and TCP flags – chosen based on the analysis (omitted for a lack of space) of the statistical characteristics across the flow groups of the field values in our datasets. One intriguing approach would be to replace the update vector U with a matrix in which each row corresponds to a particular update vector for a given set of input field values. For example, the first row could be the update vector corresponding to the packet size 0 and the FIN TCP flag while the second row could be for packet size 1, etc. However, this quickly brings to the well-known problem of search space explosion.

We avoid this problem by maintaining a single update vector, but we complement the selection of the new position with a decision tree that uses the field values to increase by one, decrease by one, or maintain the position selected by the update vector. Based on our experiments, increases/decreases of two or more give worse results.

We only consider TCP flags (FIN, RST to decrease) and packet sizes of these ranges: [0 - 359] to decrease, [360 - 1000] to maintain and [1001 - max. size] to increase the update position. We determined these values from the analysis of the difference in the distribution of packet sizes between heavy-hitters and other flows in our datasets.

We tried using the current flow size (packets or bytes) as another parameter of the decision tree, and found that it does not bring further improvements. This is not entirely unexpected because the flow state's current position is determined by the history of all cache accesses, therefore the information from the current number of packets is implicitly already used.

As this extension is agnostic of the specific way in which the update vector is determined, we can apply it to all the considered RPs. Table 3 presents the number of cache misses normalized as before obtained on the Mawi and Equinix datasets with a cache size of 8K and 128K flow states, respectively. Each cache line stores 32 flow states. The extension works well only for the policies that do not progress the flow state right to the first position in the line. The GARP still achieves the best performance but it sees a smaller improvement than S^3-LRU. This is because the GARP itself has already been optimized to the observed traffic patterns (e.g., network scans), and applying a decision tree provides only a little additional information. We leave it as future work to evolve the replacement policy together with the decision tree.

Table 3. Comparison of cache misses for heavy-hitters between extended GARP and other extended RPs. (Mawi – cache: 8K, line size: 32; Equi. – cache: 128K, line: 32)

Extended RP	Mawi			Equinix		
	v.large	large	medium	v.large	large	medium
LRU	19%	29%	10%	5%	24%	28%
SLRU	9%	18%	7%	3%	18%	17%
S^3-LRU	4%	16%	17%	0%	11%	14%
GARP	3%	7%	7%	0%	8%	9%
ORC	0.3%	1%	9%	0%	0%	0%

7 Conclusions

We proposed a paradigm shift for scalable traffic processing focused on the large flows, regarded as the problem of managing a small flow cache. By design, our scheme allows to identify and track the heavy-hitters since their first packets. We demonstrated that Genetic Algorithms can evolve cache replacement policies that obtain results close to optimal while consistently outperforming standard policies. Finally, we believe that our approach can find more general applicability in other network-based applications where performance critically depends upon cache performance such as route caching.

Acknowledgments. This work was partially supported by the BUT FIT grant FIT-10-S-1 and the research plan MSM0021630528. We thank the anonymous reviewers and our shepherd, Alan Mislove, for their many helpful comments and suggestions.

References

1. Feldmann, A., Greenberg, A., Lund, C., Reingold, N., Rexford, J., True, F.: Deriving Traffic Demands for Operational IP Networks: Methodology and Experience. IEEE/ACM Trans. Netw. 9(3), 265–280 (2001)
2. Estan, C., Varghese, G.: New Directions in Traffic Measurement and Accounting: Focusing on the Elephants, Ignoring the Mice. Trans. Comp. Syst. 21(3) (2003)
3. Bu, T., Chen, A., Lee, P.P.C.: A Fast and Compact Method for Unveiling Significant Patterns in High Speed Networks. In: Proceedings of INFOCOM 2007 (2007)
4. Ramachandran, A., Seetharaman, S., Feamster, N., Vazirani, V.: Fast Monitoring of Traffic Subpopulations. In: Proceedings of IMC 2008 (2008)
5. Canini, M., Li, W., Zadnik, M., Moore, A.: Experience with High-Speed Automated Application-Identification for Network-Management. In: Proceedings of ANCS 2009 (2009)
6. McKeown, N., Anderson, T., Balakrishnan, H., Parulkar, G., Peterson, L., Rexford, J., Shenker, S., Turner, J.: OpenFlow: Enabling Innovation in Campus Networks. SIG-COMM Comput. Commun. Rev. 38(2) (2008)
7. Goldberg, D.E.: Genetic Algorithms in Search, Optimization and Machine Learning. Addison-Wesley Longman Publishing Co., Inc., Boston (1989)

8. Kaufmann, P., Plessl, C., Platzner, M.: EvoCaches: Application-specific Adaptation of Cache Mappings. In: Proceedings of AHS 2009, pp. 11–18 (2009)
9. Karedla, R., Love, J.S., Wherry, B.G.: Caching Strategies to Improve Disk System Performance. Computer 27(3), 38–46 (1994)
10. Zadnik, M., Canini, M., Moore, A., Miller, D., Li, W.: Tracking Elephant Flows in Internet Backbone Traffic with an FPGA-based Cache. In: Proceedings of FPL 2009, pp. 640–644 (2009)
11. Molina, M.: A Scalable and Efficient Methodology for Flow Monitoring in the Internet. In: Proceedings of the 18th ITC-18 (2003)
12. Shannon, C., et al.: The caida anonymized 2008 internet traces (2008), http://www.caida.org/data/passive/passive_2008_dataset.xml

NAT Usage in Residential Broadband Networks

Gregor Maier[1,3], Fabian Schneider[2,3], and Anja Feldmann[3]

[1] International Computer Science Institute, Berkeley, CA, USA
[2] UPMC Sorbonne Universités and CNRS, LIP6, Paris, France
[3] TU Berlin / Deutsche Telekom Laboratories, Berlin, Germany

Abstract. Many Internet customers use network address translation (NAT) when connecting to the Internet. To understand the extend of NAT usage and its implications, we explore NAT usage in residential broadband networks based on observations from more than 20,000 DSL lines. We present a unique approach for detecting the presence of NAT and for estimating the number of hosts connected behind a NAT gateway using IP TTLs and HTTP user-agent strings. Furthermore, we study when each of the multiple hosts behind a single NAT gateway is active. This enables us to detect simultaneous use. In addition, we evaluate the accuracy of NAT analysis techniques when fewer information is available.

We find that more than 90 % of DSL lines use NAT gateways to connect to the Internet and that 10 % of DSL lines have multiple hosts that are active at the same time. Overall, up to 52 % of lines have multiple hosts. Our findings point out that using IPs as host identifiers may introduce substantial errors and therefore should be used with caution.

1 Introduction

Today, network address translation (NAT) is commonly used when residential users connect their computers and laptops to the Internet. Indeed, most ISPs typically offer WiFi-enabled NAT home gateways to their broadband customers. These NAT gateways enable customers to easily and swiftly connect several devices to the Internet while needing only one public IP address. The prevalence of NAT devices and the number of terminals connected through a NAT gateway thus has implications on whether a public IP address can be used as a unique host identifier and if it is possible to estimate population sizes, e.g., malware infections, using IP addresses.

We, in this paper, analyze residential NAT usage based on anonymized packet-level traces covering more than 20,000 DSL lines from a major European ISP. We examine the number of DSL lines using NAT and how many distinct devices or hosts are connected via such NAT gateways. Furthermore, for DSL lines showing evidence of activity by more than one host we also study if these hosts are used concurrently.

While common wisdom holds that NAT is widely used in residential networks and that IP addresses are problematic end-host identifiers, no recent study reported numbers on NAT penetration or quantified the error potential in IP–to–end-host mappings. Most previous studies on identifying NAT gateways and inferring the number of hosts behind such gateways rely on information available in the packet headers, e. g., IPIDs, IP TTLs, or ports. Our approach takes advantage of HTTP user-agent information in

N. Spring and G. Riley (Eds.): PAM 2011, LNCS 6579, pp. 32–41, 2011.

addition to IP TTLs. In 2002, Bellovin [2] proposed and discussed the possibility to identify end-hosts by leveraging the fact that IPIDs are usually implemented as a simple counter. He found that this approach is limited in its applicability. Nowadays some IP-stacks even implement random IPIDs, further reducing the applicability of this approach. Beverly [3] evaluated several techniques to perform TCP/IP fingerprinting and found a host count inflation due to NAT by 9 % based on a one hour trace from 2004. Phaal [10] also takes advantage of the IP TTL. Furthermore, there is work in the area of OS fingerprinting, e. g., Miller [7].

Armitage [1] performed a measurement study in 2002 by offering Quake III servers at well connected Internet sites and monitoring the incoming connections. He identified NATed players by checking for non-default Quake client ports and found that 17–25 % of the players where located behind a NAT. Xie et al. [11] track IP-to-host bindings over time for counting hosts. However, they consider all hosts behind a NAT gateway as a single host. Casado et al. [4] use active web content to analyze NAT usage and IP address churn. By comparing local to public IP addresses they find that 5–10 % of IPs contacting *the monitored web services* have multiple hosts over a 7 month period.

In previous work [5] we showed that many distinct IP addresses are assigned to the same DSL line and that IP addresses cannot be used to reliably identify end hosts. While Casado et al. [4] found relatively low IP address churn, Xie et al. [12] came to a similar conclusion as we. In this paper we show that the situation is even worse because multiple hosts share one of these fluctuating IP addresses using NAT.

Our analysis of NAT usage shows that roughly 90 % of the studied lines connect to the Internet via a NAT gateway, presenting a high potential for IP ambiguity. Indeed, in our 24 h data sets 30–52 % of the DSL lines host multiple end-hosts. When considering shorter observation periods, 20 % of the DSL lines show activity from two or more hosts at least once within 1 hour. Even with time-frames as short as 1 sec, 10 % of the DSL lines show activity from multiple hosts. These results emphasize the large error potential of techniques that rely on an IP address to uniquely identify an end-host.

The remainder of this paper is structured as follows: We describe our data sets in Section 2 and explain our methodology in Section 3. Next, we present our results on NAT usage and the number of hosts in Section 4 and the impact of shorter time-scales in Section 5. We then critically discuss our findings in Section 6 and conclude in Section 7.

2   Data Sets

We base our study on multiple sets of anonymized packet-level observations of residential DSL connections collected at a large European ISP. Data anonymization and classification is performed immediately on the secured measurement infrastructure. Overall, the ISP has roughly 11.5 million (4%) of the 283 million worldwide broadband subscribers [8]. They predominantly use DSL. The monitor, using Endace monitoring cards, operates at the broadband access router connecting customers to the ISP's backbone. Our vantage point allows us to observe more than 20,000 DSL lines. The anonymized packet-level traces are annotated with anonymized DSL line card port-IDs. This enables us to uniquely distinguish DSL lines since IP addresses are subject to churn and as such cannot be used to identify DSL lines [5]. While we typically do not

Table 1. Overview of anonymized packet traces

Name	Start date	Duration	Size
SEP08	Thu, 18 Sep 2008	24 h	$\approx 4\,\mathrm{TB}$
APR09	Wed, 01 Apr 2009	24 h	$\approx 4\,\mathrm{TB}$
AUG09a	Fri, 21 Aug 2009	24 h	$\approx 6\,\mathrm{TB}$
AUG09b	Sat, 22 Aug 2009	24 h	$\approx 5\,\mathrm{TB}$
MAR10	Thu, 04 Mar 2010	24 h	$\approx 6\,\mathrm{TB}$

experience any packet loss, there are several multi-second periods with no packets (less than 5 minutes overall per trace) due to OS/file-system interactions. Table 1 summarizes characteristics of the traces we used for our analysis, including the trace start, duration, and size.

3   Methodology

To analyze NAT usage among residential customers we have to *(i)* identify lines that use a NAT gateway (e. g., a home router) to connect to the Internet and *(ii)* differentiate between the hosts behind the NAT gateway.

3.1   Detecting the Presence of NAT

To detect whether NAT is used on a DSL line, we utilize the fact that OSes networking stacks use well-defined initial IP TTL values (ttl_{init}) in outgoing packets (e. g., Windows uses 128, MacOS uses 64). Furthermore, we know that our monitoring point is at a well defined hop distance (one IP-level hop) from the customers' equipment. Since NAT devices do routing they decrement the TTLs for each packet that passes through them. We note that some NAT implementations might not decrement the TTL, however, per Section 6, we do not find evidence that such gateways are used by our user population in significant numbers.

These observations enable us to infer the presence of NAT based on the TTL values of packets sent by customers. If the TTL is $ttl_{init} - 1$ the sending host is directly connected to the Internet (as the monitoring point is one hop away from the customer). If the TTL is $ttl_{init} - 2$ then there is a routing device (i. e., a NAT gateway) in the customers' premises.

We note that users could reconfigure their systems to use a different TTL. However, we do not expect this to happen often. Indeed, we do find that almost all observed TTLs are between $ttl_{init} - 1$ and $ttl_{init} - 3$. While there are some packets with TTL values outside these ranges, they contribute less than 1.9 % of packets (1.7 % of bytes). Moreover, approximately half of those are due to IPSEC which uses a TTL of 255 and no other TTL has more than 0.44 % of packets. Given the low number of such packets, we discard them for our NAT detection.

A NAT gateway can come in one of two ways. It can be a dedicated gateway (e. g., a home-router) or it can be a regular desktop or notebook, that has Internet connection

Table 2. First network activity example   **Table 3.** Second network activity example

From Pkt Hdr		From HTTP User-Agent			From Pkt Hdr		From HTTP User-Agent		
TTL	Proto	OS	Family	Version	TTL	Proto	OS	Family	Version
63	53/DNS	–	–	–	63	53/DNS	–	–	–
126	80/HTTP	Win2k	Firefox	2.0.1	63	80/HTTP	Linux	Firefox	3.0.1
126	80/HTTP	WinXP	Firefox	3.0.2	62	80/HTTP	Linux	Firefox	3.0.1
126	80/HTTP	WinXP	MSIE	6	126	80/HTTP	WinVista	MSIE	8
126	80/HTTP	WinXP	Firefox	2.5.1	126	80/HTTP	WinVista	Firefox	3.0.2

sharing activated. A dedicated NAT gateway will often directly interact with Internet services, e. g., by serving as DNS resolver for the local network or for synchronizing its time with NTP servers. Moreover, they generally do not surf the Web or use HTTP.

3.2   Number of Hosts Per DSL Line

We also want to count how many hosts are connected to each DSL line behind a NAT gateway to enable us to estimate the ambiguity when using IP addresses as host identifiers. A first step towards identifying a lower bound for the number of hosts per line is to count the number of distinct TTLs observed per line. Recall that Windows uses a ttl_{init} of 128 and that MacOS X and Linux use 64 and that most of the observed TTL values are within the ranges of 61–63, and 125–127. These ranges are far enough apart to clearly distinguish between them at our monitoring point. Therefore, we can use observed TTLs to distinguish between Windows and non-Windows OSes, yet we cannot distinguish between distinct Windows systems. This is unfortunate, as analyzing HTTP user-agents shows that Windows is the dominant OS in our user population.

However, we can use additional information to distinguish hosts. HTTP user-agent strings of regular browsers (as opposed to user-agent strings used e. g., by software update tools or media players) include information about the OS, browser versions, etc. This can help us differentiate between hosts within the same OS family. We find that up to 90 % of all active DSL lines have user-agent strings that contain such OS and browser version information. In addition, we often observe several different OS and browser combinations on a single line. We theorize, that home-users tend to keep pre-installed (OS and browser) software, rather than installing the same software on each of their machines.

For example, consider the summary of all network activity of one DSL line in Table 2. We see a directly connected device (TTL 63 == $ttl_{init} - 1$) that is only using DNS. According to our definition in Section 3.1 this device is classified as a dedicated NAT gateway. We also observe TTLs of 126, which is consistent with a Windows OS behind a NAT gateway. Examining the HTTP user-agent strings we see that both Win2k and WinXP are present. Thus, we can assume that there are at least two distinct hosts behind the NAT gateway. However, we also see that the WinXP OS uses several different browser families and versions. While it can happen that users use two different browser families on a single host (e. g., MSIE and Firefox), it seems rather unlikely that they use different *versions* of the same browser family on the same host. Using this rationale, the two different Firefox versions on WinXP indicate two distinct hosts, yielding a total of 3 end-hosts.

Or consider the example in Table 3. Here we also see a directly connected device (TTL 63), however there is also HTTP activity with the same TTL. We therefore classify this device as a host. We also see TTLs that are consistent with NATed Windows and Linux systems, so we conclude that the directly connected device serves a dual function: as NAT gateway and as regular computer. Moreover, we see one OS/browser combination with TTL 62—another host. For TTL 126 we see only WinVista as OS but two different browser families, which likely indicates just one host with both Firefox and MSIE installed. Overall, we infer for this example that there are 3 active hosts.

3.3 A NAT Analysis Tool

We develop a small C program, `ttlstats`[1], to implement our NAT analysis. For each DSL line, the tool records whether a particular protocol was used by that line, which TTL was used in packets of this protocol, and for HTTP which user-agents were used. To identify protocols we use their well-known ports, which works well for the protocols we consider [5].

For HTTP we parse the user-agent strings and extract the operating system (OS) version and the browser version. We limit our analysis to user-agent strings from typical browsers (Firefox, Internet Explorer, Safari, and Opera), user-agents from mobile hand-held devices (see [6]), and gaming consoles (Wii, Xbox, PlayStation). We do not consider other user-agents (e. g., from software update clients) since those often do not include OS information or host identifiers. To estimate a lower bound for the number of hosts behind a NAT gateway we use two approaches:

OS only: We only count different ⟨TTL,OS⟩ combinations as distinct hosts.

OS + browser version: For each ⟨TTL,OS⟩ combination we also count the number of different browser versions from the same browser family as distinct hosts. Firefox and Internet Explorer are examples of browser families. We do not consider different browser families as additional hosts.

In our first example above, **OS only** yields a host count of 2 while **OS + browser version** yields a host count of 3. In our second example both counting methods yield a host count of 3: one Linux system that is used as gateway and regular computer, one NATed Linux system, and one computer with Windows Vista.

3.4 NAT Analysis for Different Data Set Types

Often the kind of data (anonymized packet-level information with HTTP) we use for this NAT analysis is not available. However (anonymized) HTTP logs might be more readily available. Yet, IP/TCP header only traces are common in the measurement community as well. Thus, we compare how well NAT analysis schemes perform when less information is available. For this we use several reduced information data sets, and repeat the analysis.

---

[1] Our analysis scripts available online.

Table 4. Overview of results. Top three rows are relative to total number of active lines, remaining rows are relative to "Lines with active hosts" (B.2), i. e., for C.1–E.2 100 % is equivalent to B.2

Ref.	Description	SEP08	APR09	AUG09a	AUG09b	MAR10
A.1	Lines using NAT	89 %	91 %	92 %	92 %	93 %
B.1	Lines on which only dedicated NAT is active	9 %	10 %	14 %	18 %	10 %
B.2	Lines with active hosts (NATed and unNATed)	91 %	90 %	86 %	82 %	90 %
C.1	Lines with unNATed Windows	9 %	8 %	7 %	7 %	6 %
C.2	Lines with unNATed Linux/Mac	1 %	1 %	1 %	1 %	1 %
D.1	Total systems (OS only)	141 %	142 %	143 %	140 %	145 %
D.2	Total systems (OS + browser version)	155 %	162 %	179 %	172 %	185 %
E.1	Lines with > 1 host (OS only)	30 %	31 %	31 %	30 %	32 %
E.2	Lines with > 1 host (OS + browser version)	36 %	39 %	49 %	46 %	52 %

4 NAT Usage/Hosts Per DSL Line

In this section we present the results from our NAT analysis. We first discuss the prevalence of NAT devices at DSL lines before continuing with the number of hosts per line. Finally, we investigate NAT detection with different data set types.

4.1 NAT Usage

Overall, we find that NAT is prevalent and that the vast majority of DSL lines use NAT to connect hosts to the Internet. We also find that a significant number of lines connects more than one host. Table 4 summarizes our key findings. Note that we term a device or host *active* if it sent IP packets during the trace. More than 90 % of lines utilize NAT (Table 4, row A.1). This result differs from the findings of Armitage [1] from 2002 who only found 25 % of the IPs were behind a NAT. On 9–18 % of lines (B.1) we only observe traffic that we attribute to the NAT gateway and no traffic from regular hosts[2]. We note that this traffic could also be caused by a directly connected, unused host. However, unused hosts might still check for software or anti-virus updates using HTTP, and would thus be counted as a host. The remaining lines (82–91 %, B.2) have active hosts (those lines may or may not be NATed).

We next take a closer look at DSL lines with active hosts and determine how many of these lines are using NAT. We find that only 7–10 % (C.1 and C.2) of lines with active hosts are not NATed, i. e., there is only one host which is directly connected.

Finally, we investigate how many more hosts than lines are present: the ratio of detected hosts to the number of lines. In rows D.1 and D.2 we show the number of observed hosts relative to the number of lines with active hosts. For D.1 we use the heuristic which counts every unique TTL and OS combination as a separate host (OS only). For row D.2 we also increment the per line host count if we observe TTL-OS combinations with multiple versions of the same browser family (OS + browser version). According to our definition, we will always see more hosts than lines with active hosts.

---

[2] i. e., we observe only traffic with TTL 63 and no HTTP activity.

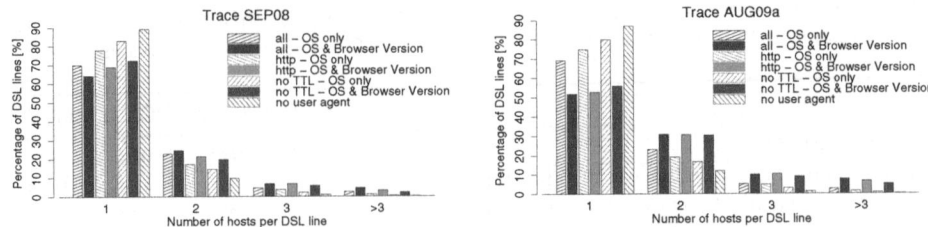

Fig. 1. Fraction of DSL lines vs. number of hosts per line for SEP08 and AUG09a

However, the differences are strikingly large—up to 1.85 times as many hosts than lines in MAR10 using the OS + browser version counting method. Independent of the estimation method the number of hosts behind NAT devices, our host counts, are far larger than the estimations by Beverly [3] from 2004, who estimated 1.09 times more hosts than IPs. This difference might be due to 6 additional years of NAT gateway deployment, different vantage points (Internet peering/exchange point vs. broadband access), different observation periods (1 h vs. 24 h), and/or information base (SYN trace vs. TTL plus HTTP logs).

4.2 Number of Hosts Per Line

Given that we see so many more hosts than lines with active hosts, we next investigate lower bounds for the number of lines with more than one host. A large fraction of such lines implies many public IP addresses with more than one host, thus limiting the utility of IPs as host identifiers. We see that 30–52 % of lines have more than one active host (Table 4, rows E.1 and E.2). We note that between APR09 and AUG09a the number of lines with more than one host increases significantly (OS + browser version, row E.2). We attribute this to an increase in browser heterogeneity: Following the release of MSIE 8 in late March 2009, we observe a significant share of MSIE 6, 7, and 8 in AUG09, while only MSIE 6 and 7 have a significant share in SEP08 and APR09. Consider the example that two hosts use a DSL-line and both have WinXP and MSIE 7. In this case we cannot distinguish between them. However, if one is upgraded to MSIE 8 while the other is not, then we can distinguish them.

In Figure 1 we present a more detailed look by plotting the fraction of lines with n hosts. We only present plots for SEP08 and AUG09a, the other traces exhibit similar behavior. We focus on the bars labeled "all" first. Note that we observe up to 7 % of lines with more than 3 hosts. We also investigate whether this high number of lines with multiple hosts is due to several computers (PCs or Macs) that are used via the same line or whether mobile hand-held devices (e. g., iPhones), or game consoles (e. g., Wii) are responsible for this. We identify these devices by examining the HTTP user-agent string. If we exclude mobile hand-held devices and game consoles, still 25–28 % (OS only; 34–45 % with OS + browser version) of lines have more than one host (not shown). Therefore, we conclude that the number of DSL lines with multiple end-hosts is only slightly influenced by mobile devices. In [6], we investigated mobile device usage in detail.

4.3 NAT Analysis with Different Data Set Types

As discussed in Section 3.4, we also use reduced data sets ("http", "no TTL", and "no useragent") and compare the NAT usage estimates to those based on the full data set available to us ("all"). Figure 1 compares the number of hosts per line for the different data sets. Note, without HTTP user-agent data there is no difference between the scheme for OS only and OS + browser version. Most accuracy is lost when relying on IP TTL only ("no useragent"). Removing the IP TTL ("no TTL") information shows slightly better results. Compared to "all" information using HTTP logs annotated with TTL information (but discarding all non-HTTP activity, "http") gives a very good estimate of NAT prevalence.

5 Impact of Shorter Time-Scales

So far we have limited our discussion to a static view of NAT behavior, i. e., we analyzed whether a DSL line is NATed and how many hosts are connected via this line. If a line has more than one host, IP addresses cannot be reliably used as host identifiers when considering time-scales of one day (our trace duration). However, it is possible that even though a line has two hosts, the first host is only active in the morning while the second host is only active in the evening. Thus, although the line has two hosts, they are not used at the same time. This can reduce the ambiguity of using IP addresses as host identifiers over smaller time intervals (e. g., by utilizing timeouts).

5.1 Analysis Approach

To answer if multiple devices are used at the same time, we compute the *minimal* inter activity time (*m*IAT) between any two HTTP requests issued by two different host on the same DSL line. If we observe an *m*IAT of T seconds then we know that two or more distinct hosts were active at this line within T seconds. As we need timestamps for this analysis we cannot use the output of the ttlstats tool (Section 3.3) as it aggregates all activity of a line for scalability reasons. Therefore, we revert to using HTTP request logs, which corresponds to the "http" data type and use the OS only counting method. These logs include timestamps for every request. We rely on Bro [9] for HTTP parsing.

5.2 Results

In Figure 2 we plot the fraction of lines with two or more hosts for increasing *m*IATs. This plot enables us to study how close in time two (or more) hosts are active via the same line. This allows us to estimate by how much ambiguity can be reduced by using a timeout, i. e., by using the IP-to-host mapping only for a limited time.

Even with intervals as low as 1 sec we observe more than 10 % of DSL lines with multiple hosts (12 % for MAR10). When considering *m*IATs of 1 h, around 20 % of lines have activity from multiple hosts (18 % for SEP08 up to 22 % for MAR10). We thus conclude that if a line has multiple hosts they are likely active at the same time or within a short time period. We see the lines starting to level off at around 10 h. This

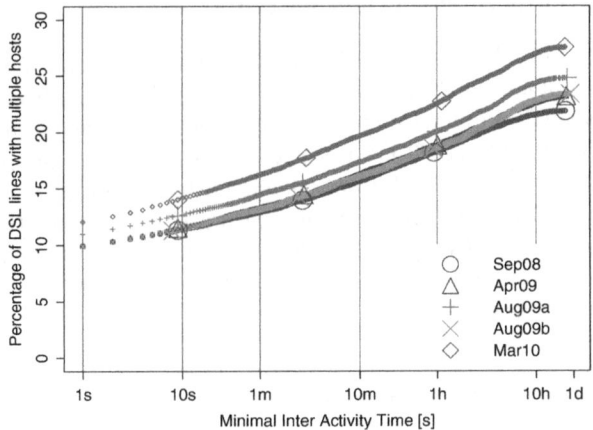

Fig. 2. Fraction of DSL lines with more than one active host within a particular time interval using OS only

is likely due to the time interval that users actively use their computers, as opposed to using them around the clock. We confirm these results by applying the static analysis (see Section 3.2 and Section 4.2) for slices of the traces, i. e., we subdivide each trace into time bins of 1, 5, 10, 30, and 60 minutes and repeat the analysis for each bin.

6   Discussion

This study aims at estimating the number of active end-host per DSL line. Our method-ology will likely underestimate the number of end hosts per lines, since we cannot dis-tinguish between hosts with identical OS and browser software. This actually renders our approach problematic for networks with homogeneous OS/software installations (e. g., businesses). However, our approach already reveals a significant number of hosts per DSL line. Furthermore, the DSL lines in our data sets are for residential customers. The ISP also offers different but comparable DSL plans for small businesses. Pars-ing additional application protocol headers might reveal additional hosts that were not counted, e. g., P2P peer IDs, however only a small fraction of DSL lines use P2P [5].

On the other hand there are factors that can bias our results towards overestimating the number of hosts per DSL line: Our method counts a computer that has two OSes installed (e. g., in a dual-boot or virtualized setup) as two different hosts. Yet, it is ques-tionable if it is wrong to count them as separate hosts. Likewise, if a user updates his browser during our observation period we also count the same machine twice. How-ever, these artifacts decrease as we consider shorter time-frames since it requires time to reboot another OS and/or update a browser. Therefore, the results for small *mIATs* are reasonable lower bounds for the number of hosts per line.

We further note that some NAT gateway might not decrement the TTL. If such a NAT gateway is used, we would classify the DSL as unNATed. However, if *multiple* hosts are connected through such a gateway, we are able to detect them. We have not found any evidence that a significant number of such non-decrementing gateways is used by our user population.

7 Conclusion

We presented a novel approach for detecting DSL lines that use network address translation (NAT) to connect to the Internet. Our approach is able to infer the presence of a NAT device and to provide lower bounds for the number of hosts connected behind the NAT gateway. For lines with multiple hosts connected we also studied the temporal behavior to see whether multiple hosts are active at the same time. Our approach relies on IP TTL information and HTTP user-agent strings and we analyze the accuracy when using less information (e. g., TTLs only, or user-agent strings only) for the NAT analysis. We find that most accuracy is lost when user-agent strings are omitted.

We find that 10 % of DSL lines have more than one host active *at the same time* and that 20 % of lines have multiple hosts that are active within one hour of each other. Overall 30–52 % of lines have multiple hosts. These results underscore the perils involved when using IPs as host identifiers.

In future work we plan to investigate NAT behavior over a number of consecutive days and to augment our analysis with IPIDs and ephemeral ports. Combining IP address churn [5] and NAT behavior, we further plan to assess the effect and potential error of utilizing IPs as host identifiers.

References

1. Armitage, G.J.: Inferring the extent of network address port translation at public/private internet boundaries. Tech. Rep. 020712A, Center for Advanced Internet Architectures (2002)
2. Bellovin, S.M.: A technique for counting natted hosts. In: Proc. Internet Measurement Workshop (IMW) (2002)
3. Beverly, R.: A robust classifier for passive TCP/IP fingerprinting. In: Barakat, C., Pratt, I. (eds.) PAM 2004. LNCS, vol. 3015, pp. 158–167. Springer, Heidelberg (2004)
4. Casado, M., Freedman, M.J.: Peering through the shroud: The effect of edge opacity on ip-based client identification. In: Proc. USENIX NSDI (2007)
5. Maier, G., Feldmann, A., Paxson, V., Allman, M.: On dominant characteristics of residential broadband internet traffic. In: Proc. Internet Measurement Conference (IMC) (2009)
6. Maier, G., Schneider, F., Feldmann, A.: A first look at mobile hand-held device traffic. In: Krishnamurthy, A., Plattner, B. (eds.) PAM 2010. LNCS, vol. 6032, pp. 161–170. Springer, Heidelberg (2010)
7. Miller, T. Passive OS fingerprinting: Details and techniques,
http://www.ouah.org/incosfingerp.htm (last modified: 2005)
8. OECD. Broadband Portal (December 2009), http://www.oecd.org/sti/ict/broadband
9. Paxson, V.: Bro: A system for detecting network intruders in real-time. Computer Networks Journal 31, 23–24 (1999), Bro homepage: http://www.bro-ids.org
10. Phaal, P.: Detecting NAT devices using sFlow,
http://www.sflow.org/detectNAT/ (last modified: 2009)
11. Xie, Y., Yu, F., Abadi, M.: De-anonymizing the internet using unreliable ids. In: Proc. ACM SIGCOMM Conference (2009)
12. Xie, Y., Yu, F., Achan, K., Gillum, E., Goldszmidt, M., Wobber, T.: How dynamic are IP addresses? In: Proc. ACM SIGCOMM Conference (2007)

The Efficacy of Path Loss Models for Fixed Rural Wireless Links

Caleb Phillips[1], Scott Raynel[2], Jamie Curtis[2], Sam Bartels[2], Douglas Sicker[1],
Dirk Grunwald[1], and Tony McGregor[2]

[1] Computer Science Department
University of Colorado, Boulder, USA
[2] Computer Science Department
University of Waikato, New Zealand

Abstract. In this paper we make use of a large set of measurements
from a production wireless network in rural New Zealand to analyze the
performance of 28 path loss prediction models, published over the course
of 60 years. We propose five metrics to determine the performance of
each model. We show that the state of the art, even for the "simple"
case of *rural* environments, is surprisingly ill-equipped to make accurate
predictions. After combining the best elements of the best models and
hand-tuning their parameters, we are unable to achieve an accuracy of
better than 12 dB root mean squared error (RMSE)—four orders of
magnitude away from ground truth.

1 Introduction

Modeling the propagation of a wireless transmitter in a complex environment
has entertained scientists for at least sixty years. The result is a staggering number of proposals of just about every shape, size, and approach imaginable. The
basis for this level of interest is solid—predicting the attenuation of transmitted signals with high precision has very important applications in the design,
trouble-shooting, and simulation of wireless systems.

Despite the large quantity of work done, we recognize an important shortcom-
ing: there have been relatively few comparative evaluations of path loss prediction models using a sufficiently representative dataset as a basis for evaluation.
Those studies that do exist make comparisons between a small number of similar
models. And, where there has been substantial work of serious rigor done, for instance in the VHF bands where solid work in the 1960's produced well validated
results for analog television (TV) propagation, it is not clear how well these
models work for making predictions outside their intended coverage (i.e., frequency, distance, environment type, etc.). The result is that wireless researchers
are left without proper guidance in picking among dozens of propagation models
from which it is not clear which is best or what the penalty is of using a model
outside of its intended coverage. This work provides a first step towards solving
that problem.

N. Spring and G. Riley (Eds.): PAM 2011, LNCS 6579, pp. 42–51, 2011.

In this paper, we describe, implement, and analyze 28 propagation models spanning 60 years of publications using five metrics to gauge performance. Although many of these models are massively different from one another, they all make use of the same basic variables on which to base their predictions: position (including height and orientation) of the transmitter and receiver, carrier frequency, and digital elevation model and land cover classification along the main line-of-sight (LOS) transmit path. These models are a mix of approaches: empirical, (purely) analytical, stochastic or some combination thereof. In the present study, we are not including ray-tracing models (e.g., [11]) or partition based models (e.g., [5]) which require substantial knowledge of the environment which is seldom available at all, and rarely at the precision required to make useful predictions. We are also not considering active-measurement models (e.g., [8]) which make use of in-situ measurements to correct their predictions. We expect to analyze these more complex models in later work.

To perform our evaluation we use a large set of active measurements collected from a production wireless network on the northern isle of New Zealand. This network spans approximately 8300 square kilometers, containing more than 368 transceivers (with 1328 possible links, 1246 of which are under measurement), and provides Internet connectivity to more than 740 clients. The network is built using commercial off-the-shelf equipment (COTSE) and operates in the popular bands of unlicensed spectrum at 2.4 and 5.8 GHz. All of the measurements we use will be released to the community to enable comparative evaluations.

2   Related Work

The vast majority of existing work analyzing the efficacy of path loss models has been carried out by those authors who are proposing their own improved algorithm. In such cases, the authors collect data in an environment of interest and show that their model is better able to describe this data than one or two competing models. Unfortunately, this data is rarely published to the community, which makes comparative evaluations impossible. One noteworthy exception is the work of the COST-231 group in the early 1990's, which published a benchmark dataset (900 MHz measurements taken in European cities) [3]. This effort produced a number of well-validated models which are tuned for 900 MHz transmitters in urban environments. We consider all of the proposed COST-231 models in our analysis here. The COST-231 data, being collected in an urban environment, is inappropriate for our present work, but we expect to use it in future work.

There are several studies similar to our own that compare a number of models with respect to some data. In [4], the authors compare five models with respect to data collected in rural and suburban environments with a mobile receiver at 910 MHz. They discuss the abilities of each model, but abstain from picking a winner. In [1], the authors compare three popular models to measurements collected at 3.5 GHz. The authors highlight the best of the three, which turns out to be the ECC-33 model proposed in [6]. In [9], Sharma et al. do a very similar analysis, but instead focus on measurements made in India at 900 and 1800 MHz. In contrast to [1], they find that the SUI and COST-231 models perform best. We believe our work here is the first to do an in-depth and rigorous analysis of a *large number of diverse propagation models* using a *large and realistic dataset from a production network*. And, it is the first such comparative study looking at results for the widely used 2.4 and 5.8 GHz bands.

3   Measurement

The network used in our study is a large commercial network that provides Internet access to primarily rural segments of the Waikato region in New Zealand. Every two minutes, each device on the network transmits a measurement frame at each supported bit-rate. For this study we only use measurements from the lowest bit-rate for each protocol (1 Mbps for 802.11b/g and 6 Mbps for 802.11a). Meanwhile, each device uses a monitor mode interface to log these measurement frames.

The back-haul network is composed of long distance 802.11a links operating at 5.8 GHz[1]. These are commonly point-to-point links that use carefully steered highly directional antennas. The local access network is composed of predominantly 802.11b/g links which provide connectivity to client premise equipment (CPEs). Often, an 802.11g access point with an omnidirectional or sector an-

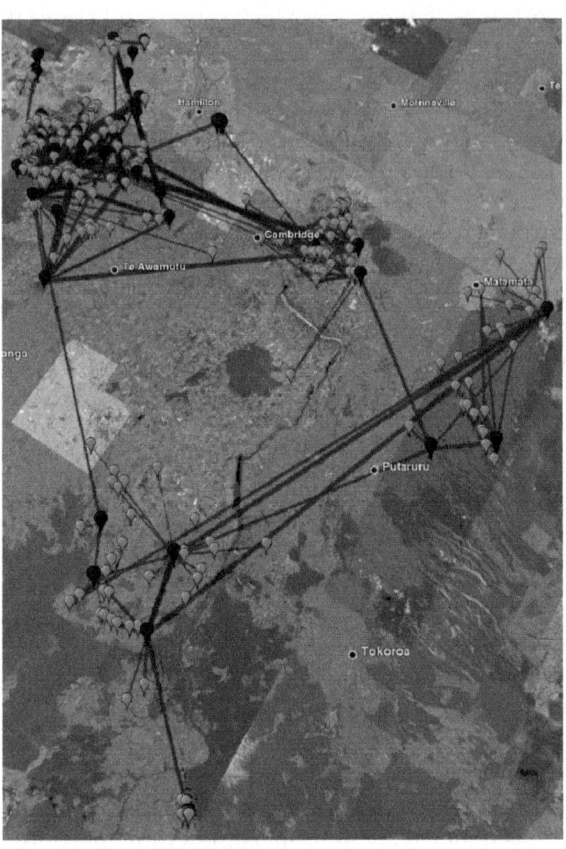

Fig. 1. The largest of three disconnected sections of the network (80x100km). Link width indicates strength. Back-haul nodes (mainly 5.8 GHz) are dark/black and CPEs are light/white.

tenna will provide access to a dozen or more CPE devices which have directional (patch panel) antennas pointing back to the access point. With few exceptions, each node in the network is an embedded computer running the Linux operating system which allows the use if standard open-source tools to perform measurement and monitoring. All nodes under measurement use an Atheros-brand radio and the MadWifi driver is used to collect frames in monitor mode and record received signal strengths. In [2], we showed that this hardware is able to measure signal strength at a sufficient accuracy for path loss modeling.

After collection, the data requires fairly substantial scrubbing. We discard any frame that arrives with its checksum in error or those from a source that produces less than 100 packets. The remaining packets are used as an oracle to analyze the performance of the propagation models. For this particular analysis we use one week of data collected between July 25th, 2010 and August 2nd, 2010. Because detailed documentation about each node simply did not exist prior to our study, some assumptions were made for analysis. The locations of nodes for which there is no specific GPS reading are either hand-coded, or in the case of some CPEs, geo-coded using a street address. Antenna orientations for directional antennas are assumed to be ideal—pointing in the exact bearing of their mate. All nodes are assumed to be positioned 3m off the ground, which is roughly correct for the vast majority of nodes. While these assumptions are not perfect, and are clearly a source of error, we feel that they are as accurate as is feasible for a network of this size and complexity. Certainly, any errors in antenna heights, locations, or orientations are on the same scale as those errors would be for anyone using one of the propagation models we analyze to make predictions about their own network.

In the end, our scrubbed data for a single week constitutes 19,235,611 measurements taken on 1328 links (1262 802.11b/g links at 2.4 GHz and 464 802.11a links at 5.8 GHz) from 368 participating nodes. Of these nodes, the vast majority are clients and hence many of the antennas are of the patch panel variety (70%). Of the remaining 30%, 21% are highly-directional point-to-point parabolic dishes, 4.5% are omnidirectional, and 4.5% are sector antennas. We believe this dataset is of sufficient scope and diversity to justify the claim that it is representative of a large class of wireless networks which have similar characteristics and operating frequency.

4   Models

Table 1 provides details of the models evaluated in this study. We subdivide models into five categories: *Foundational* models, which are purely theoretical and (often) form the core of more advanced models, *Basic* models, which are the majority and typically include empirical corrections from measurements and often require special tuning parameters for the environment type, *Terrain* models, which expand on the basic models by including terrain features into their calculations, and *Supplementary* models, which are not able to stand on their own but instead are used to make corrections to existing models.

At a high level, a model's task is to predict the value of $L_t + L_s$ in this log-domain equation:

---

[1] Atypically liberal power regulations in New Zealand and Australia around 5.8 GHz allow for much longer links than can be seen in most other places in the world.

Table 1. Models Studied along with their categorization, citation, and year of (initial) publication

Name	Short-Name	Category	Year
Friis' Freespace	friis	Foundational	1946
Egli	egli	Basic	1957
Hata-Okumura	hata	Basic	1968
Edwards-Durkin	edwards	Basic/Terrain	1969
Alsebrook-Parsons	alsebrook	Basic/Terrain	1977
Blomquist-Ladell	blomquist	Basic/Terrain	1977
Longley-Rice Irregular Terrain Model (ITM)	itm	Terrain	1982
Walfish-Bertoni	bertoni	Basic	1988
Flat-Edge	flatedge	Basic	1991
COST-Hata/Cost-231	cost231	Basic	1993
Walfish-Ikegami	walfish	Basic	1993
Two-Ray (Ground Reflection)	two.ray	Foundational	1994
Hata-Davidson	davidson	Basic	1997
Erceg-Greenstein	erceg	Basic	1998
Directional Gain Reduction Factor (GRF)	grf	Supplementary	1999
Rural Hata	rural.hata	Basic	2000
ITU Terrain	itu	Terrain	2001
Stanford University Interium (SUI)	sui	Basic	2001
Green-Obaidat	green	Basic	2002
ITU-R/CCIR	itur	Basic	2002
ECC-33	ecc33	Basic	2003
Riback-Medbo	fc	Supplementary	2006
ITU-R 452	itur452	Terrain	2007
IMT-2000	imt2000	Basic	2007
deSouza	desouza	Basic	2008
Effective Directivity Antenna Model (EDAM)	edam	Supplementary	2009
Herring Air-to-Ground	herring.atg	Basic	2010
Herring Ground-to-Ground	herring.gtg	Basic	2010

$$P_r = P_t - (L_t + L_s + L_f(t)) \tag{1}$$

Where P_r and P_t are the received and transmitted power and the total path loss is the sum of L_t, the trivial free-space path loss, L_s, the loss due to shadowing/slow-fading from large unmoving obstacles like mountains and buildings, and $L_f(t)$, the small-scale/fast fading due to destructive interference from multipath effects and small scatterers (which varies with time t). Models cannot, without perfect knowledge of the environment, be expected to predict the quantity $L_f(t)$. In most applications, this additional error is computed "stochastically" using a probability distribution. For the protocols used in our study, however, this quantity tends to be small due to the averaging effect of wide-band modulation schemes [10].

It is worth noting that among the models we study, only very few were designed with the exactly sort of network we are studying in mind. Indeed, some are very specific about the type of environment in which they are to be used.

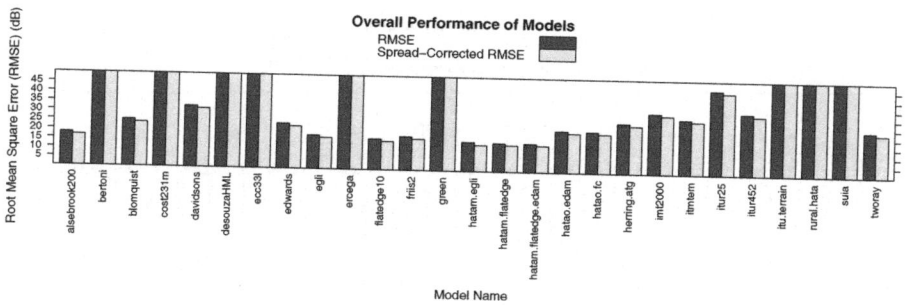

Fig. 2. Overall model performance as described by (residual) root mean squared error (RMSE) and spread-corrected RMSE (SC-RMSE). Spread corrected error is adjusted (reduced) by the expected measurement spread on a given link.

In this work, we pay little attention to these coverage requirements because we observe that they are not largely followed in the literature (the Longley-Rice Irregular Terrain model, in particular, is frequently used well outside of its intended coverage). In this study both appropriate and "inappropriate" models are given an equal chance at making predictions for our network. We have no starting bias about which should perform best.

5   Results

To obtain results, we ask each model to offer a prediction of median path loss for each link in our network. The model produces an estimate of the loss $\hat{L}$ which we combine with known values to calculate the predicted received signal strength P_r:

$$P_r = P_t + G_t(\theta) + G_r(\phi) - \hat{L} \qquad (2)$$

Where G_t is the antenna gain of the transmitter in the azimuthal direction (θ) of the receiver and G_r is the antenna gain of the receiver in the azimuthal direction (ϕ) of the transmitter. These gains are drawn from measured antenna patterns (one for each type of antenna)[2]. The transmit power (P_t) is set to 18 dBm for all nodes, which is the maximum transmit power of the Atheros radios our nodes use. For a given link, we calculate the median received signal strength value across all measurements ($\bar{P}_r$). Then, the prediction error, ϵ, is the difference between the prediction and the median measured value: $\epsilon = \bar{P}_r - P_r$.

Some models come with tunable parameters of varying esotericism. For these models, we try a range of reasonable parameter values without bias towards which we expect to be best. To conserve space, in the following discussion and figures we show results from only the 27 best performing models/configurations.

Figure 2 provides the overall performance of each algorithm in terms of its RMSE. To account for underlying variance in the measurements, we use a "spread corrected" RMSE ($\hat{\epsilon}$) where the link's measured standard deviation ($\bar{\sigma}$) is subtracted from the prediction error: $\hat{\epsilon} = |\epsilon| - \bar{\sigma}$. This corrected RMSE

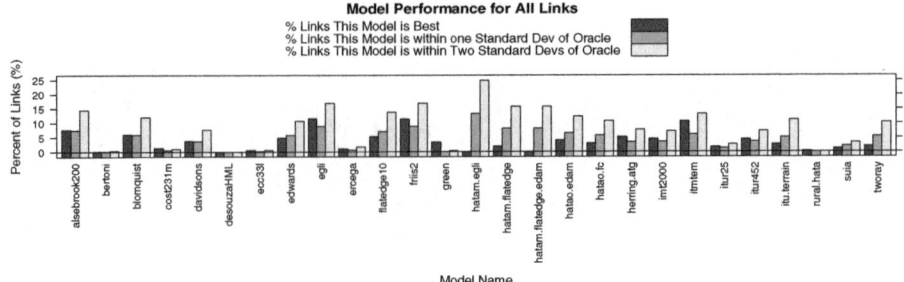

Fig. 3. Competitive and Individual Performance. Competetive performance is the percentage of links a given model is the best predictor for. Individual performance is the percentage of links a model makes a prediction within one (or two) standard deviations of the correct value.

gives an idea of error in excess of expected variance due to temporal variation (i.e., fast-fading and intrinsic/diurnal periodicity)[2]. As we can see, the best performing models achieve an RMSE on the order of 15 dB. The best models are the Alsebrook model (with its terrain roughness parameter set to 200m) at just under 18 dB RMSE (16.7 dB when corrected), and the Flat-Edge model (with 10 "buildings" presumed) at 16.5 dB RMSE (15.3 dB when corrected)[3].

Figure 3 provides two domain-oriented metrics that describe models' competitive and individual "goodness". The competitive metric is the percentage of links that a given model produces the best prediction for (and hence sums to 100). We can see that no given model dominates the competition—the honor of best prediction is spread fairly evenly among half a dozen models that each achieve the best prediction between 10 and 15 percent of the time. The other metric is an individualistic definition of success—the percentage of links a given model's prediction is within the expected spread (measurement standard deviation). The best performing models are "correct" 10% of the time using this metric. If we lower the bar to making a prediction within two standard deviations of the measured median value, the best performing models (Egli, Friis (with $\alpha = 2$), Flat-Edge, ITM, ITU Terrain, and Two-Ray) achieve between 10 and 15% correct.

Figure 4 plots our next metric: ability to order links. In some applications it may be sufficient for a propagation model to order two or more links by strength. In this scenario, we imagine that the predicted path loss isn't itself expected to be absolutely correct, but instead simply a relational performance compared to other links in the same network. In this figure, we plot Spearman's non-parametric rank order coefficient ρ for each model. For this metric, a value of

---

[2] Although we are careful to correct for this measurement variation, it is on the whole rather small: 1.31 dB median standard deviation and 1.67 dB at the third quantile.

[3] Some models perform substantially better when we consider only the fraction of cases that are in their intended coverage. The ITM, for instance, has a competitive spread-corrected RMSE of 17.3 dB when only error-free predictions are considered.

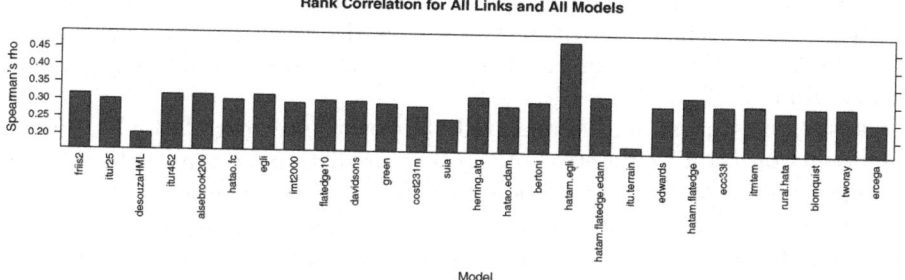

Fig. 4. Ability to order links, computed using Spearman's ρ. A value of 0 indicates a random ordering (relative to the oracle order) and a value of 1 would be a perfect ordering.

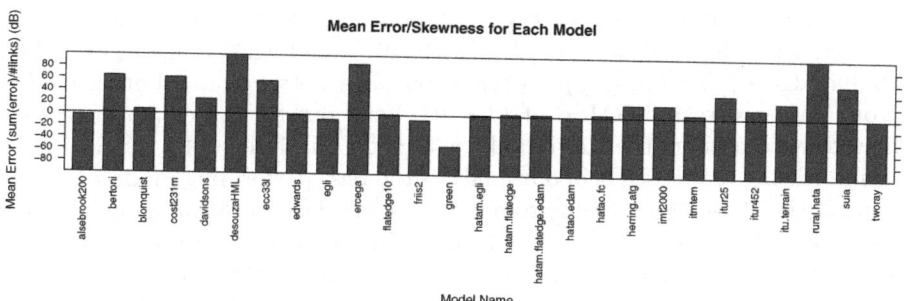

Fig. 5. Prediction Error Skewness, computed as the sum of error divided by the number of total links. Models that make an equal amount of over and under predictions acheive a value near zero. Models that make a majority of under or over predictions have a large negative or positive value respectively.

zero indicates no correlation (random order) and a value of 1.0 or -1.0 indicates perfect positive or negative correlation. We can see that with few exceptions, all models score in the neighborhood of 0.25 to 0.30 indicating a small positive correlation. The best model (hatam.egli) performs around 0.45 and the worst model (itu.terrain) acheives less than 0.20 correlation.

Our final metric is skewness, which is shown in figure 5. For many applications an over or under estimate of path loss can come with a high price. This metric plots the sum of all residual error for each model. A model that makes an equal amount of over and under estimations should produce a skewness of 0. A model that systematically over-predicts path loss (i.e., under-predicts the received signal strength at sites) will have a large positive value and a model that systematically under-predicts path loss will have a large negative value.

We see that even in the mean case, the best models, with their best parameter settings cannot achieve an error of less than 15 dB—five orders of magnitude from the correct value! Even our more permissive performance metrics show the models are unable to widely succeed at seemingly simple tasks of rank-ordering links, or making predictions within two standard deviations of the measured value. This raises the question: is there some common source of error that is affecting all models?

To answer this question, we analyzed the covariance (correlation) between "best prediction error" (the error of the best prediction from all models) and various possible factors. We found no significant correlation between carrier frequency (and therefore neither modulation scheme nor protocol) or antenna geometry. We did however find that link distance is significantly correlated with error for a large number of models. This makes sense: many models were designed with particular lengths of links in mind and we are using them outside of their coverage in this study. It also raises the question: can a hybrid model which uses one of two or more other models at different link lengths produce a model which is better performing than any single model alone?

To answer this question, we implemented two hybrid models. The first uses the Hata model (for medium cities) for links under 500m (where it is well performing) and the Flat-edge model (with 10 "buildings") for longer links (hatam.flatedge10). This model performs marginally better than all other models, producing a corrected RMSE of 14.3 dB. Very slightly better performance is achieved by combining the Hata model with the Egli Model (14.2 dB RMSE).

It is interesting to note that in our analysis the best performing models would *not* typically be chosen for this environment. The two best performing individual models are Flat-Edge and Alsebrook. The Flat-Edge model attempts to calculate the path loss after the signal diffracts over some number of interfering "screens". Here, we pick 10 as the number of screens and obtain decent results, better in fact than the models which take the true terrain profile into account when they make predictions. The Alsebrook model is a simple plane-earth (two-ray) model with some corrections from measurements and an optional static correction for terrain "roughness". In the version that performs best for our measurements, we arbitrarily set the terrain "roughness" to 200m and the "street width" and average "building height" to the suggested default values of 5 and 20m. Perhaps comporting with Occam's Razor, the simplest models (Friis, Egli, Two-Ray) are often as well performing and in many cases better performing than the more complex models with respect to our metrics.

6   Conclusion

Overall our results show that even with the best models, hand-tuned for our environment, we can expect an RMSE in excess of 12 dB (4 orders of magnitude from correct and a far cry from the 3 dB repeated-measures variation which we treat as the gold standard [7]—a result that precludes use in all but the least demanding applications. More forgiving performance metrics show similarly bleak results: no model is able to obtain better than 25% of predictions within two standard deviations of the true value and the best models are typically 20% wrong when it comes to placing links in an order relative to all other links.

We have also shown that picking a "good looking" model at random from the literature and applying it to a new (or even seemingly congruent) domain is a precarious task which can produce substantially wrong predictions. Given this, we believe attempts to model path loss in even more complex environments, such as indoors, are premature. Instead, we advocate a renewed focus on rigorous cross validation using publicly available data sets. We also caution users of these models to be wary of their predictions and to do in-situ validation whenever possible. In future work we expect to explore more complex models for path loss prediction such as those that make use of active correction from measurements (e.g., [8]).

References

1. Abhayawardhana, V., Wassell, I., Crosby, D., Sellars, M., Brown, M.: Comparison of empirical propagation path loss models for fixed wireless access systems. In: VTC 2005-Spring, vol. 1, pp. 73–77 (May 2005)
2. Anderson, E., Phillips, C., Sicker, D., Grunwald, D.: Modeling environmental effects on directionality in wireless networks. In: 5th International Workshop on Wireless Network Measurements (WiNMee) (2009)
3. Cichon, D.J., Kürner, T.: Digital mobile radio towards future generation systems: Cost 231 final report. Tech. rep., COST European Cooperation in the Field of Scientific and Technical Research - Action 231 (1993)
4. Delisle, G.Y., Lefévre, J.P., Lecours, M., Chouinard, J.Y.: Propagation loss prediction: A comparative study with application to the mobile radio channel. IEEE Trans on Ant and Prop VT 34, 86–96 (1985)
5. Durgin, G., Rappaport, T., Xu, H.: Measurements and models for radio path loss and penetration loss in and around homes and trees at 5.85 ghz. IEEE Trans. on Comms. 46(11), 1484–1496 (1998)
6. Erceg, V., Hari, K., et al.: Channel models for fixed wireless applications. Tech. rep., IEEE 802.16 Broadband Wireless Access Working Group (2001)
7. Rizk, K., Wagen, J.F., Gardiol, F.: Two-dimensional ray-tracing modeling for propagation prediction in microcellular environments. IEEE Trans. on Veh. Tech. 46(2), 508–518 (1997)
8. Robinson, J., Swaminathan, R., Knightly, E.W.: Assessment of urban-scale wirelesss networks with a small number of measurements. In: MobiCom (2008)
9. Sharma, P.K., Singh, R.: Comparative analysis of propagation path loss models with field measured databases. International Journal of Engineering Science and Technology 2, 2008–2013 (2010)
10. Shin, H.: Measurements and Models of 802.11B Signal Strength Variation Over Small Distances. Master's thesis, University of Delaware (2010)
11. Sridhara, V., Bohacek, S.: Realistic propagation simulation of urban mesh networks. Computer Networks 51(12), 3392–3412 (2007)

Dissecting 3G Uplink Delay by Measuring in an Operational HSPA Network

Markus Laner[1], Philipp Svoboda[1], Eduard Hasenleithner[2], and Markus Rupp[1]

[1] Vienna University of Technology, Austria
mlaner@nt.tuwien.ac.at
[2] Telecommunications Research Center Vienna (ftw), Austria

Abstract. Users expect mobile Internet access via 3G technologies to be comparable to wired access in terms of throughput and latency. HSPA achieves this for throughput, whereas delay is significantly higher.

In this paper we measure the overall latency introduced by HSUPA and accurately dissect it into contributions of USB-modem (UE), base station (NodeB) and network controller (RNC). We achieve this by combining traces recorded at each interface along the data-path of a public operational UMTS network. The actively generated sample traffic covers real-time applications.

Results show the delay to be strongly dependent on the packet size, with random components depending on synchronization issues. We provide models for latency of single network entities as well as accumulated delay. These findings allow to identify optimum settings in terms of low latency, both for application and network parameters.

1 Introduction

In the past few years the number of mobile devices accessing Internet via 3rd Generation (3G) technologies experienced a significant grow. Novel gadgets such as smartphones and netbooks captured a new market, providing Internet access paired with high mobility. Their users expect a connection quality comparable to wired Internet access in terms of throughput and delay. In contrast to their wired counterpart mobile broadband connections have to deal with varying channel conditions depending on a manifold of parameters such as user position, mobility and total number of users in a cell. This causes challenges in hiding limitations of the access technology from the end-application and user.

The state of the art (2010) radio access technologies are High Speed Downlink Packet Access (HSDPA) and High Speed Uplink Packet Access (HSUPA), specified in the 3rd Generation Partnership Project (3GPP). These technologies allow for throughput comparable to wired access, whereas the access delay is still significantly higher. Although improved compared to former releases [1], HSUPA introduces high latency. The reason being the wireless channel as communication resource shared among unsynchronized users and the master-slave hierarchy in 3G networks, meaning the Base Station (NodeB) has to grant access to the User

N. Spring and G. Riley (Eds.): PAM 2011, LNCS 6579, pp. 52–61, 2011.

Equipment (UE) before data can be send. Hence, realtime applications claiming very low latency encounter difficulties when connected via 3G networks. Such realtime applications may be online games or machine-to-machine communication [2]. Application designers can exploit knowledge about delay characteristics of mobile wireless connections to improve user experience. On the other hand, networks can be optimized in terms of latency, given precise information about its origin. Having reached wired data rates, reduction of delay is one of the main goals for next generation wireless networks.

This work investigates the overall uplink One-Way Delay (OWD), Δ, introduced by an operational HSUPA network and analyses the exact delay contribution of every single network component. We confine ourselves to measure OWD because the up and downlink are strongly asymmetric, hence, Round-Trip Time (RTT) measurements have weak significance. Furthermore, we assess latency of the 3G network only, since it constitutes the first *hop* in terms of packet communication. Data packets have been traced and accurately timestamped on each communication link, from the destination PC throughout the UMTS Terrestrial Radio Access Network (UTRAN) up to the Internet gateway. Since each packet is subject to changes in protocols and size, we particularly monitor Internet Protocol (IP) packets, for which the mobile network is transparent. We pay special attention to the packet size, which has strong influence on the OWD.

To the best of our knowledge this is the first work reporting accurate OWD measurements from a HSUPA network, providing latency statistics of each network component. In [3] the authors performed end-to-end measurements of OWD with high timestamping accuracy, however, without intermediate measurement points. They give results for three different network operators. Their traffic generation method differs significantly from ours. The authors of [4] and [5] provide OWD measurements with low timestamping accuracy from multiple network operators. They use *ICMP ping* messages as measured data traffic, in order to highlight the importance of the right data generation method, which has to be *RCF 2330* [6] compliant in their opinion. RTT measurements from a HSUPA testbed are presented in [7], where data was generated by the *ping* program. In [8] large-scale RTT measurements from a Wide-band Code Division Multiple Access (WCDMA) network are presented, resulting from captured Transmission Control Protocol (TCP) acknowledgement packets. Parts of the presented measurement setup have been reused for this work. Furthermore, possible reasons for variability in delay in wireless networks are highlighted, which do mostly apply for HSUPA as well, e.g. radio channel conditions or scheduling and channel assignment. Finally, the authors of [9] investigate OWD introduced by the Serving GPRS Support Node (SGSN), a 3G network component. Although reusing parts of their measurement setup, results cannot be compared because 3GPP specifies that from Rel. 7 on data traffic bypasses the SGSN.

This paper is structured as follows. Section 2 explains the measurement setup in detail. The results are presented in Section 3 and analyzed in detail. We conclude with Section 4, giving an outlook on future networks.

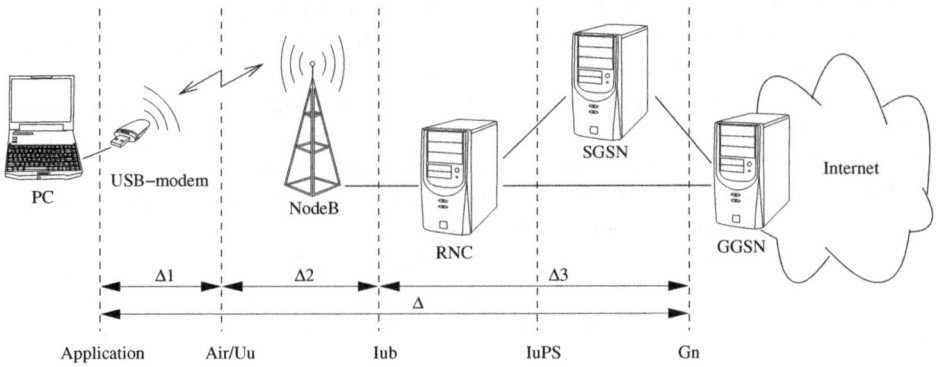

Fig. 1. The UMTS network and its components, 3GPP Release 7

2 Measurement Setup

The measurements were carried out in the operational Universal Mobile Telecommunication System (UMTS) network, of one of the biggest operators in Austria, EU. An overview of the data path of this network is given in Fig. 1. The dashed lines indicate the names of the different interfaces between network components. $\Delta 1$ to $\Delta 3$ indicate the delay contributions of the single elements, Δ the accumulated delay. In the following the components are explained briefly.

- *PC.* The computer on which the end-application is running and application interface traces are captured.
- *USB-modem.* The USB-modem used for measurements is manufactured by Option [10] and equipped with Rel. 7 HSUPA functionality.
- *NodeB.* The Base Station (NodeB) receives and decodes the packets. For controllable measurement conditions an indoor NodeB was chosen.
- *RNC.* The Radio Network Controller (RNC) is the controlling entity in the UTRAN. It coordinates multiple NodeBs. It handles tasks such as ciphering, soft-handover and radio connection manipulations.
- *SGSN.* The Serving GPRS Support Node (SGSN) controls the radio connection and handles mobility issues. Since Rel. 7 it is not part of the data path any more.
- *GGSN.* The Gateway GPRS Support Node (GGSN) is the gateway to the Internet. It sends plain IP-packets towards their destination.

All interfaces shown in Fig. 1, except IuPS, were traced in order to carry out delay measurements of each separate network component. The exact methodology is explained in Section 2.2 for each interface separately. The reason for not tracing the IuPS interface is the *direct tunneling* feature taking effect in Rel. 7. This feature allows the SGSN to remove itself from the data path. Consequently, the expected delay between IuPS and Gn interface is negligible and not considered further.

2.1   Traffic Generation

The traffic patterns sent over the network in order to measure latency were generated actively. According to the proposals in IP Performance Metrics (IPPM) RFC2330 [6], they consist of packets with random size and random-inter arrival time. The importance of the right choice in traffic patterns is highlighted in [5], where the authors reason that invariant traffic generation models such as used by the *ping* command are not adequate for latency measurements in 3G networks. We chose User Datagram Protocol (UDP)-packets for transmission, whereas we allow for large packets up to 10 kByte. This approach is unusual for network measurements, because big packets are segmented into smaller packets of maximum Packet Data Unit (PDU) size. However, the 3G network is transparent for IP packets and interprets segments just as extra payload. Furthermore, such packet sizes are demanded by latency sensitive applications [11], and therefore considered in this work. In order to guarantee the USB-modem is operating in HSUPA mode, we kept the mean data rate above 1 kbit/s. Otherwise the network scheduler would release the HSUPA connection and force the modem to WCDMA Forward Access Channel (FACH) operation, in order to save radio resources. Consequences of such a fallback are observed in [4] and [3], resulting in very high delay values for small packet sizes. In the context of this study these effects are undesired and hence avoided.

2.2   Measurement Devices

OWD measurements require careful consideration of (i) time synchronization of the measurement entities and (ii) accurate packet recognition. In our measurement setup we use Global Positioning System (GPS) receivers for time synchronization, which allow for a precision better than 1 μs. This precision is satisfactory for our purposes, since we plan to achieve a maximum resolution of 100 μs. We use full IP and UDP headers to distinguish between packets at different interfaces. Since the whole 3G network, from UE to GGSN corresponds to one *hop* in terms of IP-networking, both packet headers are not altered during the propagation. In the following sections measurement methods and devices are described.

Gn Interface. As depicted in Fig. 1, the Gn interface connects the GGSN to the rest of the 3G network. We passively monitor this link by means of wiretaps and dedicated tracing hardware, i.e. Endace DAG cards [12] with GPS synchronization. The system has been developed in an earlier project in collaboration

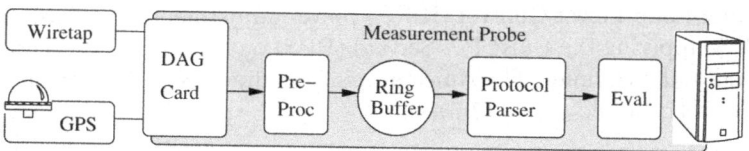

Fig. 2. Measurement setup at the Gn and Iub interfaces

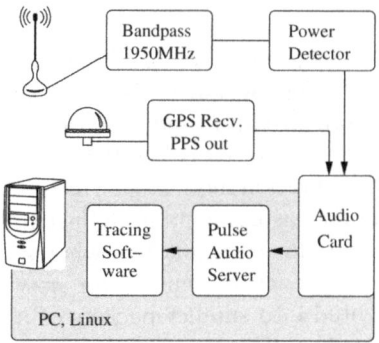

Fig. 3. Transmit power measurement setup (air interface)

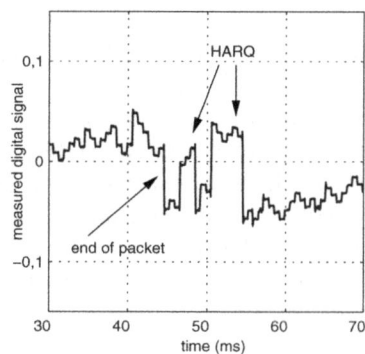

Fig. 4. Measured transmit power of UE (digital domain)

with Telecommunications Research Center Vienna (ftw), see [13] and [14]. An outline of the measurement setup is given in Fig. 2. The timestamping accuracy is specified by the manufacturer with less than 200 ns.

Iub Interface. For data acquisition at the Iub interface the same measurement setup as for Gn has been deployed, see Fig. 2. Tracing at this interface appears particularly challenging because of the complex protocol hierarchy, ciphered payload and *soft handover* [15]. IP packets do not appear in one piece at this interface but split into single Radio Link Control (RLC) frames which are timestamped separately.

Air Interface. Packet sniffing (fully decoding) at the air interface we consider too challenging for our purposes. Instead, we can identify start and end time of single packets by monitoring the transmission power of the UE. This is HSUPA specific, since the NodeB assigns extra transmission power to the UE via Relative Grant Channel (RGCH), in order to transmit data in uplink [1]. This method allows to identify packet transmissions, as long as the inter-arrival time of packets is big enough to guarantee a change in allocated transmission power between packets. Depending on the payload size we varied this time from 10 ms to 100 ms. The measurement setup is depicted in Fig. 3. An antenna with bandpass filter (1920 - 1980 Mhz) and attached power detector [16] is placed nearby the UE. The measured signal is fed into a standard audio device of a PC, with a sampling rate of 44.1 kHz and 16 bit resolution. Figure 4 shows the resulting digital signal. Here we observe the end of a packet transmission (44 ms) with Hybrid Automatic Repeat Request (HARQ) retransmission (46 ms, 50 ms). The small steps result from the Inner Loop Power Control (ILPC) power adjustments. Synchronization is achieved by applying the Pulse Per Second (PPS) output of a GPS receiver [17] at the second audio channel. The timestamping accuracy is limited by the inter-sample time of the audio card (22.7 μs).

Application Interface. We chose the traffic generating application and the application-interface traffic monitoring tool to reside on the same PC. Therefore

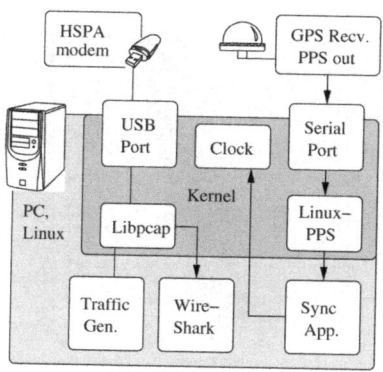

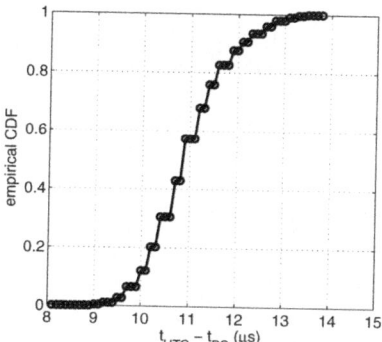

Fig. 5. Application interface measurement setup

Fig. 6. Synchronization quality

we verify the CPU load to not exceed 20 % during measurements and hence assume the mutual influence of applications to be negligible. Packet capturing was performed by the use of *libpcap* [18] and the *Wireshark* tool, see Fig. 5. In order to achieve correct timestamping of the traffic, we synchronize the software-clock of the PC to Coordinated Universal Time (UTC). We deploy a GPS receiver [17] attached at the serial port and the *LinuxPPS* toolkit [19] to adjust the PC clock, see Fig. 5. The synchronization accuracy was verified with a rubidium oscillator, results yield roughly $10\,\mu s$, see Fig. 6.

3 Results

The measurement results presented in the following are obtained from a protected environment. Although, the NodeB to which we established connections is operational and publicly available, it is deployed in an indoor scenario (office) with low cell load and a relatively small number of users. Furthermore, it communicates with the RNC via Asynchronous Transfer Mode (ATM) connection and the Transmission Time Intervals (TTIs) have 10 ms duration. HSUPA also provides 2 ms TTIs for improved latency, hence, the presented results constitute a worst case scenario. The channel conditions were stationary and the data rate was constant in the long run. As pointed out in [8], the deployment scenario strongly influences OWD. We publicly advertise a sample data set [20], enabling reproduction of the following results.

3.1 Single Components

In the following we provide delay measurement results focusing on the single network components, named $\Delta 1$ to $\Delta 3$ in Fig. 1. This information allows to identify main sources of latency and to detect network settings which are improvable in terms of delay.

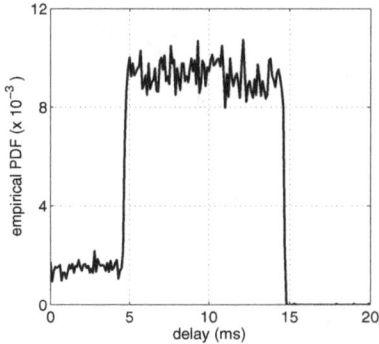

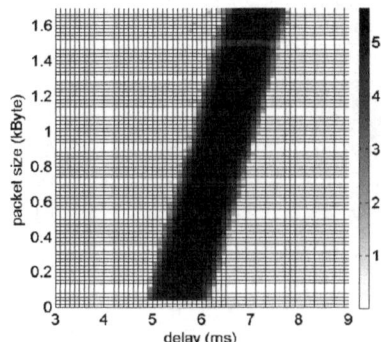

Fig. 7. Delay $\Delta 1$, empirical PDF   **Fig. 8.** $\Delta 2$ over size, log. histogram

UE. The latency contribution of the USB-modem, $\Delta 1$ (see Fig. 1), is shown in Fig. 7. The delay PDF results from timestamps obtained by tracing at the application interface and the rising edge of the transmission power at the air interface. Thereby the packet size varies from 1 to 1500 Bytes. The delay distribution is concentrated between 5 to 15 ms, where it exhibits uniform character. This can be explained as a contribution of 5 ms caused by the USB-modem due to data processing and a random contribution of up to 10 ms while waiting for a transmission window. The start of a transmission can only take place at the beginning of a TTI, whereas data appears randomly in the transmission queue and hence, is kept for a random time until the outset of the next TTI. This delay contribution can be removed by designing HSUPA aware software applications. The small amount of packets yielding a delay below 5 ms are measurement artifacts. They result from retransmitted packets or control information, misinterpreted as part of the user data. Increasing the packet inter-arrival time would improve the situation but, as explained in Section 2.1, this would increase the probability of switching to normal Dedicated Channel (DCH) operation. Figure 11(a) shows a histogram of delay and size for $\Delta 1$. In contrast to Fig. 7, the falling edge of the transmission power is used to obtain the timestamps, thus, transmission delay is included as well. We model the delay contributed by the UE, the queuing and the transmission as

$$\Delta 1 \;=\; 5\text{ms} + X \cdot 10\text{ms} + \lceil l/\alpha \rceil \cdot 10\text{ms} \,, \tag{1}$$

whereas X is a uniformly distributed random variable between 0 and 1, l is the payload length of the transmitted packet, α denotes the length-factor, equivalent to the step hight in Fig. 11(b) (e.g. 800 Bytes) and $\lceil \cdot \rceil$ is the ceiling operation.

NodeB. In Fig. 8 the reader finds a logarithmic histogram of delay $\Delta 2$ and packet size, thus, corresponding to the delay introduced by the NodeB. Thereby the value assigned to different colors of the grid corresponds to the natural logarithm of the number of packets corresponding to one parcel of the grid. The delays are calculated by subtracting the timestamp of the falling edge of the

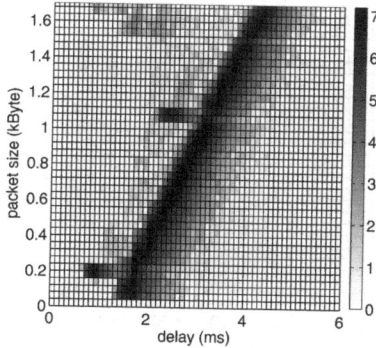

Fig. 9. Delay $\Delta 3$ over packet size, log. histogram

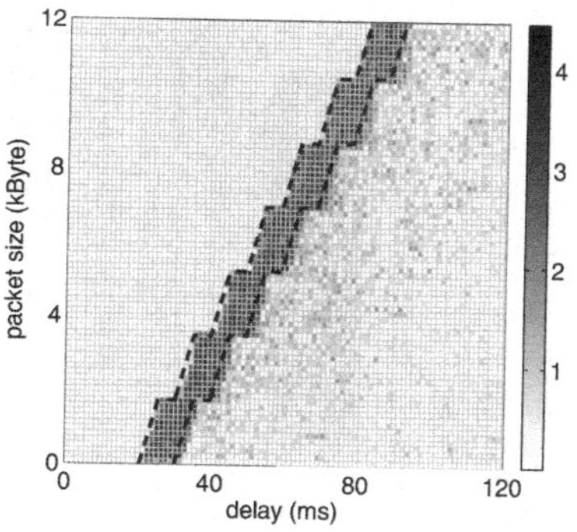

Fig. 10. $\Delta 1 + \Delta 2 + \Delta 3$ over packet size, log. histogram

transmission power at the air interface from the last RLC frame transmitted over the Iub interface. The minimum is 5 ms, whereas up to 7 ms of latency are experienced depending on the packet size. The contribution of the NodeB can thus be modeled as

$$\Delta 2 \;=\; 5\text{ms} + (l\%\alpha) \cdot 1\text{ms/kByte} , \tag{2}$$

whereas % denotes the modulo operator and the expression $(l\%\alpha)$ introduces extra delay growing linearly with packet size.

RNC. Figure 9 shows the delay characteristics of the RNC, $\Delta 3$ (see Fig. 1). The delay is the difference in time of the last RLC packet fragment at the Iub interface and the last IP packet fragment at the Gn interface.

The minimum latency introduced by the RNC is 1.5 ms. Additionally the packets experience an extra delay up to 4 ms, depending on the packet size. This can be modeled in the same way as for the NodeB by

$$\Delta 3 \;=\; 1.5\text{ms} + (l\%\alpha) \cdot 2\text{ms/kByte} . \tag{3}$$

3.2 Accumulated Delay

Accumulated delay is the delay experienced by the user application. Figure 10 displays this accumulated delay for a large variation of packet sizes. The dashed lines correspond to the model illustrated below. Furthermore, Fig. 11 shows the accumulation of the latency throughout the 3G network. In other words those figures show the delay contributed by the first *hop* of the communication link.

By combining the Eqn. (1), (2) and (3), we obtain an expression for the accumulated latency,

$$\Delta \;=\; 11.5\text{ms} + X \cdot 10\text{ms} + \lceil l/\alpha \rceil \cdot 10\text{ms} + (l\%\alpha) \cdot 3\text{ms/kByte} . \tag{4}$$

This expression accurately models the regions of high density in Fig. 10 and 11(c). The parameter α is strongly dependent on a manifold of parameters, such as data

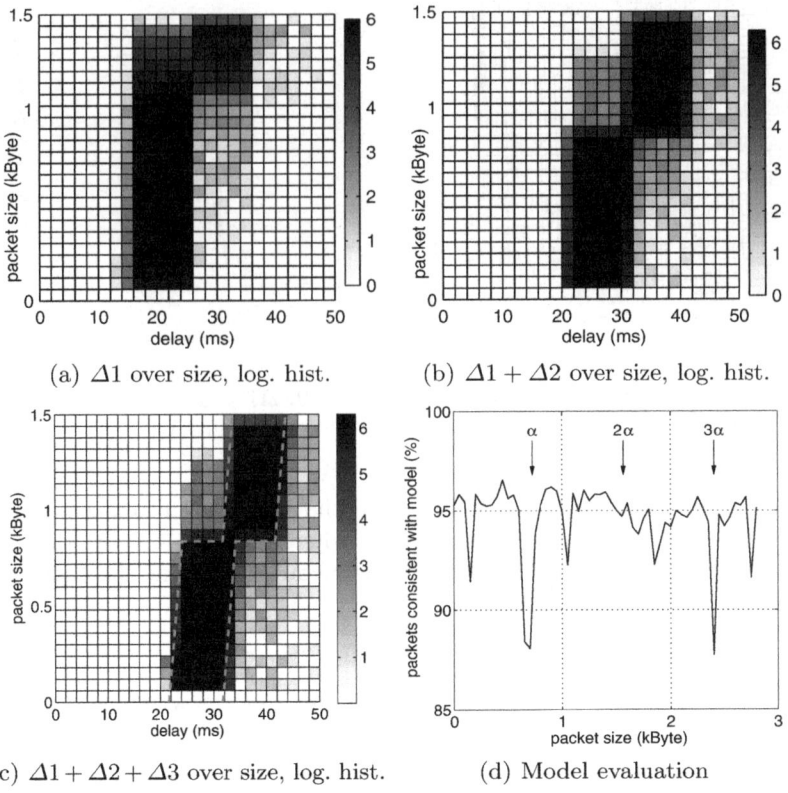

(a) $\Delta 1$ over size, log. hist.

(b) $\Delta 1 + \Delta 2$ over size, log. hist.

(c) $\Delta 1 + \Delta 2 + \Delta 3$ over size, log. hist.

(d) Model evaluation

Fig. 11. Accumulated delay

rate and channel quality, and is defined by the HSUPA scheduler. Comparing Fig. 10 and 11(c) we estimate α as 1800 Byte and 800 Byte respectively, which is a considerable variation, although in the measurement setup only the mean data rate changed. All possible values for α are listed in [21], Annex B. Nevertheless, we expect α not to drop below 200 Bytes for reasonable channel conditions.

The accuracy of the model can be visually evaluated from Fig. 10 and 11(c). The dashed lines show the lower and upper bounds, within which the model assumes a uniform distribution. In Fig. 11(d) a numerical evaluation of the accuracy is depicted. Thereby a data set of packet sizes up to 3 kByte is compared to the model. The result shows that 90 - 95 % of all packets are consistent with the model.

4   Conclusion and Outlook

In this paper we present measurements, analysis and models of latency components of 3G HSUPA communication. We inspected the network elements - user equipment (UE), base station (NodeB) and network controller (RNC) - in live operation. The average delay value for a 1kByte packet is 30 ms (UE: 66%, NodeB:

20%, RNC: 14%). Therefore the 3GPP Long Term Evolution (LTE) delay performance target of 5ms makes improvements in the core network mandatory. Based on the analysis of the results we designed a model for each of the delay components. It provides an average performance of 95%.

Acknowledgments. We would like to thank Sebastian Caban, Robert Langwieser and Michael Fischer for contributing technical expertise. Furthermore, we thank *A1 Telekom Austria* and *ftw* for technical assistance and the *EU FP7 LoLa Project* for financial support.

References

1. Holma, H., Toskala, A.: Hsdpa/Hsupa For Umts. In: High Speed Radio Access for Mobile Communications. Wiley, Chichester (2006)
2. LoLa consortium. D2.1 Target Application Scenarios (2010), http://www.ict-lola.eu/
3. Arlos, P., Fiedler, M.: Influence of the Packet Size on the One-Way Delay in 3G Networks. In: Krishnamurthy, A., Plattner, B. (eds.) PAM 2010. LNCS, vol. 6032, pp. 61–70. Springer, Heidelberg (2010)
4. Fabini, J., Karner, W., Wallentin, L., Baumgartner, T.: The Illusion of Being Deterministic – Application-Level Considerations on Delay in 3G HSPA Networks. In: Fratta, L., Schulzrinne, H., Takahashi, Y., Spaniol, O. (eds.) NETWORKING 2009. LNCS, vol. 5550, pp. 301–312. Springer, Heidelberg (2009)
5. Fabini, J., Wallentin, L., Reichl, P.: The importance of being really random: methodological aspects of IP-layer 2G and 3G network delay assessment. In: ICC 2009, Dresden, Germany (2009)
6. Paxson, V., Almes, G., Mahdavi, J., Mathis, M.: Framework for IP Performance Metrics (1998), http://www.ietf.org/rfc/rfc2330.txt
7. Liu, J., Tapia, P., Kwok, P., Karimli, Y.: Performance and Capacity of HSUPA in Lab Environment. In: VTC Spring 2008, Singapore (2008)
8. Vacirca, F., Ricciato, F., Pilz, R.: Large-Scale RTT Measurements from an Operational UMTS/GPRS Network. In: WICON 2005, Budapest, Hungary (2005)
9. Romirer-Maierhofer, P., Ricciato, F., Coluccia, A.: Explorative analysis of one-way delays in a mobile 3G network. In: LANMAN 2008, Cluj-Napoca, Romania (2008)
10. Option Wireless Technology, http://www.option.com/
11. LoLa consortium. D 3.2. Network related analysis of M2M and online-gaming traffic in HSPA (2010), http://www.ict-lola.eu/
12. Endace DAG, http://www.endace.com/
13. The Darwin Project, http://userver.ftw.at/~ricciato/darwin/
14. Ricciato, F.: Traffic monitoring and analysis for the optimization of a 3G network. IEEE Wireless Communications 13, 42–49 (2006)
15. 3GPP. TS 25.401, UTRAN overall description, http://www.3gpp.org/
16. Linear Technology, LT5534 - RF Power Detector, http://www.linear.com/
17. SiRF star III GPS Receivers, http://www.csr.com/products/technology/gps
18. libpcap - library for network traffic capture, http://www.tcpdump.org/
19. LinuxPPS Project, http://wiki.enneenne.com/index.php/LinuxPPS_support
20. Vienna University of Technology, Institute of Telecommunication - Downloads, https://www.nt.tuwien.ac.at/downloads/featured-downloads
21. 3GPP. TS 25.321, MAC protocol specification, http://www.3gpp.org/

On the Potential of Fixed-Beam 60 GHz Network Interfaces in Mobile Devices

Kishore Ramachandran[1], Ravi Kokku[1], Rajesh Mahindra[1],
and Kenichi Maruhashi[2]

[1] NEC Laboratories America Inc., Princeton, NJ
[2] NEC Corporation, Tokyo, Japan

Abstract. The small form-factor and significantly high bandwidth of 60 GHz wireless network interfaces make them an attractive technology for future bandwidth-hungry mobile devices. To overcome several challenges in making such 60 GHz communication practical, beamforming is widely accepted as an integral part of 60 GHz devices. In this paper, we perform a first-of-its-kind user study to answer a rather unconventional question: *can users explicitly assist* in aligning fixed-beam directional antennas on the transmit/receive side? Our measurements involving 30 users show significant promise, and lean us towards answering the question in the affirmative. The implication of these observations is in substantially simplifying the design of 60 GHz interfaces for mobile devices.

1 Introduction

Recent years have seen a surge of interest in using mm-wave or 60 GHz radios for short range (<10 meters), multi-Gbps communication [1,2,3,9,17]. The WiGig alliance [17] envisions that 60 GHz communication will be common place in multiple deployment scenarios (Figure 1). These can be categorized into static-to-static, handheld-to-static and handheld-to-handheld communications, of which we focus on the latter two scenarios in this paper. Examples of the handheld-to-static scenarios include sync-and-go applications such as movie and music downloads from public kiosks, content prefetching for future disconnected operations, "google-in-the-pocket" by saving large amounts of user-relevant data locally, aggregation and upload of non-real-time sensor data from mobile devices, etc. Examples of handheld-to-handheld scenarios include file sharing applications between users.

For any deployment involving 60 GHz radios, directional transmission is crucial to leverage their high bandwidth potential. Directional transmission can be achieved with (a) fixed directional antennas, (b) switched-beam antennas, or (c) adaptive beamforming. These approaches ((a) to (c)) are in the order of increasing complexity, cost and power consumption, and at the same time increasing flexibility or adaptability to changing conditions; selecting the appropriate approach hence engenders a tradeoff during system design [12].

To assist in striking the tradeoff effectively, in this paper, we ask the following question: *can users assist in aligning fixed-beam antennas on the transmit/receive*

N. Spring and G. Riley (Eds.): PAM 2011, LNCS 6579, pp. 62–71, 2011.

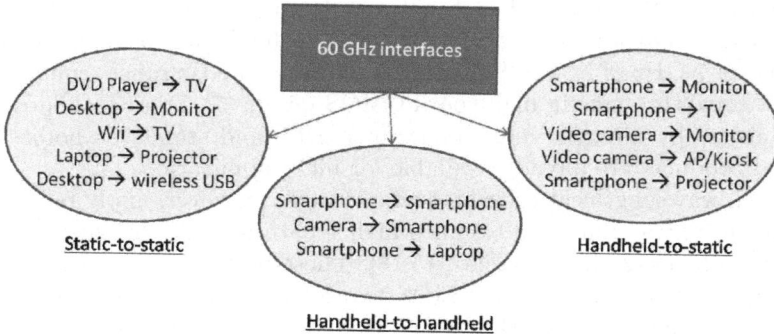

Fig. 1. Deployment Scenarios for 60 GHz wireless interfaces

side for 60 GHz communications? If the answer is yes, it could simplify the design of mobile devices by making the antenna a passive element, thereby reducing the initial cost and continuous power consumption. We ask this question based on the intuition that 60 GHz communication is predominantly line-of-sight. And for enabling short distance line-of-sight communications, our hypothesis is that human intuition (along with minimal feedback from the system) is good enough to align the transmitter receiver pairs. A challenge, however, is that at these frequencies, the wavelength is ∼5mm, and hence even a small movement can cause significant signal fluctuation.

Our measurement study includes using 60 GHz radios as transmitter and receiver, with 30 users who perform repeated data transfer sessions, spanning over multiple days. The study with handheld-to-static scenario shows several interesting observations: (1) Users with little prior practice can align the antennas very well 80% of the time getting close to 1 Gbps throughput, when the distance between the transmit and receive antennas is within 1 meter. (2) Human-assisted alignment is *bimodal*; i.e. users either align very well or go completely out-of-alignment. Once mis-aligned, users correct it within a short period of time (92% of the time users re-align within 2 seconds) to achieve high throughput again, owing to the feedback provided by the system. (3) With time, users learn how to align the antennas, and hence get high throughput continuously. We make similar observations with the handheld-to-handheld scenario.

The rest of the paper is organized as follows. Section 2 provides a brief background on 60 GHz radios and directional transmission. Section 3 describes our measurement methodology. Section 4 discusses the results and their implications in detail. Section 5 discusses the limitations of this study, and Section 6 concludes with future directions.

2   Background on 60 GHz Radios

Recent years have seen a surge of interest in using 60 GHz radios due to several reasons: (1) the rapid emergence of sophisticated mobile devices and personal area applications that demand high network bandwidth, (2) the lack of scope for such high bandwidth in other short-range technologies [5,12], and (3) the availability of 7 GHz of license-free spectrum in the 60 GHz range, coupled with the recent breakthroughs in high-speed CMOS design [7]. Draft standards have been published by multiple industry forums [2,17] and standards bodies [1,9], and initial products are already available for niche applications [3].

The small wavelengths at these frequency ranges, however, imply reduced antenna aperture areas that lead to much higher path loss [7] and increased susceptibility to blockage by obstacles [15,18]. These additional losses along with the high noise figure of 60 GHz CMOS transceiver implementations, and the low-power requirements make the feasibility of delivering Gbps speeds challenging even at distances of 10 meters. Consequently, focused transmission through beamforming is considered an integral part of 60 GHz communication [2,17] (unlike cellular and WLAN standards where beamforming is included as an optional feature), and also receives significant research focus [11,13,14,16].

In this paper, we explore the potential of *user assistance* in aligning fixed-beam antennas for focused transmission. Fixed-beam antennas are significantly simpler than adaptive beamforming antennas and consume lower power, thus making them more attractive for handheld devices.

3   Measurement Setup and Methodology

Our measurement testbed mainly consists of 60 GHz radios with fixed-beam directional antennas. Specifically, our experiments focus on the following questions:

1. What is the throughput achieved by users in such settings? How does it fluctuate due to users holding such a device in their hands?
2. How long does it take for users to re-align once alignment is broken?
3. Does user-assisted alignment improve over time, i.e. can users "learn" alignment over a period of time?

We consider two different application contexts: (a) when a user is interacting with static infrastructure (i.e. *handheld-to-static*), e.g. smartphone-to-display, and (b) when a user is interacting with another user (i.e. *handheld-to-handheld*), e.g. smartphone-to-smartphone.

User population: Our population mix consists of users with and without a technical background: out of our thirty users, twenty four have at least some engineering background, and the remaining are from the legal/administration/janitorial departments. All users are male or female adults between 25-50 years of age.

Setup: Our setup is shown in Figure 2. The 60 GHz transceivers in our study are described in detail in [10]. Briefly, these transceivers operate at a carrier frequency of 60.3 GHz with a channel bandwidth of 1.6GHz. Taken together with

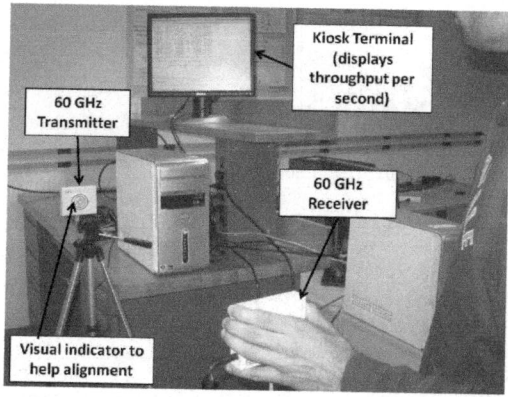

Fig. 2. Measurement setup, with tripod-mounted transmitter and handheld receiver

amplitude shift-keying (ASK) modulation, a $36°$-Horizontal beamwidth (measured) antenna, and an output power of 10.4dBm, these transceivers can support a data rate of 1.25Gbps within a 7-10m range. All our experiments are however carried out within a 2m range such that packet losses are mostly due to user-induced mis-alignment. We use two Dell desktop SMP machines running Linux. We use *nuttcp v6.1.2* [4] to generate traffic at the transmitter, and *gulp* [8] for packet capture on the receiver. We also tune the kernel buffers to ensure that the bottleneck is indeed the wireless link. Packets are marked with monotonically increasing sequence numbers to enable computing different metrics.

Metrics: To quantify performance, we measure *packet delivery rate (PDR)* and *throughput*, which are relevant to the target network-intensive applications. The per-second throughput is also made visible to the users on the Kiosk terminal, which helps them detect misalignment and realign better. We also measure the *re-alignment time* using the packet sequence numbers, i.e. how long it takes for users to re-align their transceivers once alignment is broken.

4   Results

Effectiveness of User-assisted Alignment: We first conduct experiments to study the performance of user-assisted alignment in the handheld-to-static scenario. In this set of experiments, thirty users try to align the handheld receiver with the tripod-mounted transmitter, while receiving 1 GB of data (731000 UDP packets with 1470-byte payload at 1Gbps). At the receiver, we determine the start and end time of each experiment using nuttcp's control packets. These control packets utilize the wired interface between the transmitting and receiving machines. For every user, we repeat the experiment five times (i.e. have five different data transfer sessions).

Figure 3(a) shows the sorted average throughput in each session at different distances from the static transceiver for all users. We observe that users are able

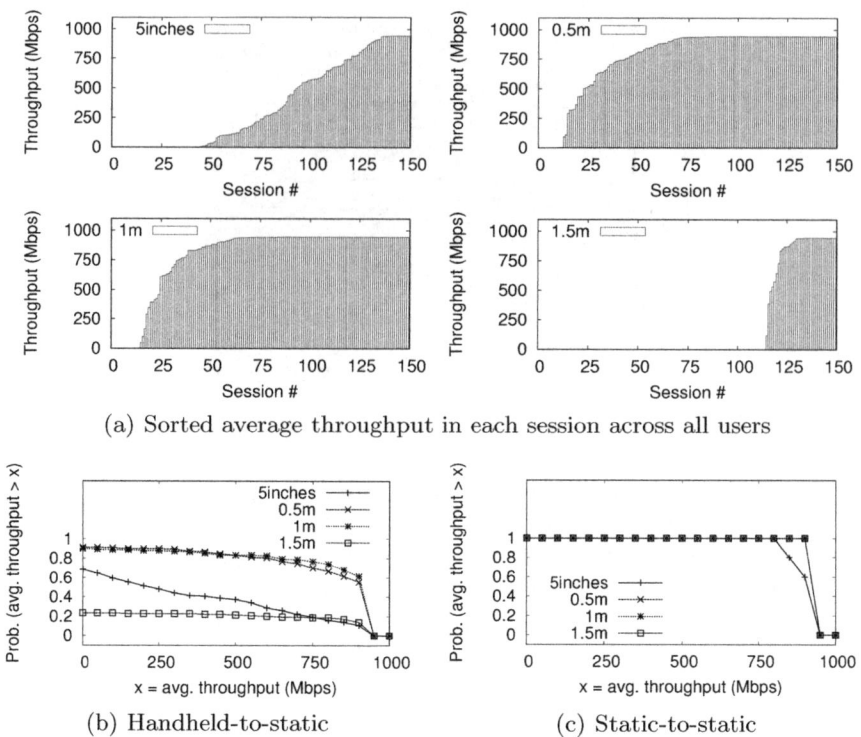

(a) Sorted average throughput in each session across all users

(b) Handheld-to-static

(c) Static-to-static

Fig. 3. Average throughput for all users in the handheld-to-static scenario

to achieve much higher throughput on average at the 0.5m and 1m distances than at the 5 inches and 1.5m distances. For comparison, we also repeat the experiment multiple times with a static-to-static scenario with both the transceivers mounted on tripods and carefully aligned. Figures 3(b) and 3(c) show the average throughput distribution in the handheld-to-static setting (across all users) and the static-to-static setting respectively. At 0.5m and 1m, the graphs show that users are able to achieve high throughput (700Mbps 80% of the time), much like the static-to-static scenario. At 5 inches and 1.5m, users are unable to achieve such high throughput continuously, although the properly-aligned static-to-static scenario can achieve full throughput.

To understand the underlying packet loss behavior due to mis-alignment by users, we plot the probability density function (PDF) of the PDR (discretized into 5% buckets) at different distances in Figure 4. The hardware we use drops packets locally if the link is not aligned, as determined by PHY-layer pilot signals. The PDR is computed in 100ms intervals. Surprisingly, we observe a *bimodal* packet loss distribution—packet loss is either negligible and PDR is close to one, or all packets in the interval are lost. Further, the low average throughput at 5 inches and 1.5m is explained by the high frequency with which PDR is zero in both these cases (60% of the time at 5 inches and 80% of the time at 1.5m).

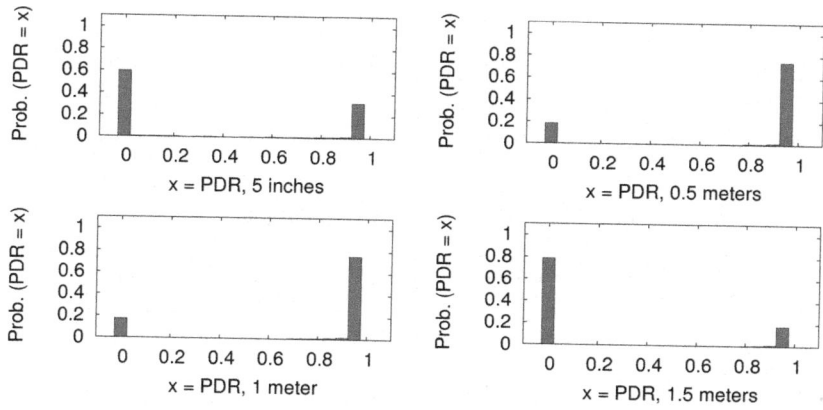

Fig. 4. PDF of PDR in the handheld-to-static scenario

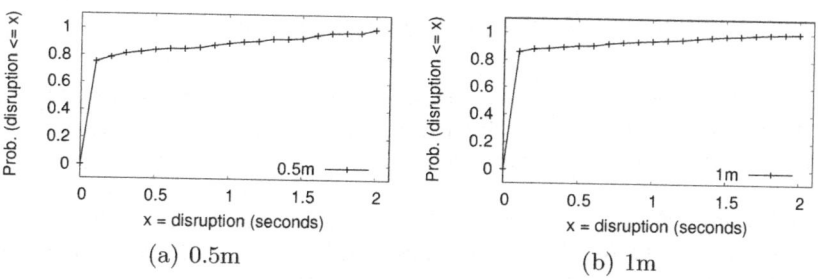

(a) 0.5m   (b) 1m

Fig. 5. CDF of connectivity disruption durations due to mis-alignment

At 1.5m, we observe that users find it hard to align the transceivers with the visual input we provided. Many users requested for additional input either in the form of a laser-pointer or in the form of device vibration (common in today's smartphones). We believe that the high packet loss at 5 inches is due to the well-known receiver saturation problem [6]. This hypothesis is confirmed by holding the transceiver slightly higher or lower than the intuitive alignment height that reduces the received signal; we observe increased throughput by doing so. Independently, some users observed this behavior over time and used it to improve their throughput at 5 inches. We made similar height adjustment for the static-to-static scenario in Figure 3(c).

The bi-modal loss behavior has the advantage that it simplifies the feedback given to applications and users. In practice, users are more likely to be able to understand (and adopt) systems with simpler feedback.

Figures 5(a) and 5(b) show the distribution of connectivity disruption (intervals greater than 10ms in which no packets were received) across all users. The graph shows that 80% of the time, disruption is only about 100ms. Such fine-timescale disruptions can be handled by backoffs and retransmissions at the MAC layer, thereby avoiding their exposure to higher layer protocols like TCP.

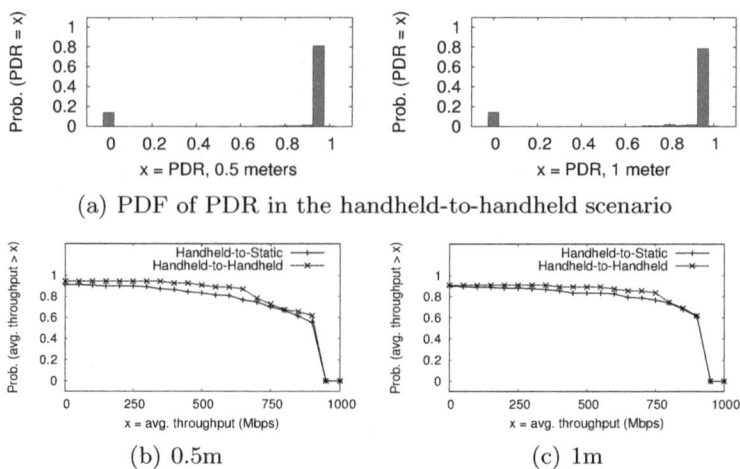

(a) PDF of PDR in the handheld-to-handheld scenario

(b) 0.5m   (c) 1m

Fig. 6. PDR and average throughput comparison

These results show that there is a region in which users can comfortably align fixed-beam 60 GHz transceivers, which should be taken into consideration when designing systems using such transceivers.

Handheld-to-handheld scenario: Figure 6 shows the result of the same experiments with both transceivers being handheld. We run this experiment with 12 different pairs of users. We observe that the PDR and throughput behavior is similar to the handheld-to-static scenario—the PDR is bimodal and the throughput distribution is similar.

Re-alignment time: Once connectivity breaks due to mis-alignment, we measure how long it takes for users to align back. We ran experiments in which ten users were asked to re-align their receiver after explicit (and sudden) alignment changes to the transmitter. To carry out these alignment changes, we rotate the transmitter at random instances of time when data transfer is taking place. After each rotation, we wait for the user to re-align the handheld receiver (and stabilize the throughput), and then initiate the next re-alignment sequence. Such a methodology ensures that the drop in PDR or throughput was specifically due to the explicitly induced re-alignment. Figure 7(a) shows the CDF of the realignment delay from these experiments. At 0.5m, we see that users are able to re-align their transceivers within 2 seconds 92% of time and take atmost 4 seconds to re-align. At 1m, we see that the re-alignment delay is slightly higher. This experiment also gives us an idea of the initial alignment time for users.

Improvement in alignment over time: We repeat our first experiment of 1 GB data transfer with 10 users with lowest throughput. We compare the total data transferred in their two iterations in Figure 7(b). At 0.5m, users are able to transfer 5-764% more data in Iteration 2. Even at 1m, seven out of the ten users

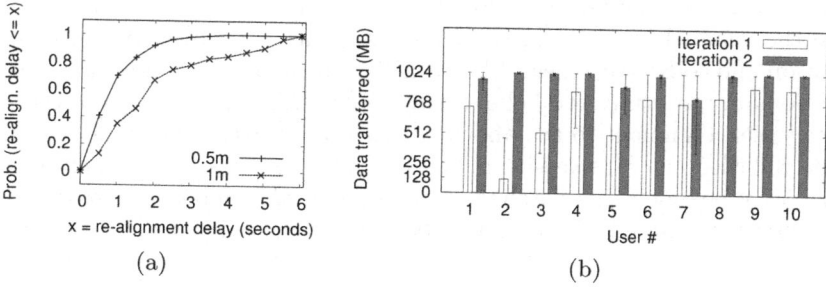

Fig. 7. (a) Re-alignment delay in seconds, and (b) two iterations of data transfer (in MB) showing learning behavior at 0.5m

could improve the average amount of data transferred from 7-140% (results not shown here). We attribute this improvement to users "learning" to improve their alignment over time by figuring out the sensitivity of the device to mis-alignment.

In summary, at close enough distances, we observe that users are able to align fixed-beam antennas well, thereby motivating their consideration for adoption in power- and complexity-constrained mobile handheld devices.

5 Discussion and Limitations

Fixed-beam antennas are also useful in static-to-static scenarios in a managed deployment, as long as line-of-sight is ensured. Alternately, handheld-to-static and handheld-to-handheld can be converted to a static-to-static scenario by aligning the devices on a stable platform. Nevertheless, the particular scenario instantiated with a given pair of devices is mainly a matter of users' convenience.

Like most user studies, this study is also done on a small set of users. To understand the sensitivity, we use the data obtained for Figure 3, and plot the throughput distribution with different numbers of users. In Figure 8(a) and Figure 8(b), we see that the throughput distribution does not change much beyond 10 users, thereby indicating that small number of users can provide sufficiently representative results.

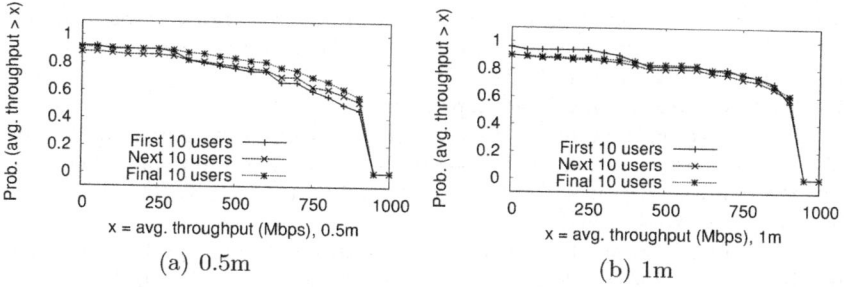

Fig. 8. Throughput distribution for different numbers of users (handheld-to-static)

Unfortunately, we did not have access to the internals of the current hardware to tune the channel bandwidth, transmit power, antenna beamwidth, and the modulation and coding schemes. While this limitation does not affect the general observations in our study, we believe that future work should explore the sensitivity of user alignment to the above parameters. Further, the paper relies on conventional wisdom that fixed-beam antennas are more cost- and power-efficient than adaptive beamforming antenna systems; as hardware becomes more accessible, future work should explore quantifying the cost and power benefits.

6   Conclusion and Future Directions

This paper focuses on answering the following question: *Can users explicitly assist* in aligning fixed-beam directional antennas on the transmit/receive side of a 60 GHz communication link? Our study reveals three useful conclusions: (1) Users can align the antennas very well 80% of the time getting full throughput at reasonable distances. (2) When mis-aligned, users correct it within a short period of time to achieve full throughput again. and (3) With time, users learn how to align the antennas, and hence get near full-throughput continuously. Using fixed-beam antennas can significantly simplify 60 GHz interfaces on mobile devices, thereby making them cheaper and energy-efficient—both of which are attractive benefits to mobile equipment manufacturers.

The work raises several interesting questions: What are the design considerations for a MAC to mask off the effects of mis-alignment? Can such a MAC ensure that traditional higher-layer protocols are completely unaffected? While the user attempts to align the antennas, can another omni-directional antenna or a wider beamwidth antenna allow for low rate communication, to ensure that the user sees more graceful throughput degradation? We plan to explore these directions in our future work.

References

1. MAC and PHY Specifications for High Rate WPANs, mm-wave-based alternative PHY extension. IEEE Std 802.15.3c-2009 (Amendment to IEEE Std 802.15.3-2003), pp. c1–187 (October 2009)
2. WirelessHD Specification Overview (August 2009), http://tinyurl.com/2ehkq6f
3. WirelessHD Product Listing (2010), http://tinyurl.com/2d3f8gr
4. Fink, B., Scott, R.: nuttcp traffic generator,
   http://www.lcp.nrl.navy.mil/nuttcp/nuttcp-6.1.2/
5. Daniels, R., Heath, R.: 60 GHz Wireless Communications: Emerging Requirements and Design Recommendations. IEEE Vehicular Tech. Mag. (September 2007)
6. Dixon, R.C.: Radio Receiver Design. Section 5.2, vol. 104, pp. 109–111. Marcel Dekker AG, New York (1998)
7. Doan, C., Emami, S., Sobel, D., Niknejad, A., Brodersen, R.: Design Considerations for 60 GHz CMOS Radios. IEEE Comm. Mag. 42(12) (December 2004)
8. gulp. Lossless Gigabit Remote Packet Capture With Linux,
   http://staff.washington.edu/corey/gulp/

9. IEEE TGad. PHY/MAC Complete Proposal Specification (approved as TGad D0.1) (May 2010), http://tinyurl.com/2fqlkxx

10. Ohata, K.: NEC Corporation. Application of 60 GHz WPAN, https://mentor.ieee.org/802.15/dcn/04/15-04-0653-01-003c-application-60ghz-wpan.ppt

11. Lee, H.-H., Ko, Y.-C.: Efficient Codebook-based Symbol-wise Beamforming for Millimeter-wave WPAN System. In: ACM mmCom Workshop (2010)

12. Park, C., Rappaport, T.: Short-Range Wireless Communications for Next-Generation Networks: UWB, 60 GHz Millimeter-Wave WPAN, And ZigBee. IEEE Wireless Communications 14(4), 70–78 (2007)

13. Park, M., Pan, H.K.: Effect of Device Mobility and Phased Array Antennas on 60 GHz Wireless Networks. In: ACM mmCom Workshop (2010)

14. Ramachandran, K., Prasad, N., Hosoya, K., Maruhashi, K., Rangarajan, S.: Adaptive Beamforming for 60 GHz Radios: Challenges and Preliminary Solutions. In: ACM mmCom Workshop (2010)

15. Singh, S., Ziliotto, F., Madhow, U., Belding, E.M., Rodwell, M.: Blockage and Directivity in 60 GHz Wireless Personal Area Networks. In: IEEE JSAC (2009)

16. Tsang, Y.M., Lin, S., Poon, A.S.: Fast Beam Training for mmWave Communication System: from Algorithm to Circuits. In: ACM mmCom Workshop, Chicago, Illinois, USA, pp. 27–32 (2010)

17. WiGig Alliance. WiGig Specifications (May 2010), http://tinyurl.com/29sql4q

18. Xu, H., Kukshya, V., Rappaport, T.: Spatial and Temporal Characteristics of 60 GHz Indoor Channels. IEEE JSAC 20(3), 620–630 (2002)

On the Feasibility of Prefetching and Caching for Online TV Services: A Measurement Study on Hulu

Dilip Kumar Krishnappa, Samamon Khemmarat, Lixin Gao, and Michael Zink

University of Massachusetts Amherst, USA
{krishnappa,khemmarat,lgao,zink}@ecs.umass.edu

Abstract. Lately researchers are looking at ways to reduce the delay on video playback through mechanisms like prefetching and caching for Video-on-Demand (VoD) services. The usage of prefetching and caching also has the potential to reduce the amount of network bandwidth usage, as most popular requests are served from a local cache rather than the server containing the original content. In this paper, we investigate the advantages of having such a prefetching and caching scheme for a free hosting service of professionally created video (movies and TV shows) named "hulu". We look into the advantages of using a prefetching scheme where the most popular videos of the week, as provided by the hulu website, are prefetched and compare this approach with a conventional LRU caching scheme with limited storage space and a combined scheme of prefetching and caching. Results from our measurement and analysis shows that employing a basic caching scheme at the proxy yields a hit ratio of up to 77.69%, but requires storage of about 236GB. Further analysis shows that a prefetching scheme where the top-100 popular videos of the week are downloaded to the proxy yields a hit ratio of 44% with a storage requirement of 10GB. A LRU caching scheme with a storage limitation of 20GB can achieve a hit ratio of 55% but downloads 4713 videos to achieve such high hit ratio compared to 100 videos in prefetching scheme, whereas a scheme with both prefetching and caching with the same storage yields a hit ratio of 59% with download requirement of 4439 videos. We find that employing a scheme of prefetching along with caching with trade-off on the storage will yield a better hit ratio and bandwidth saving than individual caching or prefetching schemes.

Keywords: Video-on-Demand services, Hulu, Cache, and Prefetching.

1 Introduction

The Internet has emerged as a prime medium for TV shows, radio programs, movies, and the exchange of videos for personal as well as commercial use. The advent of websites such as Hulu [1] and Netflix [2], which offer streaming of TV shows and movies, has made the Internet a major source for digital entertainment in the US. The

N. Spring and G. Riley (Eds.): PAM 2011, LNCS 6579, pp. 72–80, 2011.

growing use and popularity of content streaming among users is closely tied to the increasing popularity of broadband Internet connection in homes. The greater adoption of broadband in the US has motivated television channels such as NBC and ABC to offer their prime-time programming to online viewers via the media content provider hulu. In parallel, Netflix, a DVD rental company began to take advantage of the click-and-view streaming of full-length films and television episodes with a subscription service.

In the measurement study described in this paper, we focus on hulu as it is free and offers ad-supported streaming video of TV shows and movies from NBC, Fox, ABC, and many other networks and studios [3]. The advantage of hulu is that it is owned by these corporations, and the shows that air on their traditional TV channels are available for Internet users the next day for free (but not free of ads). This is popular in university campuses as many students would not have a TV in their dorm rooms and rely on Internet content for entertainment. Apart from TV shows, movies and video clips from other commercial sources are also hosted for free on hulu.

Due to the high popularity of TV shows and movies hosted on hulu, many people watch the same content in a certain time period. Our analysis of how hulu requests are distributed reveals that the requested videos are streamed from original servers hosting the content even when multiple clients request the same video, which shows that there is no proxy employed. This redundancy in streaming the same video from a server which is far away leads to an unnecessary increase in the network traffic.

In this paper, we investigate, through trace-based simulations, how prefetching and caching of videos requested from a campus network could reduce the consumption of network bandwidth by reducing multiple downloads of the same video from the origin server(s). We evaluate three different schemes: conventional caching scheme, popularity based prefetching scheme [5] and a combined scheme. The popular videos list is obtained from the hulu website, which is updated on a weekly basis. In our popularity-based prefetching simulation, we download the top-100 videos from that list to our local cache. Next to reducing bandwidth consumption, prefetching and caching can also reduce the potential of delayed playout, and pauses during video playback since videos streamed from the proxy are not prone to congestion or outages in the backbone network.

We evaluate the proposed caching and prefetching schemes with user browsing pattern data collected from a university network. Results from our trace-driven simulation show that a conventional caching scheme at the proxy with no limit on storage yields a hit ratio of up to 77.69%. A prefetching scheme where the top-100 popular videos of the week are downloaded to the proxy yields a hit ratio of 44% with a storage requirement of 10GB and download requirement of 100 videos. A LRU caching scheme with a storage limitation of 20GB can achieve a maximum hit ratio 55% % but downloads 4713 videos to achieve such high hit ratio compared to 100 videos in prefetching scheme, whereas a scheme with both prefetching and caching with the same storage yields a hit ratio of 59% with download requirement of 4439 videos. We find that employing a prefetching scheme along with caching with limited storage will yield a better hit ratio than individual caching or prefetching schemes.

Although caching and prefetching are not new mechanisms [6, 7], we believe that, to the best of our knowledge, our work is the first that systematically investigates their effectiveness on the hulu VoD service based on trace-driven simulations.

2 Methodology

In this section, we describe our methodology to monitor the traffic between clients in our campus network and hulu servers. The methodology allows us to understand how a client receives a video stream from hulu and to obtain the hulu usage statistics in our campus network. Also, we explain the extraction of hulu requests from the captured trace.

The measurement equipment used to monitor the traffic between clients in our campus network and hulu servers is a commodity PC installed with a DAG card [4] to capture packet headers. It is placed at the gateway router of UMass Amherst, connected via optical splitters to the Giga-bit access link connecting the campus network to a commercial ISP. The TCP and IP headers of all the packets that traverse these links are captured by the DAG card along with the current timestamp. In addition, we capture the HTTP headers of all the HTTP packets going out to www.hulu.com. Note that all the recorded IP addresses are anonymized. (A more detailed description of the measurement setup can be found in [8].)

For each outgoing packet through the gateway router, its timestamp, source IP address, destination IP address and the HTTP request header are extracted from the captured trace files. Out of these packets, the ones containing only hulu requests are filtered using the filtering pattern "/watch/" and the destination IP address of hulu servers. The video requests that are unique in the trace were filtered using sort and eliminate duplicates algorithm to obtain information about the number of duplicate requests present in the trace.

3 Dataset

In this section, we present the dataset obtained by the measurement process described in the previous section.

Table 1. Day-to-Day statistics of the trace

Trace	Total Video Requests	Unique Videos	Percentage (%)
Day1	3511	1109	31.58
Day2	3461	1101	31.81
Day3	3616	1113	30.77
Total	10588	2363	22.31

3.1 Trace Details

For our analysis we captured a three day network trace using the measurement setup described in Section 2. The trace was captured during fall 2010 semester when students were back in full numbers. The trace captured was filtered for hulu data as explained in Section 2. There were 10,588 hulu video requests in a three day period where only 2,363 distinct videos were requested in total. Table 1 provides the day-to-day and total statistics of the hulu trace used in our analysis. It should be noted that the total unique videos value of 2,363 is not the sum of the unique videos of each day as seen from the table. This is an artifact of subdividing the trace into single day data and shows that videos are repeatedly requested not only in a 24-hour time span but also over several days. The table also shows that there are only 22.31% distinct video requests, which leaves us with 77.69% of the video requests being two or more requests for the same video. This is an important result since this indicates the feasibility of prefetching and caching.

To give an overview of the usage of hulu on campus, we use the trace details to show the number of requests for each unique video during the period of the trace. Figure 1 shows the CCDF plot of the popularity graph describing the requests per video similar to [8]. We can see that the number of unique videos requested only once are about 48.92% (1,156 videos), which leaves us with a majority 51.08% (1,207 videos) requested multiple times, demonstrating the popularity of the content provided in hulu.

3.2 Popular Video List Details

In addition to the network trace, to validate our proposed prefetching approach, we obtain the list of most popular videos watched by viewers for a particular week preceding the capture of the traces. The hulu website provides a list of videos which are ranked in the order of their popularity for a particular day, week or month. We chose the weekly popularity list since many TV shows are updated on a weekly basis rather than daily or monthly basis. Our experiment shows that change in popularity of videos over a week is minimal. Thus, popularity list on a weekly basis serves best for prefetching. We use 'wget' to obtain the HTML page that contains popular videos list from the hulu website. We then parse the obtained HTML page to extract the URLs of the popular videos. These data are later used to simulate the prefetching of the videos from the hulu server to our local storage.

4 Simulation and Results

In this section, we present a simulation methodology for the evaluation of our proposed approaches. Through trace-driven simulations, we compare the performance of the cache-only and prefetch-only schemes. We also evaluate the performance of an approach that combines both caching and prefetching. Also, the impact of storage size on the performance of our proposed schemes and the overall bandwidth consumption is evaluated.

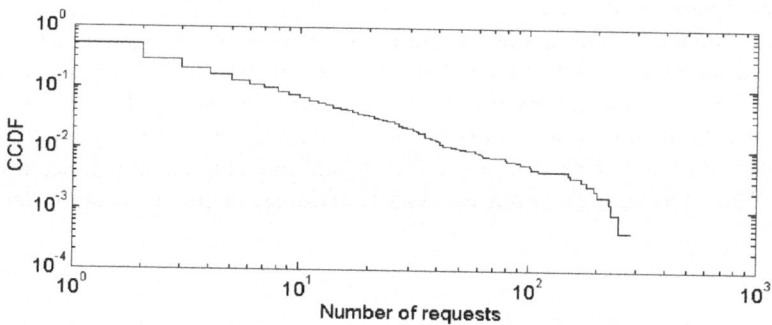

Fig. 1. CCDF popularity plot of the hulu trace

4.1 Evaluation Metrics

We simulate the proposed prefetching and caching schemes from real user request patterns by issuing video requests based on the network trace presented in Section 3.1. Prefetching is simulated by maintaining a prefetching storage which keeps track of the list of popular videos list obtained from the hulu website. Similarly, the caching scheme is simulated by providing storage on the proxy which holds the videos requested by viewers, if not already present in the storage.

We perform our simulation of the caching scheme for cases where the storage space is unlimited and also the case where there is limited storage space. For simplicity, the storage space size is defined by the number of slots where each slot can hold one hulu video. Based on our measurement on the size occupied by HD hulu video, it is approximated as each hulu video requires about 100MB of space, which corresponds to the size of each slot in our storage.

In this study, we use hit ratio as the metric to evaluate the proposed prefetching and caching schemes. Hit ratio is defined as a fraction of the number of requests for a video that can be served from the prefetching/caching storage (called hit requests) over the total number video requests.

$$hit\ ratio = hit\ requests/all\ requests$$

A higher hit ratio means we can serve more requests from the prefetching/caching storage, resulting in a reduction of bandwidth usage.

4.2 Performance of Caching without Storage Limit

We first present the performance of the caching scheme without any limit on the storage required to cache the videos. The caching scheme is simulated as follows: Each video requested by the user is downloaded to the local proxy placed on the edge of the campus network[1]. Video requests from clients are directed to the proxy. If the video is already cached at the proxy, it will be streamed from here; if not, the request is forwarded to the hosting server, and the video is streamed from the server through the proxy to the requesting client. Using this scheme a hit ratio of 77.69% is obtained. Although this scheme provides a very high hit ratio, the amount of storage required increases significantly as the number of video requests from clients increase. To implement this scheme, 236GB storage would be required, which corresponds to the 2,363 unique videos present in our trace. Also, the amount of bandwidth required to download all the videos into the local storage increases with the number of unique videos. Though 236GB storage seems reasonable, when this approach is applied to a bigger access network or a week-long trace, the amount of storage required increases considerably. Thus, this scheme is not necessarily feasible for implementation on a larger network.

---

[1] For all caching schemes mentioned in this paper we assume so called "write-through" caching [9]. In this case, a video that's not already cached is streamed from the origin server through the proxy to the requesting client.

4.3 Performance of Caching With Storage Limit

Next, we present the evaluation results for a caching scheme that is slightly modified from the one presented in Section 4.2. In comparison to the previous approach, storage on the proxy is now limited. Let N represent the number of videos that can be cached in the storage. We evaluate this scheme by varying N from 100 to 2000 which corresponds to varying the storage limit from 10GB to 200GB. Figure 2(a) shows the resulting hit ratio of such a scheme. Once the storage limit is reached, LRU caching scheme is employed to remove the least accessed video.

The figure shows that the hit ratio increases gradually for small storage spaces till N=1000 after which the increase in hit ratio is minimal as we increase the number of videos that are cached and reaches the maximum hit ratio of 77.69% as in case of caching without storage limit. As seen from Figure 2(a), a storage limit of 50GB will yield a hit ratio of 67%, while doubling the storage space yields a hit ratio of 73.86%. Though the improvement in hit ratio is minimal, the amount of bandwidth savings is increased as we increase the storage space.

For example, the number of videos that need to be streamed[2] from the origin server to obtain a hit ratio of 67% which corresponds to the storage size of 50GB is 3494, whereas this number decreases to 2767 (resulting in a hit ratio of 73.86%) when the storage size on the proxy increases to 100GB. Thus, increase in storage space yields higher hit ratio and bandwidth savings. Also, there exists a trade-off between the hit ratio desired and storage space provided.

4.4 Performance of Prefetching Popular Videos List

After analyzing the limited and unlimited caching scheme, we now evaluate the performance of prefetching the popular videos list obtained as explained in Section 3.2. Let P represent the number of popular videos prefetched. We evaluate this scheme by varying P from 20 to 100 which corresponds to varying the prefetching storage from 2GB to 10GB. Figure 2(b) shows the hit ratio of such a scheme.

The figure depicts the variation of hit ratio with the increase in prefetching of most popular videos of the week from 20 to 100. It can be observed from the figure that the hit ratio increases gradually till P = 60, and then the increase in hit ratio is relatively minimal. The maximum hit ratio of 44.2% is obtained when P=100 which corresponds to storage space of 10GB. Though the LRU caching scheme as mentioned in section 4.3 yields a hit ratio of 45.53% for the same storage space, the important point to be noted in this evaluation is the fact that the number of videos downloaded to the prefetch cache is just 100 compared to 5767 videos in case of LRU cache. Thus the amount of bandwidth savings is very high in prefetching scheme compared to the caching scheme.

---

[2] The amount of videos downloaded is not proportional to the numbers mentioned in Table 1. Videos are downloaded only when LRU scheme decides to remove a video due to space constraint.

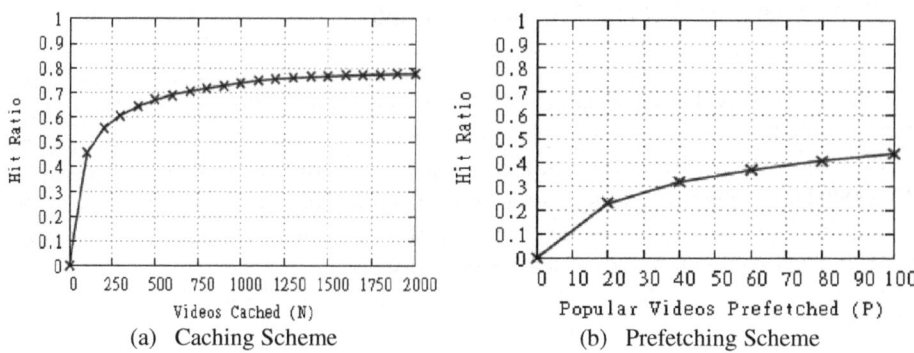

Fig. 2. Hit Ratio with varying storage limits

In addition, our simulation shows that 100% of the popular videos from P = 20 to P = 60 list were requested by the clients, whereas it is 95% for P = 80 and P = 100. This shows that almost all videos in the top-100 popular videos list are watched at least once by the clients in a three day period of our trace. Also the change in the popular videos list is minimal over a week period as we consider the popular videos of a week in our analysis. Thus, it is feasible and advantageous to implement the prefetching of popular videos scheme.

4.5   Combining Caching and Prefetching

In the previous section, we have shown that the bandwidth savings that can be obtained with the prefetching scheme is high. On the other hand, the videos served by the top-100 videos prefetched at the proxy are only 44.2% of the total requests, which leaves us with more than half of the videos in the trace left unattended by the prefetching scheme. Some of these unattended videos from the prefetching scheme can be taken care of by employing a caching scheme. Thus, the combinination of prefetching and caching schemes called prefetch-and-cache scheme serves more videos and uses less bandwidth than individual schemes.

The simulation of the combination of caching and prefetching scheme is carried out as follows: (i) a storage is maintained on the proxy with a fixed part and a variable cache part. The fixed part of the storage holds the prefetched popular videos. (ii) all user requests are directed to the proxy. The video requested is searched for both in the prefetch or cache part of the storage (iii) if the video requested by the user is not present in the storage, then the request is sent to the hulu server hosting the video. The resulting stream from the hulu server is cached in the variable part of the storage. (iv) if the variable part of the storage is filled, videos are removed from the variable part of the storage using LRU scheme.

Figure 3 shows the hit ratio resulting from the prefetch-and-cache scheme. The combination of two schemes increases the hit ratio by 3-5% for the same amount of storage as in the caching-only scheme. For example, a storage limit of 20GB in caching-only scheme will hold about 200 videos and yields a hit ratio of 55.5% as seen in Figure 2(a). The same storage limitation in prefetch-and-cache scheme with 100 videos prefetched and 100 videos cached would yield a hit ratio of 59%, which is a slight improvement over the caching only scheme.

The combination is also an improvement over the prefetch-only scheme. As seen, the prefetch scheme offers a maximum hit ratio of 44.2% and the other videos cannot be served by employing prefetching scheme. By combining both prefetching and caching, all the requests by the clients can be served from the cache with increase in hit ratio compared to prefetching only or caching only scheme. Again it is a trade-off between the storage available and the hit ratio desired, but the advantage of this combination scheme is that the storage required to obtain the desired hit ratio is less than the cache-only scheme.

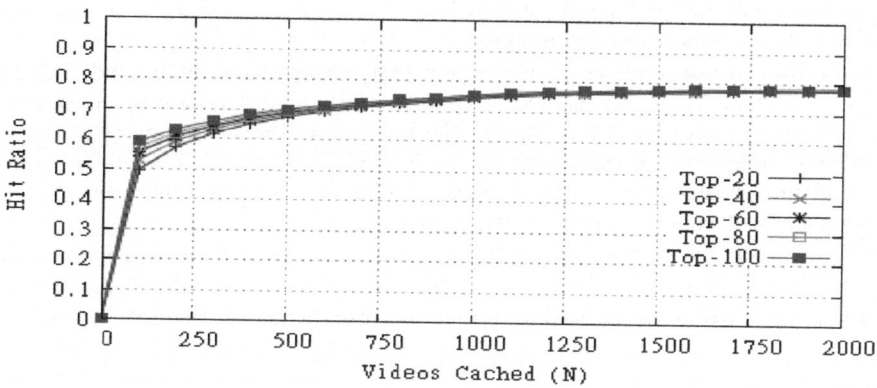

Fig. 3. Hit Ratio for combination of prefetching and caching

The combination of prefetching and caching scheme also improves the bandwidth usage as compared to prefetching-only and caching-only schemes. Prefetching-only scheme provides a maximum hit ratio of 44.2% but bandwidth consumption is very less as only 100 videos are downloaded to the cache, whereas a caching-only scheme uses more bandwidth by downloading 5767 videos to provide a higher hit ratio of 45.5% with storage space of 10GB. The combination scheme with 100 prefetchied videos and 100 cached videos will yield a hit ratio of 59% and requires 4439 videos to be downloaded where as the caching scheme of 20GB storage which offers a hit ratio 55.5% requires 4713 videos to be downloaded. The hit ratio and bandwidth savings increase in the combination scheme with increase in storage space. Thus, implementing a combined scheme of prefetching and caching works well for serving more requests from the local storage and reducing the amount of bandwidth usage in the backbone network.

5 Conclusion

In this paper, we present a measurement study of hulu traffic in a large university campus network. The analysis of the measurement data reveals that 77.69% of the video requests for hulu content are multiple requests for the same content. This is significantly higher than earlier findings on the analysis of YouTube traffic [9] where only 25% of the requested videos are requested more than once.

We analyze three different schemes, prefetching-only, caching-only and a combination of prefetching and caching, respectively. The advantage of such proxy-based distribution schemes is the fact that a viewer can access the video content faster and, since popular videos are prone to be requested multiple times, the amount of streams originating from the hulu server is reduced, resulting in a reduction of backbone bandwidth consumption. Results from our trace-based simulations show that, in the case of hulu, prefetching popular videos to the proxy is more efficient in bandwidth savings than simple caching. Prefetching the 100 most popular videos yields a hit ratio of 44.2% while a caching scheme that requires the same storage space results in a hit ratio of 45.5% with download requirement of 5767 videos. A scheme that combines prefetching and caching enhances the hit ratio by an additional 3 to 5% with less bandwidth consumption.

To the best of our knowledge, this is the first measurement-based study of hulu traffic in a large university campus network. Hulu is different than most other Internet-based services like YouTube and Netflix since it offers a variety of TV shows immediately after their broadcast on the traditional TV network. Our measurement and simulation results show that prefetching and a combined prefetching and caching approach are well suited for such a VoD service.

In future work, we plan to execute a long term measurement study to evaluate the influence of the weekly popularity of videos by the release schedule of new content and if that information can be used to further optimize the prefetching mechanism.

References

1. Hulu, http://www.hulu.com
2. Netflix, http://www.netflix.com
3. Wikipedia on Hulu, http://en.wikipedia.org/wiki/Hulu
4. Endance DAG Network Monitoring Interface, http://www.endance.com
5. Liu, W., Chou, C.T., Yang, Z., Du, X.: Popularity-wise Proxy Caching for Interactive Media Streaming. In: Proceedings of LCN Conference, Tampa, Florida (2004)
6. Sen, S., Rexford, J., Towsley, D.: Proxy Prefix Caching for Multimedia Streams. In: Proceedings of IEEE INFOCOM (1999)
7. Wu, K.-L., Yu, P.S., Wolf, J.L.: Segment-based Proxy Caching of Multimedia Streams. In: Proceedings of the 10th International Conference on World Wide Web, pp. 36–44. ACM, New York (2001)
8. Zink, M., Suh, K., Gu, Y., Kurose, J.: Watch Global, Cache Local: Youtube Network Traffic at a Campus Network – Measurements and Implications. In: Proceedings of SPIE/ACM Conference on Multimedia Computing and Networking (MMCN), Santa Clara (2008)
9. Zink, M.: Scalable Video on Demand: Adaptive Internet-based Distribution. John Wiley and Sons, Ltd, Chichester (2005)

On the Feasibility of Bandwidth Detouring

Thom Haddow[1], Sing Wang Ho[1], Jonathan Ledlie[2],
Cristian Lumezanu[3], Moez Draief[1], and Peter Pietzuch[1]

[1] Imperial College London, United Kingdom
[2] Nokia Research Center, Cambridge, MA, USA
[3] Georgia Institute of Technology, Atlanta, GA, USA

Abstract. Internet applications that route data over default Internet paths can often increase performance by sending their traffic over alternative "detour" paths. Previous work has shown that applications can use detour routing to improve end-to-end metrics such as latency and path availability. However, the potential of detour routing has yet to be applied where it may be most important: improving TCP throughput.

In this paper, we study the feasibility of bandwidth detouring on the Internet. We find that bandwidth detours are prevalent: between 152 Planetlab nodes, 74.8% of the paths can benefit from detours with at least 1 Mbps and 20% improvement. To understand how to exploit bandwidth detours in practice, we explore the trade-offs between network- and transport-level mechanisms for detouring. We show, both analytically and experimentally, that direct, TCP-based detour routing improves TCP throughput more than encapsulated, IP-based tunneling, although the latter provides a more natural interface.

1 Introduction

The Internet was designed for best-effort data communication. It is limited to a basic role—to provide connectivity—and does not guarantee good path performance between hosts in terms of latency, bandwidth or loss. Not surprisingly, direct end-to-end routing paths may be more congested, longer, or have lower bandwidth than necessary. To overcome these inefficiencies and improve network performance, distributed applications can use *detour routing* [17]. Detour routing constructs custom paths by concatenating multiple network-level routes using an overlay network.

Existing proposals use detour routing to improve latency [13] and availability [1,3]. However, an important potential benefit of detour routing—improving end-to-end bandwidth—is still unrealised. Bandwidth is critical for many Internet applications. For example, emerging data-intensive applications, such as HD video streaming and content-on-demand systems, require consistently high bandwidth in order to operate effectively. Further, as enterprises begin to store their data in "cloud" data centres, access to high throughput paths is critical.

Discovering and exploiting bandwidth detours is challenging. Unlike latency or path availability, bandwidth is more expensive to measure. Bandwidth measurement tools generally require many probes of differing sizes sent over long periods

N. Spring and G. Riley (Eds.): PAM 2011, LNCS 6579, pp. 81–91, 2011.

of time [5,18]. Available bandwidth also varies with the volume of cross-traffic on the path: measurements must be done not just once, but continuously.

In this paper, we study the feasibility of bandwidth detouring and lay the groundwork for a general Internet detouring platform for bandwidth. We explore the variability of bandwidth measurements and the properties of detour paths. Our measurements on the PlanetLab testbed show that 74.8% of the paths can benefit from at least 20% and 1 Mbps bandwidth increase. Bandwidth detours are often symmetric, benefiting both forward and reverse paths at the same time, and last for more than 90 minutes.

To understand how to build a bandwidth detouring platform, we investigate the trade-off between network- and transport-level mechanisms for detour routing and the relationship between detours for different path metrics. We provide evidence, both analytically and experimentally, that TCP-based detouring, rather than IP detouring, achieves better performance. In addition, we show that employing cheaper latency probes to find bandwidth detours is not effective.

The rest of the paper is organised as follows. In §2 we review related work. We consider Internet bandwidth measurement and analyse properties of bandwidth detour paths in §3. In §4 we propose how detour paths can be exploited. We conclude in §5.

2   Related Work

Routing overlay networks exploit detours to improve the performance and robustness of packet delivery [1,13,3,15]. They delegate the task of selecting paths to applications, which can choose paths that are more reliable, less loaded, shorter, or have higher bandwidth than those selected by the network. Gummadi et al. [3] found that path failures occur frequently, but can be circumvented through random detours. *iPlane* [15] uses measurements from PlanetLab nodes to build a structural map of the Internet that predicts path performance properties, such as latency, bandwidth and loss. While this previous work focused on path availability and end-to-end latency, our focus is on bandwidth.

Prior research has studied bandwidth-aware overlay routing. Lee et al. [11] describe *BARON*, a method for switching to an overlay path with higher available bandwidth. It relies on periodic all-to-all network capacity measurements, which are less transient than available bandwidth measurements. When searching for possible alternative paths, BARON uses high capacity to infer potential for high available bandwidth on a path. Since evaluation results are simulated, it is unclear how a deployment would perform. In contrast, we evaluate the discrepancy between predicted and measured bandwidth on a live system.

Zhu et al. [19] propose an overlay-based approach for selecting a path with high available bandwidth; because their focus is on fairly small networks, they re-measure bandwidth to a large fraction of the network with each path adjustment, which is not scalable. Jain et al. [6] are able to implicitly learn available bandwidth through a video streaming application; they disseminate this information through a link-state protocol with limited scalability.

Split-TCP [7] improves end-to-end throughput by establishing a relay between the two endpoints of a TCP connection. Its benefits have been thoroughly studied in many domains, especially for mobile devices [8]. While our approach for TCP bandwidth detouring benefits from splitting TCP connections, the bulk of improvements result from carefully choosing the right detour nodes (cf. §4).

3 Detour Properties

In this section, we use measurements to demonstrate the existence of bandwidth detours. We show that most measured paths could benefit from detours with higher bandwidth. We also investigate how bandwidth detours change over time and how they compare with latency detours.

PlanetLab. We use PlanetLab to demonstrate the feasibility of bandwidth detouring. Nodes are selected from independent sites to maximise path diversity and avoid known bandwidth restrictions. We created a list of 256 nodes with a bandwidth cap higher than 10 Mbps on May 3rd, 2010. Some experiments used fewer nodes due to node failures or bandwidth limits on PlanetLab. In these cases, we state the actual number of used nodes in the text.

UkairoLab. To circumvent the above limitations and validate measurement results, we also use our own *UkairoLab* testbed hosted on corporate and university machines. It consists of 10 geographically-dispersed nodes located in the US, India, Kenya, UK and France. Their network connectivity is provided by commercial hosting companies, which results in a lower median bandwidth: 4.87 MBps on UkairoLab versus 6.54 MBps on PlanetLab. Machines are virtualised but are dedicated with full kernel access.

3.1 Bandwidth Measurement

To discover detour paths, we must measure a particular bandwidth metric. Since our focus is on the TCP protocol, we consider *bulk transfer capacity (BTC)*, which is the steady-state throughput (in terms of successfully transmitted data bits) of a TCP connection[1]. We measure BTC using the standard *Iperf* tool[2], which observes the throughput of an elastic TCP transfer. We deploy Iperf on 256 PlanetLab nodes and collect all-pairs measurements with a 5 second timeout. We ensure that each node makes only one inbound and one outbound measurement at any point in time. On average, each Iperf measurement takes 8 seconds and consumes 10.8 MBytes.

To understand the variability of bandwidth measurements, we perform repeated measurements at 30 sec, 5 min, 30 min, and 1.5 hour intervals. To stay

---

[1] We use the terms BTC, throughput and bandwidth interchangeably in this paper.
[2] We explored the use of available bandwidth predictions tools such as Pathload [5] for estimating BTC with lower measurement overhead. However, on average, Pathload took 50 seconds to measure a path, which is too slow for a large deployment.

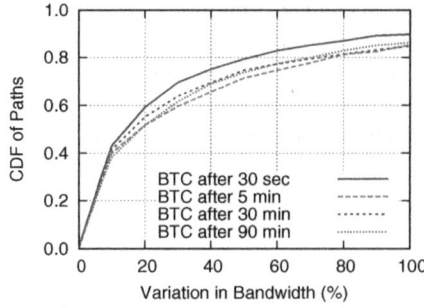
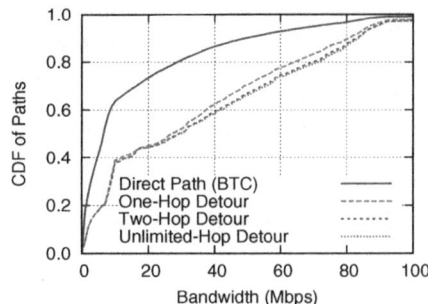

Fig. 1. Bandwidth measurements vary significantly over time.

Fig. 2. Detouring via a node increases bandwidth but more hops have little effect.

within Planetlab's 10 GB daily limit, 48 Planetlab nodes measure to 20 randomly-chosen nodes within those 48 nodes. This is repeated three times at different times, measuring 920 paths. As Figure 1 shows, bandwidth can vary significantly, even when measured in quick succession, as confirmed by others [12]. Approximately half of the paths have a 20% variation in bandwidth, regardless of when remeasured. This means that good bandwidth detours have to be significantly better to compensate for this variation.

3.2   Bandwidth Detouring

We want to understand how often traffic between two Internet hosts can benefit from a detour path with higher bandwidth than the direct path. Of the 20 323 successful BTC measurements between 152 PlanetLab nodes, we examined whether detour paths via another node have higher bandwidth. We consider the bandwidth of a detour path as the minimum bandwidth of the paths between the source and the detour node and the detour node and the destination.

Figure 2 shows the cumulative distribution of path bandwidth. We find that 96.6% of all pairs of nodes have a detour path with higher bandwidth. The median increase in path performance is 18.6 Mbps (i.e. a factor of 2.24). We also noted 74.8% of the paths can improve by at least 20% and 1 Mbps. Because detouring via one node can significantly increase bandwidth, we also investigate if additional detour nodes yield similar gains. As the figure shows and confirmed by Lee et al. [11], this is not the case and it provides only minimal additional benefits. We also observe that 40% of paths cannot benefit from detours with more than 10 Mbps bandwidth. This is likely because many PlanetLab paths have 10 Mbps network capacity.

In Figure 3, we compare the relative improvement from bandwidth detouring to latency and loss detouring, discovered by brute-force search. Bandwidth detouring has a significantly larger gain: half the paths can double in bandwidth, while only 13.5% of paths are half the average path latency. We measure loss by

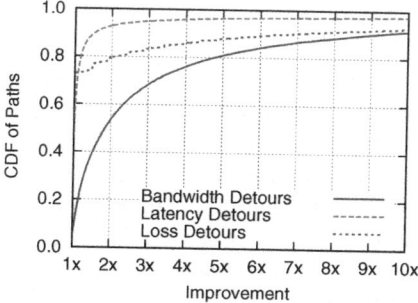
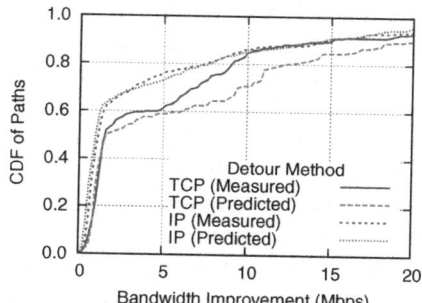

Fig. 3. Bandwidth can be improved signif- icantly more than latency using detouring.

Fig. 4. TCP detouring improves actual bandwidth between nodes significantly more than IP detouring on UkairoLab.

sending 1200 UDP probes with a payload of 1472 bytes and an interval of 100 ms, which is similar to the rate of VoIP connections [15]. Only 27.2% of paths benefit from detouring for loss because most paths suffer no loss at this low rate.

Why are there such a large number of good detour paths with higher bandwidth? Previous studies show that latency detours are due to ISP routing policies [14], which we believe also cause bandwidth detours. We have preliminary evidence that good detours can be found by avoiding one or more autonomous systems (AS) in the default path: for 32% of the pairs of PlanetLab nodes, for which we have complete AS paths, at least one AS in the direct path is avoided more than half the time by the detour. For 29% of the pairs of nodes, the detour paths traverse all the ASes on the direct path. These detours may be due to Internet congestion or differences in intra-domain routing policies.

We expect that "similar" paths in terms of their AS-links would benefit from the same detour nodes. This idea has been exploited in latency detouring [4]—we aim at exploring analogous mechanisms for bandwidth detouring. We leave further investigation of this to future work.

3.3   Bandwidth Detour Properties

Symmetry. We define a detour to be symmetric if the same detour node benefits both the forward and reverse direction of the direct path. Since congestion in the forward path rarely affects the reverse path, we expect bandwidth to be different for each direction. However, our results show that 89% of the 18 036 paths for which we have measurements in both directions, have at least one symmetric detour. We believe this happens because the quality of a detour path is dominated by the properties of the detour node (such as download and upload speed), which are the same in both directions, rather than by congestion on the path. Symmetric detours are better than average: they improve the median path performance by 39% compared to 16% for the asymmetric detours.

Skewness. Detour nodes that have lower latency to the source or destination are more likely to provide higher throughput for TCP transfers. We define the *skewness* of a detour path as the ratio of the absolute difference between the latencies from the detour node to the source and destination to the maximum of the two latencies. As their skewness decreases towards 0, detours are more likely to improve the bandwidth of the direct path: the median skewness value for good detours is 0.43 compared to the median (0.54) of all detours. The reverse case is also true: as skewness increases towards 1, detours are less beneficial for the direct path. In our measurements, the detours that do not benefit the direct path at all have a median skewness of 0.58. These results suggest that low skewness values may be associated with detours that have high-capacity links, and which in turn have a higher probability of being good detours.

Persistence in Time. Given the variability of bandwidth measurements, we investigate the longevity of detour paths: for a detouring platform, short-lived detours would be less useful. Our measurements show that approximately two-thirds of all bandwidth detours persist for more than 90 minutes. This suggests that a platform can make long-term decisions about detour paths.

4   Exploiting Detours

Applications must be able to discover and exploit good bandwidth detours. Here we examine the challenges in implementing a detour routing platform when it consists of cooperative edge or near-edge nodes. In particular, we find that low-level kernel access is not required for good detouring performance.

4.1   Detouring Mechanisms

Two options exist for routing between a pair of Internet hosts via a tertiary detour node: (a) network-level *IP detouring* or (b) transport-level *TCP detouring*.

IP detouring works by encapsulating every IP packet on egress from the source node and sending it to the appropriate detour node, which in turn forwards it to the destination node. From an application standpoint, IP detouring is the more natural approach: (1) it can be deployed transparently because it only operates at the IP layer; (2) it supports both TCP and UDP traffic; and (3) the same detouring mechanism can be used for other metrics such as latency. However, it also has a major disadvantage: the detour path is composed of two complete end-to-end Internet paths. This increases the network-level hop count compared to the direct path. The associated increase in loss probability and latency adversely affects TCP throughput [10].

The alternative to IP detouring is to break the TCP connection at the detour node and use TCP detouring, which is analogous to *split-TCP* [7]. By splitting a long TCP connection into two separate connections terminated mid-path, the feedback-based control loop of TCP becomes more responsive due to reduced path latency. Although this comes at the cost of increased state within the network, this may be acceptable when TCP connections are split by end hosts, instead of network routers [9]. For TCP detouring, we deploy SOCKS proxies at potential detour nodes and use application-level "socksifying" software to redirect connections via the appropriate detour proxy. This retains the benefit of being transparent to destination nodes and preserves path symmetry.

To compare IP and TCP detouring, we deploy both detouring mechanisms on UkairoLab[3]. We then perform an all-to-all-via-all measurement: for each pair of nodes, we predict and measure the throughput achievable via each of the potential detour nodes using both IP and TCP detouring. For TCP detouring, we predict the throughput of the detoured connection to be the minimum of the throughput of the two paths, i.e. the narrow link [2]. For IP detouring, we also predict the throughput analytically as described in §4.2.

Figure 4 shows the predicted and measured detouring improvement for each method. The results match the intuition that the long TCP paths created by IP detouring adversely affect performance. In contrast, splitting the TCP connection significantly boosted most pairs; for example, 40% of paths improved by at least 5 Mbps. However, the discrepancy between measured and predicted TCP detouring performance is larger for paths which are predicted to benefit more from detouring, suggesting there can exist a bottleneck in forwarding throughput at the detour node.

Although TCP detouring benefits from the effect of a split TCP connection, most improvement comes from choosing a good detour node with respect to the throughput it offers, rather than its latency to the endpoints. For example, 77% of all detours provide at least 10% and 1 Mbps bandwidth improvement; of the detours where the intermediate leg latencies are lower than the direct path latency (which stand to benefit most from a split TCP connection), only 28% provide similar improvements. While the features of IP detouring, such as transparency and UDP support, outweigh those of TCP detouring, we conclude that the performance gains of TCP detouring make it the better choice.

4.2   Analysis of IP and TCP Detouring

Using a stylised stochastic model of TCP's congestion control mechanism [16], the following square-root formula relates the steady-state throughput of a path's BTC to its packet loss probability p and its average round trip delay RTT:

$$\text{BTC} = \frac{\Phi}{\text{RTT}\sqrt{p}}. \qquad (1)$$

This formula is valid for both the case where loss is independent of the rate, in which case $\Phi = 2$, and the rate dependent case where the loss depends (linearly) on the rate, in which case $\Phi \approx 1.31$. We use this formula to perform a back-of-the-envelope calculation to derive the IP detouring bandwidth.

IP Detouring. Let us denote by BTC_1, p_1, RTT_1, and BTC_2, p_2, RTT_2 the average throughput, the loss and the round trip delay of the constituent paths

---

[3] We found that, on PlanetLab, the long delay between timeslices due to heavy load severely damaged performance of userspace IP processing.

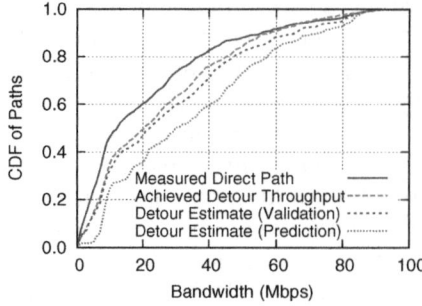
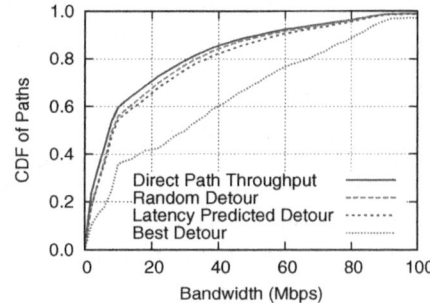

Fig. 5. Detour paths substantially increase throughput. However, bandwidth variations over time can lead to overestimating a given detour's potential improvement.

Fig. 6. Latency performs no better than random selection for discovering bandwidth detour paths.

that we will refer to as the first and second leg, respectively. The following approximates the resulting throughput:

$$\mathrm{BTC}_{\mathrm{IP}} \approx \frac{\mathrm{RTT}_1}{\mathrm{RTT}_1 + \mathrm{RTT}_2} \sqrt{\frac{(\mathrm{RTT}_2\mathrm{BTC}_2)^2}{(\mathrm{RTT}_1\mathrm{BTC}_1)^2 + (\mathrm{RTT}_2\mathrm{BTC}_2)^2}} \mathrm{BTC}_1 \qquad (2)$$

where we drop the p_1p_2 term in the corresponding square-root expression since the loss probabilities p_1 and p_2 are in general small; in the second equality, we replace p_1 and p_2 using Eq. (1). It is easy to see that the predicted throughput is always strictly smaller than the minimum of BTC_1 and BTC_2, i.e. the respective throughputs of the two legs taken in isolation.

TCP Detouring. Baccelli et al. [2] describe two coupled stochastic differential equations that govern the dynamics of the throughput of the two legs of a detour path. The coupling is dictated by the buffer at the detour node. The key feature of this model is that the TCP throughput of the composed path is, in general, the minimum bandwidth of the two constituent paths given that the buffer at the detour node is sufficiently large. In our system, we ensure this holds.

The above analysis confirms what we observed in practice in Figure 4: IP detouring provides worse performance compared to TCP detouring as predicted by the minimum of the throughputs of the two legs.

4.3   Detouring Overlay Performance

We describe our experience in deploying a TCP detouring platform on 50 Planet-Lab nodes. The experiment is divided in two phases: *prediction* and *validation*. First, we measure BTC between all pairs of nodes to predict good detours, consuming on average 571 MBytes per node. We stop after 90 minutes and find that 1845 out of 2019 paths are detourable. We estimate detour bandwidth by taking the minimum bandwidth of the two intermediate legs. In the second validation phase, we use TCP detouring to validate the best detour for each path. Since we avoid concurrent measurements, the second phase takes substantially longer: after 11 hours, we obtain 689 detourable paths. In Figure 5, we plot the distributions of (a) measured direct path bandwidth; (b) estimated detour bandwidth in the prediction phase and (c) in the validation phase; and (d) achieved detour throughput measured in the validation phase.

We make several observations. First, the median bandwidth improves significantly, from 12 Mbps to 21 Mbps, using TCP detouring. Detours improve the bandwidth on direct paths in 69% of the cases (not shown in the plot). The large increase in bandwidth of detours can justify the fixed measurement overhead per node, assuming at least a modest usage of detoured paths after their discovery to amortise measurement costs. Second, we observe the 10 Mbps egress bandwidth limit present on some PlanetLab nodes. Finally, the benefits of detouring are largely lost at around 50 Mbps, suggesting a throughput bottleneck due to limitations on node performance.

The substantial difference between the detour bandwidths at the time of prediction and the estimated bandwidth at the time of validation may be caused by the variability of bandwidth measurements (cf. Figure 1). Since detour bandwidth is constrained by the minimum bandwidth of the two legs, we see a consistent decrease of around 25% upon validating detour bandwidth a few hours later. Although the *best* detours for any given path may be constantly changing, we can still see temporal consistency in detour path performance.

4.4   Detour Transferability

To discover if good latency detours can also be effective for finding good bandwidth detours, we compare the estimated bandwidth via the best latency detour for each direct path. We measure latency and BTC on 10 265 paths between 136 PlanetLab nodes and compute the best bandwidth and latency detours between each pair of nodes for which we have measurements.

Figure 6 shows the distribution of estimated bandwidth for the best bandwidth and latency detours found through brute-force search, and the estimated bandwidth through detours chosen randomly. As discussed earlier, the best possible detour results in significant improvements over the direct path, although these are likely unachievable due to bandwidth flux. Employing the best latency detour for bandwidth detouring results in performance equal to a random detour. This implies that discovery methods for finding good bandwidth detour based on latency detours are not effective.

5   Conclusions

To understand how to exploit bandwidth detouring on the Internet, we addressed several key questions in this paper. We illustrated the preponderance and longevity of potential bandwidth detour routes: 74.8% of paths had a detour that improved bandwidth by at least 20% and 1 Mbps; and most detours lasted for more than 90 minutes. Contrary to our initial goals of providing transparent IP-level detouring, we gave evidence that significantly better performance can be achieved through the use of TCP-level detouring. Interestingly, this also means that kernel access is not required for overlay participation, perhaps broadening adoption of a general detouring platform. More research is needed to explore practical and scalable methods for detour discovery and how wide-spread bandwidth detouring would interact with traffic engineering policies by ISPs.

Acknowledgements. We thank Nokia Research IT and David Eyers for hosting UkairoLab machines. Thom Haddow is supported by a Doctoral Training Grant from the UK Engineering and Physical Sciences Research Council (EPSRC).

References

1. Andersen, D.G., Balakrishnan, H., Kaashoek, M.F., Morris, R.: Resilient Overlay Networks. In: SOSP, Chateau Lake Louise, Banff, Canada (2001)
2. Baccelli, F., Carofiglio, G., Foss, S.: Proxy Caching in Split TCP: Dynamics, Stability and Tail Asymptotics. In: INFOCOM 2008, pp. 131–135 (2008)
3. Gummadi, K.P., Madhyastha, H., Gribble, S.D., et al.: Improving the reliability of internet paths with one-hop source routing. In: OSDI (2004)
4. Ho, S.W., Haddow, T., Ledlie, J., Draief, M., Pietzuch, P.: Deconstructing Internet Paths: An Approach for AS-Level Detour Route Discovery. In: IPTPS (2009)
5. Jain, M., Dovrolis, C.: Pathload: A Measurement Tool for End-to-End Available Bandwidth. In: PAM, Fort Collins, CO (2002)
6. Jain, M., Dovrolis, C.: Path Selection using Available Bandwidth Estimation in Overlay-based Video Streaming. Com. Networks 52(12), 2411–2418 (2008)
7. Karbhari, P., Ammar, M.H., Zegura, E.W.: Optimizing End-to-End Throughput for Data Transfers on an Overlay-TCP Path. In: Boutaba, R., Almeroth, K.C., Puigjaner, R., Shen, S., Black, J.P. (eds.) NETWORKING 2005. LNCS, vol. 3462, pp. 943–955. Springer, Heidelberg (2005)
8. Kopparty, S., Krishnamurthy, S.V., Faloutsos, M., Tripathi, S.K.: Split TCP for Mobile Ad Hoc Networks. In: GLOBECOM (2002)
9. Ladiwala, S., Ramaswamy, R., Wolf, T.: Transparent TCP Acceleration. Com. Communications 32(4), 691–702 (2009)
10. Lakshman, T., et al.: Performance of TCP/IP for Networks with High Bandwidth-delay Products and Random Loss. IEEE/ACM Trans. Netw. 5(3), 336–350 (1997)
11. Lee, S.J., Banerjee, S., Sharma, P., Yalagandula, P., Basu, S.: Bandwidth-Aware Routing in Overlay Networks. In: INFOCOM, Phoenix, AZ (2008)
12. Lee, S.-J., Sharma, P., Banerjee, S., Basu, S., Fonseca, R.: Measuring Bandwidth Between PlanetLab Nodes. In: Dovrolis, C. (ed.) PAM 2005. LNCS, vol. 3431, pp. 292–305. Springer, Heidelberg (2005)
13. Lumezanu, C., Baden, R., Levin, D., Bhattacharjee, B., Spring, N.: Symbiotic Relationships in Internet Routing Overlays. In: NSDI (2009)
14. Lumezanu, C., Baden, R., Spring, N., Bhattacharjee, B.: Triangle Inequality and Routing Policy Violations in the Internet. In: Moon, S.B., Teixeira, R., Uhlig, S. (eds.) PAM 2009. LNCS, vol. 5448, pp. 45–54. Springer, Heidelberg (2009)
15. Madhyastha, H.V., Isdal, T., Piatek, M., Dixon, C., et al.: iPlane: An Information Plane for Distributed Services. In: OSDI, Seattle, WA (2006)

16. Padhye, J., Firoiu, V., Towsley, D.F., Kurose, J.F.: Modeling TCP Throughput: A Simple Model and Its Empirical Validation. In: SIGCOMM (1998)
17. Savage, S., Anderson, T., Aggarwal, A., Becker, D., Cardwell, N., Collins, A., Hoffman, E., Snell, J., Vahdat, A., Voelker, G., Zahorjan, J.: Detour: Informed Internet Routing and Transport. IEEE Micro. 19(1), 50–59 (1999)
18. Strauss, J., Katabi, D., Kaashoek, M.F.: A Measurement Study of Available Bandwidth Estimation Tools. In: IMC (2003)
19. Zhu, Y., Dovrolis, C., Ammar, M.H.: Dynamic Overlay Routing based on Available Bandwidth Estimation: A Simulation Study. Com. Networks 50(6), 742–762 (2006)

Can Network Characteristics Detect Spam Effectively in a Stand-Alone Enterprise?

Tu Ouyang[1], Soumya Ray[1], Michael Rabinovich[1], and Mark Allman[2]

[1] Case Western Reserve University, Cleveland, OH, USA
[2] International Computer Science Institute, Berkeley, CA, USA

Abstract. Previous work has shown that the network dynamics experienced by both the initial packet and an entire connection carrying an email can be leveraged to classify the email as spam or ham. In the case of packet properties, the prior work has investigated their efficacy based on models of traffic collected from around the world. In this paper, we first revisit the techniques when only using information from a single enterprise's vantage point and find packet properties to be less useful. We also show that adding flow characteristics to a model of packet features adds modest discriminating power, and some flow features' information is captured by packet features.

1 Introduction

Spam email is an ever-present irritant in the modern Internet: it uses scarce server and network resources, costs users' productivity, spreads malware, scams users and recruits bots for all manner of malicious purposes. Hence, judging whether a particular email is spam or ham—i.e., legitimate—is a crucial for operators and users. Many different approaches have been investigated and a handful now enjoy regular use. The most useful techniques to-date have been those that leverage (i) properties of the host sending the email (e.g., IP address black- or grey-lists, domain keys [3], etc.) or (ii) properties of the email messages themselves in the form of filtering in mail servers (e.g., SpamAssassin [2]) or users' mail applications (e.g., Apple Mail).

A new class of techniques has emerged, which attempt to use properties of the network traffic to determine whether a message is spam. Beverly and Sollins [4] used transport-level features (e.g., round-trip time, TCP advertised window sizes) as the basis for predicting whether a particular TCP connection is carrying spam. Hao et al. [10] used mostly lower-than-transport traffic features and in particular found that properties of a single SYN packet from an incoming SMTP connection can effectively identify spam. These "content-blind" techniques are attractive because they leverage properties that are hard to manipulate and can help discard spam quickly and at less computational cost. This previous work raises two sets of pertinent questions:

First, Hao et al. [10] show that single-packet features are effectively detect spam using models developed via a global email reputation service with about 2,500 subscribing institutions which provides for a diverse vantage point. However, do these findings hold for a stand-alone organization that does not subscribe to a global service and hence has a relatively narrow vantage point? Further, while Hao et al. studied their classifiers as a

N. Spring and G. Riley (Eds.): PAM 2011, LNCS 6579, pp. 92–101, 2011.

replacement for blacklists, most enterprises will likely use such classifiers *in addition to* blacklists. Will packet features still be effective in this case?

Second, Beverly and Sollins [4] find that transport-level features are effective in spam detection while Hao et al. [10] arrive at a similar conclusion regarding single-packet features. Further, in our prior work [13], we observed that though flow features are useful in discriminating ham from spam, examination of the resulting classifiers indicates that in many cases they potentially serve as "proxies" for features that could be computed from a single packet. Given that packet-level features allow one to discard spam more quickly, a key question is whether the more expensive "flow features"—requiring multiple packets—add discriminating power to the packet features. Hao et al. [10] consider a similar question with regard to their packet and message feature sets but do not focus on flow features.

In this paper, we evaluate these questions with a seven month dataset of emails to users at the International Computer Science Institute (ICSI). We develop three key findings. First, neither single-packet features nor flow features by themselves are effective classifiers at the enterprise level. In particular, packet features are much less effective than suggested in [10]. We identify underlying causes, one of which points to fundamental limitations of single packet features for spam detection. Second, while we find that neither single-packet nor flow features are operationally useful by themselves, we find their effectiveness increases when combined, indicating that flow features capture relevant discriminating information beyond packet features. However, even the combination is not as accurate in our setting as reported in prior work. Finally, the above results hold for two methods we used to analyze the data, giving a preliminary indication that these results are independent of the choice of the analysis method and reflect the underlying discriminating power of the features in question.

2 Data and Features

Our dataset includes all incoming email to ICSI from the 11th–18th of each month over 7 months. We work from packet traces with full packet contents. Some of these connections are blocked by the DNS blacklists, for which the SMTP transaction is terminated before email content is transmitted to the monitored servers. We exclude these connections from our analysis, except where noted. We use *Bro* [14] to re-construct the messages and derive some of the features. We additionally use *SpamFlow* [4] and custom tools to derive certain traffic features. The overall characteristics of our data are given in Table 1. A more in-depth description of our methodology is given in [13].

Ground Truth. We cannot manually classify messages in our dataset due to both the scale and the sensitivity of dealing with real users' email. Therefore, we developed an automated procedure to label the messages (as fully developed in [13]). Each message is processed by four content-based spam filters—SpamAssassin [2], SpamProbe [5], SpamBayes [12] and CRM-114 [1]. With the exception of SpamAssassin—which is used in non-learning mode—these tools are trained using the 2007 TREC email corpus [6]. A message is considered spam if any one of the tools flags it as such. Checking all the ham messages in the corpus involving the fourth author as well a 2% sample of email marked as spam by at least one of tools reveals this process yields the correct

Table 1. Data overview: The first row shows the total number of email messages, rows 2–6 show messages removed from the analysis and the last two rows give the number of hams and spams

	May	Jun	Jul	Aug	Sep	Oct	Nov
Msgs.	279K	302K	317K	292K	300K	223K	249K
Outbound	41K	38K	49K	54K	46K	37K	43K
DNSBL	165K	185K	174K	165K	172K	116K	105K
Unknown	11K	21K	31K	20K	24K	12K	10K
No Msg.	9K	7K	8K	6K	7K	7K	7K
Other	5K	8K	8K	5K	7K	9K	8K
Spam	30K	26K	30K	26K	27K	25K	55K
Ham	18K	18K	18K	15K	17K	17K	21K

classification in 98% of the cases with a false positive rate of 1.23% (standard deviation 0.11%), and a false negative rate of 0.55% (standard deviation 0.07%). We evaluated a majority voting scheme as well, but that procedure was found to be less effective [13].

Packet Features. The upper part of Table 2 lists the single packet features we use. The geoDistance, senderHour, AS-Spamminess, and NeighborDist features are used in [10] although we derive the last three differently, as follows. We do not translate sender's hour into the ratio of ham to spam that were sent during that hour, because sender's hour itself is a numeric feature directly suitable for inclusion in our models. Hao et al. use the AS number directly as a numeric feature in their work. However, AS numbers are individual labels which do not lend themselves to meaningful aggregation in models (e.g., just because ASes 3 and 12 show some common behavior does not mean that ASes 4–11 share that behavior). Further, if treated as discrete values, the number of distinct AS values is problematic for classification methods. So we translate sender's AS number into a numerical value that reflects the prevalence of spam originating in the AS. The value for this feature is derived by using all messages in a training sample to develop a database of the "spamminess" of an AS. If a test message came from an AS that did not occur in the training set, we assign the average spamminess over all ASes as the value of this feature for that message.

To calculate the neighbor distance, NeighborDist, Hao, et al. first split their dataset into 24-hour bins. The NeighborDist is then the average distance to the 20 nearest IPs among preceding senders in the same bin, or among all the neighbors if there are fewer than 20 preceding senders [10,9]. This procedure is not suitable for our enterprise environment because a one-day bin does not provide enough email to accumulate enough history. Further, since the database is smaller, boundary effects due to insufficient number of neighbors in the beginning of each bin influence the results greatly. This is illustrative of our first contribution (discussed in more detail below): a single edge network's myopic view thwarts development of accurate models. To mitigate this effect, we build IP databases using an entire training sample—consisting of 9/10 of the data for each month, given we use 10-fold cross validation. We then use this database to produce NeighborDist values for the training and test data. Note that because of our procedure, each fold of our experiments uses different databases for the AS-Spamminess and NeighborDist features. We refer to these two features as "database features" below.

Table 2. Message features. Features marked with H and B are from [10] and [4], respectively.

Feature	Description
$geoDistance^H$	The geographical distance between the sender and ICSI, based on the MaxMind GeoIP database [11].
$senderHour^H$	The hour of packet arrival in sender's timezone.
$AS\text{-}Spamminess^H$	Num. of spams from AS divided by total msgs. from AS in the training set.
$NeighborDist^H$	Avg. numerical dist. from sender's IP to the nearest 20 IPs of other senders.
OS	OS of remote host as determined by *p0f* tool from SYN packet.
ttl	IP TTL field from SYN received from remote host.
ws	Advertised window size from SYN received from remote host.
$3whs^B$	Time between the arrival of the SYN from the remote host and arrival of ACK of the SYN/ACK sent by the local host.
$fins\_local^B$	Number of TCP segments with "FIN" bit set sent by the local mail server.
$fins\_remote^B$	Number of TCP segments with "FIN" bit set received from the remote host.
$idle^B$	Maximum time between two successive packet arrivals from remote host.
$jvar^B$	The variance of the inter-packet arrival times from the remote host.
$pkts\_sent\ /$ $pkts\_recvd$	Ratio of the number of packets sent by the local host to the number of packets received from the remote host
$rsts\_local^B$	Number of segments with "RST" bit set sent by the local mail server.
$rsts\_remote^B$	Number of segments with "RST" bit set received from remote host.
$rttv$	Variance of RTT from local mail server to remote host.
$rxmt\_local^B$	Number of retransmissions sent by the local mail server.
$rxmt\_remote^B$	Approximate number of retransmissions sent by the remote host.
$bytecount$	Number of non-retransmitted) bytes received from the remote host.
$throughput$	*bytecount* divided by the connection duration.

Hao et al. also use a feature that requires port scanning the sending IP. This is operationally problematic as it is time consuming and may trigger security alarms on remote hosts. Further, while we have historical packet trace data, we do not have historical port scanning data and mixing current port scans with historical packet traces would be a dubious experimental procedure. While we deleted or modified several single packet features we also added several features: senders' OS, IP's residual TTL, and TCP's advertised window (from prior work [4,13]).

Flow Features. The lower part of Table 2 shows the set of flow features we use to describe messages. This list is not identical to that used in prior work [4] (with common features tagged with a B)). We added several features we believe may help discriminate ham from spam. In addition, we removed three features: *packets* (in each direction), *cwnd0* and *cwndmin*. The number of packets is closely related to the *bytecount* and *pkts_sent/pkts_recvd* features in our list. A more detailed description of these features can be found in [13].

3   Empirical Evaluation

We use two algorithms in our experiments: decision trees [16] (from Weka [18]) and Rulefit [7]. Decision trees use the idea of *recursive partitioning*: at each step, they

Table 3. Results for packet features with AS-spamminess. The TPR is reported at 1% FPR.

Month	Rulefit			Decision Trees		
	Acc	TPR	AROC	Acc	TPR	AROC
May	0.674	0.483	0.944	0.663	0.464	0.783
Jun	0.573	0.280	0.926	0.564	0.266	0.785
Jul	0.555	0.299	0.940	0.563	0.312	0.805
Aug	0.580	0.338	0.940	0.543	0.280	0.773
Sep	0.560	0.279	0.933	0.586	0.322	0.783
Oct	0.609	0.353	0.938	0.640	0.406	0.779
Nov	0.504	0.315	0.904	0.507	0.319	0.660

choose a feature and use it to split the data until a partition only has examples from a single class. Rulefit—used in [10]— constructs a linear classifier that uses the primitive features as well as Boolean tests on feature values as predictors. We perform 10-fold stratified cross validation on each month's data by randomly dividing the trace at the granularity of SMTP sessions into ten folds such that all folds have the same spam/ham ratios as the entire dataset. We train our models using every set of nine folds and test it on the remaining folds. Throughout the paper, we consider spam as the target class; thus our true positive rate (TPR) is the fraction of spam classified as spam and false positive rate (FPR) is the fraction of ham misclassified as spam. We report (averaged over ten folds) accuracy, the area under ROC (AROC) [15], an alternative quality measure, and TPR at a given FPR (0.2% unless stated otherwise), obtained from the ROC graph for the classifier. The ROC, or receiver operating characteristic, graph relates the TPR and FPR as a threshold is varied over the confidence of the predictions.

3.1   Packet-Level Features at the Enterprise

Prior work [10] reports that properties of the first SYN packet from an incoming SMTP connection could be sufficient to filter out 70% of spam with 0.44% false positives (0.2% when adding features beyond single-packet). However, this result was obtained using models derived from 2,500 organizations, in a pre-blacklist setting. Our first question is whether single-packet features could be similarly effective in a stand-alone enterprise mail service using only its own vantage point. To study this, we run decision trees and Rulefit on each month's data, using only the single packet features (in the upper part of Table 2) to describe each message.

We first observed that the unmodified algorithms we used had an average FPR of almost 20% across the months (18.74% for decision trees and 19.83% for Rulefit), and our attempts to reduce FPR by thresholding the confidence degraded the TPR to single-digit percentages. This is clearly not operationally usable. To remedy this, we produce cost sensitive classifiers, trained to penalize FP errors more than FN errors. We use a cost ratio of 175:1 in our experiments for decision trees and 20:1 for Rulefit. The results are shown in Table 3. While the FPR drops significantly compared to the unweighted case, it does not reach 0.2% for decision trees—even when increasing the cost ratio significantly. Analysis of the classifiers reveals that the AS-spamminess feature—from the training data—is chosen as highly predictive in each case. However, it appears to be less predictive on the test data, possibly because even using 90% of our data from a month does not result in a comprehensive database. Thus, even though our results confirm previous findings (e.g., [17]) that AS origin differs for spam and ham, we find the utility of this feature in an enterprise environment limited.

Next, we remove AS-spamminess from the analysis, forcing our classifiers to use other features. The results are shown in the "Rulefit" and "Decision Trees" columns of Table 4. In this case, we are able to obtain an FPR of 0.2%. We further observe that though the classifiers produced achieve a low FPR, their TPR is low as well—as low as 10% and never reaching beyond 36%. This is significantly different from the result in prior work [10], where a TPR of 70% was achieved at FPR=0.44%, as we discussed above (while we omit our full results for 0.44% FPR due to space, Rulefit produced 29% TPR in May and at best 16% in other months; without AS-spamminess, the results improved to 47% in May and 18-31% in other months). Further, the result in [10] was achieved with unweighted Rulefit by purely thresholding confidence [9], while as mentioned earlier, this did not produce usable results in our setting. Thus it generally appears that packet features are significantly less useful in our setting. Further we observe that both decision trees and Rulefit exhibit quite similar results in our experiments. Thus the lack of utility of the single packet features is (at least to some extent) not a function of the learning algorithm they are used with, but purely a consequence of the limited information they convey about the message in this setting.

One might wonder if it is possible to increase the TPR or decrease the FPR further. However, this is difficult with just packet features to describe each message. It is intuitively plausible that looking at a single packet reveals limited information about the message, and one can only construct few features from this information (we use seven). This set of features generally describes the characteristics of a group of hosts sending email. But unless the granularity is extremely fine, such a group will sometimes send ham and sometimes spam. We therefore found many instances where messages were described by identical packet features but had opposing labels, i.e., some were labeled as spam and some as ham. For example, in the May data, 4K messages out of 48K total had a counterpart with the identical feature values but opposite label. This clearly is problematic for any classifier and may increase the FPR and lower the TPR. On the other hand, if granularity is decreased (e.g., imagine using the IP address—with a range of 4 billion values—as a feature), then significantly more data will need to be collected to train a useful classifier. This appears to be a fundamental limit of single packet features for spam detection.

Hao et al.'s work evaluated the utility of packet features in a *pre*-DNS blacklist setting. Although using such a blacklist is natural and common in an enterprise setting, we perform a similar analysis on our data to establish a direct comparison. This experiment follows Hao et. al.'s methodology–using the same classifier (Rulefit) and reports TPR at the same FPR (0.44%)—except it employs the cost-sensitive classifier with cost ratio of 100:1, as lower cost ratios degraded FPR to non-usable levels. In this case, we include messages that were blocked by ICSI's operational DNS blacklist setup ("DNSBL"+"Ham"+"Spam" in Table 1) since their first SYN packet is still available for analysis. We label all messages blocked by the DNS blacklist as spam. In this pre-blacklist experiment we train and evaluate on all messages including those blocked by the DNS blacklist (the results are shown in the "Pre-blacklist" column in Table 4),

Table 4. Results for packet features *without* AS-spamminess. The TPR is reported at 0.2% FPR for the post-blacklist and at 0.44% for the pre-blacklist experiments.

Month	Post-Blacklist(Rulefit)			Post-Blacklist(Decision Trees)			Pre-Blacklist (Rulefit)		
	Acc	TPR	AROC	Acc	TPR	AROC	Acc	TPR	AROC
May	0.600	0.359	0.909	0.594	0.348	0.768	0.824	0.808	0.967
Jun	0.492	0.139	0.882	0.454	0.072	0.652	0.346	0.290	0.964
Jul	0.478	0.171	0.906	0.438	0.108	0.666	0.467	0.421	0.962
Aug	0.506	0.216	0.905	0.479	0.172	0.660	0.714	0.691	0.969
Sep	0.509	0.189	0.892	0.497	0.169	0.663	0.644	0.612	0.967
Oct	0.515	0.191	0.901	0.488	0.145	0.683	0.520	0.462	0.957
Nov	0.421	0.197	0.884	0.436	0.218	0.826	0.709	0.670	0.943

while in all other experiments, we train and evaluate on messages that passed through and have not been filtered out by the DNS blacklist. We observe that the "Pre-blacklist" results vary significantly across months. For some months, our results are comparable to, even exceed, the 70% TPR reported by Hao et al. However, for other months, we find the TPR is far lower (e.g., 29% in June). Such variability reduces the operational utility of packet features for spam detection. While the reason for the variability is unclear, one possibility is that it is due to the enterprise's vantage point. Another possibility is that it is a fundamental property of packet features, and was not observed by Hao et al. since their data was collected over a period of only 14 days.

3.2 Effect of Flow-Level Features

Given the limited accuracy of packet features, we next consider whether adding flow-level features to the message description adds value by making the classifier more accurate. To check this, we compare two settings. First, we use only the flow features in the lower half of Table 2 to classify messages. Then we add the flow features to the packet features (without AS-spamminess) and use the full set in the same way. For these experiments, we use decision trees as the learning algorithm. This is because our prior results show that any patterns we see generalize to Rulefit as well, yet Rulefit is significantly more expensive to run (a cross validation runtime of hours, compared to a few seconds for trees). Further, trees are easier to interpret. The results are shown in Table 5.

Comparing these results to the results in Table 4, we observe that using the flow features by themselves improves TPR at a given FPR as against using the packet features by themselves. (In other experiments, not shown here, we also found that including AS-spamminess in the packet features reversed this trend, so that packet features had a higher TPR at a given FPR; however, as stated above, in that case the comparison was made at 1% FPR since the packet features with AS-spamminess do not achieve 0.2% FPR.) Further, we observe that using all of the features generally achieves a higher TPR at a given FPR as compared to either feature set on their own. This indicates that these two feature sets capture different kinds of information about packet traces.

Even though our results show that flow features can improve spam detection rates in conjunction with packet features in our post-blacklist, enterprise setting, the absolute TPRs do not reach the 70% found in the setting of prior work [10]. A question is whether

Table 5. Results for decision trees using flow features (left), all features (without AS-spamminess) (right). TPR is reported at 0.2% FPR.

Month	Flow Features			All Features		
	Acc	TPR	AROC	Acc	TPR	AROC
May	0.583	0.330	0.709	0.632	0.410	0.759
Jun	0.555	0.244	0.689	0.546	0.230	0.686
Jul	0.547	0.281	0.701	0.564	0.308	0.748
Aug	0.538	0.266	0.691	0.576	0.327	0.754
Sep	0.558	0.270	0.681	0.582	0.309	0.711
Oct	0.488	0.145	0.633	0.529	0.215	0.675
Nov	0.417	0.191	0.823	0.449	0.236	0.788

Table 6. Left: Average accuracy, TPR at 0.2% FPR and AROC when only one single-packet feature is used. Right: Average accuracy, TPR and FPR when one single-packet feature is left out.

Feature	Use one feature			Use all but one feature		
	Accuracy	TPR	AROC	Accuracy	TPR	AROC
All single-packet	0.594	0.348	0.768	0.594	0.348	0.768
geoDistance	0.473	0.153	0.667	0.546	0.271	0.746
senderHour	0.378	0(FPR=0)	0.500	0.595	0.35	0.769
NeighborDist	0.378	0(FPR=0)	0.519	0.522	0.233	0.704
OS	0.378	0(FPR=0)	0.500	0.597	0.353	0.770
ws	0.38	0.004	0.622	0.596	0.352	0.768
ttl	0.378	0(FPR=0)	0.500	0.564	0.30	0.721

an effective pre-filter can be constructed using such a classifier, so that only messages that cannot be classified with high probability are sent to computationally expensive content filters. We are currently investigating this question.

3.3 Utility of Individual Features

Next, we examine which packet and flow features are most useful in discriminating between ham and spam. We consider three situations. First, we look at the accuracy of our classifiers when only a single packet feature is used, and when we leave a single packet feature out from all the packet features (results in Table 6). Next, we start with the full set of packet features and add flow features one at a time to determine the value added by each flow feature. Finally, we look at what happens if we start with the full feature set and leave one flow feature out (results in Table 7).

Table 6 shows *geoDistance* to be the most useful packet feature. The other packet features, when used in isolation, result in zero or near zero TPR. This is because they produce an empty (or nearly empty in the case of *ws*) tree that always predicts "ham" in order to minimize the cost with a high FP cost. Further, only *geoDistance* and *Neighbor-Dist* result in large drops in TPR when they are left out of the feature set. This indicates that though *NeighborDist* is not useful by itself, it has some discriminating power when used in conjunction with other packet features. For the other packet features, the TPR

Table 7. Left: Average accuracy, TPR at 0.2% FPR and AROC when all single-packet features and only one flow feature are used. Right: Results when one flow feature is left out, and all other flow and single-packet features are used.

Feature	Use one feature			Use All but one features		
	Accuracy	TPR	AROC	Accuracy	TPR	AROC
All packet and flow features	0.632	0.410	0.759	0.632	0.410	0.759
All single-packet features	0.594	0.348	0.768	0.594	0.348	0.768
3whs	0.586	0.336	0.720	0.643	0.427	0.784
fins_local	0.611	0.376	0.772	0.615	0.382	0.729
fins_remote	0.598	0.354	0.770	0.628	0.403	0.759
idle	0.597	0.353	0.770	0.633	0.411	0.759
jvar	0.594	0.348	0.771	0.632	0.410	0.759
pkts_sent/pkts_received	0.599	0.356	0.770	0.618	0.386	0.759
rsts_local	0.595	0.349	0.768	0.632	0.410	0.759
rsts_remote	0.595	0.349	0.770	0.623	0.395	0.788
rttv	0.606	0.367	0.770	0.618	0.386	0.751
rxmt_local	0.596	0.351	0.768	0.629	0.404	0.759
rxmt_remote	0.595	0.350	0.769	0.624	0.396	0.751
bytecount	0.598	0.354	0.768	0.632	0.409	0.759
throughput	0.607	0.369	0.793	0.625	0.398	0.729

stays the same or increases slightly when they are dropped, indicating that they do not provide much added value beyond the remaining features. In particular, our results do not show *senderHour* to be useful for spam detection despite previous findings that spammers and non-spammers display different timing properties [8].

From the results in Table 7, we observe that adding any one flow feature to the set of single packet features improves the performance of the classifier, though by a small margin. In particular, *fins_local*, *rttv* and *throughput* provide the greatest additional discriminating power beyond the single packet features. Further, *fins_local*, *rttv* and *pkts_local/pkts_remote* result in the largest drops in performance when they are dropped, indicating that they are also useful in conjunction with the other features (i.e. no other feature captures their information). Some flow features such as *rsts_local* and *3whs* either do not change the TPR or increase it when they are dropped, indicating that they do not provide much added value beyond the remaining features. This contradicts prior results [4,13] that found that *3whs* was the most useful in discriminating ham from spam, if *only* flow features were used. However, it appears that the information in *3whs* is subsumed by the other features, perhaps by packet features such as *geoDistance*.

4   Summary

This paper addresses two questions: whether an organizational mail server can detect a sizable amount of spam based on the first packet of an incoming connection, and the relative effectiveness of single-packet and flow features in detection. Our primary finding indicates that from an organizational perspective, single-packet features are much less effective than was observed in prior work. "Database" features such as AS-spamminess and sender's neighborhood density are less effective in this situation, and the limited information conveyed by packet features leads ambiguity and hence non-useful models. Also, adding flow features to packet features improves accuracy, but the net effect is still modest.

Some questions still remain. While we find that network features may not be useful in the enterprise setting, it would be useful to study other such organizations to strengthen our findings. Finally, though network features only filter 20-40% of post-blacklist spam, avoiding content-based processing of these messages may still be a net win for mail servers, which we are quantifying in ongoing work.

Acknowledgments. Robert Beverly provided his SpamFlow tool. Shuang Hao and Nick Feamster clarified the methodology used in [10]. This work was funded in part by NSF grants CNS-0916407, CNS-0831821 and CNS-0433702.

References

1. Crm114 - the controllable regex mutilator, http://crm114.sourceforge.net/
2. SpamAssassin, http://spamassassin.apache.org/
3. Allman, E., Callas, J., Delany, M., Libbey, M., Fenton, J., Thomas, M.: Domain-Based Email Authentication Using Public Keys Advertised in the DNS (DomainKeys) (May 2007) RF 4871
4. Beverly, R., Sollins, K.: Exploiting Transport-Level Characteristics of Spam. In: 5th Conference on Email and Anti-Spam (August 2008)
5. Burton, B.: SpamProbe, http://spamprobe.sourceforge.net/
6. Cormack, G., Lynam, T.: TREC Public Spam Corpus (2007), http://plg.uwaterloo.ca/~gvcormac/treccorpus07/
7. Friedman, J.H., Popescu, B.E.: Predictive learning via rule ensembles. Annals of Applied Statistics 2(3), 916–954 (2008)
8. Gomes, L.H., Cazita, C., Almeida, J.M., Almeida, V.A.F., Meira Jr., W.: Characterizing a spam traffic. In: IMC, pp. 356–369 (2004)
9. Hao, S., Feamster, N.: Personal Communication (2010)
10. Hao, S., Syed, N.A., Feamster, N., Gray, A.G., Krasser, S.: Detecting spammers with SNARE: Spatio-temporal network-level automatic reputation engine. In: Usenix Security Symp. (2009)
11. MaxMind, http://www.maxmind.com
12. Meyer, T., Whateley, B.: SpamBayes: Effective Open-Source, Bayesian Based, Email classification System. In: Proc. First Conference on Email and Anti-Spam (June 2004)
13. Ouyang, T., Ray, S., Allman, M., Rabinovich, M.: A Large-Scale Empirical Analysis of Email Spam Detection Through Transport-Level Characteristics. Technical Report 10-001, International Computer Science Institute (January 2010)
14. Paxson, V.: Bro: A System for Detecting Network Intruders in Real-Time. In: Proceedings of the 7th USENIX Security Symposium (January 1998)
15. Provost, F., Fawcett, T., Kohavi, R.: The case against accuracy estimation for comparing induction algorithms. In: 15th Int. Conf. on Machine Learning, pp. 445–453 (1998)
16. Quinlan, J.: C4.5: Programs for Machine Learning. Morgan Kaufmann, San Francisco (1993)
17. Ramachandran, A., Feamster, N.: Understanding the Network-Level Behavior of Spammers. In: ACM SIGCOMM (2006)
18. Witten, I.H., Frank, E.: Data Mining: Practical machine learning tools and techniques, 2nd edn. Morgan Kaufmann, San Francisco (2005)

Detecting and Analyzing Automated Activity on Twitter

Chao Michael Zhang[1] and Vern Paxson[1,2,⋆]

[1] University of California, Berkeley, CA
[2] International Computer Science Institute, Berkeley, CA

Abstract. We present a method for determining whether a Twitter account exhibits automated behavior in publishing status updates known as *tweets*. The approach uses only the publicly available timestamp information associated with each tweet. After evaluating its effectiveness, we use it to analyze the Twitter landscape, finding that 16% of active accounts exhibit a high degree of automation. We also find that 11% of accounts that appear to publish exclusively through the browser are in fact automated accounts that spoof the source of the updates.

1 Introduction

Twitter is a microblogging service that allows its members to publish short status updates known as *tweets*. Over 180 M visitors interact with Twitter each month, generating 55 M tweets/day [13]. User accounts and their status updates are public by default, accessible by the general public via Twitter's two application program interfaces (APIs). The large number of users, low privacy expectations, and easy-to-use API have made Twitter a target of abuse, whether relatively benign in the form of spam and disruptive marketing tactics [5], or malicious in the form of links to malware [17] and phishing schemes [8]. Often abuse on Twitter employs automation for actions such as publishing tweets, following another user, and sending links through private messages.

Prior research on Twitter has studied the properties of the social network [10], characteristics of users and their behavior [11], and social interactions between users [9], but not specifically regarding the issue of automation on Twitter (other than our own use of the technique we develop here to assist with finding Twitter "career" spammers [7]). In this work we present a technique for determining whether a Twitter account appears to employ automation to publish tweets, as manifest in fine-grained periodicities in tweet timestamps. Our approaach has the benefit of being able to find legitimate accounts compromised by spammers who employ automation. We evaluate the test's effectiveness and describe its weaknesses, including the ability for determined adversaries to evade it by directly mimicking human posting patterns. Finally, we examine various facets of Twitter as a service and discuss the prevalence of automation in each.

2 Background and Measurement Data

Tweets are short messages (limited to 140 characters) posted to a Twitter account using a browser, a stand-alone application, an API, or SMS messages. Information associated

---

⋆ This work was supported by NSF grants CNS-0831535, CNS-0905631, and NSF-0433702, and ONR MURI Grant N000140911081.

N. Spring and G. Riley (Eds.): PAM 2011, LNCS 6579, pp. 102–111, 2011.

with each tweet includes the time at which the update was created and the source by which the status appears to have been posted. Users on Twitter can subscribe to the tweets of another account by choosing to *follow* that account. The user will then receive that account's tweets through the main "timeline" prominently displayed on the Twitter website and via separate applications, or via SMS messages. Accounts have two main privacy settings: *Public* accounts have their content visible to the general public regardless of whether the visitor is logged in or not, while *protected* accounts can only be viewed by users who have had follow requests accepted by the account owner.

Twitter's "Verified Account" program allows people and companies to show that their account in fact belongs to them. Twitter only makes this program available to a modest number of accounts that deal with mistaken identity or impersonation problems; at the time of this writing there are 1,738 *verified* accounts.

Twitter is a real time communication service, and at any given time there may be certain topics that are widely discussed among members in the community. These *trending topics* are featured prominently to provide users with an up-to-date glimpse at what the community is talking about. Twitter uses algorithms to constantly determine these popular topics, publishes them to the website, and makes them available through APIs.

Twitter provides two APIs through which developers can interact with the service. The "REST API" provides methods for reading and writing data to the main service, while the "Search API" handles queries for searching tweets and obtaining trending topics. The API can be accessed through basic authentication using an account's username and password, or can be accessed through OAuth [2], allowing users to provide third-party applications with access to their data stored on Twitter.

For our purposes we term any account that publishes a significant portion of its tweets automatically using a computer program as a *bot*. We refer to tweets published in real-time by a human as *manual*, or *organic*, tweets.

Data Used in the Study. We draw upon public data associated with accounts and status updates. We evaluated 106,573 distinct accounts using data from 3 weeks in April 2010. Since we rely on public information, we only examine accounts with "public" privacy. For each account, the REST API can return the latest 3,200 tweets, with 200 updates returned per call (we examined a maximum of 300 tweets per account, to avoid skew due to API timeouts). Tweets returned by the API include a timestamp indicating when Twitter received the tweet (1 sec precision), the account's followers and privacy settings, the client program from which the tweet apparently originated, and whether the account has been "verified."

3   Detecting Tweet Automation

We base our detector on the premise that highly automated accounts will exhibit timing patterns that do not manifest in the tweet times of non-automated users. In particular, a human user posting updates to Twitter organically is most likely indifferent towards what second-of-the-minute or what minute-of-the-hour they post updates.[1] Therefore, an organic sequence of update times should appear to be randomly drawn from a uniform distribution across seconds-of-the-minute and minutes-of-the-hour. The upper left

---

[1] This will certainly be the case if their posting is well-modeled as a Poisson process.

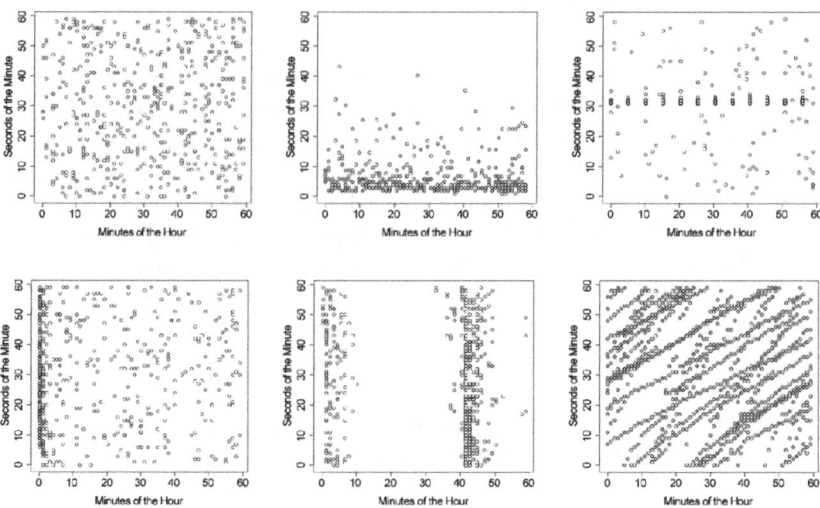

Fig. 1. Timing plots for different Twitter accounts. Each point represents a single tweet. The x-axis gives the tweet's minutes-in-the-hour and the y-axis the seconds-in-the-minute. The upper left plot passes our χ^2 test for expected uniformity, presumably reflecting organic behavior. The others all fail, exhibiting different patterns of non-uniformity, except for the lower right, which exhibits *hyper-uniformity*, too good to be produced by a random-uniform process.

plot in Figure 1 shows a typical *timing graph* for human-generated tweet times. While not completely uniform, they lack noticeable groupings or patterns.

Automated accounts, on the other hand, may exhibit timing distributions that lead to detectable non-uniformity (or excessive uniformity) due to a number of reasons. First, automation is often invoked by job schedulers that execute tasks at specified times or intervals, and these are usually specified in round quantities such as minute-granularity. Furthermore, Twitter imposes a limit of 1,000 tweets/day (as well as finer-grained limits for smaller units of time), so there is no apparent benefit in scheduling automated tweets more often than say one a per-minute basis. Given scheduling at minute-granularity, the seconds-within-the-minute when such tweets appear are unlikely to be uniformly distributed across the minute. The upper middle plot in Figure 1 shows a timing graph of a user who exhibits this type of automated behavior. While the times are distributed somewhat uniformly for minutes-of-the-hour, the user clearly tends to publish updates towards the beginning of the minute.

If scripts publish tweets at scheduled times in each hour, then we will find tweet times clustering at those scheduled minutes. On the other hand, if a script publishes updates on a per-minute basis, it may exhibit a timing pattern that is *too uniform*, which also distinguishes it from organic activity. The upper right plot in Figure 1 shows the timing graph of a user that publishes tweets every 5 minutes in the hour; the lower left plot shows an account that automatically posts updates at the beginning of the hour; and the lower middle plot shows an account that publishes nearly all of its updates during two particular times of the hour.

Non-uniform timing can also arise from delay-based automated behavior: scripts programmed to pause for a certain amount of time after each tweet. Delays that always run the script at the same minutes-of-the-hour will manifest as either extremely non-uniform across minutes-of-the-hour, or, in rare cases, too uniform across minutes-of-the-hour. This latter arises when run times creep into delay-based automation, meaning that small delays that should lead to non-uniformity instead appear to exhibit excessive uniformity. The lower right plot in Figure 1 shows the timing graph of an account that is perfectly uniform across seconds-of-the-minute and minutes-of-the-hour due to what appears to be slowly drifting times. *Thus, we can conclude the presence of automation if we find tweet times either not uniform enough, or too uniform.*

Testing for Automated Behavior. We use Pearson's χ^2 test to assess whether a set of update times is consistent with the uniform second-of-the-minute and minute-of-the-hour distributions expected from human users. The p-value returned by the χ^2 test is the probability of the observed distribution of times arising if the account is indeed publishing updates uniformly across seconds-of-the-minute or minutes-of-the-hour. If the probability is too low, it indicates that the account exhibits non-uniform behavior in choosing which second-of-the-minute or minute-of-the-hour to publish a post; likewise, if the probability is too high, it suggests that the account is using a mechanism that causes it to publish tweets with a level of uniformity that is unlikely to be observed from natural human use.

For our test we use a two-sided significance level of 0.001, or 0.1%, as the threshold for failing the test. We chose this level after preliminary examination of a small subset of the accounts. We selected a quite low level to avoid incurring many statistical false positives due to the large volume of accounts that we examine. Thus, we expect only 2 in 1,000 human accounts with uniform distributions to fail each test.

A common rule of thumb for Pearson's χ^2 test is that 80% of bins should have an expected count of at least 5 [6]. Therefore if we have 300 timestamps for an account we use 60 bins for assessing seconds-of-the-minute and minutes-of-the-hour. If we have fewer, then we use only 6 bins, unless the account has fewer than 30 tweets, in which case we exclude it due to insufficient data. Eliminating such accounts does not significantly impair our study as we presume that the interesting uses of automation occur when accounts regularly tweet.

Automated accounts can exhibit non-uniform timing patterns for both seconds-of-the-minute and minutes-of-the-hour, both indicative of automation. Therefore, we perform a separate χ^2 test for each, with a failure of either indicating automation.

4   Evaluating the Test

An important issue is that we lack ground truth regarding whether accounts are truly automated or organic, and also whether automation reflects unwanted activity. However, we form a partial assessment as follows. From an initial evaluation of 18,147 accounts we found that 975 accounts had seconds-of-the-minute p-values less than 0.001, and 15 accounts had p-values greater than 0.999. The same figures for minutes-of-the-hour are 2,599 p-values less than 0.001 and 76 greater than .999.

We manually examined hundreds of timing graphs to confirm they exhibited clear non-uniform or hyper-uniform behavior, and randomly selected dozens of accounts for manual verification. (Accounts that did not visibly manifest non-uniform behavior, but were flagged by the test, generally turned out to indeed use third party applications that automate tweets.) This latter included an examination of the user's profile and their first page of recent status updates. In nearly all cases we could determine that the account exhibited strong evidence of likely automation not reflecting social human use, based on status updates (i.e., number of updates, sources, frequency, and contents) and other features of the account's Twitter page (i.e., user icon, background image, screenname, number of followers and friends, and website URL). See below for further discussion of our evaluation of false positives and false negatives.

This assessment gives us confidence that a significance level of 0.001 can effectively capture accounts that exhibit anomalous timing behavior. However, we also note that such a stringent significance level can cost us the opportunity of observing *hybrid* accounts that publish with a mix of manual and automatic updates. Some hybrid users may utilize different applications for these two kinds of updates, allowing us to separate these sources in order to evaluate our test. For example, one hybrid we identified used the third-party applications TweetDeck [3] and HootSuite [12], both applications that provide an interface for reading and creating tweets. However, TweetDeck does not offer functionality for automating tweet creation, while HootSuite provides a scheduling feature. This account's timing graph exhibits distinct periodicity. Testing only the tweets posted from TweetDeck, however, does not exhibit such patterns (and passes the χ^2 test), while tweets originating from "HootSuite" exhibit updates at five minute intervals, failing the χ^2 test.

False Positives. A false positive occurs an account fails our test but is in fact organic. Along with statistical fluctuations (which will contribute about 2 false positives per 1,000 accounts we assess), these can arise due to legitimate organic use that deviates from uniform timing. For example, a student who only publishes Twitter updates in between class periods may fail our test because their tweets will tend towards certain minutes-of-the-hour.

An example of an account that fails our test but otherwise appears to be organic is the account of television personality Phil McGraw, also known as Dr. Phil [1]. After inspecting the account, we found that it consistently publishes one update per day shortly before the show begins to remind followers to watch. Although these updates are manually generated, they are skewed towards the first half of the hour.

While we discovered a few false positives along these lines, we note that all of them concerned accounts that failed on minutes-of-the-hour for the type of reason described above. We have not discovered any apparently legitimate human account that exhibits anomalous timings for seconds-of-the-minute.

False Negatives. On the other hand, our false negative rate is likely considerably higher for a number of reasons. First, as discussed above, hybrid behavior can mask automated posting due to blending it with organic posting. We could potentially detect more such instances by using a less stringent significance level, but at the cost of more statistical false positives. Second, automated accounts that exhibit uniformity in some fashion will of course be missed by our test. In particular, one form of this can arise from *copycat automation*, i.e., an automated account that posts in reflection of non-automated timings. For example, an automated accounts triggered by an RSS feed will reflect the timings of the source rather than a specific schedule.

Evasion. One can easily design an automated account to evade the χ^2 test by uniformly spreading its tweets across seconds-of-the-minute and minutes-of-the-hour. For example, the account could post whenever a known-organic account posts; or simply generate exponentially distributed interarrivals. There does not seem to currently exist any incentive for automated accounts to be intentional about exhibiting uniformity. However, if Twitter adopts a test like ours as a countermeasure to detect possible abuse, then accounts may begin evading the test in this way.

5   Analyzing Twitter's Landscape

Using the χ^2 test, we analyzed public tweets and accounts to determine the prevalence of automated accounts on the service and how the use of automation varies with respect to different factors. We sampled the public timeline of global tweets via the REST API, which makes available the 20 most recent tweets, refreshed every minute. We were therefore able to obtain a sample of 1,200 tweets per hour. In addition, we used the Search API to query for samples based on keywords and to obtain trending topics. For a range of keywords, we performed a search every minute and recorded the accounts behind the 10 most recent results, for which we then analyzed the posting account. We sampled search results for between two and four days for each keyword. In addition to the constantly changing public timeline and sampled search results, we also obtained accounts from various static lists, including verified users, most-followed users, and followers of the most-popular account, collecting up to 300 tweets for each account.

For each account we have six possible dispositions. *Passed* accounts pass the χ^2 test while *Failed* accounts do not. *Insufficient* accounts do not have the 30 status updates necessary to perform the test. *Protected* accounts have their privacy settings set to protected, so we could not test them. *Suspended* accounts have been suspended by Twitter for reasons such as spamming and abusing the API. These accounts are rendered completely inaccessible through the API. However, their user IDs may persist for a time in various places on Twitter, and therefore may be included in our analysis. *Not Found* accounts no longer exist on Twitter. When an individual or business deactivates their Twitter account, the API returns an error when requesting data from that account. However, the user ID may persist on various pages of Twitter for up to 30 days, and may be detected by our analysis.

Table 1 summarizes our results. We note that accounts might exhibit varying degrees of automation depending on temporal factors such as time of the day or day of the week. For example, an account may syndicate news from a news source that publishes more heavily during the waking hours of the day, or may publish from a source that is inactive on weekends. Therefore, a more accurate assessment of automated activity on Twitter may monitor activity over the course of weeks or months in order to determine average levels of automation. Our present analysis does not take these considerations into account, which we leave for future work. Finally, we emphasize that our estimates

Table 1. Automation testing results for different facets of the Twitter landscape (lower bounds)

Facet	Total	Passed	Failed	Insufficient	Protected	Suspended	Not Found
Public timeline accounts	19,436	15,330	2,817	1,176	66	47	0
Public timeline tweets	18,331	14,790	2,475	983	59	24	0
Verified users	1,738	1,531	113	66	17	6	5
Most followed (all)	1,000	862	121	15	1	0	1
(verified)	400	373	25	2	0	0	0
(not verified)	600	489	96	13	1	0	1
Trending topics	14,230	13,260	617	286	58	8	1

likely reflect lower bounds, as we will overlook both low-rate automation (too few samples to apply the χ^2 test) and automation that already employs randomization to avoid appearing regular.

Public Timeline. The Twitter public timeline provides a sample of the thousands of tweets being sent via the service each minute. Thus, we can use it to estimate the prevalence of automation for public statuses on Twitter overall. The *Public timeline accounts* line of Table 1 reflects a sample from two days in April 2010. Of the 19,436 accounts examined during this period, we could test 18,147 using our χ^2 method. We find that 16% of the accounts publishing tweets exhibit discernible automation.

A study conducted in August 2009 analyzed 11.5 million accounts, classifying those publishing >150 updates per day as bots [15]. The report concluded that at least 24% of all tweets were generated by automated bots. Around this time, Twitter began to focus on reducing spam in the service, and in March 2010 published the claim that the tweet spam rate had fallen below 1% [5]. To test these claims, we also ran a separate analysis (on different, somewhat smaller data) of the public timeline weighted by tweet rather than by account (*Public timeline tweets* row). We find that 14% of public tweets come from automated sources, suggesting that Twitter has indeed reduced the amount of unwanted automation on the service (if the methodology used by [15] has an accuracy comparable to ours). However, unless the vast majority of these automated tweets are not spam, our results also indicate that the problem of spam is still far from being solved.

Verified Users. That verified accounts are often owned by celebrities and popular companies (and Twitter manually approves accounts in the program) argues against these accounts exhibiting strong automation in their tweets. A heavily automated account may reflect badly on fans and customers, and would likely be harder to have approved by Twitter. The *Verified users* row in Table 1 shows the results of our analysis of these accounts. We find that 6.9% failed our test—the amount of automation seen in verified accounts is indeed less than the proportion in the general Twitter population. Among the verified accounts that failed were: (1) popular bands reminding fans of concerts and TV appearances, (2) TV shows reminding their fans of episodes each day, (3) political figures and parties publishing links to news articles, (4) journalists publishing links to their organizations, (5) non-profit organizations sharing links to issues around the world, and (6) government organizations publishing news and alerts to the public. Thus, common reasons for verified accounts failing our test were that they syndicated news, shared links, or sent reminders to followers in an automated way.

Table 2. Profiles of different sources used to publish tweets

Source	Overall Use	Automation Rate	Bot Rate	Bot Exclusivity	Organic Rate	Organic Exclusivity
Web	31%	6.4%	11.8%	85%	37%	82%
Ubertwitter	9.4%	2.3%			11.9%	87%
Twitterfeed	7.5%	62.0%	27.8%	94%	3.7%	95%
Tweetdeck	6.6%	3.9%	1.5%	76%	8.2%	77%
REST API	5.9%	60.0%	21.0%	96%	3%	92%
Echofon	4%	2.1%			5%	77%
Mobile	2%	1.9%			2.5%	73%
Tweetie	1.6%	3.0%			2%	73%
Txt	1.6%	2.6%			2%	75%
Hootsuite	1.4%	51.0%	4.1%	84%		

Most Followed Users. Although Twitter does not publish a list of most-followed users, certain 3rd-party websites do. Using the list provided by TwitterCounter [16], we analyzed the 1,000 most-followed accounts on Twitter. We find that 12% of the testable accounts failed our χ^2 test (*Most followed (all)* row). Only 6.3% of the verified accounts (next row) failed, slightly lower than the 6.9% found when analyzing all verified Twitter accounts. Of the remaining 600 not-verified accounts, significantly more (16%) were likely to be automated. Manually examining the 96 non-verified accounts that failed, many of them were news websites, blogs, and TV shows that use Twitter to broadcast new content to followers.

Trending Topics. Twitter publishes a constantly updated list of the 10 most popular words or phrases at any given time, providing users with a realtime glimpse at the topics being discussed by the Twitter community. Since many users follow trending topics by reading the latest tweets that contain those particular terms, it would seem profitable for automated accounts to target currently trending topic keywords. To test the trending topics for automation, we performed a search for the first trending topic once per minute, and tested the accounts behind the resulting tweets. As the results Table 1 show, we found that only 4.7% of accounts participating in the trending topic discussions on Twitter exhibited strongly automated behavior—significantly less than the 16% automation found in the public timeline.

This lower rate of automation may indicate that Twitter is careful in preventing automated tweets from polluting the trending topic discussions, since the tweets posted in response to trending topics are frequently viewed by both members and visitors. Alternatively, perhaps the number of human users is simply proportionally higher in searches for trending topics compared to the public timeline, or spammers have not widely adopted this tactic yet.

Keyword Search Results. Using the Twitter Search API, we evaluated the accounts behind the search results for 24 keywords that we believed might result in varying levels of automation. (Our aim here is to obtain a qualitative sense of automated-vs.-non-automated topics, rather than a representative assessment.) Sorted in descending order by the proportion of testable accounts that appear automated, the words were: *mortgage*

(48%), *jobs, insurance, news, discount, free, money* **(31%)**, *click, sex, poker, photography* **(24%)**, *video, download, bot, video, viagra* **(17.5%)**, *porn, school, tv, bieber, jesus* **(8.3%)**, *happy, bored, god* **(5.0%)**.

Most keywords tested had automation rates higher than the global 16% automation rate, particularly keywords commonly associated with spam ("discount", "free", "sex", "poker", and "download"). Likewise, keywords with lower automation rates often reflect terms not commonly associated with spam ("jesus", "happy", "bored", "god"). It is surprising though to find that "photography" had a higher rate of automation than "viagra". However, manually searching these keywords indeed reveals a significant amount of automated linking to photography-related articles and websites, while "viagra" often appears in lighthearted messages or jokes posted organically.

A more comprehensive study might directly analyze the frequencies of words that appear in the updates of automated/organic accounts. We leave this for future work.

Tweet Sources. For each account tested, we also analyzed the source appearing most often in that account's tweets. Table 2 summarizes the usage of the most popular sources. *Overall Use* is the percentage of tweets we examined that used the given source. *Automation Rate* is the proportion of those tweets belonging to accounts that we identified as automated. The next two columns reflect what proportion of automated accounts used the given source, and of those, how many used *only* that source ("Exclusivity"). The final two columns summarize the same information for non-automated accounts. Empty table entries reflect that the given entry corresponded to marginal activity (not in the top ten sources for either bots or organic activity, respectively).

We see sharp differences in usage patterns depending on the sources employed. Activity from Twitterfeed, REST API, and Hootsuite is very often automated, while other sources exhibited automation rates far below the overall average rate of 16%. Indeed, many of the services favored by organic users (e.g., UberTwitter [4], TweetDeck [3], and Echofon [14]) do not offer any scheduling features. This suggests that consideration of publishing source might prove beneficial for identifying unwanted/malicious Twitter activity. However, just about all of the top sources are also used organically, so we cannot simply filter by source without considering other factors.

Based on these findings, a possible way to improve our testing would be to examine the publishing times of each of an account's sources separately. Doing so might readily identify both hybrid accounts and *hijacked* accounts for which an attacker usurps use of what is otherwise a legitimate, organic account.

6   Summary

We have presented a method for detecting instances of automated Twitter accounts using only the publicly available timestamp associated with each of an account's tweets. We find that automated accounts exhibit distinct timing patterns that we can not only observe visually, but also detect in a mechanized fashion using Pearson's χ^2 test.

Testing 19,436 accounts from the public timeline, we find 16% exhibit highly automated behavior, and that 12% of automated accounts spoof their tweet source as "web," apparently to appear organic. (Note that these at best reflect evasive postings, because legitimate automation would presumably use the API rather than a web browser.) We also find that verified accounts, most-followed accounts, and followers of the most-followed account all have lower automation rates than the public timeline (6.9%, 12%, and 4.2%, respectively). Trending topic search results were found to have a lower rate as well, with 4.7% automation. We also find that keywords more associated with spam generally have higher automation rates than other keywords. We also examined the apparent source of tweets, finding that automated sources utilize services that provide automation and scheduling, while organic users often use Twitter's web interface or other non-automated services.

A practical application of our methodology could be to use it in conjunction with existing spam prevention measures such as community flagging of inappropriate or abusive accounts. The ability to quickly assess that an account operates in an automated fashion would allow operators to expedite paying attention to such complaints, allowing them to more quickly and effectively combat cases of serious spam and other abuse.

References

1. Dr. Phil (DrPhil) on Twitter (2010), http://twitter.com/DrPhil
2. OAuth FAQ 2010, http://apiwiki.twitter.com/OAuth-FAQ
3. TweetDeck (2010), http://www.tweetdeck.com/
4. UberTwitter (2010), http://www.ubertwitter.com/
5. Chowdhury, A.: State of Twitter Spam (2010),
   http://blog.twitter.com/2010/03/state-of-twitter-spam.html
6. D'Agostino, R.B., Stephens, M.A. (eds.): Goodness-of-Fit Techniques. Marcel Dekker Inc., New York (1986)
7. Grier, C., Thomas, K., Paxson, V., Zhang, M.: @spam: The Underground on 140 Characters or Less. In: Proc. ACM CCS (2010)
8. Harvey, D.: Trust And Safety (2009),
   http://blog.twitter.com/2010/03/trust-and-safety.html
9. Huberman, B.A., Romero, D.M., Wu, F.: Social networks that matter: Twitter under the microscope. Technical report, Social Coputing Laboratory, HP Labs (2008)
10. Java, A., Song, X., Finin, T., Tseng, B.: Why We Twitter: An Analysis of a Microblogging Community. In: Zhang, H., Spiliopoulou, M., Mobasher, B., Giles, C.L., McCallum, A., Nasraoui, O., Srivastava, J., Yen, J. (eds.) WebKDD 2007. LNCS, vol. 5439, pp. 118–138. Springer, Heidelberg (2009)
11. Krishnamurthy, B., Gill, P., Arlitt, M.: A few chirps about Twitter. In: Proc. ACM SIGCOMM Workshop on Online Social Networks (2008)
12. Media, I.: HootSuite (2010), http://hootsuite.com/
13. Miller, C.: Twitter Makes Itself More Useful (2010),
    http://bits.blogs.nytimes.com/2010/04/14/
    twitter-makes-itself-more-useful/
14. naan studio. Echofon (2010), http://www.echofon.com/
15. Sysomos. Inside Twitter: An In-Depth Look at the 5% of Most Active Users (2009),
    http://sysomos.com/insidetwitter/mostactiveusers
16. TwitterCounter.com. The 1000 most popular Twitter users (2010),
    http://twittercounter.com/pages/100/
17. Zetter, K.: Trick or Tweet? Malware Abundant in Twitter URLs (2009),
    http://www.wired.com/threatlevel/2009/10/twitter_malware/

A Practical Approach to Portscan Detection in Very High-Speed Links

Jakub Mikians*, Pere Barlet-Ros, Josep Sanjuàs-Cuxart, and Josep Solé-Pareta

UPC BarcelonaTech, Barcelona, Spain
{jmikians,pbarlet,jsanjuas,pareta}@ac.upc.edu

Abstract. Port scans are continuously used by both worms and human attackers to probe for vulnerabilities in Internet facing systems. In this paper, we present a new method to efficiently detect TCP port scans in very high-speed links. The main idea behind our approach is to early discard those handshake packets that are not strictly needed to reliably detect port scans. We show that with just a couple of Bloom filters to track active servers and TCP handshakes we can easily discard about 85% of all handshake packets with negligible loss in accuracy. This significantly reduces both the memory requirements and CPU cost per packet. We evaluated our algorithm using packet traces and live traffic from 1 and 10 GigE academic networks. Our results show that our method requires less than 1 MB to accurately monitor a 10 Gb/s link, which perfectly fits in the cache memory of nowadays' general-purpose processors.

1 Introduction and Related Work

Every day both individuals and companies depend more on the reliability and safety of Internet connections. However, even today, entire industry branches or countries can be a target of an attack (e.g., `Stuxnet` [3]). Most attacks start with a recognition phase, where an attacker looks for attack vectors in one or several victim systems. Port scanning is arguably the most widely used technique by both worms and human attackers to probe for vulnerabilities in Internet systems.

Given the large implications in network security, several previous works have addressed the problem of how to efficiently and reliably detect port scans. Most proposed solutions require tracking individual network connections (e.g., [6,15,14]). This approach however does not scale to very high-speed links, where the number of concurrent flows can be extremely large. For example, a naive solution based on a hash table would require large amounts of DRAM (e.g., to store flow identifiers) and several memory accesses per packet (e.g., to handle collisions). Nevertheless, access times of current DRAM technology cannot keep up with worst-case packet interarrival times of very high-speed links (e.g., 32 ns in OC-192 or 8 ns in OC-768 links).

Traffic sampling is considered as the standard solution to this problem. Unfortunately, recent studies [7,5] have shown that the impact of sampling on

---

* J. Mikians' work was partially supported by an FI grant from Generalitat de Catalunya.

N. Spring and G. Riley (Eds.): PAM 2011, LNCS 6579, pp. 112–121, 2011.

portscan detection algorithms is extremely large. Another alternative is the use of probabilistic, space-efficient data structures, such as Bloom filters [16,11], which significantly reduce the memory requirements of detection algorithms. This way, the required data structures can fit in fast SRAM, which has access times below 10 ns. Although we are not aware of any survey paper covering the use of Bloom Filters for portscan detection, [11,15] provide a good overview on the work in this area.

In this paper, we present a practical method to detect TCP port scans in very high-speed links that follows this second approach. A key assumption behind our method is that, apart from data traffic, we can even discard most TCP handshake packets and still be able to successfully detect port scans.

First, we ignore legitimate handshakes using a *whitelist* of active server IP-port pairs. Second, we discard those failed connections that do not correspond to scans, such as TCP retransmissions, packets from other network attacks (e.g., SYN floods) or configuration errors (e.g., P2P nodes down or misconfigured domain servers). In order to discard handshake packets, we use two Bloom filters. Surprisingly, we show that this simple solution can drop about 85% of all handshake packets with negligible loss in accuracy. This significantly reduces the number of memory accesses, CPU and memory requirements of our algorithm.

After filtering most part of the traffic, we still need to track the number of failed connections for the remaining sources. Although there is a potentially very large number of active sources, most of them will fail very few handshakes, while scanners will fail many. Thus, the detection problem can be seen as the well-known problem of finding the top-k elements from a data stream [8]. In order to efficiently detect port scans, we use an efficient top-k data structure based on the *Stream-Summary* proposed in [9], which has a constant memory usage.

We evaluated our algorithm in 1 and 10 GigE academic networks [1]. Our results show that our method requires less than 1 MB to accurately monitor a 10 Gb/s link. Therefore, it can be implemented in fast SRAM and integrated in router line cards, or reside in cache memory of general-purpose processors.

The rest of this paper is organized as follows. Sec. 2 describes our portscan detection algorithm in detail. Sec. 3 evaluates the performance of the algorithm with both packet traces and live network traffic. Finally, Sec. 4 concludes the paper and outlines our future work.

2   Detection Algorithm

Port scans are characterized by a simple feature: they attempt to connect to many targets but only get few responses. This imbalance in the number of attempts and successes is the basis of several portscan detection algorithms. A portscan detection algorithm can then be divided into two different problems: (1) detecting failed connections, and (2) tracking the sources responsible for them. Both (1) and (2) are challenging in high-speed networks, since they require a significant amount of memory and computing power to process packets at line speed. As already discussed in Sec. 1, a naive solution based on a hash table is impractical in this case, although it can be used in small networks.

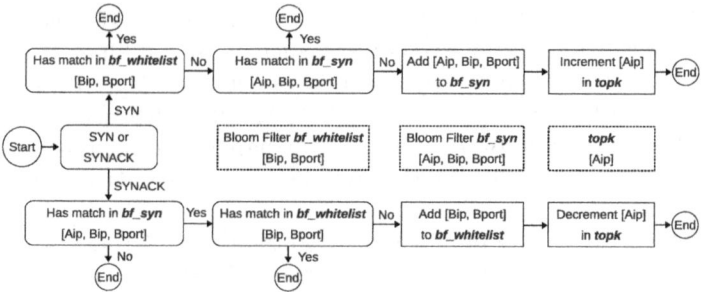

Fig. 1. Algorithm description

In this section, we present a practical solution that copes with these two problems by reducing both the volume of processed traffic and the memory requirements of the detection algorithm. In Sec. 2.1, we describe a simple method to discard unnecessary traffic using Bloom filters, which significantly simplifies problem (1), while Sec. 2.2 concentrates on identifying scanners using a lightweight counting structure that addresses problem (2).

For the sake of clarity, throughout this section, we will refer to the client host that initiates the handshake as A, with IP address A_{ip}, and to the server that receives the connection as B, with address B_{ip} and port B_{port}.

2.1 Detecting Failed Connections

We can define a failed connection as one for which a client does not get a $SynAck$ response from the server after having sent the corresponding Syn packet. Therefore, to detect failed connections, we can ignore data traffic and focus only on $Syn/SynAck$ packets. According to our traces (described later in Sec. 3), these control packets represent only 1.5% of all TCP traffic.

In addition, we can ignore legitimate handshakes to detect port scans, given that a scanner will always fail a large number of connections compared to a normal host. In order to efficiently discard connections directed towards a working service, we can use a Bloom filter that maintains a whitelist of active server IP-port pairs (*bf_whitelist*). In particular, for every new $SynAck$ response, we add the tuple $[B_{ip}, B_{port}]$ into this Bloom filter.

Since we are especially interested in those clients that connect to many unique destination addresses and ports, we can also discard those repeated connection attempts to the same destination. Besides standard TCP retransmissions, many applications try to reconnect several times (even hundreds) to the same destination after a failed connection (e.g., P2P nodes, misconfigured proxies, mail servers or VPN applications). Surprisingly, repeated Syn packets are extremely common according to our traces (see Sec. 3). In order to efficiently drop duplicated Syn packets to the same destination IP-port pair, we use a second Bloom filter (*bf_syn*). For every Syn packet observed, we store the tuple $[A_{ip}, B_{ip}, B_{port}]$ in the Bloom filter. As we will see later, using this second filter has the additional advantage of protecting the *bf_whitelist* from being saturated by many $SynAck$

packets sent by a malicious user (i.e., *SynAck* packets are ignored if they are not an answer from a previous *Syn*).

Although Bloom filters can have false positives, they have a negligible impact on our method as we show in Sec. 3. In addition, in case that one or both filters get saturated (e.g., if they are not properly dimensioned), the algorithm will produce False Negatives instead of False Positives, which is an important feature for systems automatically blocking port scanners [16].

Fig. 1 presents our algorithm in detail. After a packet arrival, we check if it is a *Syn* or a *SynAck* packet. Otherwise, the packet is dropped. In case it is a *Syn* packet, we check if the $[B_{ip}, B_{port}]$ tuple corresponds to a known destination in the *bf_whitelist*. In this case, the packet is directly dropped. If not, we check if it is a repeated connection attempt in the *bf_syn* filter. In this case, the packet is also dropped. Otherwise, the $[A_{ip}, B_{ip}, B_{port}]$ tuple is stored in the *bf_syn* filter and the A_{ip} source is incremented in the counting structure (described later in Sec. 2.2). For a *SynAck* packet, we first check if it is a response from a previous *Syn* packet in the *bf_syn* filter. Otherwise, the packet is dropped. Next, we check if the $[B_{ip}, B_{port}]$ tuple is already in the *bf_whitelist*. If not, the destination $[B_{ip}, B_{port}]$ is stored in the whitelist and the $[A_{ip}]$ source is decremented. Therefore, we use the *bf_whitelist* for two different purposes: (*i*) to keep track of active destinations, and (*ii*) to check if a source needs to be decremented after the connection has been established.[1]

2.2   Identifying Scanners

The algorithm described in Sec. 2.1 produces a series of increments and decrements for new connections and completed handshakes respectively. From this sequence, we want to identify the most active producers of failed connections, which will very likely correspond to port scanners. This can be seen as the well-known problem of identifying the top-k most frequent elements in a data stream.

For this purpose, we need a data structure that has limited memory usage and supports both incrementing and decrementing. Fortunately, the recent literature provides us with several efficient top-k algorithms [8]. From those, we selected the *Stream-Summary* data structure [9], since it uses a constant (and small) amount of memory. However, our algorithm is not bound to a particular top-k data structure. Although the original *Stream-Summary* does not support decrementing, we made a straightforward extension to support a limited number of decrements. We called this extension *Span-Dec*. As we will see in Sec. 3, in the particular context of portscan detection, the data structure behaves almost like an ideal hash table, but using much less memory. Although the particular implementation details of the top-k data structure are not essential to understand

---

[1] Note that using *bf_whitelist* to check which decrements are needed can introduce errors of 1 unit in the counting structure if several *Syn* packets from different sources are sent to an active destination before it enters the whitelist. Although this unusual situation cannot be exploited by an attacker, it could be easily solved by adding a filter similar to *bf_syn* for *SynAck* packets.

our algorithm, for the sake of completeness, we include below a short description of both mentioned structures.

Stream-Summary. This structure is part of the *Space-Saving* algorithm [9] that finds the most frequent elements in a data stream. It is able to observe up to $elem_{max}$ distinct elements at once. Every element e_i has an assigned counter cnt_i. All counters with the same value are linked into the same bucket. The buckets are linked together and they can be dynamically created and destroyed. When an element e_i is incremented, it is detached from its bucket and attached to a neighbor bucket with the new value. When the maximum number of observed elements ($elem_{max}$) is reached, a new incoming element evicts the element with the smallest counter. Each element has a maximum overestimation ε_i that depends on the value of the evicted element. The element frequency is estimated as $freq(e_i) = cnt_i - \varepsilon_i$. The algorithm is lightweight and it requires only $\frac{1}{\epsilon}$ counters for a specified error rate ϵ. See [9] for a more detailed description.

Span-Dec. The original *Stream-Summary* does not support decrementing. However, we need to discount those established connections for which the corresponding *Syn* has passed both Bloom filters. Therefore, we made a simple modification to the original *Stream-Summary* to support a limited number of decrements. In particular, instead of having a single counter per element, we use two counters: $cnt_L(e_i)$ and $cnt_H(e_i)$. We also specify a maximum allowed difference between both counters $span_{max}$, which controls the tradeoff between the number of allowed decrements and the error ε_i of the estimate. When an element is incremented, $cnt_H(e_i)$ is moved as in the original *Stream-Summary*. In case that the difference between both counters is greater than $span_{max}$, the $cnt_L(e_i)$ is also incremented. In order to decrement an element e_i, the $cnt_H(e_i)$ is decremented, but never below the value of $cnt_L(e_i)$. This solution can be understood as an "undo" operation, where $span_{max}$ is the "undo" depth. The frequency of an element e_i is estimated as $freq(e_i) = cnt_H(e_i) - \varepsilon_i$. The technical report [10] provides a detailed description of this extension.

As shown in Fig. 1, our detection algorithm uses *Span-Dec* to maintain the count of failed connections per source $[A_{ip}]$. This solution is useful to detect both horizontal and vertical port scans. However, if we are interested only in a particular type of scan, we can use instead $[A_{ip}, B_{port}]$ to detect horizontal port scans and $[A_{ip}, B_{ip}]$ to detect vertical ones.

3   Results

In the evaluation we used four traces. trace A was captured from the 1GigE access link of UPC, which connects about 50,000 users. trace A0 is a modified version of trace A that we describe later. trace B was taken from the MAWI Working Group Traffic Archive [2]. trace C was captured from the 10GigE link that connects the Catalan Research and Education Network to the Internet. This link connects more than seventy universities and research centers. Due to

Table 1. Statistics of the traces. `trace C` only accounts for $Syn/SynAck$ packets.

| | trace A | trace B | trace C | trace A0 |
	30min @ 1GigE	2h @ OC-3	30min @ 10GigE	30min @ 1GigE
date	2010-05-18	2010-04-16	2010-07-29	2010-05-18
TCP packets	228,848,927	144,885,865	13,978,845	97,380,742
TCP sources	188,136	263,055	467,264	89,086
TCP flows	2,892,334	5,199,928	11,526,323	1,133,392
average usage	879.1 Mb/s	185 Mb/s	3.5 Gb/s	n/a

the link speed, for `trace C` we only collected $Syn/SynAck$ packets. Statistics of the traces are presented in Tab. 1. We published all the packet traces used in this work, with anonymized IP addresses, at [1].

For the evaluation, we needed a ground truth trace to check if a detected scanner was a real scanner or a (misclassified) legitimate source. For this purpose, we modified `trace A` by removing all real scanners. We scanned the trace using Bro [12] with both its standard algorithm and the TRW algorithm. Although Bro is an online tool that does not guarantee an accurate ground truth, we used a low alarm threshold (25) and removed all the flows from the reported IP addresses to make sure that no scanning traffic is left, even if some legitimate traffic was also removed. Later, following the methodology proposed in [11], we injected artificial scans to build a ground truth: 1000 scanners with success ratio 0.2 and 1000 benign sources with success ratio 0.8. The interval between Syn-$SynAck$ packets was taken uniformly from the range $(0, 450ms)$, while the backoff time between $Syns$ was modeled using an exponential distribution [11]. All modifications resulted in `trace A0` that serves as the ground truth for Sec. 3.1. Traces B and C were not modified.

3.1   Evaluation

This section covers the evaluation of our algorithm. First, we present an example of how it is dimensioned. Next, we check the performance and validate its accuracy with packet traces. Finally, we deploy it in an operational 10 GigE link.

Dimensioning. We followed a conservative approach to handle an unexpected growth of traffic or peaks. For $bf\_whitelist$, we checked the mean number of distinct $[B_{ip}, B_{port}]$ tuples in the trace, multiplied this value by 3 and we assumed a maximum collision probability of $p_{coll} = 0.01$. We used an arbitrary length of the measurement window of 2 minutes. Although in this paper we do not evaluate this parameter, its value is important. As the filters are reset at the end of every period, the window size represents a tradeoff between the memory usage of the algorithm and its ability to detect slow scanners. With those values, we calculated the optimal size of the Bloom filter. We repeated the procedure for bf_syn using the unique number of $[A_{ip}, B_{ip}, B_{port}]$ tuples. The value of $span_{max}$ depends on the number of Syn packets concurrently sent by a source to distinct active destinations, which are not yet in the whitelist. We set this value according

Table 2. Configuration parameters for the evaluated traces

	trace A	trace B	trace C	trace AO
bf_syn size	256KB	256KB	1MB	64KB
bf_whitelist size	128KB	128KB	512KB	32KB
$span_{max}$	6	4	10	5

to 95th percentile of the traffic. For *topk* we arbitrarily set $elem_{max}$ to 10000 elements, unless otherwise noted. Resulting parameters are presented in Tab. 2. More details about the dimensioning procedure can be found in [10].

Detection Threshold. To present the results for traces A, B and C, we follow the methodology used in [13]. Fig. 2 depicts the results when running the algorithm on our traces with the parameters described in Tab. 2. We plot the total number of sources reported as scanners as a function of the detection threshold. The threshold is the number of failed connections over which we classify a source as a scanner. The embedded plots show the whole range of data in a log-log scale, while the main plot presents only the part where the number of reported sources grows rapidly, in a linear scale. The "hash table" line presents the results obtained using hash tables to count distinct *Syn* and *SynAck* packets. In this scenario, all packets are counted with perfect accuracy. Results placed above this line indicate the presence of False Positives (FP), while those placed below the line imply False Negatives (FN). "Span-dec" line plots the results obtained when our counting structure was used. Both lines almost overlap indicating that our algorithm is close to an ideal tracking scheme using a hash table, but without its memory constraints. In particular, for high threshold values our algorithm features almost perfect performance. "Original top-k" shows the results obtained with the original *Stream-Summary* structure [9]. The large number of FP shows the necessity of supporting decrements in the counting structure.

Accuracy. The results in Fig. 2 were not enough to validate the actual accuracy of our algorithm. For this purpose, we used the ground truth trace AO, for which we knew the actual scanners and legitimate hosts. Our results show that, for thresholds higher than 20, the algorithm obtained perfect accuracy (i.e., 0 FP, 0 FN, and 100% detected scanners). More details about the accuracy of our algorithm and the impact of each configuration parameter are given in [10].

Filter Performance. Tab. 3 presents the performance of the filters. The *Space usage* row shows the maximum space usage of each Bloom filter and (in brackets) the empirical collision probability. The probabilities are very small, even negligible. The *evictions* row shows the rate of traffic dropped by each filter (relative to the input packets of that filter). *Total packets evicted* gives the total ratio of handshake packets discarded by any of the two filters. Both filters together drop about 85% of all handshake packets. Thus, only 15% of all *Syn/SynAck* packets result in increments or decrements in the counting structure. Given that the counting error depends directly on the number of introduced elements, with a smaller number of entries we achieve better accuracy with less space.

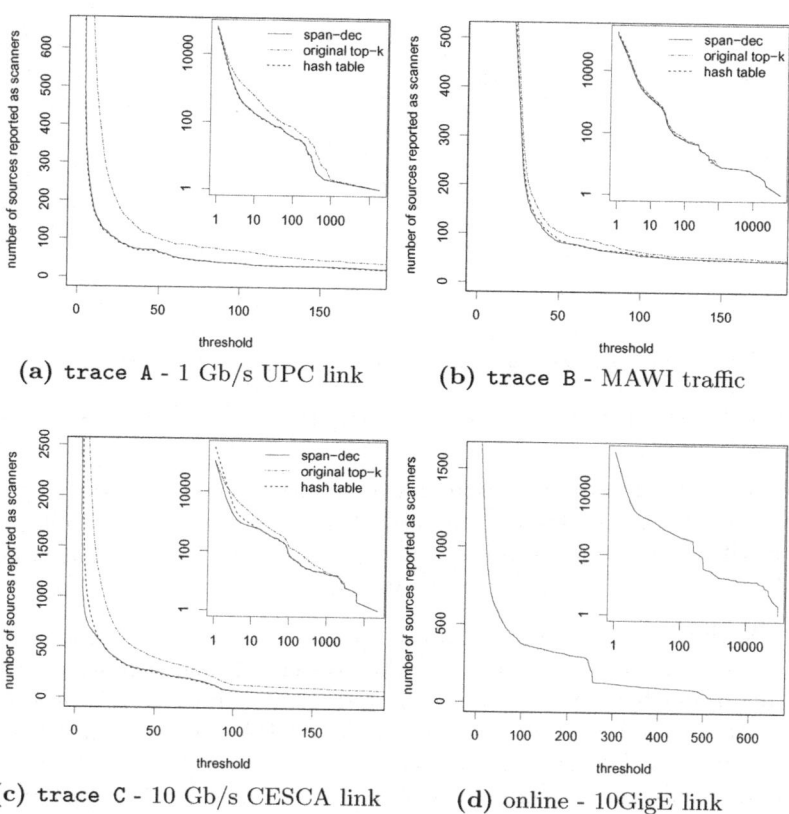

(a) trace A - 1 Gb/s UPC link   (b) trace B - MAWI traffic

(c) trace C - 10 Gb/s CESCA link   (d) online - 10GigE link

Fig. 2. Evaluation results on the traces - number of sources reported as scanners vs. detection threshold. Main graphs show a part of the data in a linear scale, embedded graphs show the whole range of data in a logarithmic scale.

Table 3. Usage of the filters during the evaluation (evictions: *Syn* / *SynAck*)

	trace A	trace B	trace C
space usage: *bf_whitelist*	6.78% (6.59e-09)	1.90% (8.94e-13)	4.66% (4.77e-10)
space usage: *bf_syn*	13.27% (7.25e-07)	29.07% (1.75e-4)	11.02% (1.97e-07)
evictions: *bf_whitelist*	52.7% / 67.1%	24.7% / 76.2%	54.3% / 77.9%
evictions: *bf_syn*	61.2% / 65.0%	54.3% / 72.0%	55.4% / 64.2%
total packets evicted	84.3%	73.5%	84.4%

Memory Size. Finally, we evaluated the impact of the memory size on the accuracy of the detection algorithm using trace C. First, we examined the impact of the size of the Bloom filters using 10000 entries in the *topk* structure. Results are presented in Fig. 3a. Filters below 96KB present FN due to collisions, as discussed in Sec. 2.1. With filters of 192KB (128KB+64KB) and a threshold above 100, the algorithm performs very close to the optimal. Using these filters, we

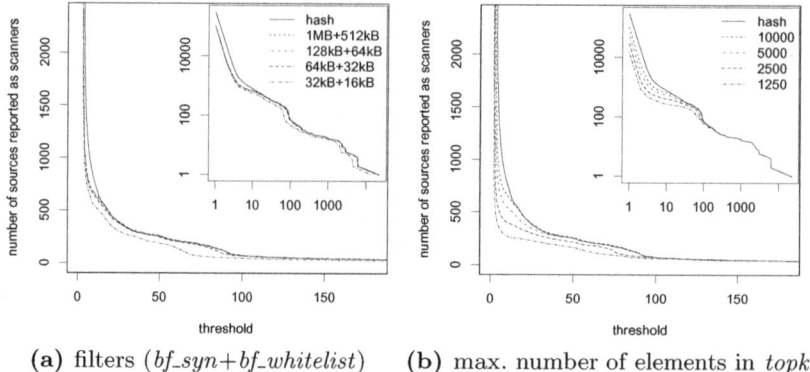

(a) filters (*bf_syn+bf_whitelist*)   **(b)** max. number of elements in *topk*

Fig. 3. Impact of the memory size compared to an ideal scheme (`trace C`)

examined the influence of the maximum number of elements ($elem_{max}$) in the *topk*. The results are presented in Fig. 3b. We can see that, for thresholds above 100, even with 2500 elements in the *topk* we still obtain very good accuracy. In our implementation, this configuration occupies only 417KB for a 10 GigE link.

Online Deployment. In order to evaluate the real-time performance of the algorithm, we implemented it in the CoMo system [4] and deployed it on the 10GigE link from where `trace C` was collected. The hardware platform consisted of a PC with an Intel Xeon at 2.40GHz with two DAG 5.2SXA cards. A filter to discard non-*Syn/SynAck* packets was set in both cards. The filtering also can be done easily in software, since it requires only checking *Syn* and *Ack* flags in a TCP header. We ran the program for 100 min. (13-12-2010 at 10:50). The average traffic in the link was 5.4 Gb/s. The CPU load was about 5% during the whole experiment. For both filters, the maximum usage was 18.5% with a maximum collision probability of 7.31e-06. The threshold-alarm graph is presented in Fig. 2d.

4   Conclusions and Future Work

In this paper, we presented a practical approach to detect port scans in very high-speed links. The key idea behind our approach was to discard as much traffic as possible at early processing stages in order to reduce both the CPU and memory requirements of our algorithm. We used two simple Bloom filters that maintain a whitelist of active destinations and efficiently track TCP handshakes, and combined them with an efficient top-k data structure to track failed connections. Both Bloom filters together can early discard about 85% of all handshake packets in our traces.

Our evaluation with four traces from different scenarios showed that our algorithm can achieve almost perfect accuracy with very little memory. We also deployed our algorithm in an operational 10GigE link and showed that it can work online. Also, we made a new dataset available to the research community, so that our results can be validated and compared with other solutions.

Although in the paper we focused only on TCP port scans, we are currently investigating how to extend the algorithm to detect UDP scans. A possible solution is to define which address blocks are behind the network to be protected. Another limitation of the algorithm is that it focuses on detecting top sources of port scans, and therefore it is not designed to reliably detect slow scans or more sophisticated attacks, like distributed scans.

References

1. UPC/CESCA traces, http://monitoring.ccaba.upc.edu/portscan/traces
2. MAWI Working Group Traffic Archive, http://mawi.wide.ad.jp/mawi/
3. http://www.bbc.co.uk/news/world-middle-east-11414483 (2010)
4. Barlet-Ros, P., et al.: Load shedding in network monitoring applications. In: Proc. of USENIX ATC (2007)
5. Brauckhoff, D., Tellenbach, B., Wagner, A., May, M., Lakhina, A.: Impact of packet sampling on anomaly detection metrics. In: Proc. of ACM SIGCOMM IMC (2006)
6. Jung, J., et al.: Fast portscan detection using sequential hypothesis testing. In: 2004 IEEE Symposium on Security and Privacy (2004)
7. Mai, J., Sridharan, A., Chuah, C.N., Zang, H., Ye, T.: Impact of packet sampling on portscan detection. IEEE J. Select. Areas Commun. (2006)
8. Manerikar, N., Palpanas, T.: Frequent items in streaming data: An experimental evaluation of the state-of-the-art. Data & Knowledge Engineering (2009)
9. Metwally, A., Agrawal, D., Abbadi, A.E.: Efficient computation of frequent and top-k elements in data streams. In: Eiter, T., Libkin, L. (eds.) ICDT 2005. LNCS, vol. 3363, pp. 398–412. Springer, Heidelberg (2005)
10. Mikians, J., et al.: Span-Dec data structure in portscan detection. Technical report (2010), http://monitoring.ccaba.upc.edu/portscan/portscan-report.pdf
11. Nam, S., Kim, H., Kim, H.: Detector SherLOCK: Enhancing TRW with Bloom filters under memory and performance constraints. Computer Networks (2008)
12. Paxson, V.: Bro: a system for detecting network intruders in real-time. Comput. Netw (1999)
13. Robertson, S., et al.: Surveillance detection in high bandwidth environments. In: Proc. of DARPA Information Survivability Conference and Exposition (2003)
14. Schechter, S.E., Jung, J., Berger, A.W.: Fast detection of scanning worm infections. In: Jonsson, E., Valdes, A., Almgren, M. (eds.) RAID 2004. LNCS, vol. 3224, pp. 59–81. Springer, Heidelberg (2004)
15. Sridharan, A., Ye, T., Bhattacharyya, S.: Connectionless port scan detection on the backbone. In: Proc. of IPCCC (2006)
16. Weaver, N., Staniford, S., Paxson, V.: Very fast containment of scanning worms. In: Proc. of the 13th Conf. on USENIX Security Symposium (2004)

Omnify: Investigating the Visibility and Effectiveness of Copyright Monitors

Rahul Potharaju*, Jeff Seibert*, Sonia Fahmy, and Cristina Nita-Rotaru

Purdue University
{rpothara,jcseiber,fahmy,crisn}@cs.purdue.edu

Abstract. [1] The arms race between copyright agencies and P2P users is an on-going and evolving struggle. On the one hand, content providers are using several techniques to stealthily find unauthorized distribution of copyrighted work in order to deal with the problem of Internet piracy. On the other hand, P2P users are relying increasingly on blacklists and anonymization methods in order to avoid detection. In this work, we propose a number of techniques to reveal copyright monitors' current approaches and evaluate their effectiveness. We apply these techniques on data we collected from more than 2.75 million BitTorrent swarms containing 71 million IP addresses. We provide strong evidence that certain nodes are indeed copyright monitors, show that monitoring is a world-wide phenomenon, and devise a methodology for generating blacklists for *paranoid* and *conservative* P2P users.

1 Introduction

Peer-to-peer (P2P) applications possess fundamental advantages over the traditional client-server model and fixed-infrastructure content distribution networks like Akamai. Specifically, P2P systems offer increased performance, availability, and scalability by leveraging resources (e.g., bandwidth, storage, and computing power) contributed by each peer. As a result, P2P systems enable a wide range of services such as data sharing, voice-over-IP (VoIP), and video streaming. Popular applications that use P2P systems include file sharing systems such as BitTorrent [1] and Gnutella [2], VoIP systems such as Skype [3], and video streaming systems such as PPLive [4]. Several studies have indicated that P2P systems contribute towards more than 60% of the overall network traffic [5].

Users exchange content via P2P file sharing networks for many reasons, ranging from the legal exchange of open source software to the illegal exchange of copyrighted material. The latter activities, however, are perceived as a threat to the business models of the copyright holders. To protect their content, copyright holders monitor P2P networks and the sharing behavior, collecting evidence of infringement, and then issue any infringing user a notice. In the United States, this notice is called a *Digital Millennium*

---

* Both authors contributed equally.

[1] Entry for PAM Award: This paper contributes a novel *Reverse Infohash* database containing more than 1.75 million infohash → title mappings. The dataset and more information can be obtained at: http://omnify.info/

N. Spring and G. Riley (Eds.): PAM 2011, LNCS 6579, pp. 122–132, 2011.
© Springer-Verlag Berlin Heidelberg 2011

Copyright Act (DMCA) [6] takedown notice. The notices are formal requests to stop sharing particular data, and are typically sent to the authorities responsible for the IP addresses of the infringing users. These authorities then forward these notices to the respective users inside their network. Unfortunately, this simple approach of monitoring is prone to a wide variety of errors. Piatek *et al.* [7] describe techniques for implicating arbitrary network endpoints in illegal content sharing, and demonstrate their effectiveness by experimentally attracting real DMCA complaints for devices such as IP printers and wireless access points.

Our work was motivated by our recent experience of being mistakenly implicated for copyright infringement, when in fact we were performing performance measurement experiments on the PlanetLab testbed [8], an overlay network for developing and accessing a broad range of network services. This problem can be partly solved by using existing blacklists [9], consisting of IP subnet ranges of clients suspected of monitoring activities. However, blacklists such as those constructed by iBlocklist [9] use help from various user communities and no empirical research exists to prove their integrity or effectiveness. In this paper, we derive a methodology for constructing different types of blacklists. It is important to note that we are *not* encouraging unlawful sharing of copyrighted material, but rather showing that the patterns we reveal can be useful in designing conservative research experiments, as such experiments are critical for improving the BitTorrent ecosystem. Our results can also be leveraged by copyright monitors to improve their detection accuracy, thus enabling them to reduce the rate of false positives.

Contributions. Our work reveals a number of findings, confirming known types of undesirable behavior in the BitTorrent network, and uncovering new patterns that provide strong evidence of monitoring. Our contributions include:

- We develop a systematic methodology for obtaining the file name for a given infohash (a SHA-1 identifier for a BitTorrent file that is globally unique), thereby constructing the first *Reverse Infohash* database containing mappings for 1.18 million infohashes. This dataset has several applications such as understanding the extent of swarm redundancy (how many swarms share the same file), and current trends in file sharing. We are making this data publicly available for the benefit of other researchers.
- We introduce the Ω-factor that utilizes the BitTorrent crawls we collected from more than 2.75 million BitTorrent swarms and the *Reverse Infohash* database to distinguish normal peers from suspicious ones in a P2P system. We then leverage the Ω-factor to identify copyright monitors.
- We reveal a number of patterns in the activity of different hosts (identified by IP addresses), which we use to establish strong evidence supporting the existence of copyright monitors. For instance, we show instances when certain IP addresses participate in hundreds of swarms serving the same file. Leveraging these observations and the Ω-factor, we design and present the methodology for creating two blacklists of suspicious IP addresses: *paranoid*, useful for users who are privacy-conscious and *conservative*, useful for users who are more lenient.

The rest of this paper is organized as follows: Section 2 provides relevant background on our data collection process and the methodology for constructing the *Reverse Infohash* database. We then use this database to calculate the participation extent of each IP address using the novel metric we introduce called the Ω-factor. We use two threshold schemes to derive two blacklists. In Section 3, we examine the blacklists in detail and give insights on the effectiveness of copyright monitors. Finally, we summarize related work in Section 4 and conclude in Section 5.

2 Methodology

We seek to study peer activity patterns to identify possibly atypical behavior, with the ultimate goal being to derive blacklists consisting of IP addresses belonging to suspicious clients. To achieve this, we rely on measuring the extent of participation of each IP address in swarms so that we can filter out normal user clients from the list of active IP addresses. We make the key observation that a normal client typically participates in at most one swarm to download a certain file, whereas a copyright monitor would want to participate in as many swarms (that serve the same file) as possible to increase its effectiveness. In order to determine whether multiple swarms are serving the same file, we utilize our *Reverse Infohash* database to groups similar swarms together. We then, to distinguish normal clients from those exhibiting abnormal behavior, introduce the Ω-factor that captures these groupings and the activity pattern of a client.

We first present the background on our data collection methodology. Next, we explain how we construct the *Reverse Infohash* database and use this database to calculate the Ω-factor for each IP address in our dataset. Finally, we use two threshold schemes on the Ω-factor to derive two blacklists.

2.1 Data Collection

The methodology oftentimes used for crawling BitTorrent swarms is to find torrent metafiles by first crawling a BitTorrent aggregator website that hosts them, and then querying the associated tracker for clients [7, 10]. However, as aggregator websites usually only attract users associated with a particular language, this technique would result in only revealing copyright monitoring in certain parts of the world. Therefore, we do the *reverse*: we first crawl a tracker that is not associated with an aggregator website and is highly popular all over the world, called "OpenBitTorrent" [11], and afterwards we discover the content that the swarms we find are serving. We note that while we use a particular tracker, our methodology is extensible to multiple trackers.

When crawling the tracker, we extract a list containing the infohash and number of seeders and leechers for every swarm it is tracking. In BitTorrent lexicon, the infohash is a 20-byte SHA-1 hash of information contained in a `.torrent` metafile. In May 2010, for every hour over 8 days, we obtained this list and crawled each swarm that had at least one leecher. Typically, a single crawl consists of over 5 million IP addresses in one million swarms. We discovered 71 million unique IP addresses in 2.75 million swarms over the 8-day period.

2.2 Building the Reverse Infohash Database

We now focus on finding the file name associated with an infohash and then group similar file names together. We apply a number of heuristics to construct the *Reverse*

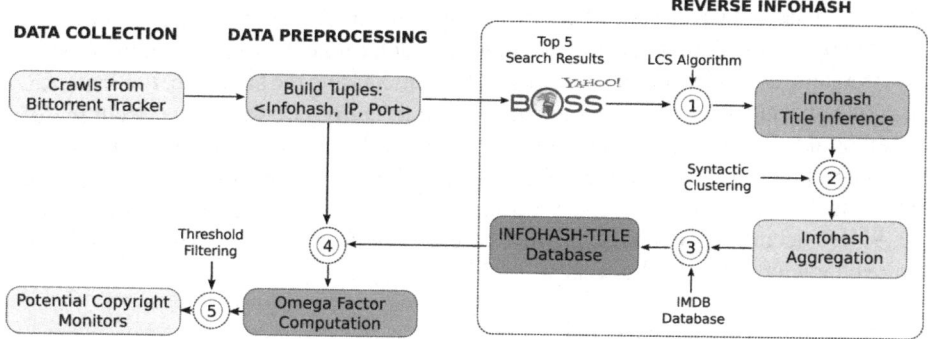

Fig. 1. Schematic overview of the proposed methodology: Starting from our BitTorrent crawls, we use a number of techniques to derive the *Reverse Infohash* database which is used for computing Ω, a metric for distinguishing a normal peer from undesirable peers

Infohash database. Figure 1 gives an overview of how we accurately determine the file name associated with an infohash. Our initial step is to query a search engine for the infohash, giving a rough approximation of the file name. As Google rate-limits search queries, we use the Yahoo! Search BOSS API [12], which imposes less stringent constraints on their API usage. We consider the top five results returned by each search query, and use the *Longest Common Subsequence*(LCS) algorithm [13] for constructing a single title using the five search results. Our heuristic performs an exhaustive comparison to find the best possible match. For instance, the algorithm outputs "Iron Man 2 D" for an input of {"Iron Man 2 DivX", "Iron Man 2 DVD", "Iron Man 2 DirectSubs"}.

At this stage, we leverage the Shingling technique [14] to determine the syntactic similarity of the strings in our database. Intuitively, this method helps us determine if two strings are "roughly the same" *i.e.*, for determining when they have the same content except for modifications such as lost characters etc. We view each string in our database as a set of subsequences of tokens $T(S, w)$. A contiguous subsequence contained in S is called a *shingle*. Given a string S, we define its *w-shingling* $T(S, w)$ as the set of all unique shingles of size w in S. For instance, the *2-shingling* or the character bigram shingles of the string *"iron man"* is the following set: {"ir", "ro", "on", "n ", " m", "ma", "an"}.

Given two strings, we build a *shingling* set for each, and then use a distance metric to measure the similarity. As a distance metric, we use the Jaccard Index [15] which is a measure used for comparing the similarity and the diversity of sample sets. It is the ratio of the size of the intersection of the sets to the size of the union of the sets. For instance, if $J(A, B)$ is the Jaccard Index between sets A and B, then:

$$J_{(A,B)} = \frac{|A \cap B|}{|A \cup B|} \tag{1}$$

We build a similarity index represented by an adjacency matrix for the list of strings in our database, and use a threshold of 0.8 (determined through manual inspection and represents only those strings which are nearly similar to each other) to prepare the final list. At this stage, we have reduced the string grouping problem to an instance of finding *connected subgraphs* [16]. From the result, we can determine if two different infohashes served the same *entity*. We define *entity* as all torrents sharing the same file. For instance, all torrents sharing Iron Man 2 constitute a single *entity*. To verify the accuracy of our methodology, we manually checked 1330 infohashes which were suspected to be serving the same file, "Iron Man 2." We searched Google for information related to an infohash and matched it with ours. We were able to manually match 1265 out of the 1330 (95.1% accuracy). The false positives were for entries such as "Irina," a fictional vampire character in the Twilight Saga.

2.3 Identifying Activity Patterns

Our ultimate goal is to distinguish normal P2P users from copyright monitors. Due to the vast number of IP addresses we collected, we do not attempt active measurements or probing of clients, but rely solely on analyzing the data collected. Since oftentimes the IP address, port number, and AS number are not revealing, we must identify patterns that would be indicative of an organization monitoring copyrighted material. We now outline a list of identifiable patterns and why we consider them.

An IP address participates in a large number of swarms. The vast majority of IP addresses seen in our crawls participate in very few swarms. To demonstrate this, we plot in Figure 2.3 a CDF of the number of swarms every IP address participates in (over our eight-day crawl). For example, 84% of IP addresses participate in 10 swarms or fewer. However, some IP addresses appear in hundreds, and even thousands, of swarms. We suspect that since monitors aim to observe the transfer of copyrighted material in the BitTorrent community, they would participate in every relevant swarm.

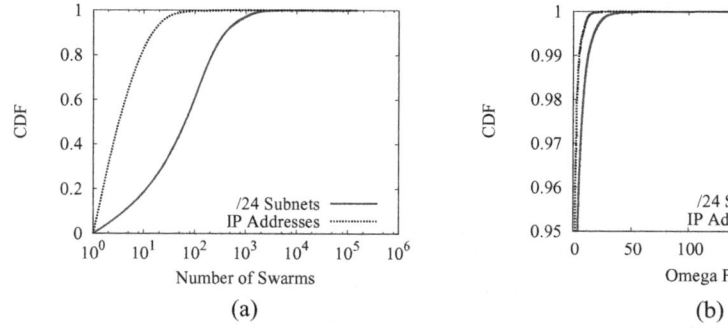

Fig. 2. (a) CDF of the number of swarms every IP address participates in over our eight-day crawl. Observe that 84% of the IP addresses participate in 10 swarms or fewer. (b) CDF of the Ω-factor for IP addresses and subnets. Most IP addresses have $\Omega = 1$, meaning they only participate in a single swarm corresponding to a particular *entity*.

An IP address participates in multiple swarms that correspond to the same *entity*. As mentioned earlier, we discovered over a thousand swarms that corresponded to the same "Iron Man 2" movie. We would expect a normal user, if desiring to download such a movie, to simply participate in one of these swarms. In contrast, a copyright monitor would participate in many swarms, attempting to observe as many downloaders as possible by utilizing all its available resources. Thus, we introduce the Ω-factor, which intuitively measures how effective a host (with a certain IP address) is at monitoring entities, carefully adjusting for entities with a fewer/larger number of swarms. We define the Ω-factor as follows:

$$\Omega_{IPAddress} = \frac{\sum_{i=0}^{n} t_i s_i}{\sum_{i=0}^{n} t_i} \tag{2}$$

where t_i is the total number of torrents corresponding to *entity* i, and s_i is the total number of torrents corresponding to *entity* i where the IP address is actually seen. Let us consider an example of a user downloading "Iron Man 2" and "Valentine's Day" from two swarms. In our dataset, the number of distinct torrents we observed for the former swarm was 1526 and for the latter, 431. Thus, $\Omega = \frac{1526(1)+431(1)}{1526+431} = 1$. A copyright monitor, in contrast, typically aims to monitor multiple torrents corresponding to an *entity*. For the same entities, assuming that the monitor participates in 120 swarms related to "Iron Man 2" and 100 swarms related to "Valentine's Day", we would get $\Omega = \frac{1526(120)+431(100)}{1526+431} = 115.59$. Thus, by using the number of swarms an IP address is participating in as the weight for the total number of torrents corresponding to an *entity*, we are able to detect the outliers.

We evaluate the Ω-factor for every IP address that appears in our database and present the results in Figure 2.3. Unsurprisingly, most IP addresses have a factor of 1, meaning they only participate in a single swarm corresponding to a particular *entity*. However, there are several outliers that have values greater than 40, implying suspicious behavior.

2.4   Generating Blacklists

We now leverage the values of the Ω-factor to derive two blacklists. The first blacklist, called the *paranoid* dataset, is useful for users who are privacy-conscious and do not want to be bothered by any kind of a monitor including a copyright monitor, spambot, or researchers conducting measurements. The second blacklist we constructed, called the *conservative*, is a restrictive subset of the *paranoid* dataset that comprises IP addresses that are all highly likely copyright monitors.

The *paranoid* dataset is obtained by applying a threshold scheme on the Ω factor, and then filtering out all the IP addresses that participate in fewer than 100 distinct swarms. We choose this threshold as most IP addresses participate in fewer than 100 swarms; otherwise, they would seem ineffective as copyright monitors. From Figure 2.3, we chose Ω to be 5.0, therefore including many suspicious IP addresses. The total number of IP addresses in this blacklist is 53,752. The *conservative* dataset is obtained in a similar manner by setting Ω to 20.0 to only select highly suspicious clients participating in more than 100 distinct torrents. The total number of IP addresses in this blacklist is 5,719 – much smaller than *paranoid*. We have verified that these IP addresses do not belong to a known botnet and are not in a spam database.

3   Evaluation

In this section, we show that using our methodology, we can automatically generate blacklists that are able to effectively identify copyright monitors. We also identify interesting characteristics of these monitors and discuss how they can avoid detection in the future.

Identifying Monitors. To evaluate if the *conservative* dataset accurately reflects behavior consistent with a copyright monitor, we manually verified the 100 IP addresses with the largest values of Ω. We provide a snapshot of the details of the entities they are monitoring in Table 1. In this table, we provide the AS number and country where the IP address is located, and also the entities that they are heavily monitoring. We determine their *effectiveness* at monitoring copyright infringement by calculating the percentage of swarms that they participate in that correspond to a particular *entity*.

For example, in the first entry in the table, we find that a particular IP address in AS-9167 is heavily monitoring swarms related to the *"Percy Jackson and the Olympians: The Lightning Thief"* entity, which is a popular movie distributed by 20th Century Fox. Using our reverse infohash database, we map 310 different torrents to this *entity*. We observed that this IP address in particular monitors 174 different torrents, giving it an effectiveness of 55.10%. While we do not dig into the details of the other ASes, we show a few more in Table 1.

Table 1. Using the Ω factor to pinpoint a copyright monitor: The AS numbers shown in this table had IP addresses that exhibited high Ω factors. Upon further inspection, they were found to participate in a large number of torrents serving the same *entity*.

AS Number	Effectiveness %	Country	Entity
9167	55.10	Denmark	Percy Jackson & the Olympians
9167	53.54	Denmark	Percy Jackson & the Olympians
9167	36.5	Denmark	Alvin & the Chipmunks 2 The Squeakquel
33650	84.94	United States	Alex Jones Show
1213	5.4	Ireland	Iron Man 2
30023	17.45	United States	Iron Man 2
30023	15.65	United States	Iron Man 2, Princess and The Frog
30023	6.26	United States	Iron Man 2, Valentine's Day
558	5.81	United States	Iron Man 2, Valentine's Day
9167	49.27	Denmark	Jennifer's Body

Pervasiveness of Monitoring. For every swarm we find how many monitors are participating and also the fraction of monitors in that swarm and plot CDFs of these values in Figure 3 and Figure 3, respectively. We find that 11% (20%) of the 2.75 million swarms are being monitored in the conservative (paranoid) dataset. We also find that sometimes hundreds of monitors are used and that in 0.6% (3%) of swarms the majority of participants are monitors.

Geolocating Monitors. We geolocate the IP addresses in our *conservative* dataset using the MaxMind database [17], and plot the results in Figure 4. As can be seen, most countries in Europe are densely populated with monitors. In addition, several Asian countries, such as Japan, South Korea, and the Philippines are densely populated. While

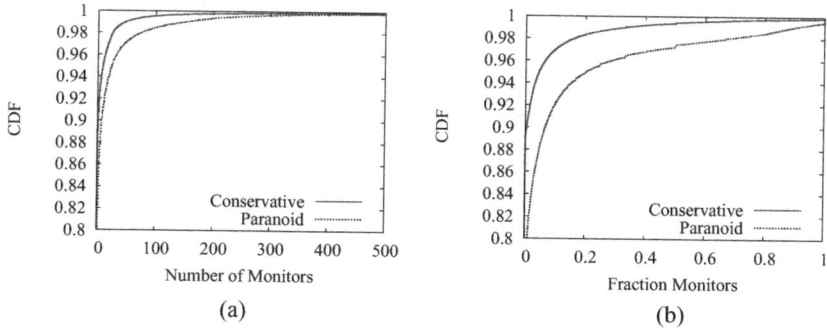

Fig. 3. CDF of the number and fraction of IP addresses classified as monitors participating in each swarm in our eight-day crawl

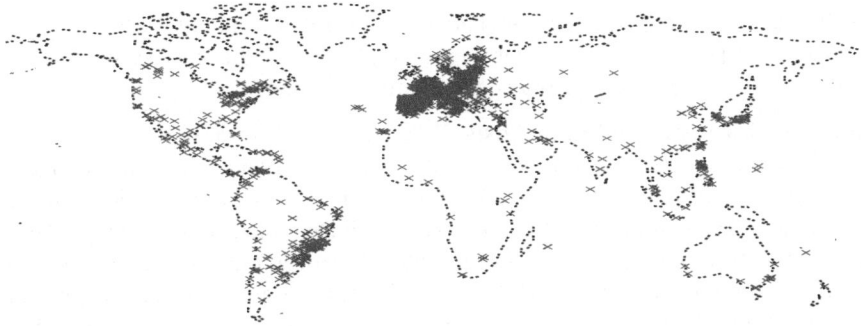

Fig. 4. Map showing the geolocated positions of all IP addresses from our *conservative* dataset

we are not legal experts, we suspect that copyright and privacy laws in each country highly influence the number of monitors there.

Monitors Exhibit Temporal Patterns. From the *paranoid dataset*, we find that copyright monitors do indeed own subnets and use them in interesting ways. To illustrate this, we choose two suspected monitors that have multiple subnets, and give each IP address an identifier in the order of the first time it is observed in the crawls. We plot a point for every crawl where we observe the IP address. The results are depicted in Figure 5. As there is large overlap in the swarms each IP address is monitoring, we suspect that this type of pattern can be attributed to an automated monitor that, when crawling, uses a different subset of IP addresses every time. For example, the monitor in Figure 3 seems to use several different IP addresses every hour, while the monitor in Figure 3 has a more diurnal pattern, using approximately 100 different IP addresses to crawl once a day.

Spammers Utilize BitTorrent. We note that the *paranoid* dataset captures behavior beyond that of a copyright monitor. We found several consecutive subnets in AS-5384 which contained IP addresses that were participating in over 60,000 swarms, which were some of the most often seen. We checked Project Honey Pot [18], which is a database of known email spammers, and found that many of them were contained in

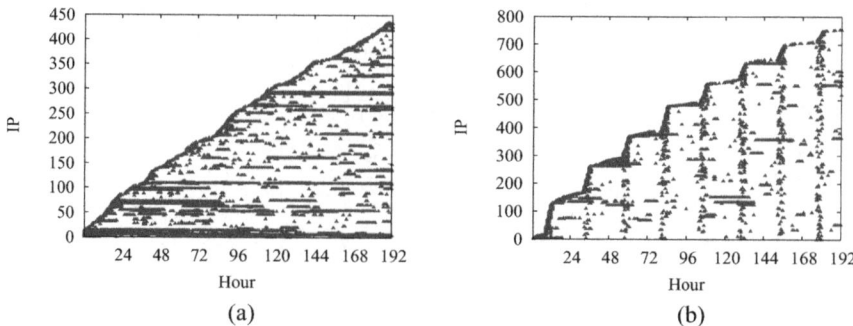

Fig. 5. An instance when multiple IP addresses belonging to the same subnet exhibit similar activity patterns

that list. We suspect that these clients are harvesting information about BitTorrent users. Thus, while they are not necessarily copyright monitors, we believe most that privacy-conscious users would prefer to avoid contact with such clients.

Comparison with Real-World Blacklists. We investigate several blacklists of IP addresses that are suspected to be owned by copyright monitors. These are collected from an aggregator of blacklists [9] and include IP addresses of organizations that are involved with trying to stop file sharing (e.g., MediaDefender, MediaSentry). These blacklists are P2P community-driven and accepted; however, they are usually only extended after users have received a DMCA takedown or similar notice. We find that our *conservative* and *paranoid* datasets overlap with 2,051 and 2,507 IP addresses in these blacklists, respectively. This indicates that algorithmic techniques for determining copyright monitors can be effectively used to supplement existing blacklists.

Improving Stealth and Effectiveness of Monitors. We now present a few suggestions for copyright monitors that can improve their stealth and effectiveness. First, they can use our methodology for finding torrents and not rely on crawling aggregator websites. This increases their effectiveness, because they will be able to find more entities. Second, to improve their stealth, they must utilize more hosts (IP addresses) and intelligently use them by distributing among them the swarms that belong to the same *entity*. This will obscure them from most pattern-mining algorithms. Third, using better measurement techniques by leaving a swarm immediately after getting the list of peers, their IP addresses can remain below a detection threshold that relies on hours of activity or the number of times an IP is seen.

4   Related Work

Copyright monitors and the techniques they use to infer copyright infringement in Bit-Torrent have been studied by Piatek *et al.* [7]. They discover that copyright monitors use indirect and thus inconclusive evidence to serve DMCA takedown notices, and show that it is possible to frame arbitrary IP addresses of infringement. The authors also crawl popular torrent aggregation sites and crawl tens of thousands of swarms. They evaluate the potential of blacklists to identify copyright monitors, and find that there are suspicious IPs participating in many swarms. Our work takes this a step further by crawling millions of swarms, identifying suspicious activity patterns, and narrowing down the list to the most suspicious clients.

Deviant client behavior in BitTorrent swarms was studied by Siganos *et al.* [10]. They implement a client that exchanges control messages with other BitTorrent clients to discover if they exhibit suspicious behavior. They crawl 600 popular torrents over 45 days, and find behavior indicative of copyright monitors and peers involved in botnets. In contrast, our work introduces metrics that can be used to infer copyright monitor behavior.

5   Conclusions

In this paper, we have reported our findings on the effectiveness of monitoring agencies in the wild. We constructed a novel reverse infohash database which we used in computing what we refer to as the Ω-factor, a measure that differentiates entities in a P2P system, to shortlist potential copyright monitors. We applied our techniques on data we collected from more than 2.75 million BitTorrent swarms containing 71 million IP addresses, and discussed our methodology for arriving at a list of potential copyright monitors. In particular, we prepared two datasets: a *paranoid* dataset that contains a list of copyright monitors along with hosts that could be potential spambots, and a *conservative* dataset that contains hosts that are suspected to be copyright monitors with a high probability.

References

1. Cohen, B.: Incentives build robustness in BitTorrent. In: Workshop on Economics of Peer-to-Peer systems (2003)
2. Matei, R., Iamnitchi, A., Foster, P.: Mapping the Gnutella network. IEEE Internet Computing 6(1), 50–57 (2002)
3. Baset, S., Schulzrinne, H.: An analysis of the skype peer-to-peer internet telephony protocol. Arxiv preprint cs/0412017 (2004)
4. Huang, Y., Fu, T.Z., Chiu, D.-M., Lui, J.C., Huang, C.: Challenges, design and analysis of a large-scale p2p-vod system. In: SIGCOMM (2008)
5. Cho, K., Fukuda, K., Esaki, H., Kato, A.: Observing slow crustal movement in residential user traffic. In: CONEXT (2008)
6. Kao, A.: RIAA v. Verizon: Applying the Subpoena Provision of the DMCA. Sch. L. Rev. 63, 64 (2003)
7. Piatek, M., Kohno, T., Krishnamurthy, A.: Challenges and directions for monitoring P2P file sharing networks–or–Why my printer received a DMCA takedown notice. In: 3rd USENIX Workshop on Hot Topics in Security, HotSec (2008)
8. Chun, B., Culler, D., Roscoe, T., Bavier, A., Peterson, L., Wawrzoniak, M., Bowman, M.: Planetlab: an overlay testbed for broad-coverage services. ACM SIGCOMM Computer Communication Review 33(3), 3–12 (2003)
9. TBG Blocklist, http://tbg.iblocklist.com/
10. Siganos, G., Pujol, J.M., Rodriguez, P.: Monitoring the bittorrent monitors: A bird's eye view. In: Moon, S.B., Teixeira, R., Uhlig, S. (eds.) PAM 2009. LNCS, vol. 5448, pp. 175–184. Springer, Heidelberg (2009)

11. OpenBittorrent, `http://www.openbittorrent.com`
12. Yahoo! Search Boss, `http://developer.yahoo.com/search/boss/`
13. Hirschberg, D.: Algorithms for the longest common subsequence problem. Journal of the ACM (JACM) 24(4), 664–675 (1977)
14. Broder, A., Glassman, S., Manasse, M., Zweig, G.: Syntactic clustering of the web. Computer Networks and ISDN Systems 29(8-13), 1157–1166 (1997)
15. Tan, P., Steinbach, M., Kumar, V.: Introduction to data mining. Pearson Addison Wesley, Boston (2006)
16. Khuller, S.: Approximation algorithms for finding highly connected subgraphs. In: Approximation Algorithms for NP-hard Problems, pp. 236–265 (1996)
17. MaxMind, L.: GeoIP (2006)
18. Project Honey Pot, `http://www.projecthoneypot.org`

Internet Censorship in China: Where Does the Filtering Occur?

Xueyang Xu, Z. Morley Mao, and J. Alex Halderman

Department of Computer Science and Engineering, University of Michigan,
2260 Hayward Street, Ann Arbor, MI 48109
{xueyang,zmao,jhalderm}@umich.edu
http://www.cse.umich.edu

Abstract. China filters Internet traffic in and out of the country. In order to circumvent the firewall, it is helpful to know where the filtering occurs. In this work, we explore the AS-level topology of China's network, and probe the firewall to find the locations of filtering devices. We find that even though most filtering occurs in border ASes, choke points also exist in many provincial networks. The result suggests that two major ISPs in China have different approaches placing filtering devices.

Keywords: Censorship, topology, network measurement.

1 Introduction

In this work, we explore where Intrusion Detection System (IDS) devices of the Great Firewall of China (GFC) are placed for keyword filtering at AS and router level. Knowing where IDSes are attached helps us better understand the infrastructure of the firewall, gain more knowledge about its behavior and find vantage point for future circumvention techniques.

China has the world's most complex Internet censorship system, featuring IP blocking, keyword filtering, DNS hijacking and so on [1]. IP blocking is the earliest filtering mechanism. It is easy to circumvent, because webmasters can always change their IP and DNS record. Besides, censors are very prudent to do DNS hijacking nowadays due to the risk of affecting the network in other countries [2]. In this paper, we focus on the most effective filtering mechanism of GFC, keyword filtering.

According to [4], the filtering occurs more at AS-level rather than strictly along the border routers. This paper answers the question whether all censorship occurs at border AS, and how filtering occurs inside those ASes. We first explore the AS-level topology of China's network. In this part, we explore which Chinese ASes are directly peered with foreign ones and which are internal ones. We call those peered with foreign network *border AS*, and the others *internal AS*. The resulting AS-level topology shows that the best vantage point to place filtering device is in the border ASes.

To find where IDS devices are attached at router level, we select a set of web servers in China and probe with HTTP GET packets that contain known

N. Spring and G. Riley (Eds.): PAM 2011, LNCS 6579, pp. 133–142, 2011.

keywords. In order to find more filtering devices, we manually select web servers to ensure their geographical diversity, as opposed to previous work that uses top websites in search result. This diversity is desirable, because it helps us to find more routing paths across China, and with more paths, we can discover more filtering devices.

The result shows that most filtering devices are in the border ASes, but a small portion is not. It is possible that there is a trend of placing filtering devices outside of border ASes. The number of router interfaces that have filtering devices attached for CHINANET is stable since 2007, while the second largest filtering force CNCGROUP has increasing number of filtering interfaces. Moreover, CHINANET's filtering is decentralized, while CNCGROUP has their IDS devices mostly in the backbone. A decentralized placement of filtering devices can facilitate censor to monitor domestic traffic.

The rest of the paper is organized as follows. Section 2 introduces the related work on measurement of the China's network censorship. Section 3 presents our result on AS topology of China's network. We locate filtering devices at router level in Section 4 to find how they are related to AS-level topology and the device placement strategies of different ISPs. Section 5 concludes the paper.

2   Related Work

An early work in the censorship measurement field is [3]. This paper analyzes the keyword filtering mechanism of GFC, and is a good source of background knowledge. They claim that the mechanism is based on an out-of-band intrusion detection system at border routers. The system emits forged reset packet to both destination and source, but packets themselves go through the router unhindered. Therefore, both source and destination ignoring forged reset packet makes the system entirely ineffective. They also claim that the firewall does not maintain a state.

An influential paper in this field is [4]. In the measurement study part, the most significant discovery is that unlike commonly believed, the censorship system in China is like a panopticon, where filtering does not occur strictly at border routers, but rather more centralized at AS level. They find that some filtering occurs 13 hops past border. In our work, we provide a more fine-grained analysis of where those filtering devices are located, answering whether all filtering occurs at border AS, and where IDS devices are attached at router level. They also discover that the firewall is stateful, namely a GET packet with keyword itself will not trigger the firewall. Rather, a complete TCP handshake is required. This contradicts with [3]. The paper also demonstrates that the RST packets sent by IDS devices are more complicated than before. The TTL of RST is now crafted, so we cannot identify the location of IDS devices by simply looking at the TTL values. Therefore, we identify the location of filtering devices by sending probe packets with increasing TTL values, and see when we receive RST packets from censors, as proposed in this work.

The most recent work in this field is [5]. This paper reports the discontinuation of keyword filtering in HTTP response on most routes, while that in HTTP GET request is still prevalent. They investigate whether the firewall has a state and yield a result that the firewall is stateful only in part of the country. All 3 works have conflicting views of whether the firewall is stateful. Their latest tests have done in August 2009.

3   China's AS-Level Topology

Crandall et al. [4] claims that the firewall is better described as a panopticon, where filtering does not strictly occur at the border and suggests that the filtering is more at AS-level. Inspired by their work, we want to explore whether only border ASes are involved in the filtering and how filtering occurs inside those ASes. This knowledge is important, because if internal routers also have filtering devices attached, censors would have the capabilities to monitor and filter domestic traffic, which is considered not true before. It is believed that Chinese censors do not filter domestic websites technically, presumably because of the heavy domestic traffic flow; rather, the domestic Internet censorship is about social control, human surveillance, peer pressure, and self-censorship. [15]

In this section, we provide a more comprehensive view of China's AS-level topology that lays the foundation for Section 4.

3.1   Methodology

The first step is to find the mapping between AS numbers that belongs to China and their corresponding IP prefixes. Finding the mapping between IP prefix and AS number is known to be hard. We propose a methodology that yields a coarse-grained result. We first get the list of ASes that headquarter in China from APNIC [6]. An estimated mapping between IP prefix and AS number is extracted from the archival file obtained from Routeview [7] and RIPE [8] collectors. For each prefix entry in the archival files, we claim that its corresponding AS is the last AS in AS_PATH.

We acknowledge that the methodology is an estimation, because 1) we do not address the inaccuracies introduced by router interfaces that have addresses belonging to neighboring AS, and 2) the list of ASes is incomplete as the assignment record from APNIC does not capture all traffic originated from China.

We take the archival data collected between May and June 2010 from all collectors of Routeview and RIPE. We parse more than 300 MRT files, and this effort yields 408,688 AS-prefix mappings. Among them, 11,824 are in China's address space. In 136 AS numbers assigned to China, we find 76 corresponding prefixes of them.

In order to get as many peerings between China and other countries as possible, we traceroute from PlanetLab [14] nodes all over the world. A script is written to traceroute from each PlanetLab node outside of China to each of 76 Chinese ASes that we have their corresponding IP prefixes. We take the first IP in a prefix as the sample IP to which we traceroute.

For each hop in the traceroute result, we attempt to map them back into AS number using our estimated mappings. For those that we fail to map back, the whois server of Team Cymru [9] that returns IP to ASN mapping is consulted.

From the traceroute result, we construct an estimated AS-level topology of China's network. Once the first hop inside China's address space is noted, we add its corresponding AS number to a graph and denote it as a border AS. The corresponding AS numbers of all following hops are also added and are denoted as internal ASes. In addition, we also include the immediate AS that precedes each border AS, annotated as external AS.

CIDR report [16] analyzes the BGP table within AS2.0 and generates an aggregation report for each individual AS. For each AS, the report contains a list of its adjacent ASes and its announced prefix. To include the result of CIDR report into our topology, we crawl its website. For the report of each AS, we download the list of its adjacent ASes. We use the largest AS in China (AS4134) to bootstrap, and do a breadth-first search over its adjacent AS list. The search terminates whenever we encounter an AS not belonging to China.

In the resulting topology graph, the names of ASes are obtained from [9]. We use the name to imply the ISP that an AS belongs to.

3.2 Results

We find 138 internal, 24 border and 92 external ASes. Our result shows 133 unique peerings with external ASes. Among them, 62 belong to CHINANET and 23 belong to CNCGROUP. These two ISPs possess 63.9% of China's total peerings with other countries. Table 1 shows the breakdown of ISPs in China that have the most number of unique peerings with foreign ASes according to our experiment. The resulting topology serves as the foundation of the experiment in the second part of the paper, while the following are some interesting observations that are worth further investigation.

Table 1. Chinese ISP with most number of unique peerings to foreign AS

ISP	AS Numbers	Peerings
CHINANET	4134, 4809, 4812, 23724, 17638	62 (46.6%)
CNCGROUP	4837, 9929, 17621, 4808	23 (17.3%)
TEIN	24489, 24490	8 (6.0%)
CNNIC	37958, 24151, 45096	8 (6.0%)
CERNET	4538, 4789	9 (6.8%)
Other	9808, 9394, 4847, 7497, 9298, 23911	23 (17.3%)

It is observed that some border ASes do not peer with any internal AS at all. These include 37958, 24151, 45096, 24489 and 24490. The first three belong to CNNIC, the national Internet registry of China. Even though it is possible that the lack of internal peering is due to our experimental error, we speculate that the CNNIC ASes are used for special purposes. A future work could be exploring whether these ASes have different filtering rules. Another owner of this kind of AS is Trans-Eurasia Information Network, the traffic through which should be transit traffic, which means that both the source and destination are not in China's address space. We do not expect to see filters being installed in Trans-Eurasia ASes.

Our result indicates that border ASes in this country are peered with at least 20 foreign countries. Among them, U.S. is the largest one that has a peering count of 52. Hong Kong and Japan follows U.S., and have 21 and 11 peerings respectively. This information is useful in future work to find whether GFC defines different policies for different countries.

3.3   Discussion

We then organize the resulting topology hierarchically. In order to do that, we select border ASes as roots and grow trees under them with internal ASes as children. The depth of the tree is only 2, meaning that to get to any AS we discovered in China, we only need to traverse at most 2 other ASes. In fact, only 18 out of 138 internal nodes are at level 2.

Most of the internal ASes (87.0%) are within direct reach of border ASes. The names of border ASes suggest that most of them belong to backbone, and there are just 24 of them. This implies that the best vantage points for efficient content filtering are in the border/backbone ASes since they can easily serve as choke points, given that IDS devices have enough power and the censors do not intend to monitor domestic traffic.

4   Locating Filtering Devices

As the key step of this study, we make efforts to find as many filtering devices as we can to see their relationship with AS topology. Before we get started, here we provide some brief background of the firewall. As suggested by [3], IDS devices are attached externally to routers and thus out-of-band. The IDS terminates TCP connection by sending multiple spoofed RST packets to both ends of the communication. Within a period after that, all traffic between these two parties is blocked by RST packets, no matter whether a keyword is included in the packets.

For detailed description of the behavior of GFC, please refer to [3]. In this section, we discover to router interfaces at which locations IDS devices are attached.

4.1   Statefulness of the Firewall

A firewall being stateful means that we need to establish a TCP connection with a legal handshake to trigger the firewall [3]. If we directly send a TCP packet that contains an HTTP GET with a known keyword but without a handshake, a stateful firewall would not send any RST packet. On the other hand, if the firewall is not stateful, any TCP packet with keyword, regardless of the existence of TCP connection, would trigger it.

Previous works [3] and [4] have contradicting result of whether the firewall is stateful, and [5] claims that part of the firewall is stateful. After sending a single packet with known keyword to the first IP of 11,824 Chinese prefixes, we observe no firewall activity at all. Assuming that the firewall behaves the same for all IPs in a prefix, the result indicates that the firewall is now totally stateful.

The firewall being stateful is meaningful. It can at least make probing in this kind of studies difficult. With a stateful firewall, we need to find servers in China that accept TCP connection to determine the position of filtering devices, rather than just probe the first IP of all prefixes with a packet that contains a keyword. With a stateless firewall, we can easily get a comprehensive set of filtering devices by probing all prefixes. On the other hand, in a stateful firewall, it is time-consuming to find an active server in each prefix, because it requires port scanning. Therefore, a stateful firewall makes probing more difficult and reduces the completeness of this kind of measurement.

4.2   Websites Probed

Since we are unable to probe each prefix to get a complete list of filtering devices, it is necessary to select a set of websites that are in different part of the country to achieve better completeness. Most previous work selects websites from the top result from search engine. This is biased, because top websites are likely to be clustered in some big cities in China. A CNNIC report [13] states that 51.2% websites are in 5 provinces, and there are 32 provinces in China. The least represented 17 provinces only have 10.8% of total number of websites in China. Furthermore, 13 provinces have less than 1% representation. Therefore, we cannot achieve our goal of getting as many filtering device as possible by employing their methodology.

Consequently, we carefully select web servers geographically across the entire country to probe. Our list of website covers all provinces and three major ISPs in this country, CHINANET, CNCGROUP and CERNET. To cover all provinces, we gather a list that contains the websites of all provincial governments. This list is obtained from the website of the central government [10]. The list of websites of provincial branches of CHINANET and CNCGROUP is also collected from Google search. Moreover, from a Chinese web resource guide [11], we collect a number of popular local websites. Taking CERNET, which is not a public network but mainly serves academic institutes, into account, we include websites of many universities in different parts of the country into our list.

Our final list contains 1594 websites. To show that they are geographically diverse, we query the most popular IP geolocation database in China [17]. The result is shown in the Appendix.

4.3   Algorithm

We probe our list of Chinese websites described in 4.1.2 to find the location of filtering devices at router level. Our methodology is similar to the one used by [4] and [5]. In short, the algorithm sends probing packets that contain known keywords with increasing TTLs.

For each IP of websites in our list, we first determine if it is online and whether it accepts TCP connection by establishing a TCP connection and sending an innocuous HTTP GET request. If we receive RST packets or the connection timed out, we skip it and proceed to the next website. Otherwise, we establish another connection with it, but this time, we send an HTTP GET with a known keyword `falun` that triggers the firewall.

At this moment, we wait for 5 seconds for the connection to completely die down. This allows the real and spoofed RST exchanges among source, destination and the firewall to complete.

Since the firewall is already triggered and now all further traffic between two endpoints, no matter considered harmful or not, is blocked by the firewall for a period, a simple ACK packet would trigger the firewall. Therefore, we send ACK packets with increasing TTL, and stop whenever we receive RST from a filtering device and record the IP address revealed by the ICMP packet that the router interface to which the filtering device is attached sends. We skip and record the website if the keyword does not trigger the reset in case of whitelisted websites.

4.4   Results

We found 495 router interfaces that have filtering devices attached to in our experiment, 106 more than in [4]. The proportions of filtering interfaces that each ISP has are as follows: CHINANET has 79.4%; CNCGROUP possess 17.4%, and the rest 3.2% belong to other ISPs. We get largely identical proportion for CHINANET as in [4], but for CNCGROUP, our percentage is three times of their result. Our result suggests that the placement of IDS device of CHINANET is stable since 2007, and the filtering power of CNCGROUP is growing and now counts for almost one fifth of all filtering interfaces in the country. We can derive that the filtering capability of CHINANET is mature, as the increase in traffic has not made it too overloaded to force them adding more filtering interfaces for several years.

Table 2 shows what ASes the filtering devices belong to. We consult the whois server of Team Cymru [9] for IP to ASN mapping.

Not surprisingly, most of the filtering devices belong to the border ASes. However, we find that some of them are in internal ASes. The proportion is small (2.9%), so it is prone to errors introduced by inaccurate IP to AS number mapping. However, it is still worth noting. We will continue to monitor this number, to see if there exists a trend that censors deploy more and more filtering devices to internal ASes.

All except for two internal filtering interfaces belong to CHINANET, and none belongs to CNCGROUP. Since this is particularly questionable, we examine our

Table 2. ASes that contain filtering devices

AS Number	AS Name	Number of Filtering Interfaces
Border ASes		481
4134	CHINANET-BACKBONE	374
4812	CHINANET-SH-AP	9
4837	CHINA169-BACKBONE CNCGROUP	82
9929	CNCNET-CN	4
4538	ERX-CERNET-BKB	4
9808	CMNET-GD	5
9394	CRNET	3
Non-border ASes		14
23650	CHINANET-JS-AS-AP	4
17785	CHINATELECOM-HA-AS-AP	4
37943	CNNIC-GIANT	3
38356	TIMENET	1
17633	CHINATELECOM-SD-AS-AP	1
4813	BACKBONE-GUANGDONG-AP	1

traceroute log more carefully. As a result, we find that if the first router interface in China's address space belongs to CHINANET, it rarely conducts any filtering. Pursuing this further, we find that many filtering router interfaces do not seem to belong to the same prefix as that of the first few router interfaces into the country, so we whois CHINANET's filtering interfaces to find more.

The result is interesting. Despite the name of AS4134 suggests, only 49 of 374 filtering interfaces actually belong to the backbone of CHINANET, and the rest of them are actually belong to provincial branch companies of CHINANET. In AS4134, we find that 16 provinces have their own filtering devices. Counting Shanghai that is not represented in AS4134 but has its own AS number, 80% of 21 provinces that CHINANET serves [12] do their own filtering. The provinces that are observed not having their own filtering are Shaanxi, Gansu, Qinghai and Ningxia. According to a CNNIC report [13], the number of IP addresses in these 4 provinces only counts 2.5% of the nation's total number of IPs. Table 3 shows where the filtering devices are located in AS4134. We only list the provinces that are in the service area of CHINANET.

This implies that CHINANET, instead of filtering strictly along the border, offloads the burden to its provincial network. On the other hand, CNCGROUP has most of its filtering devices in the backbone rather than provincial network, and all its filtering is done within very few hops into China's address space. We also whois the IP address of those filtering devices, and find that 74 out of 82, or 90% of filtering devices belongs to the backbone of CNCGROUP. This indicates that two major ISPs in China have different approaches placing their filtering devices.

The total bandwidth of CHINANET's international connection is 616703Mbps, and that of CNCGROUP is 330599Mbps [13]. Moreover, the number of peerings with foreign AS of CHINANET is 3 times of that of CNCGROUP. CHINANET, as a larger operator that has international bandwidth 2 times of

Table 3. Locations of filtering devices in AS4134

Province	# Devices	Percentage
Backbone	49	13.10%
Guangdong	84	22.46%
Fujian	29	7.75%
Hunan	28	7.49%
Hubei	24	6.42%
Sichuan	22	5.88%
Yunnan	21	5.61%
Guangxi	19	5.08%
Jiangsu	19	5.08%
Zhejiang	15	4.01%
Guizhou	14	3.74%
Jiangxi	14	3.74%
Hainan	11	2.94%
Chongqing	10	2.67%
Anhui	6	1.60%
Unidentified	6	1.60%
Xinjiang	2	0.53%
Tibet	1	0.27%

CNCGROUP, needs to filter more network traffic. Placing all filtering devices in backbone might have created a bottleneck for CHINANET, and allowed some unwanted traffic to go through. This might partly explain why they have different IDS placement strategies.

Another implication is that the filtering devices being in the provincial network allows censor to inspect inter-province traffic. Even though there is no evidence that they are doing this right now, this arrangement makes the future deployment of stricter firewall that censors domestic traffic easier.

5   Conclusion

Chinese censors impose strict restrictions on international Internet traffic. In order to understand the national-scale intrusion detection system better, this is the first study dedicated to explore both AS and router-level structures of China's censored network.

As a preparation, the first part of the paper presents our approximate result of China's AS-level Internet topology. We manage to collect the peering among 265 China-related ASes. In the second part of our work, we probe the firewall in an attempt to gather as many filtering interfaces as we can and to relate AS topology to the location of those filtering devices. We find that most filtering occurs in border ASes, but two major filtering ISP's have different approaches placing their filtering devices. CHINANET does not place most of its filtering devices in its backbone, but rather distribute the work to provincial networks. This makes censoring domestic traffic easier.

References

1. The Great Firewall Revealed,
   http://www.internetfreedom.org/files/WhitePaper/
   ChinaGreatFirewallRevealed.pdf
2. China's Great Firewall spreads overseas,
   http://www.networkworld.com/news/2010/
   032510-chinas-great-firewall-spreads.html
3. Clayton, R., Murdoch, S., Watson, R.: Ignoring the Great Firewall of China. In:
   Danezis, G., Golle, P. (eds.) PET 2006. LNCS, vol. 4258, pp. 20–35. Springer,
   Heidelberg (2006)
4. Crandall, J., Barr, E.: ConceptDoppler: A Weather Tracker for Internet Censorship.
   In. In: 14th ACM Conference on Computer and Communications Security (2007)
5. Park, J., Crandall, J.: Empirical Study of a National-Scale Distributed Intrusion
   Detection System: Backbone-Level Filtering of HTML Responses in China. In. In:
   The Proceedings of the 30th International Conference on Distributed Computing
   Systems (2010)
6. APNIC delegated internet number resource,
   http://ftp.apnic.net/stats/apnic/delegated-apnic-latest
7. University of Oregon Route Views Archive Project,
   http://archive.routeviews.org/
8. RIPE NCC Projects, http://www.ripe.net/projects/ris/rawdata.html
9. Team Cymru, http://www.team-cymru.org/Services/ip-to-asn.html
10. The Central People's Government of the People's Republic of China,
    http://www.gov.cn/zwgk/2008-04/23/content_952239.htm
11. Dao Hang Wang, http://www.daohang.com/
12. China Comservice, http://www.chinaccs.com.hk/eng/about/history.htm
13. The 26th Statistical Reports on the Internet Development in China, http://www.
    cnnic.cn/uploadfiles/pdf/2010/7/15/100708.pdf
14. PlanetLab, http://www.planet-lab.org
15. The Connection Has Been Reset, http://msl1.mit.edu/furdlog/docs/atlantic/
    2008-03_atlantic_fallows_chinese_firewall.pdf
16. CIDR Report, http://www.cidr-report.org/as2.0/
17. Chunzhen IP geolocation database, http://www.cz88.net

Appendix: Geographical Locations of Probed Websites

This is a list of provinces represented in our probed websites. It is a result after
querying the database of [17] dated December 30, 2010. The number in bracket
is the number of probed websites in that province.

Shanghai (24), Yunnan (36), Inner Mongolia (29), Beijing (94), Hubei (48),
Guangdong (115), Fujian (59), Jilin (25), Sichuan (65), Liaolin (63), Tianjin (16),
Ningxia (15), Anhui (43), Shandong (73), Shanxi (31), Guangxi (39), Xinjiang
(28), Jiangsu (82), Jiangxi (45), Hebei (48), Henan (63), Zhejiang (69), Hainan
(21), Hunan (44), Gansu (35), Shaanxi(36), Tibet (4), Guizhou (28), Chongqing
(15), Qinghai (5), Heilongjiang (28), Other (268)

Route Flap Damping Made Usable

Cristel Pelsser[1], Olaf Maennel[2], Pradosh Mohapatra[3], Randy Bush[1], and Keyur Patel[3]

[1] Internet Initiative Japan
Tokyo, Japan
{cristel,randy}@iij.ad.jp
[2] Loughborough University
United Kingdom
O.M.Maennel@lboro.ac.uk
[3] Cisco Systems
San Jose, CA, USA
{pmohapat,keyupate}@cisco.com

Abstract. The Border Gateway Protocol (BGP), the de facto inter-domain routing protocol of the Internet, is known to be noisy. The protocol has two main mechanisms to ameliorate this, MinRouteAdvertisementInterval (MRAI), and Route Flap Damping (RFD). MRAI deals with very short bursts on the order of a few to 30 seconds. RFD deals with longer bursts, minutes to hours. Unfortunately, RFD was found to severely penalize sites for being well-connected because topological richness amplifies the number of update messages exchanged. So most operators have disabled it. Through measurement, this paper explores the avenue of absolutely minimal change to code, and shows that a few RFD algorithmic constants and limits can be trivially modified, with the result being damping a non-trivial amount of long term churn without penalizing well-behaved prefixes' normal convergence process.

1 Introduction

Despite the huge success of the Internet, the dynamics of the critically important inter-domain routing protocol, the Border Gateway Protocol (BGP), remain a subject of research. In particular, despite a large number of research efforts, the convergence of BGP[6, 11], and lately, the chattiness of BGP, also called BGP churn [3], are still not well understood. Further observations have been made of duplicated and/or 'unnecessary' updates [15]. These all ultimately lead to slow protocol convergence.

Understanding the BGP mystery is critical. In the case of convergence, vendors may improve code based on insights into propagation patterns, which in turn could lead to less churn, and thus lower load, a more robust network, and faster response to failure events. Researchers suggesting replacement protocols could design them with an in-depth understanding of what works today, what does not work well, and why.

This paper aims at one facet in this spectrum: how, with absolutely minimal code change, to better differentiate the *normal* path-vector protocol convergence process from *abnormal* activity, such as heavily flapping prefixes. It has been shown that a single triggering event can cause multiple BGP updates elsewhere in the Internet [5, 6]. We say a BGP route is flapping or unstable if a router *originates* multiple BGP update

N. Spring and G. Riley (Eds.): PAM 2011, LNCS 6579, pp. 143–152, 2011.

messages (reachable or unreachable) for the prefix in a 'short' time interval and prop-agates those changes to its neighbors. However, BGP, being a path-vector protocol is also subject to *topological amplification*, sometimes called *path exploration*. One trig-gering event can cause multiple BGP updates at a topologically distant router. Studies using BGP beacons [12] have illustrated this effect. It is important to understand that this is a property (or artifact) of the BGP protocol itself and does not correspond to con-stantly changing topology. In fact, studies of BGP update behavior and traffic flow have found little correlation [20]. The traffic may continue to reach its destination despite the constant noise of BGP update messages.

While this is conceptually very simple, it is not easy to distinguish real topological changes from path exploration in the BGP signal. Ideally, we would like to maximize the speed topological information is propagated, while minimizing exchanged messages required to *converge* to a stable path. However, the root cause of a BGP update typically cannot be known. Therefore mechanisms to reduce BGP's chattiness face the dilemma of finding appropriate algorithms and parameters.

Huston [8] has observed that a small portion of the prefixes generate a high number of BGP update messages. In Figure 1 we show a similar observation. Most prefixes receive very few updates. Only 3% of the prefixes are responsible for 36% percent of the BGP messages. The plot shows the number of update messages that are received at a router in our measurement setup (Fig. 3) for each prefix during the week from Sept. 29th to Oct. 6th, 2010.

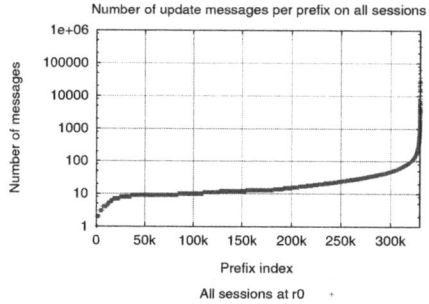
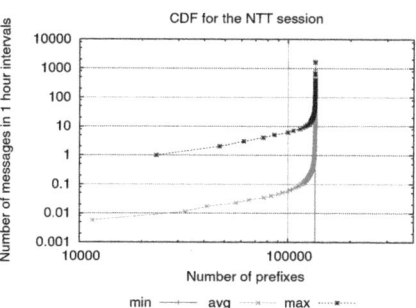

Fig. 1. Update count per prefix at $r0$ during the week of Sept. 29th to Oct. 6th 2010

Fig. 2. Update count per prefix from a single BGP session in one hour bins

Figure 2 illustrates the churn, i.e. update messages per hour that are received on a session with a tier-1 ISP. The y-axis depicts the number of updates received for a particular prefix per one hour bin, while the x-axis shows the prefixes sorted by the number of update messages received. The majority of prefixes account for few updates, while a small number of prefixes account for a very high number of updates within a short time period. The figure shows three curves, the minimum (vertical line), the average (lower curve) and maximum (top curve) number of updates in one hour bins.

Router $r0$ receives a full routing table, 326,575 routes, from NTT. One might expect that most of those routes would be stable and not receive any updates at all. However, we observe updates for 153,773 prefixes during *one week* of observation. And the router receives up to 1,647 updates in one hour for the prefix with the highest churn (see right most point on the top curve in Figure 2), there are less than ten updates for more than 100,000 of the prefixes for which there were any updates. Most prefixes for which we observe BGP update messages are quiet most of the time. Only 0.01% of the prefixes are always present in the trace, with one prefix having a minimum of 913 BGP updates per hour over the whole trace (which explains the vertical line in Figure 2). These observations confirm that most prefixes are very quiet, and only a very small number of the prefixes are responsible for the majority of the BGP churn.

For some prefixes the router received hundreds and thousands of update messages, over arbitrarily long time-periods. We hypothesize those updates are being caused by some periodic events and/or flapping. This cannot be 'normal' protocol convergence. This is causing an unnecessary load on the global routing system.

2 Background

There are many causes for route flapping. One common cause is a router or a link going up and down due to a faulty circuit or hardware. Another cause is a BGP session being reset. BGP policy changes can also lead to the readvertisement of routes and can thus be interpreted as a route flap, this also includes policy changes for traffic engineering. Furthermore, IGP cost changes may cause BGP updates which then propagate across the Internet [17]. Duplicate advertisements [15] are probably the best example of 'unnecessary' updates that do not contain any new topological information. Lastly, the BGP protocol is known to be inherently unstable [1, 4, 7].

Today, two approaches attempt to make the trade-off between convergence time and message count [6]. First, the MinRouteAdvertisementInterval timer (MRAI) [16] specifies the minimum time between BGP advertisements to a peer. While it is recommended to be a per prefix timer, existing implementations typically use a per-peer timer for all prefixes sent via that peering. By default, it is 30 seconds (jittered) for an eBGP peer, and five seconds for iBGP. The idea is that the router waits for the 'path exploration' downstream to finish, before sending any updates. However, as mentioned earlier, no technique can reliably discriminate between flapping routes and routes that are 'converging'.

The second technique is Route Flap Damping (RFD) [19]. It is more complex and fine-grained, as routers maintain a penalty value per prefix and per session. Routes with a penalty above a given threshold are damped, e.g., newly received announcements are suppressed and not considered as suitable alternatives to reach a destination. The idea is that heavily flapping paths are putting a large burden on the routing system as a whole and to protect the Internet from such routes, it is better to disregard the path and drop its traffic than to let such prefixes potentially cause cascading failures due to system overload. Of course, despite observations, stable routes are not supposed to be affected by this mechanism. Thus, there is still room for research in this area. For instance, the work of Huston [10] is promising in that it aims to categorize updates and determine the types that are potential indicators of path hunting. However, live detection of such updates is much more CPU and memory intensive than the brutally simple approach explored in this paper.

Using RFD [19], each prefix accumulates a penalty which is incremented on receipt of an announce or withdraw message for that prefix. This penalty is a simple counter and the values added to the penalty are listed in Table 4. When the penalty reaches a given threshold, the 'suppress penalty', the route is damped, i.e. quarantined. It is not advertised by the router until the penalty gets below another threshold, the 'reuse penalty'. The penalty value of a damped route is decremented using a 'half-life', i.e. it is divided by two after 'half-life' seconds. Upon the receipt of further updates the penalty continues to grow. However, there is a 'max suppress time', which constitutes a maximum time the route can be damped. E.g., provided that the route is not receiving any further updates, a damped prefix is typically released after one hour. This translates into a 'maximum suppress penalty', which is computed using the suppress threshold, the reuse threshold and the half-life time. For example, with Cisco default parameters a penalty of 12,000 will result in a suppression of one hour if no further updates for that prefix arrive. We refer to the work of Mao et al. [13] for a detailed study of the RFD algorithm.

RFD has been reported to be harmful [2] in that, with current default settings and recommendations [14], it penalizes routes which are not flapping, but receiving multiple updates due to path exploration. This severely impacts convergence. Reachability problems for over an hour have been observed where there was no physical outage, network problem, or congestion that would justify any packet drops. In fact, it has been shown that perfectly valid and fine paths can be withdrawn due to RFD [2]. As a consequence most operators have disabled RFD. On the other hand, we see serious BGP noise affecting router load and burdening the whole system [9].

Can research on BGP dynamics lead to an appropriate recommendation of RFD parameters? What would happen if we adopted a strategy to select only the 'heavy hitters', the heavily flapping routes, or 'elephants' as we call them – but leave the converging routes, or 'mice', in peace? BGP churn should decrease significantly compared to the current situation where RFD is turned off, yet the BGP convergence for prefixes with 'normal' BGP activity would not be affected. In this paper, we try to find and propose such appropriate parameters.

3   Measurement Setup

In this section, we present our experimental design. We describe a change to Cisco's IOS XR BGP implementation to enable the collection of damping statistics, the location of the router in the Internet and the BGP feeds that it receives. Then we explain how we collected and analyzed the RFD data.

Router $r0$ in Figure 3 is a Cisco 12406 running a minimally modified version of Cisco's IOS XR software to enable us to perform a detailed analysis of what the router 'thinks'. The router applies the RFD algorithm using the normal penalty values. The modified code does not actually damp the routes, instead it records the calculated penalty values of each route and its supposed status, active or damped. The other modification was that no 'Maximum Suppress Penalty' was imposed, e.g., the penalty values could increase above 12,000.

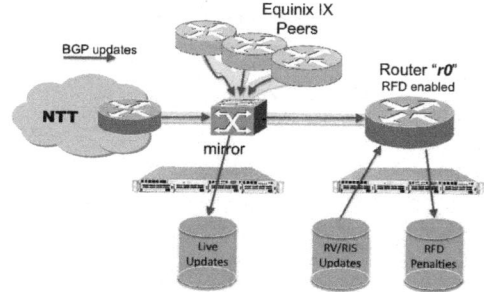

	Parameter	Value
1	Half-life time	15 min
2	Max suppress penalty	12,000
3	Max suppress time	60 min
4	Suppress penalty	2,000
5	Reuse penalty	750
6	Withdrawal penalty	1,000
7	Re-advertisement penalty	0
8	Attribute change penalty	500

Fig. 3. Measurement Topology Setup

Fig. 4. Cisco's default RFD values

Figure 3 shows our measurement infrastructure. Router $r0$ is directly connected to a large public Internet Exchange over which it receives both full and partial feeds. In addition, the router connects to a global tier-1 provider for another full BGP feed.

We pulled statistics from the router at regular intervals for one week, from September 29 through October 6, 2010, using the clogin command from the rancid tool. Data included details of all route flap damping counters, although the router code did not actually damp any route. The time to pull the data from the router depended on how quickly the router responded to our queries, but was typically in the order of 4–5 minutes. Missing counter values due to slow router response time did not significantly affect our observations in subsequent sections, as there were very few of them. The 95% quantile was under ten minutes. However, in some circumstances it was longer, up to 45 minutes in one instance! We believe this was due to CPU utilization peaks.

4   Results

We investigate the penalty values assigned to the prefixes received by our modified router, $r0$ (Figure 3). We then provide recommendations for new RFD parameter settings.

Figure 5 shows the Cumulative Distribution Function (CDF) of the penalties assigned to prefixes by the router during the one week experiment. Let us assume there are n snapshots during the week's experiment. We define an 'instance' $i_{p,t}$ as the RFD penalty of prefix p in snapshot t. Figure 5 shows the proportion of instances with penalties smaller than or equal to x over the whole set of instances. Intuitively, this is the proportion of prefixes which would have been damped in the time-prefix-space.

We observe that 14% percent of the instances reached a penalty greater or equal to $2,000$ in the measurement period. $2,000$ is a critical threshold as this is the default value for RFD suppression on Cisco routers. This gives a feeling for how 'bad' it is, if one turns on default RFD those instances would have been damped. Further, we observe in Figure 5 that a suppress threshold of $4,000$, $5,000$ and $6,000$ leads to the damping of 4.2%, 2.8% and 2.1% of the instances respectively. The number of damped instances decreases very quickly. Finally, we note that very few of the prefixes are assigned a very high penalty. Only 0.63%, 0.44% and 0.32% have a penalty value above $12,000$,

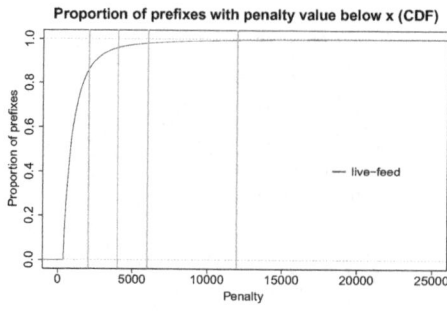

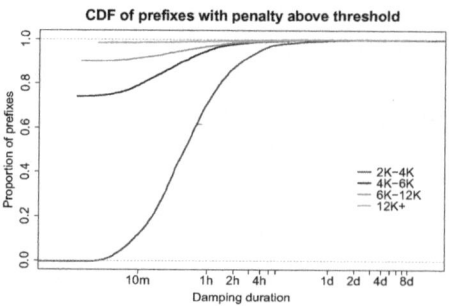

Fig. 5. Distribution of penalty values. Vertical lines are 2,000, 4,000, 6,000, and 12,000.

Fig. 6. CDF of the proportion of prefixes with penalty values above a threshold

15,000 and 18,000, respectively. Thus, very few prefixes flap heavily for long in the time-prefix-space. However, we observed earlier that those few prefixes are responsible for a disproportionate part of the BGP churn. The maximum penalty value assigned to a route during the experiment was 48,000. This value is huge compared to the median penalty of 818 (Fn(818)=0.5).

We recommend conservative operators set the 'suppress threshold' to 12,000, 15,000 or 18,000, as these values likely penalize only the very heavy hitters. We show later that, while values in the range [12,000 − 18,000] enable a non negligible BGP update rate reduction, a suppress threshold in the range [4,000 − 6,000] damps far fewer prefixes compared to current defaults and the BGP update rate is significantly reduced.

How long do prefixes typically stay at high penalty values? Figure 6 shows the CDF of the durations a prefix is above a certain penalty value, and thus would be damped if this was the threshold. The red solid curve shows the damping duration for the current threshold of 2,000. Many prefixes have a penalty above 2,000 for a very short time. For example, 68% of prefixes stay above 2,000 for up to one hour during the one week of the experiment. This means the current default suppresses a lot of prefixes that are unstable for a relatively short time. We suspect that many of those prefixes are inappropriately damped following a single event. They are given a penalty value above 2,000 during BGP convergence simply because of path exploration. We should not damp those prefixes!

The other curves show suppression times for penalty values between 2K and 4K, between 4K and 6K, 6K–12K, and above 12K relative to those prefixes in the 2K class. If a prefix is not suppressed at all, then the duration is zero and thus the curve starts at this point on the y-axis. Not surprisingly, the number of prefixes in each category varies quite a lot (721 prefixes above 12K, top most curve; 4,429 prefixes between 6K–12K, 2nd from top; and 11,546 prefixes between 4K–6K, 3rd from top; and 44,846 prefixes between 2K–4K, lowest curve). Furthermore, there are very few prefixes that have a high penalty for a long time (e.g. rightmost points). There are 57 prefixes in the 2K–4K band that stay in this band for more than two days, but only 12 prefixes in the above 12K-band that stay for more than two days. We noticed some prefixes change bands, e.g., stay for a few hours/days in the 2K–4K band and then also stay a few hours/days in a higher band. Overall, it is possible that high churn prefixes stay for quite some time in lower bands; but we have also shown that 'normal converging' prefixes stay in those bands. Therefore, we need to find a trade-off in the parameter space, that does not penalize prefixes that only experience path exploration.

Figure 7 shows the number of prefixes which would be damped given the different candidate thresholds. Clearly, (32,089) mice would be spared using a suppress threshold of 4,000 or above. Moreover, we see that the number of prefixes damped with higher suppress thresholds does not vary much. High thresholds are much more suitable to prevent damping of prefixes affected by normal BGP path exploration than the current default threshold. Our intuition here is that a 'badly behaving prefix' will flap for a long time and thus hit high penalty values; while 'normal converging prefixes', which just receive multiple updates due to path exploration, will not be penalized.

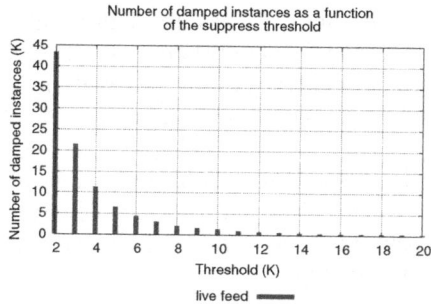

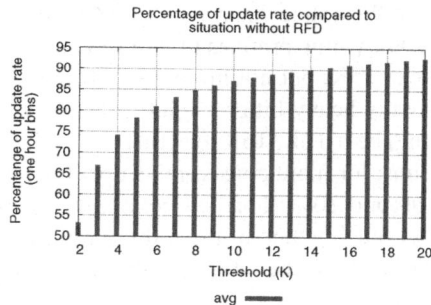

Fig. 7. A suppress threshold of 4,000 (and above) already damps many fewer prefixes

Fig. 8. A threshold of 6,000 enables an average churn reduction of 19%

Increasing the value of the suppress threshold above today's default will increase the BGP churn rate, but it will save many mice and still be less churn than a router with RFD turned off. Figure 8 illustrates this. The x-axis is the candidate value of the suppress threshold. On the y-axis we show the update rate on a per minute average in 60 minute bins. 100% is the churn when RFD is disabled.

Here, we try to estimate how churn could change if we activate RFD at various thresholds. Unfortunately, we face two problems: (1) the accuracy of timestamps and (2) we are looking at only one router and not studying interactions in complex topologies. With regard to (1) we record incoming updates via tcpdump with sub-second accuracy. However, the router provides us with less frequent snapshots of the penalty values. We therefore have only an estimate of the penalty. Especially, we do not know the exact time of onset, e.g., when an update would have been damped. Updates often come in bursts with short inter-arrival times but the arrival process of bursts is rather uniformly distributed in time, and thus within the snapshots. If a prefix has a penalty above the considered threshold in the current snapshot, all its updates in the coming interval are marked as being potentially removed. This provides an estimation of the update rate. By averaging over the whole trace, the error smooths out. We tag all updates that cross our 2K, 3K,... thresholds within a certain time-window. With respect to (2) we cannot predict how MRAI and best path selection processes will or will not delay updates.

While we believe that the overall properties of update behavior are comparable, we leave it for future work to study the impact in complex topologies.

We observe a 47% reduction of the average update rate with a penalty of 2,000, compared to a situation without RFD, in Figure 8. 4,000, 5,000 and 6,000 correspond to an average update rate reduction between 26% and 19%. Thus, it is worthwhile changing the default suppress threshold value. Our proposal is a very simple modification which is rather effective compared to more complex solutions such as [10].

We further note that the churn reduction is similar for all thresholds above 12K. Damping thresholds of 12K, 15K and 18K suppress an average of 11.26%, 9.51% and 8.12% of the updates, which is still non negligible for such a trivial change as we propose.

To compare the really heavy hitters in the intervals 12K-15K, 15K-18K, and above 18K, we concentrate on 64 prefixes which have a damped duration of six hours or longer. We notice that 53 of those 64 prefixes (83%) at some point pass the high point of 18K. Only nine prefixes (14%) stay in the 12K-15K range, and only two prefixes (3%) go over 15K, but not up to 18K. This strengthens our confidence that the 'evil' guys, the really heavy hitters which constantly flap, will be caught by almost any threshold setting, be it 12K, 15K, or 18K.

Thus, for more conservative operators that desire to spare most of the mice and still see around 10% churn reduction, we recommend values 12K and above. It does not matter much which of these three values are chosen. If a prefix is flapping so hard that it reaches 12K, then it is also likely to go higher at some time.

5   Other Feeds

A critical question is whether the observations and recommendations in the previous section hold for other locations in the Internet topology? Can we make a generic recommendation for the 'suppress penalty' value? To understand this, we replayed additional varied BGP traces from Route Views into $r0$ (see 'RV/RIS Updates' in Figure 3) in pseudo real-time. Again, $r0$ logged the RFD penalties of the received routes.

We performed two additional experiments. Figure 10 describes the additional workload traces that were replayed to the router. These were in addition to the in vivo feeds from the tier-1 ISP and the Exchange Point.

These experiments were designed to determine if different update patterns recorded at different places in the Internet topology would affect our conclusions.

Figure 9 shows the penalty values for prefixes with the new feeds replayed from Route Views. It shows that the distributions are exceedingly similar to those from the live feeds. Similar to Figure 5, this plot shows a CDF of penalties assigned by $r0$ to the different instances in the time-prefix-space. The green curve is the workload from the live feed plus a BGP feed from an African peering point. The blue curve is the 1.5 day live workload with the 10 additional Route Views feeds. The red curve is the one week workload (live feed), previously shown (see Figure 5) for comparison. We observe that all three curves have a similar shape. Adding more feeds just leads to more prefixes that flap but the number of 'elephants' is very similar.

Therefore, our damping suppression threshold recommendation does not change for BGP feeds from varying points in the Internet topology.

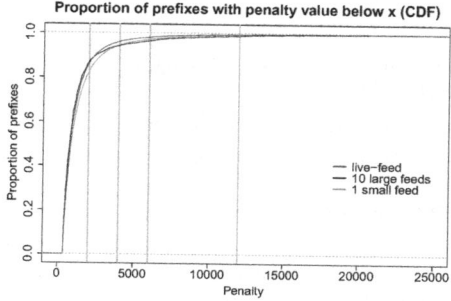

Proportion of prefixes with penalty value below x (CDF)

Fig. 9. Distribution of penalty values

10 large feeds: Ten Route Views [18] feeds which received the maximum number of updates from August 5 to mid-day August 6, 2010 (1.5 days).

1 small feed: A small selected African Exchange, route-views.kixp. Data were collected from August 27 to September 1, 2010 (5 days).

Fig. 10. Additional feeds

6 Conclusion

We studied the impact of RFD on the Internet. As previously observed by many other researchers, a small fraction of prefixes is responsible for a significant portion of the update churn. RFD was developed to reduce this noise, but the current default parameters do not properly take into account properties of the BGP protocol. Any path-vector protocol is by it's very design noisy due to *path exploration*.

We therefore looked at the effect of an absolutely minimal change, only adjusting RFD parameters, to get moderate churn reduction without adversely impacting normally converging prefixes. Our recommendation derived from this study would be to damp a route when it reaches a penalty above 12,000. The suppress threshold can be set to any value between 12,000 and 18,000. Such a setting will suppress the BGP churn of routes that flap heavily while keeping paths for prefixes which only slightly contribute to BGP churn. For operators extremely concerned about churn, a suppress threshold of 4,000 to 6,000 is a far better compromise than today's default parameters. It may still damp some normally converging prefixes, but will also significantly reduce the BGP update rate.

We do not recommend changing the maximum suppress time, but we strongly recommend the limit of the maximum suppress threshold value be raised. A maximum suppress time of one hour is very reasonable to achieve recovery once the flapping stops (and heavy hitters will anyway broadcast continuously), but the maximum suppress threshold needs to be able to allow higher values than 12,000.

Acknowledgments

We are very grateful to Cisco for the code modification that made those measurements possible, and for engineering support, equipment, and funding. Google, NTT, and Equinix contributed significant support. We are thankful to Matthew Roughan for many comments on earlier versions of this idea. We would also like to thank Nate Kushman for the inspiring discussions.

References

1. Basu, A., Ong, C.H.L., Rasala, A., Shepherd, F.B., Wilfong, G.: Route Oscillations in I-BGP with Route Reflection. In: Proc. ACM SIGCOMM (2002)
2. Bush, R., Griffin, T., Mao, Z.M.: Route Flap Damping: Harmful? RIPE 43 (2002), http://www.ripe.net/ripe/meetings/archive/ripe-43/presentations/ripe43-routing-flap.pdf
3. Elmokashfi, A., Kvalbein, A., Dovrolis, C.: BGP Churn Evolution: A Perspective from the Core. In. In: Proceedings of INFOCOM (2010)
4. Griffin, T.G., Wilfong, G.: Analysis of the MED Oscillation Problem in BGP. In: Proceedings of the International Conference on Network Protocols (2002)
5. Griffin, T.G.: What is the Sound of One Route Flapping? IPAM (2002)
6. Griffin, T.G., Premore, B.J.: An Experimental Analysis of BGP Convergence Time. In: Proc. ICNP (2001)
7. Griffin, T.G., Wilfong, G.: On the Correctness of iBGP Configuration. SIGCOMM Comput. Commun. Rev. 32(4), 17–29 (2002)
8. Huston, G.: The BGP Instability Report (2006), http://bgpupdates.potaroo.net/ instability/bgpupd.html
9. Huston, G.: BGP Extreme Routing Noise. RIPE 52 (2006), http://www.ripe.net/ripe/meetings/ripe-52/presentations/ripe52-plenary-bgp-review.pdf
10. Huston, G.: Update damping in BGP (2007), http://www.potaroo.net/presentations/2007-10-25-dampbgp.pdf
11. Labovitz, C., Ahuja, A., Bose, A.: Delayed Internet Routing Convergence. In: Proceedings of SIGCOMM, pp. 175–177 (August 2000)
12. Mao, Z.M., Bush, R., Griffin, T.G., Roughan, M.: BGP Beacons. In: Proc. ACM IMC (2003)
13. Mao, Z.M., Govidan, R., Varghese, G., Katz, R.H.: Route Flap Damping Excacerbates Internet Routing Convergence. In: Proceedings of SIGCOMM (August 2002)
14. Panigl, C., Schmitz, J., Smith, P., Vistoli, C.: RIPE Routing-WG Recommendation for Coordinated Route-flap Damping Parameters (2001), http://www.ripe.net/ripe/docs/ripe-229.html
15. Park, J.H., Jen, D., Lad, M., Amante, S., McPherson, D., Zhang, L.: Investigating Occurrence of Duplicate Updates in BGP Announcements. In: Krishnamurthy, A., Plattner, B. (eds.) PAM 2010. LNCS, vol. 6032, pp. 11–20. Springer, Heidelberg (2010)
16. Rekhter, Y., Li, T.: A Border Gateway Protocol 4 (BGP-4) (2006), RFC 4271
17. Teixeira, R., Shaikh, A., Griffin, T.G., Voelker, G.M.: Network Sensitivity to Hot-Potato Disruptions. In: Proc. ACM SIGCOMM (2004)
18. University of Oregon RouteViews project, http://www.routeviews.org/
19. Villamiyar, C., Chandra, R., Govindan, R.: BGP Route Flap Damping (1998), RFC 2439
20. Wang, F., Mao, Z.M., Wang, J., Gao, L., Bush, R.: A Measurement Study on the Impact of Routing Events on End-to-End Internet Path Performance. In: Proc. ACM SIGCOMM (2006)

On Reducing the Impact of
Interdomain Route Changes

Kyriaki Levanti[1], Sihyung Lee[2], and Hyong S. Kim[1]

[1] Carnegie Mellon University
[2] IBM T.J. Watson Research Center
{klevanti,kim}@ece.cmu.edu, leesi@us.ibm.com

Abstract. Interdomain route changes are frequent and they can have negative impact on a network's operation: during route convergence, packets get delayed and dropped; after route convergence, changes in the egress point for reaching a destination can alter the network's intradomain traffic patterns and trigger new traffic-engineering. In this paper, we look into reducing the impact of interdomain route changes on the network's operation. First, we investigate a route decision process which avoids the selection of routes that cause egress point changes. However, this decision process does not consider the potential benefit of selecting a more preferred route even if it causes an egress point change. Then, we propose a system which only avoids route changes causing recurring intradomain traffic shifts by processing the route changes history and by selectively modifying route attributes which affect the route decision process. We evaluate both approaches using data from a major European ISP. The modified route decision process avoids 89% of the observed intradomain traffic shifts caused by interdomain route changes, whereas route attribute modifications reduce the number of traffic shifts on average by 25%, and as much as 50%.

1 Introduction

Interdomain route changes can be highly disruptive to a network's operation [1][2]. During route convergence, traffic can be delayed by routing loops or dropped by temporary loss of routes [3][4]. This is particularly harmful for low-latency and high-availability applications. Route changes also add considerable operational overhead. After route convergence, traffic may traverse the network through a different path. This can modify the network's traffic patterns and trigger new traffic-engineering in order to efficiently use the network resources. The higher the frequency of such route changes, the more time operators have to spend ensuring a balanced traffic distribution in the network.

BGP route changes are caused by a variety of external events (e.g., remote failures, new peerings, policy changes). Although BGP's pathological behavior has decreased considerably [5], many legitimate route changes still occur and can cause disruptions to the affected networks. Operators have no control over these route changes but they can leverage their network's path diversity [6] in order to

N. Spring and G. Riley (Eds.): PAM 2011, LNCS 6579, pp. 153–162, 2011.
© Springer-Verlag Berlin Heidelberg 2011

reduce the negative impact. Our work focuses on reducing the impact of inter-domain route changes on networks with sufficient path diversity by avoiding the route changes which lead to egress point changes. These changes take longer to converge [7], harming data plane performance. They also affect the network's intradomain traffic patterns and can interfere with the internal traffic-engineering (e.g., the configuration of MPLS tunnels).

First, we investigate a modified route selection algorithm called Stick-To-Egress (STE) which avoids intradomain traffic shifts by preferring alternate routes through the same egress point with that of the previously selected route. The problem with STE is that it prioritizes the aversion of the traffic shift and disregards the potential benefit of the route change (e.g., permanently switching to a shorter route advertised to another egress point). Then, we present a system which targets more intelligent route selection and only avoids the traffic shifts caused by recurring route changes. This system deviates less from the standard route decision process and allows route changes unless the route history shows that they are caused by unstable routes. It does so by boosting the route attributes of previously selected stable routes in order to avoid the recurrence of a route change. Route boosting exploits both the network's path diversity and the knowledge provided by already "seen" route changes.

We perform a measurement study of the interdomain route changes as seen by a major European ISP in a period of eight months. We find that: 1) A considerable amount of route changes have high impact: on average 46% of the route changes cause intradomain traffic shifts, and from these, only 3% are intentionally caused by the network's operators through routing policy changes. 2) 89% of the observed traffic shifts could be avoided by STE. Thus, this network possesses sufficient path diversity which can be exploited in order to make route choices with minimum impact on the network's operation. 3) 52% of the high-impact route changes are recurring. 4) The route boosting avoids on average one in four - and as much as one in two - traffic shifts caused by the observed route changes. Also, it avoids the rerouting of traffic flowing towards the top-ranking destination networks for this ISP, helping to stabilize large traffic volumes. The remainder of this paper is structured as follows: In Sections 2 and 3, we present related works and our dataset, respectively. In Section 4, we analyze the interdomain route changes observed by the ISP and emulate the STE route selection algorithm. In Section 5, we present the route boosting system and investigate its benefits and cost. Finally, we conclude in Section 6.

2   Related Work

Interdomain routing is known to be unstable: routes change often [8], and a route change can take hours to converge [9]. Several previous works are reactive; they reduce the convergence time [10][11], or minimize the negative impact of slow route convergence [12][13]. These works mitigate the impact of route changes on data plane performance but do not address the problem of managing the unstable traffic patterns caused by the route changes. Proactive methods - including our work - directly suppress unnecessary route changes. Route Flap Damping (RFD) [14] deactivates routes that flap frequently. However, RFD may suppress relatively stable routes that only flap momentarily, and thus, significantly decrease the set of available routes [15]. Instead, our work increases the preference of routes that are shown to be more stable. Also, RFD targets pathological routing instabilities whereas our work targets legitimate route changes. The latter are recurring in longer timescales and impact a larger range of prefixes (not only the unstable and unpopular ones [16]). Overall, RFD is complementary to our work. Stable Route Selection (SRS) [17] proposes a modified BGP decision process which prefers routes that have been up the longest. Route boosting also favors route stability but only for prefixes which suffer from recurring route changes. The rest of the prefixes do not necessarily benefit from stable route selection. So, route boosting lets their route selection follow the standard BGP decision process. Additionally, route boosting also opts for intradomain traffic pattern stability by favoring the selection of routes that maintain the currently selected egress point.

3   Dataset

Our dataset includes routing tables from the backbone IP network of a major ISP in Europe. This network is comprised by 13 BGP-speaking routers with 961 eBGP neighbors. Two routers are route-reflectors and maintain BGP sessions with all other routers. The network has customer-to-provider, provider-to-customer, and peer-to-peer relationships with its neighboring ASes. It has customers in four continents, peers with hundreds commodity peers, and buys transit from multiple upper tier providers. We analyze daily snapshots of routing tables over eight non-consecutive (due to missing routing tables) months in 2007 and 2008. A routing table snapshot contains approximately 200,000 distinct prefixes and as many as a million routes. It is important to note that, since we do not have access to more frequent routing table snapshots, we only see a sample of the interdomain route changes and the intradomain traffic shifts that the network experiences. Thus, we are limited to the route change granularity given by this sampling frequency. Finally, the dataset includes a summary report of the outgoing traffic volumes per destination AS for a 24-hour period.

4   Stick-To-Egress Route Selection

First, we count the number of interdomain route changes that cause intradomain traffic shifts: the new next-hop for reaching the destination prefix in the most recent routing table snapshot resides on a different egress router than the old next-hop in the previous routing table snapshot. We find that on average 46% of the route changes cause egress point changes. We characterize these route changes as *high-impact*. The rest of the route changes are mostly changes to secondary routes, or changes to the AS-path of the best route.

Then, we analyze the high-impact route changes in order to exclude the changes which are *intentionally* caused by the network's operators and not by external events. Operators change route attributes such as local-preference (LP) and Multi-Exit-Discriminator (MED) in order to make routes more or less preferable and affect the route selection process. In particular, it is common to assign a MED value at the import side of every session in order to show session preference [18]. We illustrate the methodology for counting intentional route changes:

```
#    RS1 : available routes towards prefix P in snapshot t
#    RS2 : available routes towards prefix P in snapshot t+1
#    RB1 = Best(RS1), RB2 = Best(RS2)
1.   if RB1' in RS2 where RB1.NextHop == RB1'.NextHop and
2.         (RB1.LP != RB1'.LP  or  RB1.MED != RB1'.MED),
3.              RB2' = Best(RS2 where RB1' is replaced by RB1)
4.              if  (RB2' == RB1),  intentional route change
5.   if RB2' in RS1 where RB2'.NextHop == RB2.NextHop and
6.         (RB2'.LP != RB2.LP  or  RB2'.MED != RB2.MED),
7.              RB2'' = Best(RS2 where RB2 is replaced by RB2')
8.              if  (RB2'' == RB1), intentional route change
```

We consider a route change intentional when (i) we observe a change in the LP or MED value of either the old or the new best route (lines 1-2, 5-6) and (ii) the route change would not occur if the changed route attribute remained the same (lines 3-4, 7-8). Condition (ii) is required so that, when a route attribute change with no impact on route selection coincides with a route change caused by an external event, the route change is not counted as intentional. In our dataset, we find only 3% of the high-impact route changes to be intentionally caused by the network's operators. For the rest of this paper, we focus on how to reduce the impact of the unintentional route changes.

One way to reduce the impact of interdomain route changes is to modify the route decision process and prefer routes that stick to the same egress point. The *Stick-To-Egress* (STE) route selection algorithm prefers alternate routes through the egress point of the previously selected route. Selecting such an alternate route - if existing - ensures that route convergence is faster [7] and that the traffic towards the destination prefix traverses the network via the same intradomain path. We illustrate the STE route selection algorithm:

```
Prefer routes
  1. With a higher local-preference.
  2. Advertised to the same egress point with the previously selected route.
  3. With a shorter AS-path.
  4. Originated from IGP than from EGP.
  5. With a lower Multi-Exit-Discriminator.
  6. Learned from eBGP than from iBGP.
  7. With lower intradomain routing costs.
  8. From routers with lower router IDs.
```

STE adds the second step to the standard BGP decision process. The first step ensures that business relationships are not violated given that LP mostly represents business relationships between networks [19]. STE exploits the fact that many networks have multiple routes to a single destination [6]. These networks can use their alternate routes to avoid intradomain traffic shifts.

We emulate STE in order to estimate how many of the observed traffic shifts the analyzed network could avoid by preferring routes that stick to the same egress point. We see an - on average - 89% reduction in the number of intradomain traffic shifts caused by interdomain route changes. Although the interdomain routing activity varies during the analyzed period, STE constantly avoids a high percentage of traffic shifts. Thus, the analyzed network has sufficient path diversity which makes STE highly effective in reducing the impact of interdomain route changes. We note that the cases where STE cannot prevent the egress point change are when (i) no alternative route exists, or (ii) the most frequently selected route has a different egress point from the alternative routes.

5   Route Boosting

Should all interdomain route changes causing intradomain traffic shifts be avoided? STE also suppresses beneficial route changes (i.e., route changes towards more preferred and stable routes) because it has no means of assessing whether the benefit of avoiding a traffic shift outweighs the cost of settling with a less preferred - according to the standard BGP decision process - route. Route boosting assesses the benefit of a route change by looking into the recent route history and prevents only recurring route changes caused by unstable routes. Specifically, it does not modify the route selection algorithm but suggests routing policy changes which make the most stable route *more preferable* than the unstable route that causes back-and-forth traffic shifts. The routing policy changes prevent the future recurrence of the route change. Fig. 1 presents an overview of the route boosting system.

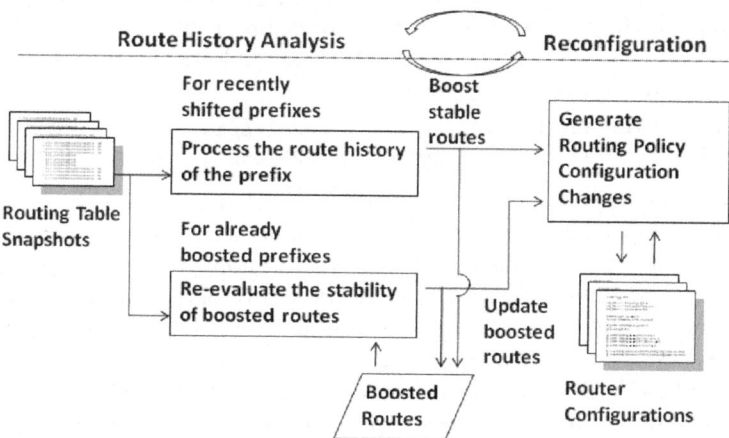

Fig. 1. High-level design of the route boosting system

5.1 Route Boosting Algorithm

We perform route boosting for the prefixes that have recently exhibited route instability, i.e. have experienced an egress point change in the past two routing table snapshots. For each of these prefixes, we perform the following steps.

Step 1: We choose the most stable route among the routes that have been chosen as best in the routing table history. The routing table history consists of the past n snapshots of the network's routing tables. The sampling frequency of the routing state poses a trade-off between accurate stability estimates and the overhead of monitoring the routing state. We refer to the most stable and previously selected route as *dominant* route D. To measure the stability of a route, we use the product of the route's *persistence* and *prevalence* [20]. Persistence represents the interval during which the route has been available before it is withdrawn or before its AS-path length changes. Both route withdrawal and AS-path length change can cause a best route change. Persistence is computed as the average of the intervals. Prevalence represents the probability of observing the route. It is computed as k/n where k represents the total number of snapshots that the route is present in the history.

Step 2: We examine whether the dominant route D is chosen as best in the most recent snapshot. If this is the case, the prefix has experienced a route change to D and we proceed to the next step which boosts D. If D is not currently the best route, we do not boost D and move on to process the next prefix. In this way, we let the current best route become dominant since the route history does not show a recurrent traffic shift and the route change could be a permanent beneficial route change.

Step 3: We identify the most preferred route over the routes that have been selected as best in the routing table history. We refer to this route as best competitor C. If C differs from D, we boost D such that D is preferred over C (i.e., $D > C$) by modifying the route attributes of D for the analyzed prefix. This can be implemented at the inbound route filter applied to the eBGP session where D is advertised. If C does not differ from D, boosting is not necessary because D is both the most stable and most preferred route among the recently selected routes. The routing policy reconfiguration follows the rules below:

```
if  D.LP  <  C.LP,  No Boosting
else if  D.LP = C.LP and D.ASP-length > C.ASP-length,  D.LP <- C.LP + 1
else if  D.LP = C.LP and D.ASP-length = C.ASP-length,  D.MED <- C.MED - 1
```

We note that we do not allow the boosting of routes that would result in violating business relationships. This means we do not boost D when D and C are received from neighbors of different business type. Also, among the range of different LP/MED values, we choose the one that is minimally better from that of C. In this way, a new route (i.e., a route which does not appear in route history) can be selected as best even after D is boosted.

Step 4: We identify the most stable secondary route S advertised to the same router as D in order to use S as a backup in the case where D is withdrawn or its AS-path is prepended. We boost S - if existing - such that S is preferred over C and D is preferred over S (i.e., $D > S > C$). This boosting follows the STE approach but only for routes that have been stable and selected in the recent history. The fail-over to S does not happen often or for long time periods because D is the most stable previously selected route in the recent route history.

We *re-evaluate* the installed route boosters on a regular basis because the stability of routes can change. If the boosted route is withdrawn or another route becomes more stable, we update the boosting. The re-evaluation process is performed for each prefix by estimating D and C given the most recent unboosted route history and by comparing them with the already installed boosters. The frequency of the re-evaluation process poses a trade-off between up-to-date route boosting and processing overhead. A short re-evaluation period imposes more processing load as required for examining all previously installed boosters. But it quickly adapts to changes in route stability. Since the stability of most routes does not change as often as a week [16], a period of a few days is a good choice.

Another issue when running the route boosting for long periods is the ever increasing number of boosted routes and policy reconfigurations. This number would stabilize if there was a comparatively constant set of unstable prefixes. However, this is the case for short-term stability [16]. For long-term stability, there are legitimate reasons for any prefix to experience instability. We maintain a maximum number of boosted routes by periodically removing boosters. We call this the *cleanup* process. The cleanup policy maintaining boosters to important and/or popular prefixes has the highest impact on the network's operation.

Finally, it is worth considering possible risks and limitations of route boosting. Firstly, boosting can cause additional traffic shifts in the rare case where both the boosted dominant D and the boosted secondary S are withdrawn. Secondly, boosting suggests configuration changes in interdomain routing policies. To avoid intradomain routing instability, we assume that the BGP-session topology and the intradomain routing metrics of the network are chosen according to the sufficient iBGP correctness conditions shown in [21]. If the iBGP configuration is correct, the route boosting can safely introduce LP and MED changes. Then, interdomain routing policy changes can interfere with routing policies in neighboring networks, leading to route oscillations and forwarding loops [22][23]. We avoid causing such routing instabilities by respecting the interdomain business relationships, as discussed earlier.

5.2   Route Boosting Emulation

We evaluate the route boosting system by emulating its operation over the longest consecutive period of our dataset (90 days). The emulator keeps track of the number of traffic shifts caused by interdomain route changes in the case where route boosting is used and in the case where it is not used. For the boosted case, we compute best routes by modifying the route attributes that the route boosting suggests and then by executing the BGP decision process with the modified routes [24]. For the original case, we extract the best routes from the routing tables. This process is repeated for each snapshot as the emulator sequentially takes the snapshots as input. The route boosting implementation includes 4000 lines of Java code and ran on a machine with a 3.8 GHz CPU and 6GB memory.

In order to deal with the limited granularity of route changes that the daily sampling of routing tables gives us, we only boost the dominant route when its stability score is much higher that its competitor's. In this way, we avoid boosting routes which are inaccurately estimated as stable. We use a routing history length of 10 days, a cleanup and re-evaluation period of 5 days, and a maximum of 2000 boosted prefixes. We omit the parameter sensitivity analysis due to space limitations. The running times of the boosting, cleanup, and re-evaluation average at 8, 1 and 13 minutes, respectively. The code can be further optimized for faster runtime if required. However, these runtimes are acceptable because the system does not need to run online since the stability of routes does not change as often [16].

In our dataset, we find that 52% of the high-impact interdomain route changes are recurring (i.e., the best route changes from route A to route B and back to route A at least once in the routing table history). In Fig. 2(a), we show the number of traffic shifts which are *experienced* by the network, *avoided*, and *caused* by route boosting for each snapshot. We count one traffic shift per each prefix whose egress point changes. The percentage of avoided traffic shifts over the total number of traffic shifts averages at 21% and goes up to 50%. This percentage is particularly low (i) after the days we miss routing table snapshots (e.g., 64th day) and (ii) after we perform booster cleanup (e.g., 31st day). This highlights the importance of the information given by the most recent snapshots in predicting the recurrence of route changes and the effectiveness of the installed boosters in avoiding high-impact route changes. When we exclude the days immediately after missing routing snapshots and after performing cleanup, the average percentage of avoided traffic shifts goes up to 25%. Also, we observe that the additional traffic shifts caused by the route boosting system are almost zero for most of the days. This is expected as the withdrawal of both the dominant and the secondary route is unlikely.

We measure the impact of route boosting by analyzing the popularity of the boosted prefixes for this network. Since our dataset does not include traffic volumes per prefix for the analyzed period, we cannot estimate the volumes of traffic not shifted because of route boosting. However, our dataset includes a summary report with the average volumes of outgoing traffic per destination AS for this network. We map each prefix whose traffic is not shifted because of route boosting to its origin AS through its AS-path. Fig. 2(b) illustrates the significance of the 1434 unique ASes originating the boosted prefixes. We observe that some of these destination ASes are very popular: 30 ASes belong to the top 250 destination ASes for this network and more than 100GB of traffic is destined to each one of these ASes per day. Thus, reducing the impact of route changes towards these ASes has significant impact on this network's outgoing traffic.

Finally, we look into the differences in route attributes between the stable routes and the more preferred competitor routes. For each avoided traffic shift, we compare the route selected when using route boosting with the route selected in the original case. Almost half of the routes chosen with route boosting are on average 1.41 hops longer than the ones chosen in the original case. When

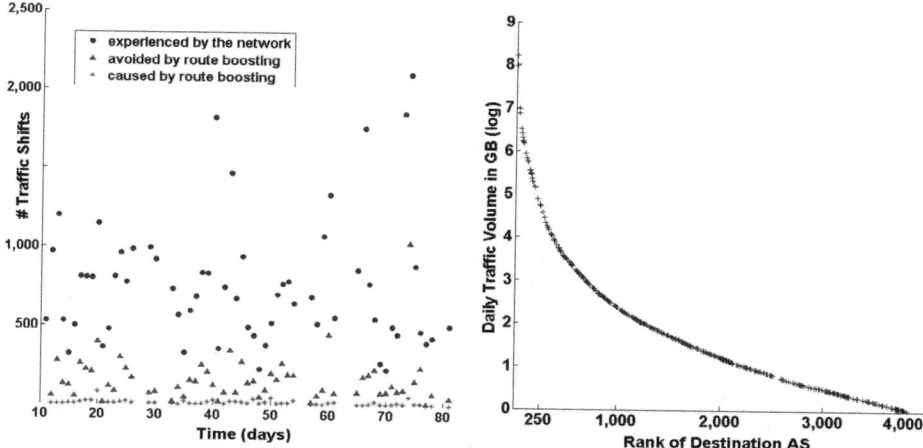

Fig. 2. (a) Number of intradomain traffic shifts per prefix experienced by the network, avoided and caused by route boosting. (b) Popularity of the destination ASes whose traffic is prevented from shifting because of route boosting.

ignoring AS-path prepending, the boosted routes are 0.82 hops longer than the unboosted routes. The difference in AS hops implies a difference in route latency but AS-path length is not a reliable indicator of route latency [3]. In almost all other cases, the boosted routes differ in assigned MED value from the unboosted routes. We note that although each network assigns MED values using different criteria, MED values are mostly used as tuning knobs for routes that are more or less equally preferred since they have the same local-preference and AS-path length [18]. To summarize, the boosted routes do not deviate significantly from the routes that would have been selected by the standard BGP decision process.

6   Conclusions

Networks experience a significant number of interdomain route changes which impact their data plane performance and disturb their traffic pattern stability. In this paper, we investigate ways of reducing the impact of these changes on networks with sufficient path diversity. We look into STE, a modified BGP decision process where routes that stick to the same egress point with the previously selected route are preferred. Then, we investigate a system which suggests routing policy reconfigurations that selectively tune the BGP decision process for unstable prefixes. The route boosting system exploits the knowledge gained from the history of route changes in order to predict recurring traffic shifts. We find that for the analyzed network recurring traffic shifts account for approximately half of the observed traffic shifts and route boosting reduces the impact of route changes on average by 25%, and up to 50%.

References

1. Agarwal, S., Chuah, C., Bhattacharyya, S., Diot, C.: "The impact of BGP dynamics on intra-domain traffic. In: Proc. ACM SIGMETRICS (June 2004)
2. Cowie, J.: Practical Instability Scoring. NANOG 45 (January 2009)
3. Wang, F., Mao, Z.M., Wang, J., Gao, L., Bush, R.: A measurement study on the impact of routing events on end-to-end Internet path performance. In: Proc. ACM SIGCOMM (2006)
4. Pucha, H., Zhang, Y., Mao, Z.M., Hu, Y.C.: Understanding Network Delay Changes Caused by Routing Events. In: Proc. ACM SIGMETRICS (June 2007)
5. Li, J., Guidero, M., Wu, Z., Purpus, E., Ehrenkranz, T.: BGP routing dynamics revisited. SIGCOMM Comput. Commun. Rev. 37(2), 5–16 (2007)
6. Teixeira, R., Marzullo, K., Savage, S., Voelker, G.: In search of path diversity in ISP networks. In: Proc. ACM IMC (October 2003)
7. Lee, S., Levanti, K., Kim, H.S.: Impact Analysis of BGP Sessions for Prioritization of Maintenance Operations, CMU-Cylab-10-018 Technical Report
8. Feldmann, A., Maennel, O., Mao, Z.M., Berger, A., Maggs, B.: "Locating Internet routing instabilities. In: Proc. ACM SIGCOMM (2004)
9. Labovitz, C., Ahuja, A., Bose, A., Jahanian, F.: Delayed Internet routing convergence. In: Proc. ACM SIGCOMM (2000)
10. Bremler-Barr, A., Afek, Y., Schwarz, S.: Improved BGP convergence via ghost flushing. In: Proc. IEEE INFOCOM (April 2003)
11. Sun, W., Mao, Z.M., Shin, K.G.: Differentiated BGP update processing for improved routing convergence. In: Proc. IEEE ICNP, Santa Babara, CA (November 2006)
12. Bonaventure, O., Filsfils, C., Francois, P.: Achieving sub-50 milliseconds recovery upon BGP peering link failures. IEEE/ACM ToN 15(5), 1123–1135 (2007)
13. Kushman, N., Kandula, S., Katabi, D., Maggs, B.M.: R-BGP: staying connected in a connected world. In: Proc. USENIX NSDI, Cambridge, MA (2007)
14. Villamizar, C., Chandra, R., Govindan, R.: BGP Route Flap Damping, RFC-2439 (November 1998)
15. Mao, Z.M., Govindan, R., Varghese, G., Katz, R.: Route Flap Damping Exacerbates Internet Routing Convergence. In: Proc. ACM SIGCOMM (2002)
16. Rexford, J., Wang, J., Xiao, Z., Zhang, Y.: BGP routing stability of popular destinations. In: Proc. ACM IMC (November 2002)
17. Godfrey, B., Caesar, M., Haken, I., Shenker, S., Stoica, I.: Stable Internet Route Selection. NANOG 40 (June 2007)
18. Roisman, D.: Effective BGP Load Balancing Using The Metric System. NANOG47 (October 2009)
19. Caesar, M., Rexford, J.: BGP routing policies in ISP networks. IEEE Network 19(6), 5–11 (2005)
20. Paxson, V.: End-to-end routing behavior in the Internet. IEEE/ACM ToN 5(5), 601–615 (1997)
21. Griffin, T.G., Wilfong, G.: On the correctness of IBGP configuration. In: Proc. ACM SIGCOMM (August 2002)
22. Griffin, T.G., Shepherd, F.B., Wilfong, G.: Policy disputes in path-vector protocols. In: Proc. IEEE ICNP, Toronto, Canada (October 1999)
23. Gao, L., Rexford, J.: Stable Internet routing without global coordination. IEEE/ACM Transactions on Networking, 681–692 (December 2001)
24. Feamster, N., Winick, J., Rexford, J.: A model of BGP routing for network engineering. In: Proc. ACM SIGMETRICS (June 2004)

Inferring the Origin of Routing Changes Based on Preferred Path Changes

Masafumi Watari, Atsuo Tachibana, and Shigehiro Ano

KDDI R&D Laboratories Inc.
{watari,tachi,ano}@kddilabs.jp

Abstract. Previous studies on inferring the origin of routing changes in the Internet are limited to failure events that generate a large number of routing changes. In this paper, we present a novel approach to origin inference of small failure events. Our scheme focuses on routing changes imposed on preferred paths of prefixes and not on transient paths triggered by path exploration. We first infer the preferred path of each prefix and measure the stability of each inter-AS link over this preferred path. The stability is measured based on routing changes of specific prefixes that regularly use the link and are advertised by the AS adjacent to the link. We then correlate the stability of other links over this path and infer the instability boundary as the origin. Our analysis using Oregon RouteViews data and trouble tickets from operational networks shows that our inference scheme can identify the origins of small failure events with very high accuracy.

1   Introduction

An inter-domain link failure in the Internet can cause routing changes of hundreds of thousands of prefixes advertised over the Internet. While some prefixes may preserve reachability through an alternative path, other prefixes may become unreachable and thus affect the data delivery of users seeking those destinations. From the ISP's point of view, operators are interested in finding the origin of these routing changes to identify possible locations of failure events. The origin information could then be used by operators to distinguish stable links from unstable links when seeking new transits. However, with the large number of routing changes observed in the Internet today, identifying the origin of these changes has been difficult [1,2].

Analyzing the sequence of update messages exchanged in Border Gateway Protocol (BGP) [3] has helped explaining the routing changes encountered by each prefix. Earlier work represented in [5,6] analyzed these routing updates across time, observation points and prefixes to locate origins. However, the use of the time threshold to group routing updates resulted in correlating unrelated updates triggered by different network events [2] and transient updates triggered by path exploration [7,8]. A more recent work in [9,10] took a different approach to capturing routing changes using the Link-Rank [11]. In [11], for each inter-AS link, the number of prefixes gained or lost is extracted from routing updates and

N. Spring and G. Riley (Eds.): PAM 2011, LNCS 6579, pp. 163–172, 2011.
© Springer-Verlag Berlin Heidelberg 2011

compared at given intervals (3-4 minutes) to find significant variations. While this approach enables routing changes to be captured efficiently, origin inference in the Internet is limited to failure events that generate a large number of routing changes because a small deviation is constantly observed for the majority of links.

In this paper, we present a novel scheme for origin inference of small failure events. Our main idea is that most prefixes have one preferred path and a routing change imposed on this path should indicate a failure or policy change at one of the nodes or links that construct the path. We thus first infer the preferred path of each prefix and extend the Link-Rank concept to measure the stability of each inter-AS link over this preferred path. The stability is measured using only the prefixes that regularly use the link and are advertised by the AS adjacent to the link to filter the noise caused by path exploration. We then correlate the stability of other links over this path and infer the instability boundary as the origin. This paper makes the following contributions. First, we present a novel approach based on preferred path changes for correlating routing updates and additionally present a scheme for effectively inferring the origins of small routing changes. Second, we describe a methodology for inferring the actual time of failure (not the time of detection) and the time of recovery, both of which provide operators with very valuable information. Third, we provide evaluation results using Oregon RouteViews data and trouble tickets from operational networks.

2   Effect of Path Exploration on Origin Inference

The effect of BGP path exploration on origin inference has not been deeply discussed in the past. In this section, we first describe how path exploration occurs and illustrate its effect on origin inference.

2.1   Path Exploration of BGP

Path exploration is a state in which a BGP router explores multiple alternative paths during convergence to a new best path. We illustrate an example using Figure 1. In the figure, AS20 to AS70 announces prefixes $p20$ to $p70$. The link between AS40 and AS60 fails and AS40 reacts by sending withdraw messages for $p60$ and $p70$ to its neighbors (#1 in Figure 1). When AS20 first receives this message, it announces to AS10 the path via AS30 as the new best path to reach $p60$ and $p70$, not knowing about the failure (#2). However, shortly after this announcement, AS20 receives a withdraw message from AS30 (#3) where it then announces to AS10 the alternative path via AS50 as the new best path (#4). In some cases, a withdraw message is observed immediately before the announce message due to possible convergence delay or an implementation bug [4]. Now suppose that at some point in time, the failed link is repaired and AS10 eventually receives the same best path observed before the link failure. Table 1 summarizes the AS paths observed for this event. As the table shows several transient paths are likely to be triggered during path exploration and selecting the update with the correct AS path is essential for an accurate origin inference.

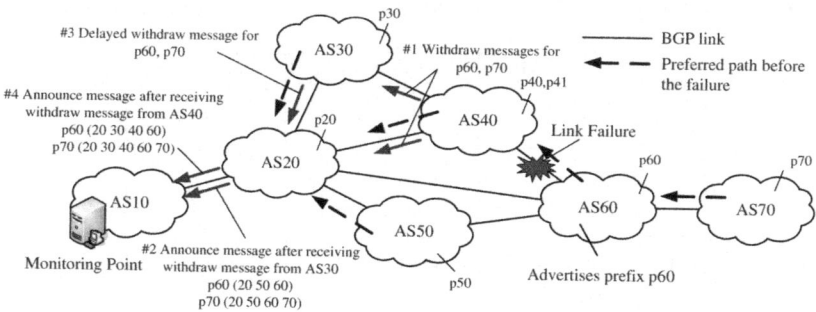

Fig. 1. Passive monitoring of BGP update messages

Table 1. AS path changes for $p70$ observed at the monitoring point. The AS path for $p60$ is the same as $p70$, only the origin is AS60.

Time	Type	AS Path	Possible Explanation
T1	Announce	10 20 40 60 70	Best path before link failure
T2	Announce	10 20 30 40 60 70	Transient path after failure
T3	Withdraw	None	Convergence delay or possible bug
T4	Announce	10 20 50 60 70	New best path after link failure
T5	Announce	10 20 30 40 60 70	Transient path after link repair
T6	Announce	10 20 60 70	Transient path after link repair
T7	Announce	10 20 40 60 70	Best path after link repair

2.2 Effect of Path Exploration on Measurement

Using the above example, we examin the effect of path exploration on origin inference. Table 2 shows the number of prefixes of each inter-AS link extracted from the routing table (Routing Information Base) created at the monitoring point. Each RIB consists of a list of prefixes and their preferred AS paths. We assume that RIB_{T1} represents the initial routing table created before the link failure. As shown in Table 2, this single failure and recovery event causes a variance of one or more prefix at all nine links. If a simple threshold is used to detect only those links that lose all prefixes as emphasized in the table, five links are still left as candidates, where two of the links are detected twice. In the Internet, failure events occur simultaneously and variance is likely to occur much more frequently making origin inference complicated and difficult.

3 Detecting Candidate Origins

In this section, we describe a methodology for detecting candidate origins. The detected candidates are correlated with other links to infer origins in Section 4.

Table 2. The number of prefixes extracted for each link using all update messages

RIB	10,20	20,30	20,40	20,50	20,60	30,40	40,60	50,60	60,70
RIB_{T1}	7	1	4	1	0	0	2	0	1
RIB_{T2}	7	3	2	1	0	2	2	0	1
RIB_{T3}	5	1	2	1	0	0	0	0	0
RIB_{T4}	7	1	2	3	0	0	0	2	1
RIB_{T5}	7	3	2	1	0	2	2	0	1
RIB_{T6}	7	1	2	1	2	0	0	0	1
RIB_{T7}	7	1	4	1	0	0	2	0	1

Table 3. The number of prefixes extracted for each link using routing updates of specific prefixes that regularly use each link

RIB	10,20	20,30	20,40	20,50	20,60	30,40	40,60	50,60	60,70
RIB_{T1}	1	1	2	1	0	0	1	0	1
RIB_{T2}	1	1	2	1	0	0	1	0	1
RIB_{T3}	1	1	2	1	0	0	0	0	0
RIB_{T4}	1	1	2	1	0	0	0	0	1
RIB_{T5}	1	1	2	1	0	0	1	0	1
RIB_{T6}	1	1	2	1	0	0	0	0	1
RIB_{T7}	1	1	2	1	0	0	1	0	1

3.1 Selection of Measurement Prefixes for Each Link

The observation from the previous example suggests that we must avoid unwanted variations that occur during path exploration after link failure and after link recovery. To achieve this, for each link we focus on a set of prefixes that are regularly advertised over the link and from the AS adjacent to the link. Specifically, for link (X,Y), we use prefixes that are advertised from Y regularly through X. Using the dashed lines in Figure 1 as the preferred path of each prefix, Table 3 shows the number of specific prefixes extracted for each inter-AS link. As the table shows, variations only occur at the origin link (40,60) and the edge link (60,70) and not at other links. Note that links (20,60), (30,40) and (50,60) are considered temporary links and variations are no longer measured since none of the prefixes advertised by AS40 and AS60 prefer these links.

To infer preferred paths of prefixes in the Internet, we use the path preference inference scheme based on usage time of paths described in [8]. For example, for n AS paths (except NULL paths = withdrawn) observed for prefix p_i, denoted as $\{path_1^i, path_2^i, ..., path_n^i\}$, we measure the cumulative duration of the usage time of each path, denoted as $\{Tpath_1^i, Tpath_2^i, ..., Tpath_n^i\}$. We then calculate for each $path_j^i$ the usage ratio $Rpath_j^i$ using Equation 1. The path with the highest ratio $Rpath_{pref}^i$ is inferred as the preferred path for p_i.

$$Rpath_j^i = \frac{Tpath_j^i}{\sum_{k=1}^{n} Tpath_k^i} \tag{1}$$

We validate this scheme using BGP data collected at two monitoring points provided by Oregon RouteViews [12] over the month of September 2009. AS22388 (TRANSPAC2) is a high-speed research and education network connecting the Asia-Pacific region with networks in the U.S. AS3356 (LEVEL3) is one of the Tier 1 networks located in the U.S. For both monitoring points, we observed that approximately 55% of the prefixes have one preferred path ($Rpath_{pref} = 1$). These prefixes either only had one path to the monitoring point or remained stable during the entire measurement period. For approximately 97% and 92% of the prefixes, we observed $Rpath_{pref}$ to be very high (over 0.9) for AS22388 and AS3356, respectively. This indicates that for most prefixes, we can infer the preferred path with very high probability. We also found that $Rpath_{pref}$ is lower than 0.5 for less than 1% of the prefixes indicating a low probability for most prefixes to encounter significant changes in policies during a 1-month period.

3.2   Detecting Links as Candidate Origins

Table 3 showed that variations also occurs when path exploration is triggered after the link is repaired. In order to avoid detecting the same link multiple times during path exploration, we limit the detection to only when a routing change is imposed on preferred paths. In Table 3 for example, the number of prefixes at link (40,60) recover at $T5$ and drop again at $T6$, but this second drop is not detected as the path observed at $T5$ is not the preferred path of this prefix. This leaves two links as candidate origins; $T3:(40,60)$ and $T3:(60,70)$.

4   The Origin Inference Scheme

The candidate set of links may include links that are actually not origins. This can occur when the reachability of prefixes are lost due to a failure at a transit link. One approach to cope with this problem is to utilize BGP data collected from multiple monitoring points. For example, if AS60 also served as a monitoring point, stable reachability to $p70$ may be observed during the event. However, such an assumption is not effective unless all ASes work as monitoring points. There is also the question of whether a routing change can be mutually observed at different monitoring points.

Instead we correlate candidate origins with other origins detected over the preferred path and use simple heuristics to infer one candidate as the origin. This is based on our idea that most prefixes have one preferred path and a routing change imposed on this path should indicate a failure or policy change at one of the nodes or links that construct the path. The correlation of candidates is first given window time T to absorb possible delays in the detection of other candidate links due to the propagation delay among updates and prefixes. We summarize the algorithm below.

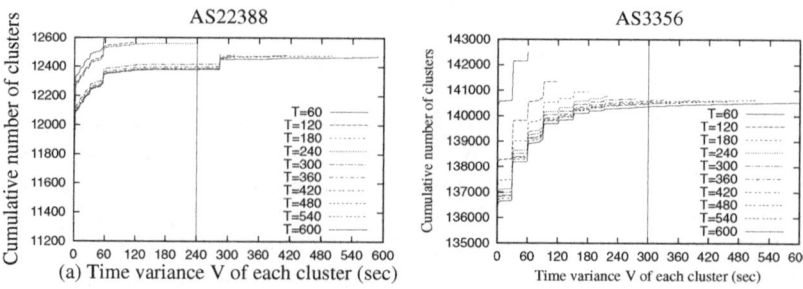

Fig. 2. Distribution of clusters created at different window times for AS22388 and AS3356

1. For each preferred path, cluster candidate origins detected within T seconds from the first detected origin.
2. If the same origin is detected within T seconds, create a new cluster from that origin. This means the link recovered once within T seconds and we consider the second detection to be from a different failure event.
3. For each cluster, infer the link closest to the monitor as the origin.

To find the most relevant window time T, we focus on the convergence delay of the monitoring network. Precisely, we look at the number of clusters created at different intervals of T and measure the time variance V $(T \geq V)$ of the detection times for each cluster. Specifically, for each cluster, we measure the difference in the detection times between the first detected link and the last detected link. If a cluster includes only a single link or includes multiple links with the same detection time, the time variance for these clusters is 0. The distribution of this variance should reflect the actual convergence delay of that network.

Figure 2 shows the number of clusters created at different window times T and the distribution of time variances V for monitoring points at AS22388 and AS3356, respectively. For the value of T, we used 60 seconds to 600 seconds at intervals of 60 seconds. As both figures show, the time variance for a large proportion of the clusters remains at $V = 0$ for all values of T. This indicates that for about 90% and 97% of the events at AS22388 and AS3356, respectively, our scheme can cluster links inferred from the same event with very high accuracy and only a few events require the window time to absorb the convergence delay. In Figure 2, the number of clusters is similar to $T = 240$ for AS22388 and from $T = 300$ for AS3356. This indicates that a possible T that reflects the convergence delay is within these ranges. For the evaluation in the following section, we use $T = 180$ for AS22388 and $T = 300$ for AS3356, where the latter is the convergence delay often referred to in the Internet [7].

What is interesting about our scheme is that we can further leverage our information to infer the time of the failure (not the time of detection) and the time of recovery. The time of failure is defined as the time when the path of a prefix first changes from its preferred path. Conversely, the time of recovery is when the path of a prefix recovers using its preferred path. In our measurement,

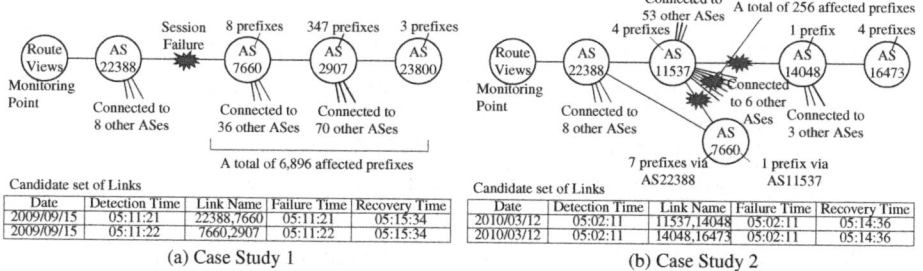

Fig. 3. Case Study: (a)Single core link failure, (b) Multiple link failure

we found cases where the failure time is several minutes before the detection time due to long lasting path exploration.

5 Evaluation

In this section, we discuss the validity of our scheme using Oregon RouteViews data and trouble tickets from several operational networks.

5.1 Evaluation Using Operational Tickets

We evaluate our scheme using operational tickets provided by TRANSPAC2 (AS22388) [13], APAN-JP (AS7660) [14] and Internet2 (AS11537) [15]. Each ticket provides information including the location, the start and end time and the cause of detected failures. For the BGP data, we use Route Views collected from AS22388. Below we describe two case studies in detail and present how our inference scheme inferred origins for each event.

Case Study 1. Tickets at TRANSPAC2 and APAN-JP describe a session failure between the two ASes beginning at 05:10 a.m. to 05:15 a.m. on September 15, 2009 (UTC) due to an exceed in the number prefixes allowed on the link. Figure 3 (a) show the results of our inference using the preferred path of AS23800 as an example. Two candidate links were detected during this period with 1 second difference in detection time. Our heuristics clustered the two links and inferred the link (22388,7660) as the origin. The same origin was also inferred for 402 other preferred paths affecting a total of 6,896 prefixes. Since the inferred origin, the failure and the recovery times all match those reported in the ticket, we confirmed that the origin was accurately inferred by our scheme. We also confirmed that no other tickets were issued nor other candidates were detected for this link during this month. Note that the failure time and the detection time are identical because path exploration was not observed for this event.

Case Study 2. A ticket at Internet2 (AS11537) describes a core router in Chicago being unavailable for several peers starting from 05:00 a.m. to 05:03 a.m. on March 12, 2010 (UTC). The reported cause was a router maintenance. Figure 3 (b) show

Table 4. The number of links inferred as origins with and without our scheme

Monitoring Point	AS22388		AS3356	
Our Scheme	Disabled	Enabled	Disabled	Enabled
Measured Links	2,533	2,092	56,172	42,364
Candidate Links	22,784	9,189	208,391	99,317
Inferred Origins	22,784	6,362	208,391	88,439

the results of our inference. Using the preferred path of AS16473 as an example, we detected two links as candidates having the same detection time and inferred the link (11537,14048) as the origin. From routing changes of other preferred paths, we inferred seven other links connected to AS11537 as origins. Since each link matched the peers described in the ticket, we confirmed that the origin was accurately inferred by our scheme. Note that the link with APAN-JP was detected using the single prefix advertised by AS7660 that preferred the path via AS11537. This demonstrates the capability of our scheme to infer origins for small failures and for simultaneous link failures. Note also that the recovery time is much longer than that reported in the ticket. Since recovery times in tickets are sometimes based on the local downtime between the two routers, we can determine the actual unreachable duration from the monitoring point.

Using 50 tickets issued over several months in 2009 and 2010, we confirmed that origins can be accurately identified for 86% of the tickets. For 6% of the tickets, origins were misinferred due to lack of prefixes (discussed in Section 6). Additionally, for 8% of the tickets that described a scheduled maintenance, no routing updates were observed and thus not detected. Note that tickets that do not generate any routing updates due to a failure event of one of the multiple links between a pair of ASes were excluded from evaluation. Unfortunately, these events cannot be detected from passive measurements.

5.2   Comparing the Number of Inferred Origins

Evaluating the effectiveness of our scheme against existing schemes is difficult since our scheme targets the detection of failures of all sizes. Instead, we compare the number of links that are inferred as origins with and without our scheme (i.e. the original Link-Rank). Table 4 shows the number of origins inferred over the month of September 2009 using AS22388 and AS3356. When our scheme is disabled at AS22388, all 2,533 links observed from updates are targeted for measurement and the number of prefixes carried by these links drops to 0 for 22,784 times. In contrast, when our scheme is enabled, we consider 17% of the links as temporary links and measure routing changes that occur over 83% of the links. The number of candidate links is 60% less and the number of origins inferred is 72% less than those detected without our scheme. This implies the importance of analyzing the routing status of each prefix during path exploration and link recovery. The results showed a similar trend for AS3356.

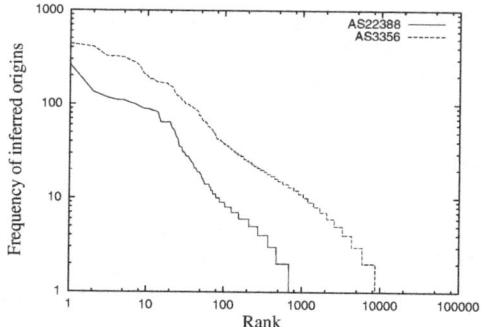

Fig. 4. Number of times a link is inferred as an origin at AS22388 and AS3356

6   Discussion

A routing change can occur not only from link failures, but also from intra-AS failures and from changes in routing policies. Although ideally we should be able to distinguish between them, we believe that inferring the adjacent link can still help operators diagnose the reachability issues. On the other hand, our scheme may misinfer origins when no prefix is extracted at transit links. In our evaluation, we identified this percentage to be 6.5% and 2.9% for AS22388 and AS3356, respectively. For these links, we must use prefixes advertised by other ASes for measuring stability, which is work to be addressed in the future.

Nonetheless, we believe our scheme can sufficiently identify origins for most events. Figure 4 shows the frequency of links inferred as origins for AS22388 and AS3356. As the figure shows, a small number of links is repeatedly inferred. This indicates the possibility of these links or the adjacent nodes being very unstable. The figure shows a Zipf-like distribution, where 86% to 95% of all failures are located in 20% of all links. This result matches many of the previous studies on stability of prefixes which found that a large number of routing updates were from routing changes of a very small number of prefixes [16]. On further analysis, we discovered that 87% to 89% of these links are edge links. While this indicates that the core transit links are much more stable than the edge links, some of the links were transit links for hundreds of prefixes.

7   Conclusion and Future Work

In this paper, we presented a methodology for sufficiently inferring the origin of routing changes observed in the Internet. We studied the negative effect of path exploration on origin inference of small failure events. We then presented a measurement scheme that focuses on the stability of some prefixes and preferred paths to identify origins. This has allowed us to infer the origin of small failure events and for the first time to further infer the time of failure and the time of recovery. Evaluation using BGP data showed that the number of origins inferred using our scheme is 72% less than those detected without our scheme.

Our future work includes finding the most relevant duration for measuring the preferred path of prefixes. We also plan to evaluate our scheme using BGP data from multiple monitoring points.

Acknowledgment

The authors would like to thank Route Views for providing the BGP data, and the NOC teams for providing operational tickets publically available. The authors are also thankful to the anonymous reviewers for their insightful comments.

References

1. Teixeira, R., Rexford, J.: A Measurement Framework for Pin-Pointing Routing Changes. In: Proceedings of ACM SIGCOMM Workshop on Network Troubleshooting (August 2004)
2. Xu, K., Chandrashekar, J., Zhang, Z.L.: A First Step Toward Understanding Interdomain Routing Dynamics. In: ACM SIGCOMM MineNet Workshop (August 2005)
3. Rekhter, Y., Li, T., Hares, S.: A Border Gateway Protocol 4 (BGP-4), RFC 4271 (January 2006)
4. Labovitz, C., Malan, G., Jahanian, F.: Internet Routing Instability. In: Proceedings of ACM SIGCOMM (September 1997)
5. Chang, D., Govindan, R., Heidemann, J.: The Temporal and Topological Characteristics of BGP Path Changes. In: Proceedings of IEEE ICNP (November 2003)
6. FeldMann, A., Maennel, O., Mao, Z.M., Berger, A., Maggs, B.: Locating Internet Routing Instabilities. In: Proceedings of ACM SIGCOMM (September 2004)
7. Mao, Z., Bush, R., Griffin, T., Roughan, M.: BGP Beacons, In. In: Proceedings of the 3rd ACM SIGCOMM Conference on Internet Measurement, pp. 1–14 (October 2003)
8. Oliveira, R., Zhang, B., Pei, D., Zhang, L.: Quantifying Path Exploration in the Internet. IEEE/ACM Transactions on Networking 17(2), 445–458 (2009)
9. Lad, M., Oliveira, R., Massey, D., Zhang, L.: Inferring the Origin of Routing Changes using Link Weights. In: Proceedings of IEEE ICNP (October 2007)
10. Campisano, A., Cittadini, L., Di Battista, G., Refice, T., Sasso, C.: Tracking Back the Root Cause of a Path Change in Interdomain Routing. In: Proceedings of IEEE/IFIP NOMS (April 2008)
11. Lad, M., Massey, D., Zhang, L.: Visualizing Internet Routing Changes. IEEE Transactions on Visualization and Computer Graphics, 1450–1460 (November/December 2006)
12. Route Views Project (March 2010), http://www.routeviews.org/
13. TRANSPAC2 NOC (March 2010), http://noc.transpac.org/
14. APAN-JP NOC (March 2010), http://www.jp.apan.net/NOC/
15. Internet2 NOC (March 2010), http://noc.net.internet2.edu/
16. Oliveira, R., Izhak-Ratzin, R., Zhang, B., Zhang, L.: Measurement of Highly Active Prefixes in BGP. In: Proceedings of IEEE GLOBECOM (December 2005)

A Comparative Study of Handheld and Non-handheld Traffic in Campus Wi-Fi Networks

Aaron Gember, Ashok Anand, and Aditya Akella

University of Wisconsin-Madison
{agember,ashok,akella}@cs.wisc.edu

Abstract. Handheld devices such as smartphones have become a major platform for accessing Internet services. The small, mobile nature of these devices results in a unique mix of network usage. Other studies have used Wi-Fi and 3G wireless traces to analyze session, mobility, and performance characteristics for handheld devices. We complement these studies through our unique study of the differences in the content and flow characteristics of handheld versus non-handheld traffic. We analyze packet traces from two separate campus wireless networks, with 3 days of traffic for 32,278 unique devices. Trends for handhelds include low UDP usage, high volumes of HTTP traffic, and a greater proportion of video traffic. Our observations can inform network management and mobile system design.

1 Introduction

Handheld devices—smartphones, portable music players, etc.—are quickly augmenting, and sometimes even replacing, laptops as the computing and Internet perusal platform of choice for users on the go. A 2009 EDUCAUSE study of technology on college campuses found 51% of undergraduates own an Internet-capable handheld and 12% plan to purchase one within the next 12 months [15]. A PEW study comparing 2007 and 2009 wireless Internet usage found a 73% increase in the rate Americans went online with their handhelds [10]. While the number of non-handheld portables, e.g. laptops, is also growing, usage of handheld devices is growing at a much faster pace.

In this paper, we seek to understand *how Wi-Fi traffic from handheld devices differs from non-handheld wireless clients, and what happens when handhelds override campus Wi-Fi networks*. Although many handheld users have cellular data plans, 802.11 Wi-Fi is still a preferred Internet access mechanism, when available, because of its higher bandwidth, lower latency, and lower energy usage. For our study, we use network traffic traces gathered from two independently-managed multi-AP campus wireless networks over a 3 day period. The traces have 32,278 unique clients, with 15% being handhelds.

We conduct an in-depth study of the *content and flow properties* of Wi-Fi handheld traffic. We examine transport and application protocols used, flow lengths and durations, and properties of content perused, e.g. prevalence of multimedia content and its nature and similarity in the content accessed by different users. We ignore low-level transmission, connectivity, and mobility issues as these have already been well studied [3,8,12]. To the best of our knowledge, these aspects of the differences between handhelds and non-handhelds have not been considered by prior studies. We believe that our

N. Spring and G. Riley (Eds.): PAM 2011, LNCS 6579, pp. 173–183, 2011.

examination of these issues is useful in informing future research on optimizing the performance of handheld devices operating in Wi-Fi networks. Specifically, our observations can help determine whether adopting prior approaches designed for non-handheld devices, such as those for caching, content distribution and battery life savings, are applicable or not. Our study can also inform management practices for campus networks, e.g., network-wide Class-of-Service definitions for Multimedia traffic.

Compared to non-handheld wireless users, handheld users access a different mix of Internet services and content. Applications like web browsers and email clients are used on both types of devices, but content providers tailor content differently based on device type. Furthermore, the interface on handhelds in itself places limitations on the range of Internet-based and local network-based services users can access. Thus, the network traffic of handhelds is likely to differ in several crucial respects from non-handheld devices. The goal of this paper is to quantify the extent of these differences and identify the sources of the differences, where possible.

We present a broad collection of measurement insights. Our key findings are as follows. The majority of handheld traffic (97%) is web, with small amounts of email traffic. In contrast, 82% of non-handheld traffic is web, with miscellaneous UDP traffic (14%) accounting for most of the remaining share. Handhelds tend to have smaller TCP flows and a narrower range of flow durations. However, both types of devices have similar TCP flow rates, with a median rate of 0.8 Mbps. Looking in-depth at HTTP traffic, we observe that handhelds access content from a narrower range of hosts. However, we see equivalent amounts of similarity in content accessed by the same user for both device types. The top content type for handhelds is video, accounting for 40% of handheld traffic verses 17% for non-handhelds. Streaming video flows represent the largest, fastest, and highest throughput flows of all handheld flows.

2   Methodology

We collect and analyze data from two independently-managed campus wireless networks (Net1 and Net2). Full packet traces were captured from about 1,920 APs in Net1 over a period of 3 days during April 2010, yielding 8 TB worth of data. From Net2, full packet traces were captured from 23 APs for a period of 3 days in June 2010, yielding 50 GB worth of data. As an artifact of our collection method, we do not include traffic sent between wireless clients. However, we expect inter-client traffic is rare.

The packet traces contain data from all wireless clients connected to the network—laptops, smartphones, and other devices. Since we focus on the differences between handheld and non-handheld devices, we need to differentiate traffic based on device type. We rely on user-agent strings in HTTP packets as the primary method for differentiation. We identify handheld user-agents using a keyword list based on common knowledge and published lists [18].[1] Organizationally Unique Identifiers (OUIs) contained within device MAC addresses are used to confirm our device classifications. For

---

[1] **Handheld keywords:** Android, ARCHOS, BlackBerry, CUPCAKE, FacebookTouch, iPad, iPhone, iPod, Kindle, LG, Links, Linux armv6l, Linux armv7l, Maemo, Minimo, Mobile Safari, Nokia, Opera Mini, Opera Mobi, PalmSource, PlayStation, SAMSUNG, Symbian, SymbOS, webOS, Windows CE, Windows Mobile, Zaurus. See [7] for non-handheld keywords.

the devices that do not send any HTTP packets, we use the OUIs of already classified devices to attempt classification based on OUI. Some devices (14%) remain uncategorized because their user-agent strings contain keywords associated with both types of devices, or they send no HTTP traffic and their OUI is registered to a manufacturer that makes both types of devices; we exclude these devices from our analysis.

Over the 3 day capture periods, 32,166 unique clients connect to Net1 and 112 clients connect to Net2. Table 1 lists the number of clients of each type present in the trace data. Non-handheld devices account for the majority of clients in both networks. However, network admins provided anecdotal evidence that handhelds are much more prevalent than in the past, and industry and campus studies show the number of handhelds is expected to continue increasing [15]. We see handhelds from 7 primary vendors, with Apple iPods, iPhones, and iPads accounting for over two-thirds of all handhelds.

Table 1. Client counts by device type

Device Type	Net1	Net2
Handheld	5060	9
Non-handheld	22485	90
Unknown	4621	13
Total	32166	112

Table 2. Protocol usage (% of packets)

Protocol	Net1		Net2	
	Handheld	Non-hand	Handheld	Non-hand
UDP	5.9%	25.7%	4.5%	18.4%
TCP	92.0%	74.0%	93.0%	81.4%
IPsec	0.3%	0.05%	–	0.05%
Other	1.8%	0.35%	2.5%	0.15%

3 Protocols and Services

The protocols and services used by devices impact the performance of both the device and the enterprise wired and wireless networks. Different protocols and services respond differently to bandwidth limitations and congestion and contribute flows of varying sizes, durations, and frequencies to the overall traffic mix. Protocol mix also tells operators the mechanisms they must put in place to secure and monitor their networks.

3.1 Protocols

Network and Transport Protocols: At the highest level, we categorize traffic based on network and transport layer protocols (Table 2). As expected, the majority of traffic is TCP or UDP; the remaining traffic is IPSec (encrypted IP traffic) or network control traffic (ICMP, ARP, etc.). A major difference in protocol usage between the two types of devices is the amount of UDP traffic. Over 4x as many non-handheld packets are UDP compared to handhelds. In the presence of congestion, handhelds will use a fairer-share of bandwidth, versus non-handhelds which use more congestion-unaware UDP.

Application Protocols: We identify application protocols using Bro [13]. Table 3 shows the percentage of traffic in bytes for each category of application protocols. Web protocols account for the largest volume of traffic for both handheld (97% on Net1) and non-handheld (82% on Net1) devices. Almost one-third of Net2 handheld web traffic is HTTPS (versus 3% for Net1), but this is an artifact of a small sample size and a single large connection from one handheld. Email protocols are the second most popular application but account for less than 2% of traffic for both device types. We believe clients actually generate more email traffic than this, as shown by Falaki et. al for handhelds [6];

Table 3. Application protocol usage by percent of bytes ($\prec$ *less than 0.01%, – none*)

Category	Protocols	Net1		Net2	
		Handheld	Non-hand	Handheld	Non-hand
Web	HTTP, HTTPS	97.0%	82.5%	91.1%	72.2%
Email	IMAP4, POP3, SMTP	1.51%	0.5%	–	0.04%
Chat	IRC	$\prec$	$\prec$	–	–
Remote	SSH, FTP	$\prec$	$\prec$	–	0.05%
Enterprise Services	IPP, LPD, NFS, SMB, LDAP, SQL	$\prec$	0.05%	–	0.3%
Management	DNS, NetBIOS, NTP, SNMP	0.2%	0.34%	1.52%	0.12%
Other TCP	*Unknown*	0.2%	2.9%	5.7%	8.7%
Other UDP	*Unknown*	1.0%	13.7%	1.7%	18.1%

we attribute the low usage of email protocols to the common usage of web-based email and the potential for handhelds to simultaneously use 3G and Wi-Fi. Overall, our protocol usage observations are consistent with other studies [8].

Bro's dynamic protocol detection can not identify the majority of UDP traffic for non-handhelds. More than 90% of the unidentified UDP traffic is large flows, from 1 MB to 20 MB in size. While we don't know the exact nature of this traffic, we suspect that a majority of this traffic is likely from streaming media (e.g., Internet Radio).

As handheld usage in Wi-Fi networks continues to grow, HTTP traffic will become an increasingly dominant share of the traffic mix. Admins should consider deploying network middleboxes focused on HTTP traffic, e.g. in-network security scanners or web proxies, to better serve handheld security needs without impacting device efficiency.

3.2 TCP Flow Characteristics

We compare the TCP flow characteristics of handheld and non-handheld traffic to determine *if* and *how* flows differ between the device types. We look at the flow size, duration, and rate for the downlink half of TCP connections—data flowing from remote host to the wireless client—since the majority of data flows in this direction. Flows which do not end with a *FIN* or *RESET* are excluded. In all cases, the distributions for both Net1 and Net2 are equivalent; we omit the Net2 distributions for brevity.

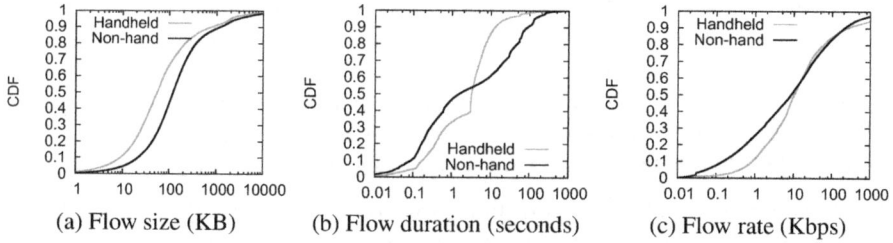

(a) Flow size (KB)   (b) Flow duration (seconds)   (c) Flow rate (Kbps)

Fig. 1. CDFs of TCP flow properties (Net1)

We observe that handhelds tend to have smaller flow sizes than non-handhelds. Figure 1a shows the median handheld flow size is 50 KB, versus 100 KB for non-handhelds. At the lower tail, there are fewer small flows for non-handhelds than handhelds; at the upper tail, the maximum flow size is larger for non-handhelds (2 GB) than handhelds (630 MB). The smaller handheld flow sizes are expected, as many content providers serve simpler or compressed content to mobile devices.

Handhelds and non-handhelds also differ in their distribution of flow duration. Figure 1b shows the median flow duration is approximately the same for both device types, but handhelds have a narrower range of flow durations. The middle 80% of handheld flows are 250ms to 15s long, compared to a range of 100ms to 75s for non-handhelds. The lack of long handheld flows can be attributed to typically short usage sessions [5]. We also look at flow durations for a few specific applications (full data in [7]). On average, web flows are 5x shorter for handhelds, which we suspect is caused by handhelds being served simplified versions of many web pages. For email traffic, receiving protocols (IMAP, POP) have shorter average flows on non-handhelds, while the sending protocol (SMTP) has shorter flows on handhelds. We hypothesize the discrepancy in SMTP is caused by a higher likelihood of non-handheld users including attachments.

Downlink flow rates are shown in Figure 1c. Both device types have the same median rate of 10 Kbps, but only 10% of handheld flows are slower than 1 Kbps compared to 30% of non-handheld flows. Other factors associated with flow rate are consistent across both device types: (i) the average round trip time for 90% of TCP flows is less than 100 ms; (ii) only 4% of flows have one or more retransmissions due to retransmission time out, and 1% of flows have one or more retransmissions due to fast retransmit. Comparing duration and size of flows (not shown), we observe for both device types that small flows tend to have long durations, while large flows tend to have short durations.

4 Web Traffic

Web traffic accounts for almost all handheld data (97%) and a large fraction of non-handheld data (82%). HTTP is used so commonly because of its wide interoperability and support for many types of content. Web usage differs between device types because of differences in the way individuals use these devices. We see variation in (i) the range and type of hosts accessed and (ii) the type and length of content. We also observe that 82% of handheld HTTP traffic is consumed by non-browser applications, compared to 10% of non-handheld. Most notably, we see a higher usage of HTTP-based streaming media services on handhelds: video accounts for 42% of handheld HTTP content, versus only 23% for non-handhelds. Our analysis excludes partial HTTP streams (due to improper reassembly) and all data from the Net2 traces (due to anonymity concerns).

4.1 Hosts

HTTP hostnames, in combination with the type of content they provide, give a rough understanding of the types of services accessed by clients. Table 4 lists the top HTTP hosts based on the size (content-length) of the data served to the devices. We observe that handhelds access more multimedia content (by volume) than non-handhelds. Over 35% of handheld HTTP content originates from googlevideo.com, followed by 18% originating from pandora.com. Multimedia-type content is also the most frequent for eight of the top ten handheld hosts. In total, the top 10 handheld hosts account for 74% of handheld data, while the top 10 non-handheld hosts account for 42% of non-handheld data. These percentages indicate a much greater diversity in hosts for non-handheld devices. In addition, non-handheld devices are more likely to receive content from hosts providing more than text or multimedia content. For example, a Microsoft site hosting application downloads, `dlservice.microsoft.com`, appears in the top non-handheld hosts with *application/octet-stream* as the primary content type.

We also look at the top hosts based on number of HTTP requests (listed in [7]). The top 10 handheld hosts account for 30% of handheld HTTP requests, compared to 32% for non-handhelds. Also, there is a greater diversity of services in the top hosts by requests: social networking, streaming media, advertising, search, and news. In summary, both device types have a great diversity in the number of hosts they request data from, but handhelds receive most of their data (by volume) from a much smaller set of hosts.

4.2 Content Type and Length

The type of HTTP content accessed by devices further identifies the services used and highlights differences in traffic characteristics. We observe the largest volume of handheld content is video (42%), while images are the top type for non-handhelds (29%) (full data in [7]). Below, we discuss each of the MIME types in detail.

Table 4. Top HTTP hosts by response size (Net1)

(a) Handheld

Bytes	Host	Top Content Types[3]
35.48%	googlevideo.com	v/mp4
18.12%	pandora.com	p/octet-stream, i/jpg
10.57%	phobos.apple.com	t/plain, i/jpg, v/mp4
2.45%	fbcdn.net	i/jpg, t/javascript, i/png
2.43%	vo.llnwd.net	v/mp4, a/mpeg
1.23%	m.nbc.com	v/mp4, i/jpg, t/javascript
1.17%	espn.go.com	t/plain, t/html, i/jpg
1.16%	video.ted.com	v/mp4
0.82%	gdata.youtube.com	t/atom+xml
0.64%	s3.amazonaws.com	a/3gpp, i/jpg, i/png

(b) Non-handheld

Bytes	Host	Top Content Types[3]
11.45%	c.youtube.com	v/flv, v/mp4
7.00%	pandora.com	p/octet-stream, i/jpg, a/mpeg
6.63%	fbcdn.net	i/jpg, i/png, t/javascript
4.63%	dlservice.microsoft.com	p/octet-stream
2.89%	vo.llnwd.net	v/wmv, a/mp4
2.80%	stileproject.com	p/octet-stream, i/jpg, v/mp4
2.53%	com.edgesuite.net	v/wmv, a/wma, p/octet-stream
1.69%	phobos.apple.com	t/plain, a/mp4, i/png
1.51%	www.facebook.com	t/html, t/javascript
0.94%	cdn.turner.com	t/javascript, i/jpg, v/flv

Application content is data associated with specific applications, e.g. documents, compressed files, or streaming media. For both device types, *octet-stream*—a simple binary data stream—is the most common subtype, accounting for 86% of handheld and 51% of non-handheld *application* type data. The average *octet-stream* is 713 KB for handhelds ($\sigma = 882$ KB) and 189 KB for non-handhelds ($\sigma = 658$ KB). The second most common *application* subtype is RSS feeds for handhelds and Shockwave Flash for non-handhelds. No handhelds access Shockwave Flash content because these devices did not support Flash until very recently [1]. Over 185 different *application* subtypes are accessed by non-handhelds compared to only 58 subtypes for handhelds. This variety results from the greater diversity of applications running on non-handheld devices.

The content for regular web browsing falls mostly into the *image* and *text* content types. Three *image* subtypes—*gif*, *jpg*, and *png*—make up the majority of image content, with JPG images being the largest (average of 13 KB for handhelds and 11 KB for

---

[3] We abbreviate the MIME content types: v = video, a = audio, i = image, t = text, p = application.

non-handhelds). HTML, CSS, JavaScript and XML are used for the web page itself. For both device types these *text* subtypes average 3-7 KB in length. Over two-thirds of the *text* content received by handhelds is *plain* text. This content is destined for non-browser applications retrieving data from a web service, e.g. a sports scores application.

The remaining MIME content types are multimedia traffic, namely *audio* and *video*. Multimedia accounts for 46% of handheld content and 29% of non-handheld content. In particular, *video* accounts for 93% of multimedia traffic in the handheld case and 80% in the non-handheld case. We examine video traffic in greater detail next.

4.3   Streaming Video

Streaming video is a major source of traffic for handheld devices. Video content accounts for 40% of all handheld traffic, compared to only 17% of all non-handheld traffic. We compare the flow characteristics of handheld streaming video, non-handheld video, and all handheld flows to understand the differences in handheld streaming media.

As expected, handheld video flows are large compared to overall handheld traffic: 80% of video flows are > 50 KB in size, whereas 50 KB is the median among all handheld flows (Figure 2a). Nearly 20% of handheld video flows are > 1 MB in size, with a 400 KB median. Non-handheld video flows are even larger, with a 3 MB median.

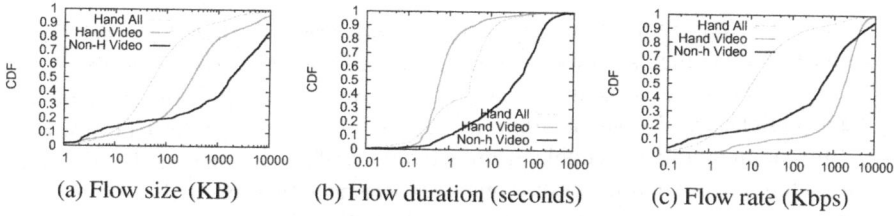

(a) Flow size (KB)   (b) Flow duration (seconds)   (c) Flow rate (Kbps)

Fig. 2. CDFs of video flow properties

Interestingly, handheld video flows appear to be of short duration. Figure 2b shows 80% of handheld video flows are less than 1 second in duration, with a median of 0.5 seconds. The median durations for all handheld flows and non-handheld video flows are significantly higher, at 5 and 50 seconds, respectively. Based on the short duration of handheld video flows, we expect high throughput rates. Figure 2c shows 80% of video flows have a rate faster than 0.8 Mbps, with a median of 2 Mbps. In contrast, the median flow rate for all handheld flows and non-handheld video flows is roughly 0.6 Mbps.

Overall, handheld video flows are long in size (although not as long as non-handheld video flows), significantly short in duration, and achieve high end-to-end throughputs which are comparable, if not slightly higher than non-handheld video flows. As handheld usage continues increasing, administrators should include Quality of Service mechanisms in their networks to support the video throughputs handhelds expect.

Video streamed to handheld devices differs from video streamed to non-handheld devices because of differences in decoding capabilities. Most streaming video services use Flash, but a lack of Flash support on handhelds results in MPEG 4 encoded content being served to them instead. In our traces, *mp4* (MPEG 4) is the top video type for handhelds and *flv* (Flash video) is the top type for non-handhelds. Video streaming sites like YouTube serve two versions: one encoded as mp4 and the other encoded as flv.

We watch the same 3 minute video [2] from YouTube on both an Android HTC Dream smartphone and a laptop to measure the differences in video content served to the two different devices. On the phone we use the standalone YouTube application and on the laptop we use Mozilla Firefox. The handheld device receives 7362 KB `video/mp4`; the non-handheld device receives 11792 KB `video/flv`. Both versions have the same resolution of 320 x 240, but different encoding rates of 200 kbps and 231 kbps, for *mp4* and *flv* respectively. The audio is encoded at 128 Kbps for the *mp4* and 64 Kbps for the *flv*. The higher quality video is the *flv* and the higher quality audio is the *mp4*, but both versions are closely comparable. The main difference in the handheld content is a smaller size—about 62% of the size of the non-handheld version.

The median size of both handheld (316 KB) and non-handheld (1.7 MB) video flows are relatively small compared to the size of the sample video. In many cases, we observe videos being streamed over multiple sequential connections—due to connection resets—resulting in a few small flows for each video. However, by comparing the combined size of these multiple flows to the size of the actual video, we observe that the size gap also results from handheld users watching only a fraction of most videos.

5   Content Similarity

In this section, we examine the similarity in the content perused by handhelds and compare it against non-handhelds. §4 focused on the *type* of content present in traffic; here we focus on the *bytes* that makeup the conent. We evaluate the potential benefits of deploying a "chunk-based" content similarity supression system, e.g. SET [14] or EndRE [4]. Eliminating duplicate chunks from network tranfsers by serving them from a local cache can improve the transfer throughput experienced by users and can help save mobile battery life by reducing network transmissions. Chunk-based schemes are more effective than object-based schemes, such as Web caches, as they are known to identify more duplicates, e.g., sub-object duplicates, uncacheable content, etc. Thus, our analysis places an upper bound on the benefits of using caching and similarity suppression.

We identify two types of similarity: that found in content accessed by the same device ("intra-user"), and that found in content accessed by a different devices ("inter-user"). We divide packet payloads into chunks (32B to 64B in size) using value sampling [16]; then we determine if the chunks have appeared in an earlier access. Unless specified, we assume 2GB of chunks are stored across all users, as done previously [4].

In Figure 3a, we show the extent of intra- and inter-user content similarity observed over every 1 million packets (0.8-2GB) worth of handheld and non-handheld traffic. We measure average redundancy as the ratio of similar bytes to all bytes in 1 million-packet trace subsets. First, we observe a greater amount of similarity in handhelds than in non-handhelds. Second, similarity due to inter-user matches is quite small: less than 2% for > 95% of both handheld and non-handheld trace subsets. Third, we observe that in more than 40% of the non-handheld trace subsets, and more than 70% of the handheld trace subsets, $\geq 8\%$ of the similar bytes are due to intra-user matches. In some cases, we observed up to 20-25% intra-user similarity for both device types. Finally, the extent of intra-user similarity is greater for handhelds than non-handhelds.

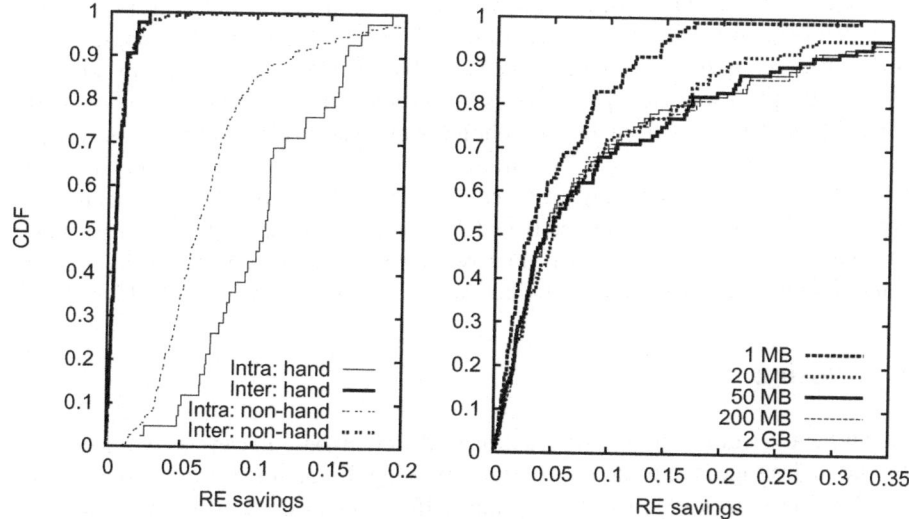

(a) Average intrauser and interuser redundancy across multiple traces

(b) Intrauser redundancy across top 100 (by bytes) handhelds for varying dictionary sizes

Fig. 3. CDFs of redundancy

Given that the dominant fraction of similar bytes belonged to intra-user traffic, we further delve intro intra-user similarity. We explore the efficacy of deploying per device caches and the cache size configuration issues therein. We split the handheld traffic on a per device basis and study the effect of different dictionary sizes on amount of similarity identified per device. Figure 3b shows the CDF of similarity across the top 100 devices by traffic volume for different dictionary sizes. Almost 80% of users have less than 20% similarity with their own traffic. However, for certain users, the similarity proportion was much higher (more than 50%). Second, we observe that most of the similarities can be identified by using only 50 MB caches—larger caches exhibit diminishing returns. As handheld usage grows, admins should consider deploying per-device caching mechanisms to improve throughput and handheld energy savings.

6   Related Work

Multiple measurement studies have analyzed traffic patterns in campus wireless network. Hederson et. al identify session and application trends at Dartmouth College and observe how usage evolved four years later [8]. Wireless AP workloads at Darthmouth are compared to the University of North Carolina by Hernandez-Campos and Papadopouli [9]. Lastly, McNett and Voelker study the wireless access and mobility patterns of students using PDAs at UCSD [12]. While all of these studies focus on campus wireless networks, none explore in detail the applications used by handheld users and the traffic characteristics thereof. In addition, mobile device usage is a rapidly changing field and trends observed five years ago are different than today's usage.

More recent studies have focused on mobile device usage in public Wi-Fi, home Wi-Fi and 3G networks. Application, session, and mobility trends in the Google Wi-Fi network in Mountain View, CA were studied in 2008 [3]. The connections between geo-location and usage of specific types of web services was studied in an urban 3G network in 2009 [17]. In 2010, logs from 43 smartphones were analyzed to find commonly used application ports and properties of TCP transfers over a combination of 3G and Wi-Fi networks [6]. A second 2010 study analyzes the protocol usage and HTTP content size and types of handheld traffic extracted from DSL traces [11]. The 2010 studies are most similar to our work, but one focuses primarily on 3G traffic and neither looks in-depth at the multimedia content served to handhelds nor the redundancy in handheld traffic.

7   Conclusion

Handhelds have become a significant fraction of the client base in campus wireless networks, and their usage is expected to continue growing. Using traces from two separate multi-AP wireless networks, we identify key differences in the Wi-Fi content access and flow-level traffic characteristics of handheld and non-handheld devices. Our findings have potential implications for network management and mobile system design:

- 97% of handheld traffic is HTTP, allowing in-network security scanners to examine a single application protocol and provide significant security benefits for handhelds.
- Over twice as much handheld traffic is video, compared to non-handhelds, making Quality of Service mechanisms an important inclusion in network design.
- Lower HTTP host diversity and significant intra-user content similarity in handheld traffic, indicates per-device redundancy elimination systems can be beneficial.
- The smaller range of TCP handheld flow durations and the lower percentage of handheld flows with rates < 1 Kbps should be taken into account when designing wireless power save mechanisms for handhelds.

Network admins and mobile designers should take these observations into account when considering design and performance. The differences between handheld and non-handheld traffic will increasingly impact Wi-Fi networks as handheld usage grows.

References

1. Adobe announces availability of flash player 10.1 for mobile,
   http://www.adobe.com/aboutadobe/pressroom/pressreleases/201006/06222010FlashPlayerAvailability.html
2. Christmas lights gone wild, http://www.youtube.com/watch?v=rmgf60CI_ks
3. Afanasyev, M., Chen, T., Voelker, G.M., Snoeren, A.C.: Analysis of a mixed-use urban wifi network: when metropolitan becomes neapolitan. In: IMC, pp. 85–98 (2008)
4. Aggarwal, B., Akella, A., Anand, A., Chitnis, P., Muthukrishnan, C., Nair, A., Ramjee, R., Varghese, G.: EndRE: An End-System Redundancy Elimination Service for Enterprises. In: NSDI (2010)
5. Falaki, H., Mahajan, R., Kandula, S., Lymberopoulos, D., Govindan, R., Estrin, D.: Diversity in Smartphone Usage. In: MobiSys (2010)

6. Falaki, H., Lymberopoulous, D., Mahajan, R., Kandula, S., Estrin, D.: A first look at traffic on smartphones. In: IMC (2010)
7. Gember, A., Anand, A., Akella, A.: Handheld vs. non-handheld traffic: Implications for campus wifi networks. Tech. rep., University of Wisconsin-Madison (2010)
8. Henderson, T., Kotz, D., Abyzov, I.: The changing usage of a mature campus-wide wireless network. Comput. Netw. 52(14), 2690–2712 (2008)
9. Hernandez-Campos, F., Papadopouli, M.: A comparative measurement study the workload of wireless access points in campus networks. In: IEEE International Symposium on Personal, Indoor and Mobile Radio Communications, vol. 3, pp. 1776–1780 (September 2005)
10. Horrigan, J.: Wireless internet use. Pew Internet & American Life Project (July 2009)
11. Maier, G., Schneider, F., Feldmann, A.: A first look at mobile hand-held device traffic. In: Krishnamurthy, A., Plattner, B. (eds.) PAM 2010. LNCS, vol. 6032, pp. 161–170. Springer, Heidelberg (2010)
12. McNett, M., Voelker, G.M.: Access and mobility of wireless pda users. SIGMOBILE Mob. Comput. Commun. Rev. 9(2), 40–55 (2005)
13. Paxson, V.: Bro: a system for detecting network intruders in real-time. In: USENIX Security Symposium, pp. 3–3. USENIX Association, Berkeley (1998)
14. Pucha, H., Andersen, D.G., Kaminsky, M.: Exploiting similarity for multi-source downloads using file handprints. In: NSDI (2007)
15. Smith, S., Salaway, G., Caruso, J.: The ECAR Study of Undergraduate Students and Information Technology. EDUCAUSE Center for Applied Research (2009)
16. Tolia, N., Kaminsky, M., Andersen, D.G., Patil, S.: An architecture for Internet data transfer. In: NSDI (2006)
17. Trestian, I., Ranjan, S., Kuzmanovic, A., Nucci, A.: Measuring serendipity: connecting people, locations and interests in a mobile 3g network. In: IMC, pp. 267–279 (2009)
18. ZyTrax: Mobile browser id strings,
   `http://zytrax.com/tech/web/mobile_ids.html`

Unveiling the BitTorrent Performance in Mobile WiMAX Networks

Xiaofei Wang, Seungbae Kim, Ted "Taekyoung" Kwon,
Hyun-chul Kim, and Yanghee Choi

School of Computer Science and Engineering,
Seoul National University, Seoul, Korea
{dobby,sbkim,hkim}@mmlab.snu.ac.kr, {tkkwon,yhchoi}@snu.ac.kr

Abstract. As mobile Internet environments are becoming widespread,
how to revamp peer-to-peer (P2P) operations for mobile hosts is gaining
more attention. In this paper, we carry out empirical measurement of
BitTorrent users in a commercial WiMAX network. We investigate how
handovers in WiMAX networks impact the BitTorrent performance, how
BitTorrent peers perform from the aspects of connectivity, stability and
capability, and how the BitTorrent protocol behaves depending on user
mobility. We observe that the drawbacks of BitTorrent for mobile users
are characterized by poor connectivity among peers, short download session times, small download throughput, negligible upload contributions,
and high signaling overhead.

Keywords: Mobile WiMAX, BitTorrent, Measurement.

1 Introduction

Over the past decade, peer-to-peer (P2P) file sharing applications have generated
dominant Internet traffic. Also, more and more users are accessing the Internet
in mobile environments due to the advances of portable devices and the increase
of wireless link capacity. These trends will lead to the increasing usage of P2P
applications in mobile networks; mobile P2P traffic is expected to be about 277
petabytes per month, 10% of the world's mobile Internet traffic by 2014 [1].

WiMAX and 3GPP LTE networks are gaining momentum as candidates for
the next generation mobile networks, aiming to provide broadband link bandwidth and mobility support. However, mobile users in these networks will experience link quality fluctuations and handovers. Therefore, mobile P2P applications
should address the following drawbacks: substantial link dynamics due to fading, disruptions during handovers, and the imbalance of link conditions between
mobile and wireline users.

Current P2P applications are however designed by assuming wireline hosts
that avail themselves of high and stable link bandwidth. Therefore measurement
and analysis of how the current P2P protocols behave in mobile environments

N. Spring and G. Riley (Eds.): PAM 2011, LNCS 6579, pp. 184–193, 2011.
© Springer-Verlag Berlin Heidelberg 2011

can be a foundation for new mobile P2P protocol designs, which motivates our measurement study of BitTorrent in mobile WiMAX networks.

Even though numerous service-oriented measurement studies, e.g., [2][3][4][5], have been carried out in real WiMAX, no work has focused on measurement of the P2P performance in WiMAX. There have been a few studies on how to design proper protocols for wireless/mobile P2P services without measurements. Huang et al. [6] proposed a new hierarchical P2P scheme that seeks to cluster nearby peers considering their network prefixes. They carry out simulations with WiFi-connected peers, without considering mobility. Wu et al. [7] designed a network architecture for a mobile P2P network consisting of ships in maritime environments. They leverage flooding to find a file among ships, which is not efficient in mobile P2P scenarios; also, they rely only on simulations. Hsieh and Sivakumar [8] discussed how cellular networks can support P2P communications; however, there was no empirical study of mobile P2P performance.

Recently Kim et al. [9] carried out preliminary P2P measurements in a commercial WiMAX network in Korea, dealing with traffic metrics, control overhead, and peers' performance. This paper is further extended based on the same log explicitly targeting the handover impact, peers' connectivity and stability, and control signaling delay. To the best of our knowledge, we are the first to carry out comprehensive empirical study of the BitTorrent performance in the mobile WiMAX networks, with following contributions:

- We empirically measure BitTorrent performance of mobile users in commercial WiMAX networks and the log data is shared in public[1].
- We measure how handovers (HOs) degrade the performance of BitTorrent. We observe that, on average, a HO reduces the throughput, number of connected peers, and number of actively transmitting peers by 32.4%, 1.4%, 14.9% in the bus case, and by 14.7%, 3.5%, 0.5% in the subway case, respectively.
- We investigate how BitTorrent behaves with user mobility in terms of connectivity among peers, download/upload duration and throughput. Frequent disconnections, short download session times, small download traffic, and negligible upload contributions characterize the BitTorrent performance in mobile environments.
- We analyze BitTorrent signaling overhead over the WiMAX network. Relatively long RTTs and link instability make the BitTorrent signaling protocol more inefficient, with longer processing time.

The rest of this paper is organized as follows. Section 2 describes measurement settings and test routes. We measure how handovers impact the BitTorrent performance in Section 3. Sections 4 and 5 analyze the application level performance of BitTorrent users and the BitTorrent signaling efficiency, respectively. Concluding remarks are given in Section 6.

---

[1] http://crawdad.org/snu/bittorrent

2   Experiment Description

2.1   Measurement Settings

We carried out the measurements in KT's mobile WiMAX network in Seoul, Korea, which has more than 300,000 subscribers as of March 2010. In the WiMAX network, one base station (BS) offers the aggregated throughput of approximately 30 to 50 Mbps, and typically covers an area with a radius of 1 to 5 km. Depending on the distance between a BS and a subscriber station (SS), the channel condition and its bit rate can vary substantially. (In this paper, we use the terms "SS" and "WiMAX host" interchangeably.) When an SS crosses the boundary between two BSs, it performs a HO, during which BitTorrent download/upload will be affected. Time-varying link conditions, inter-cell interference, and HOs adversely affect the BitTorrent performance.

We use three laptop computers, each with a WiMAX modem, for measurements. The three WiMAX modems are one KWM-U1000 and two KWM-U1800s [10]. Another desktop computer is connected to the 100 Mbps Ethernet in the campus network of Seoul National University for comparison purposes. We modify the open-source BitTorrent software, *Vuze* [11], to record logs every 0.5 second, e.g. peer list, download and upload rates. *WinDump* is used to capture the packet headers; *Wireshark* and *TCPTrace* are used to analyze the traces. We also use the XRO7000 toolkit [12] to observe the WiMAX link layer activities such as the signal strength and HO messages.

2.2   Test Routes

Based on the similar measurement studies [2][4][5][9], we consider three scenarios of WiMAX hosts: (1) **Stationary**: An SS is located stationarily inside a building in the university campus, where a single WiMAX BS and a few repeaters cover the entire campus area. The distance between the SS and the BS is about 800 meters without line-of-sight path; thus, the received signal strength is stable but not strong. (2) **Subway**: We take the subway line #4 in Seoul Metro, from Sadang station to Myeong-dong Station. The distance is about 12 km and it takes about 20 minutes; there are 10 subway stations on the route. At every subway station, a single BS is deployed, and one or more repeaters are installed between adjacent BSs to enhance the radio signal. Therefore, HOs occur whenever a subway train moves from one station to another. (3) **Bus**: We take the bus #501 from Seoul National University to Seoul Railway Station. The distance of the bus route is about 11 km and it took about 30 minutes when we carried out the measurement.

We select a popular 400 MB video file, 25 minute long sitcom; at least 300 seeds are participating in the BitTorrent network. We carry out experiments four times over four days in March, 2010; in each run, four hosts (Ethernet, stationary, subway, and bus) start downloading the same file at the same time.

3   Impacts of Handovers

WiMAX adopts a break-and-make HO approach; thus, the throughput of the WiMAX host is noticeably disrupted. We trace all HOs by observing the two IEEE 802.16e MAC frames: *MOB_MSHO_REQ* indicating the beginning of a HO, and *HO_RNG_SUCCESS* indicating the end of the HO. Then we average relevant metrics at one second intervals. The changes of metrics over time (within 5 seconds before and after the HO) are shown in Fig. 1, where the vertical line in the middle indicates the HO occurrences. We observe that in the bus case, before the HOs, the carrier-to-interference ratio (CINR) always drops below 0; hence, 0 dB may be the threshold to trigger a HO in the KT's WiMAX network. During a HO, packet transmissions are disrupted; thus, the retransmission time-out may expire, which in turn reduces the TCP congestion window. Notice that the download throughput in the bus case is nearly halved after the HO, and still keeps on decreasing due to the slow recovery of TCP congestion control. What is worse, the number of the actively transmitting peers is notably decreasing before and after HOs in the bus case. On the other hand, in the subway case the effect of HOs is less severe; the RTT around a HO increases and hence the download throughput decreases.

We calculate the average value of each metric before and after HOs, and show the changes in Table 1. On average, a HO reduces the RTT, throughput, number of connected peers, and number of active peers by 7.3%, 32.4%, 1.4%, 14.90% in

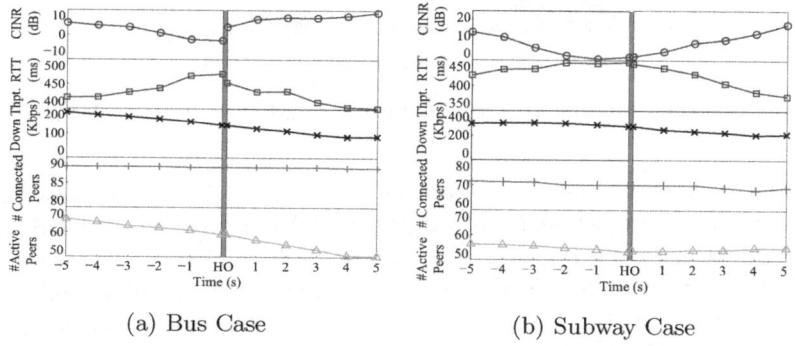

(a) Bus Case   (b) Subway Case

Fig. 1. How HOs impact the BitTorrent performance

Table 1. Calculation of How HOs Impact the BitTorrent Performance

Averaged Metrics	The Bus Case			The Subway Case		
	Before	After	Change	Before	After	Change
CINR (dB)	2.3	5.4	3.1 (N/A)	5.1	7.5	2.4 (N/A)
RTT (ms)	446.2	413.4	-32.8 (7.3%)	440.7	419.9	-20.8 (4.7%)
TCP throughput (Kbps)	174.5	117.8	-56.6 (32.4%)	287.1	244.8	-42.3 (14.7%)
#Connected peers	87.6	86.6	-1 (1.4%)	71.2	68.7	-2.5 (3.5%)
#Active peers	63.8	54.3	-9.5 (14.9%)	54.3	54.0	-0.3 (0.5%)

the bus case, and by 4.7%, 14.7%, 3.5%, 0.5% in the subway case, respectively. We observe that TCP transmissions are impacted by HOs the most significantly.

4   BitTorrent Dynamics for Mobility in WiMAX

To evaluate the behaviors of BitTorrent protocols with other peers from a WiMAX host's view, we define the following terms, which are also illustrated in Fig. 2:

- **Connection Session (CS)**: It starts from the establishment of a connection with a particular peer, and ends when the peer is disconnected. If the host is disconnected from, but reconnects to the same peer again after 1 second, we count them as two separate CSs. This term indicates the peers connectivity.
- **Download/Upload Session (DS/US)**: It means a download/upload duration during a single CS. We define that a DS/US ends if there is no packet transmissions for longer than 1 second. These terms show the download/upload stability.
- **Download/Upload Traffic (DT/UT)**: It refers to the downloaded/uploaded traffic load in bytes during a single DS/US. These terms indicate the download/upload capability.

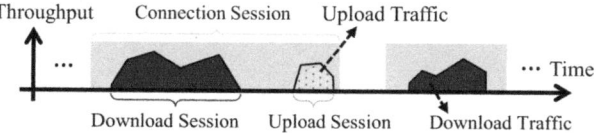

Fig. 2. An Illustration of A Peer's Connections and Downloads/Uploads

A WiMAX host may connect to (and be disconnected from) the same peer multiple times. Thus, we define a peer's **aggregated CS**, **aggregated DS/US** and **aggregated DT/UT** by summing CSs, DSs/USs and DTs/UTs with the same peer. Note that all CSs and DSs/USs are originally in unit of seconds, but normalized to the total download time of each case, respectively for comparison purposes. The total download times are 243.28s, 1208.05s , 1326.44s, and 1964.86s in the Ethernet, stationary, subway, and bus cases, respectively.

We observe that disconnections from other peers are caused by: (a) bad link conditions due to fading and mobility (passive disconnection), and (b) BitTorrent operations due to lack of incentives (active disconnection). We analyze CSs and DSs/USs of the WiMAX hosts caused by passive disconnections in the following sections to observe how WiMAX network impacts the BitTorrent performance.

4.1   Peer Connectivity

A TCP connection of a WiMAX host with a peer will be kept until it is actively closed by the peer's BitTorrent operation, or is passively disconnected due to bad

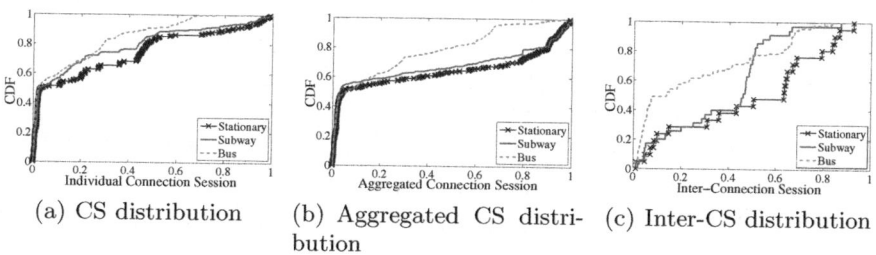

(a) CS distribution   (b) Aggregated CS distribution   (c) Inter-CS distribution

Fig. 3. Peer Connectivity

link conditions. Active and passive disconnections can be determined by checking whether there is a TCP *FIN* flag at the end of a CS. We observe that the ratio of the CSs ended by passive disconnections to all the CSs is 0%, 87.2% , 88.7% and 92.1% in the Ethernet, stationary, subway, and bus cases, respectively.

We show the cumulative distribution functions (CDFs) of CSs and aggregated CSs in Figs. 3(a) and 3(b), respectively. We observe that more than 50% of the CSs are extremely short, less than 2% of the total download time. In the bus scenario, around 80% of the aggregated CSs are shorter than half of the total download time, but in the subway and stationary scenarios, about 40% of the aggregated CSs are longer than half of the total download time. We also plot the CDF of idle durations between the adjacent CSs to the same peer, dubbed **inter-CS** times, in Fig. 3(c). In the bus case, half of the inter-CSs are shorter than 10% of the total download time, which indicates frequent disconnections and reconnections to the same peers. Frequent disconnections indicate poor connectivity to peers; the bus scenario exhibits the poorest connectivity since its wireless link is highly fluctuating while the bus moves in outdoor environments. Table 2 shows the statistical averages of CSs, aggregated CSs and inter-CSs of each scenario, and we compute that, on average, WiMAX hosts performance worse than Ethernet one, and the bus host performance the worst.

Table 2. Averages of the metrics are shown where ind., agg., inter- stand for individual, aggregated, inter-session times, respectively. All session times are normalized to the total download time in each case, and the unit of the traffic is KB.

	CS			DS			DT		US		UT	
	ind.	agg.	inter-	ind.	agg.	inter-	ind.	agg.	ind.	agg.	ind.	agg.
Ethernet	N/A	N/A	N/A	0.286	0.350	0.049	1818	1972	0.026	0.232	87	791
Stationary	0.253	0.352	0.487	0.052	0.227	0.020	227	2107	0.006	0.056	55	542
Subway	0.201	0.327	0.396	0.043	0.181	0.019	192	2113	0.005	0.081	50	855
Bus	0.155	0.210	0.259	0.021	0.088	0.013	133	1281	0.003	0.031	21	205

4.2   Download Stability

Download sessions (DSs) may be interrupted or terminated by multiple reasons: (a) bad link conditions incur large RTTs and frequent packet losses, so that

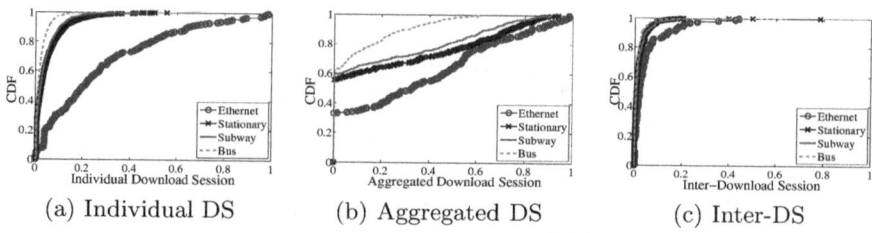

(a) Individual DS   (b) Aggregated DS   (c) Inter-DS

Fig. 4. Download Stability

TCP connections can be disrupted, (b) a chunk delivery (with chunk size of 512 KB for a 400 MB file [11] [13]) is finished successfully, (c) the host is so slow that it may be choked, (d) by the end of file download time, transmissions are withdrawn intentionally by the BitTorrent protocol. We exclude the latter three cases, which can be classified as active disconnections. We observe that DSs are passively disconnected (i.e. case (a)) with the ratios of 71.2%, 84.6%, 85.7%, and 91.6% in the Ethernet, stationary, subway, and bus cases, of all the DSs respectively.

The CDF of DSs due to passive disconnections is shown in Fig. 4(a), which reveals the stability of downloading the file. (Note that peers, which do not transmit data to the host, are not included in the figure.) The Ethernet host outperforms the WiMAX hosts significantly due to its high uplink capacity. Hosts in the WiMAX network suffer from short DSs; almost 90% of the DSs are shorter than 10% of the total download time. Fig. 4(b) shows the CDF of the aggregated DSs of the peers. Surprisingly the WiMAX hosts have negligible DSs from almost 60% of the peers, while the Ethernet host has marginal DSs from around 30% of the peers. The aggregated DSs (of peers) of the WiMAX hosts are much shorter than that of the Ethernet host. In particular, the WiMAX host in the bus scenario has the worst performance; 90% of its peers maintain aggregated DSs less than 40% of the total download time. We also plot the CDF of the **inter-DS** times, the inactive download periods, in Fig. 4(c), showing the inter-DS times are very short in the WiMAX cases, indicating that the download is terminated and recovered frequently. From Table 2, the average durations of individual and aggregated DSs (of peers) of the WiMAX hosts are quite shorter than those of the Ethernet hosts due to frequent interruptions and disconnections.

4.3   Download Traffic

During the DSs, the amount of the download traffic from remote peers to a host is time-varying depending on the link dynamics (and hence transmission rate of a channel). We measure the DT for each DS to observe how much traffic a remote peer transmits to the host. As shown in Fig. 5 (X axis is in log scale), the WiMAX host in the bus case receives the smallest DT per DS. Most of the DT to the Ethernet host are transmitted from a few peers in a short time. In

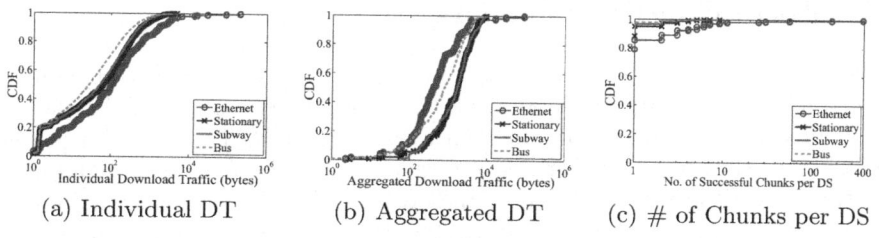

(a) Individual DT   (b) Aggregated DT   (c) # of Chunks per DS

Fig. 5. Download Traffic

contrast, the WiMAX hosts can download only a small amount of traffic from a large number of peers due to its link instability.

The effective download of a host is critical to evaluate the BitTorrent performance. We calculate the CDF of the numbers of successfully transmitted chunks during each DS. From Fig. 5(c), we observe that in the WiMAX cases, about 90% of the DSs cannot continuously download even a single chunk successfully. The average number of successful chunks per DS is 2.951, 0.218, 0.162, and 0.103 in the Ethernet, stationary, subway and bus cases, respectively. Consequently, frequent disruptions of chunk will result in retransmissions of some packets of the interrupted chunk. We suggest that reducing the chunk size may increase the efficiency of chunk delivery in mobile environments.

4.4 Upload Stability and Traffic

We evaluate upload stability and upload traffic similarly. CDFs of USs and UTs are shown in Fig. 6. Most of the individual USs of the WiMAX hosts exist for extremely short periods: 0.1% ~ 1% of the total download time. By comparison, the Ethernet host maintains higher USs due to its stable link. Fig. 6(c) shows that the UT of each of the WiMAX cases (except the bus case) is not so different from that of the Ethernet case. It is because that there is not so much need to upload even for the Ethernet host due to the huge amount of seeds, as the content is quite popular [2]. We conclude that the small uplink capacity of the WiMAX networks along with the small percentage of leechers in the "popular" swarm relieves the WiMAX hosts of uploading the chunks.

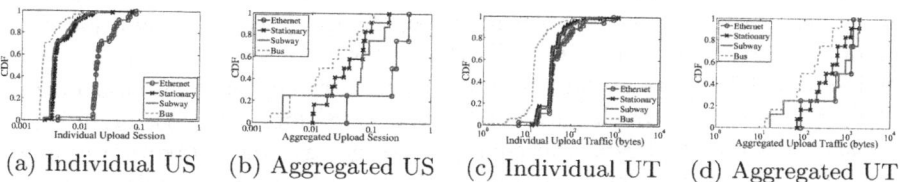

(a) Individual US   (b) Aggregated US   (c) Individual UT   (d) Aggregated UT

Fig. 6. Upload Stability and Traffic

---

[2] As we measured, about 90% of peers are seeds.

5   Protocol Control Behaviors

In this section, we evaluate the message exchange time of each BitTorrent control message, which means one RTT and the potential processing delay. We classify BitTorrent control packets [13] and then average their RTTs, as shown in Fig. 7. We observe that all control message exchanges in WiMAX cases take longer times than the Ethernet case. Thus, BitTorrent in WiMAX environments may not be able to adapt to the link dynamics timely. We also plot how long it takes to perform TCP connection setup (3-way handshake), TCP retransmission (reTX), and TCP close (2 RTTs), all of which are triggered by a host (not from a remote peer). Especially, TCP retransmissions take much longer time because they occur mostly when the link quality is not good. Consequently, large RTTs of WiMAX networks, along with TCP retransmissions, will increase the control signaling between BitTorrent peers significantly. How to optimize and revamp control signaling is crucial for BitTorrent performance in mobile environments.

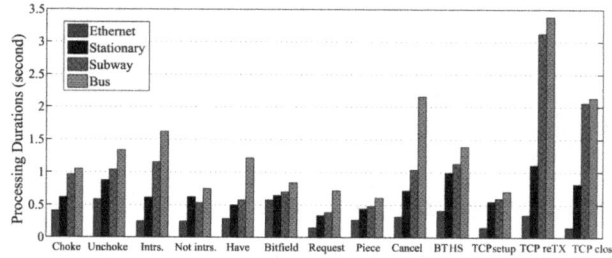

Fig. 7. The RTT of each BitTorrent control message exchange (Intrs., Not intrs., and BT HS stand for Interest, Not interest, and BitTorrent handshake, respectively.)

6   Conclusion

We comprehensively measured and analyzed the BitTorrent performance of a host in the commercial mobile WiMAX network. Based on the empirical measurements, we reach the following conclusions: (1) the wireless links in mobile WiMAX networks are quite unstable due to the fluctuation of signal strengths and handovers. Thus connections amongst peers are often in poor conditions and sometimes broken depending on mobility; (2) the poor link condition degrades download performance since TCP reduces its congestion window for packet losses; (3) handovers often terminate peer connectivity and slow down the TCP transmissions, which may not be recovered efficiently; (4) due to the large delay with remote peers, the control message exchanges take noticeable time; (5) WiMAX hosts suffer from frequent disconnections, short download sessions, small download throughput, and negligible upload contributions. Overall, the current BitTorrent protocols cannot adapt to the mobile WiMAX environments well. How to adjust BitTorrent protocols in mobile environments or even to create new protocols will be our future work.

Acknowledgment

This publication is partially based on work performed in the framework of the Project COAST-ICT-248036, which is supported by the European Community. The research is also supported partly by the NAP of Korea Research Council of Fundamental Science & Technology, and the MKE(The Ministry of Knowledge Economy), Korea, under the ITRC(Information Technology Research Center) support program supervised by the NIPA (National IT Industry Promotion Agency)(NIPA-2010-(C1090-1011-0004)). The ICT at Seoul National University provided research facilities for this study.

References

1. CISCO, Cisco visual networking index: Global mobile data traffic forecast update, 2009-2014, CISCO, Tech. Rep. (2010)
2. Kim, D., Cai, H., Na, M., Choi, S.: Performance measurement over mobile wimax/ieee 802.16e network. In: IEEE WoWMoM (2008)
3. Woo, S., Jang, K., Kim, S., Cho, S., Lee, J., Lee, Y., Moon, S.: Best-case wibro performance for a single flow. In: ACM MobiCom Workshop, MICNET (2009)
4. Wang, X., Kim, H., Vasilakos, A.V., Kwon, T.T., Choi, Y., Choi, S., Jang, H.: Measurement and analysis of world of warcraft in mobile wimax networks. In: ACM NetGames (2009)
5. Han, M., Lee, Y., Moon, S., Jang, K., Lee, D.: Evaluation of voIP quality over wiBro. In: Claypool, M., Uhlig, S. (eds.) PAM 2008. LNCS, vol. 4979, pp. 51–60. Springer, Heidelberg (2008)
6. Huang, C.M., Hsu, T.H., Hsu, M.F.: Network-aware P2P file sharing over the wireless mobile networks. In: IEEE JSAC, vol. 25 (2007)
7. Wu, H., Shi, C., Chen, H., Zhou, X., Gao, C.: An architecture for mobile P2P file sharing in marine domain. In: IEEE PerCOM (2008)
8. Hsieh, H., Sivakumar, R.: On Using Peer-to-peer Communication in Cellular Wireless Data Networks. IEEE Transaction on Mobile Computing 3(1) (2004)
9. Kim, S., Wang, X., Kim, H., Kwon, T.T., Choi, Y.: Measurement and Analysis of BitTorrent Traffic in Mobile WiMAX. In: IEEE P2P (2010)
10. KT WiBro, http://www.ktwibro.com/
11. Vuze, http://www.vuze.com/
12. XRONet Corp., http://www.xronet.co.kr/product/product_xro7000.php
13. BitTorrent Specification, http://www.bittorrent.org/beps/bep_0003.html

Peeling Away Timing Error in NetFlow Data

Brian Trammell, Bernhard Tellenbach,
Dominik Schatzmann, and Martin Burkhart

ETH Zurich, Switzerland

Abstract. In this paper, we characterize, quantify, and correct timing errors introduced into network flow data by collection and export via Cisco NetFlow version 9. We find that while some of these sources of error (clock skew, export delay) are generally implementation-dependent and known in the literature, there is an additional cyclic error of up to one second that is inherent to the design of the export protocol. We present a method for correcting this cyclic error in the presence of clock skew and export delay. In an evaluation using traffic with known timing collected from a national-scale network, we show that this method can successfully correct the cyclic error. However, there can also be other implementation-specific errors for which insufficient information remains for correction. On the routers we have deployed in our network, this limits the accuracy to about 70ms, reinforcing the point that implementation matters when conducting research on network measurement data.

1 Introduction

In the practice of network measurement, packet data is collected at one or more observation points within a network. Some combination of transformations may then be applied to the packets, such as sampling, or assembly into flows. This transformed data then undergoes some combination of export, collection, aggregation, filtering, storage, and analysis, in order to produce successively refined information from which knowledge about the network is derived, whether for research or operational purposes. Each of these stages may be seen as a function applied to the result of the previous stage. Ideally, each of these functions should lead to further refinement of the information of interest without introduction of error or loss of fidelity. Some of these stages, especially observation, export, and collection, should have no impact on the information content at all.

However, this is not the case. Each stage in the measurement process may introduce error. Some of these sources of error are well-known, such as failing to properly provision measurement devices leading to packet loss, or failing to synchronize clocks among distributed observation points. Other errors have more obscure causes. In this work, we examine a cyclic source of timing error in flow data exported via Cisco Netflow version 9 (v9) [1] which, instead of having a deployment- or implementation-time cause, is a consequence of the design of the protocol itself. Together with load-dependent export delay and long-term drift of the clocks from which timestamps are generated, we find that the accuracy of

N. Spring and G. Riley (Eds.): PAM 2011, LNCS 6579, pp. 194–203, 2011.

timestamps in flow data exported using v9 is degraded by about three orders of magnitude, to about two seconds in the worst case, instead of millisecond-level precision implied by the protocol.

After discovering this error in a flow data set collected from a national-scale network and stored as a sequence of raw NetFlow v9 export packets in received order, we set about "peeling" these layers of error away, devising an algorithm for correcting the cyclic error while compensating for delay and drift. We do this only with reference to timing information on the NetFlow v9 export packets; that is, the correction is independent of the individual flows exported. This is important both for the scalability of the approach, and for its independence on the actual content of the traffic. We find that our approach can completely remove the protocol-induced cyclic error, in the general case allowing millisecond timing resolution with NetFlow v9, even for flows exported in different export packets. This is sufficient to sequence flows occurring between one millisecond and one second apart, e.g. to determine the direction of a bidirectional flow as in [2] when the connection establishment time is more than 1ms, or to enable flow-based round-trip-time measurement for quality of service applications.

However, in practice we can only peel so far: on the Cisco 6500 and 7600 series routers that collect the data in the network we measure, additional flow-level inaccuracy of about 70ms remains, which we do not have sufficient information to correct. We thereby confirm that deployment, implementation, and design-time choices made in the systems collecting and processing the traffic data under study do not have the neutral effect one could assume on the data. We further note that this work quantitatively supports the common wisdom that router-based flow measurement is generally insufficient for applications requiring precision timing.

Section 2 characterizes the sources of timing errors we see in the examined data set and section 3 quantifies them and presents concrete examples of artifacts in the data caused by these sources. We then present and evaluate a method for correcting cyclic error based solely on the export packet headers in section 4. In section 5, we review related work in data fidelity for network measurement, and we present our conclusions in section 6.

2   Characterizing Timing Error in NetFlow Version 9

NetFlow v9 [1] exports flow data in records described by templates, allowing the flexible inline definition of record formats. However, flow start and end timestamps are expressed as with older NetFlow versions, in terms of uptime, or the time that has passed since the device started. This approach has the advantage of not requiring a real-time clock at the *metering process*, which generates flows from an observed traffic stream. We call these per-flow timestamps f_{start} and f_{end}.

Flows are exported by an *exporting process* in protocol data units called *export packets* by NetFlow v9. The exporting process stamps each outgoing packet with an export timestamp p_{export} expressed in UNIX epoch time (i.e., seconds since

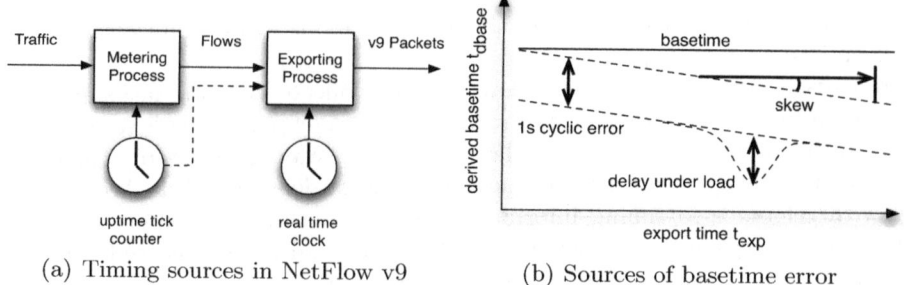

(a) Timing sources in NetFlow v9   (b) Sources of basetime error

Fig. 1. Illustrating basetime error

midnight UTC, 1 January 1970). It also exports the time since the metering process started p_{uptime}. This arrangement is illustrated in Figure 1(a)[1].

From these two timestamps, the time at which the device started (which we call the *true basetime* or t_{base}) is given by $t_{base} = p_{export} - p_{uptime}$. The start and end time in UNIX epoch seconds for each flow in the packet can then be determined by adding t_{base} to each of the per-flow timestamps f_{start} and f_{end} for each flow in the packet.

This would be the ideal situation. However, while the uptime is expressed in milliseconds, the export time is truncated to second-level precision before export due to the design of the NetFlow v9 packet header, implicitly flooring it. Therefore, the *derived basetime* from each packet is in effect given by $t_{dbase} = \lfloor p_{export} \rfloor - p_{uptime}$. The implicit floor operation causes the milliseconds part of the export timestamp not to be accounted in the basetime derivation, injecting a *cyclic error* of up to one second subtracted from the derived basetime, which can consequently cause errors in the flow timestamps leading to incorrect sequencing of flows exported in different export packets.

Further complicating this situation are two effects of the architecture and its use of separate clocks. First, the two clocks are not necessarily synchronized; that is, one second does not necessarily pass on the real time clock for each second on the uptime counter. This *clock skew* can be a result of inaccuracy in either of the two clocks. The magnitude of the skew observed in our data set is on the order of seconds per day, and appears to be stable over time. Second, the timestamp from the uptime counter and the timestamp from the real time clock are not necessarily applied simultaneously to the export packet. Export packets may be held at the Exporting Process due either to resource exhaustion or explicit export rate limiting. This *delay* can inject a further subtractive error into the derived basetime. Delays observed in our data set are uncommon, intermittent, correlated with periods of heavy load, and on the order of less than one second. These three sources of error are illustrated in Figure 1(b); here, we show the true basetime, and the dotted lines define the area within which the derived basetimes fall.

---

[1] Here we use terminology and arrangement from the IPFIX architecture [3], since the IPFIX architecture was based on that from NetFlow v9.

To see how this would affect flow measurement, consider the following example: a flow f_1 starts at 1.000s after router start (i.e., true basetime), and a flow f_2 which starts at 1.100s. The export packet containing f_1 is exported at 11.000s, and that containing f_2 at 11.950s. Assuming no drift or other delay on this time scale, we then have:

$$t_{dbase1} = \lfloor 11.000 \rfloor - 11.000 = 0, \ t_{dbase2} = \lfloor 11.950 \rfloor - 11.950 = -0.950$$
$$f_1 = t_{dbase1} + 1.000 = 1.000, \qquad f_2 = t_{dbase2} + 1.100 = 0.150$$

Even though f_1 started before f_2, the apparent sequence is reversed.

We observe a further peculiarity of export in the data from our Cisco routers: that of derived basetime *quantization*. The derived basetimes in our data set are all divisible by 4ms. Whether this is a source of error or not is uncertain without examining the implementation: the 4ms quantization could be caused either by export driven by a 4ms interrupt, or by timestamps being stored internally in 4ms units.

Due to the magnitude of these errors, applications which perform time-series aggregation with intervals greater than one second (e.g., most billing applications) are largely unaffected. However, we show in section 3 that any assumption that devices exporting NetFlow v9 are capable of millisecond-level accuracy and/or strict ordering of flows does not hold. We set out to see what could be done to improve this situation.

The most troublesome source of error on a per-flow basis is the cyclic error. The timestamps of the flows skew at the same rate as that of the basetime, so skew, while visible in the basetime series, is cancelled out for each flow. Therefore, in section 4, we will focus on correcting cyclic error, treating skew, delay, and quantization as complications to correction.

3   Quantifying Timing Errors in NetFlow v9

Our data set includes data collected from SWITCH[2], the Swiss research and education network. This network contains about 2.3 million IPv4 addresses, and the typical total traffic volume ranges from 500 megabytes to one gigabyte per second. We receive NetFlow v9 from six Cisco routers (6500 or 7600 series) deployed around the SWITCH border; we designate these routers A-F. Each router also exports flows from multiple Source IDs; these correspond to line cards. Here we examine one week of data, 26 June to 3 July, 2010.

Figure 2 shows the density of exported derived basetimes for a single source. The upper part of the figure is a density map of exported basetimes by offset from the maximum observed basetime. The lower part shows the number of export packets per second for the same time period.

The vast majority of basetimes fall within the skewed one-second cyclic error band. Note the daily seasonality in the density of basetimes. There is a maximum number of flows which can be exported in an export packet (ep), so higher

[2] http://www.switch.ch

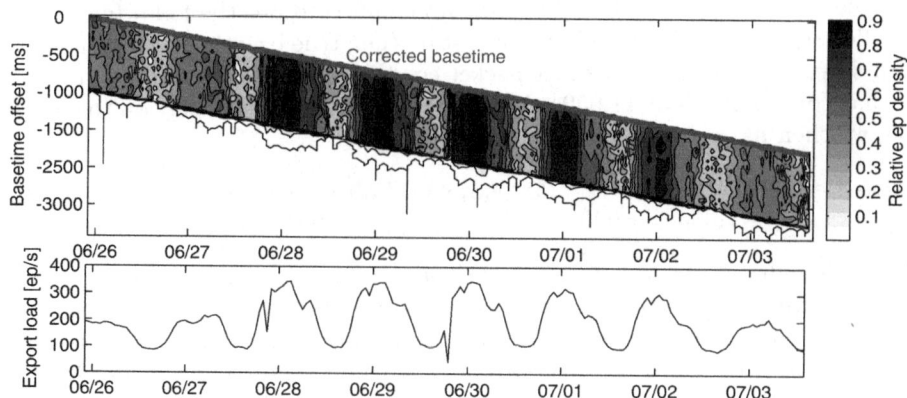

Fig. 2. Derived basetime density distribution, and basetime correction, for a single source on a single router (A/513).

traffic load leads to larger flow counts leads to larger export packet counts. This increases the number of unique derived basetimes seen per second. However, this density is not uniformly distributed among the possible values within the cyclic error band, a fact which further complicates correction. Delay also increases with traffic load, due to resource exhaustion and/or rate limiting in the exporting process. However, the number of delayed export packets is relatively low even under load.

We examine the errors on each source on each router in Table 1. Here, errors are reported in relation to the presumed real basetime as determined by the correction mechanism detailed in section 4; therefore we report the rate of unique observed derived basetimes per second and the correction interval parameter used. These will be explained further below.

Mean drift is a per-source, not a per-router parameter; we hypothesize that this is related to some physical property of the clocks on each of these line cards. Drift ranges from about -2s/day to +1s/day.

The minimum and maximum measured error show that the range due to cyclic error and delays ranges from 1050ms to 2280ms; lower values demonstrating predominantly cyclic error, with higher values as evidence of more delay. The width of the band between the 5th and 95th percentile ranges between about 950ms and 1200ms, demonstrating that the vast majority of this error is cyclic. Note that all error measurements for the routers are values divisible by four milliseconds; this is an artifact of the 4ms quantization mentioned above.

We also examined the output of the softflowd[3] NetFlow v9 metering and exporting process, which was developed independently from the Cisco codebase. softflowd was run on a small set of flows generated on an experimental local-area network, running on a Mac OS X host. We observed the same cyclic error, but negligible drift, negligible delay, and no quantization of derived basetimes.

---

[3] http://www.mindrot.org/projects/softflowd/

Table 1. Overview of timing errors for each source on each router for the examined week.

Router	Source	Drift [ms/day] mean	std.	Error [ms] max	95th	5th	min	Rate [s^{-1}] mean	std.	Correction interval [s]
A	0	-423	14.5	+344	-72	-972	-1052	0.24	0.03	10800
A	513	-228	17.0	+136	-56	-960	-1960	193.9	79.5	400
A	518	-423	7.9	+208	-56	-976	-1876	157.4	39.2	400
B	0	-2039	355.4	+280	-124	-1068	-1465	0.005	0.0008	10800
B	513	+560	41.8	+28	-48	-988	-1020	314.7	64.5	400
B	517	+81	35.4	+244	-52	-992	-1592	201.2	41.7	400
C	0	+1543	49.9	+256	+52	-848	-972	0.09	0.008	10800
C	518	+1577	70	+428	-48	-992	-1824	74.2	29.7	400
D	0	+1053	37.9	+112	+12	-924	-984	0.12	0.02	10800
D	517	+1055	21.5	+316	-52	-946	-1824	302.9	100.7	400
E	0	+239	38.3	+60	-28	-928	-1012	0.11	0.02	10800
E	513	+453	8.9	+500	-48	-952	-1600	204.6	60.8	400
E	515	-17	21.7	+280	-52	-968	-2000	333.5	101.9	400
F	0	+47	14.9	+176	-40	-936	-1044	0.07	0.005	10800
F	513	+46	20.5	+88	-48	-948	-1328	15.6	7.0	10800
softflowd		+5.5	12.0	+16	-43	-940	-1001	0.61	0.02	10800

4   Correcting Cyclic Timing Error

Having observed and quantified this error, we set out to devise a method for correcting it. Since the basetime is related to the time at which the router started, and router restarts in production networks are relatively rare events, correct basetime information could be determined out-of-band via the router's management interface (e.g., SNMP or the command line). However, this method would have two disadvantages. First, it requires the management interface of the router to be accessible to the measurement infrastructure, which is not always desirable. Second, static out-of-band basetime determination ignores the drift of the realtime clock, which is included in each of the flow timestamps; this error would then need to be corrected in any event.

Therefore, we focused on generating a *corrected basetime* estimating the true basetime from the derived basetime information. Our first attempt at this consisted of a simple robust maximum detector. The primary problem with this method is it requires a rather high packet density; otherwise it has a tendency to "follow" downward-cycling derived basetimes into the cyclic error band. The problem also initially appeared to be suited to simple linear regression, but the widely variable density of derived basetimes within the cyclic error band ruled this method out.

We therefore settled on a correction mechanism based on sliding density windows. Recalling the density diagram in Figure 2, we first take the set of derived basetimes for a specified "horizontal" (export time) interval, called the *correction interval*. We then slide a one-second "vertical" (derived basetime) interval over the correction interval, and select the position for this interval which maximizes the derived basetime density within the rectangular correction window. The top (maximum derived basetime) of this window is then taken to be the corrected basetime. For source 513 on router A, the corrected basetime is shown as the top line in Figure 2.

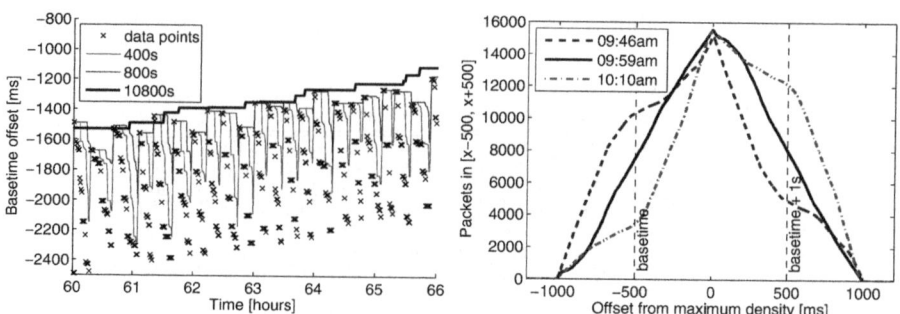

(a) Stability of corrected basetime varies (b) Density distributions within the corwith correction interval size   rection window vary over time

Fig. 3. Illustrating density-window basetime correction

The correction interval is selected based upon the density of derived basetimes for a given source, which is itself dependent on the traffic volume. In principle, it should be chosen to observe at least several wraparounds of the cyclic error. Figure 3(a) shows the effect that different correction intervals have on the corrected basetime series, observing the effects of three different windows on correcting the relatively low-density source 0 of router C. In general, longer correction intervals provide more stable and therefore more accurate corrections, but require more processing as they must consider more data points, and would lead to longer delays in reporting corrected times during stream processing. For this study, we selected a 400 second window for higher density sources, and a 10800 second (three hour) window for lower density sources.

Figure 3(b) illustrates how this correction method works in the presence of variable density of derived basetimes. Here we show the derived basetime density as a function of the position of the vertical interval for three different correction windows. Even though the density distributions differ greatly, the method leads to the same basetime correction.

4.1   Evaluation

To measure the effective accuracy of the cyclic error correction method, we compared exported flow timestamps to known flow timing. We placed a traffic-generating host on the measured network to send single-packet UDP flows to known hosts outside the network, chosen such that these flows would be routed across a known source on a known router in our collection infrastructure. We saved the injection time for each flow key, and compared this to the timestamps on the flows exported via NetFlow, both with uncorrected derived basetimes as well as basetimes corrected using the method described above.

The CDF of the deviation from known timing of per-flow timestamps over 30 hours of data over 3-4 September 2010 for source 513 on router A are shown in Figure 4(a).

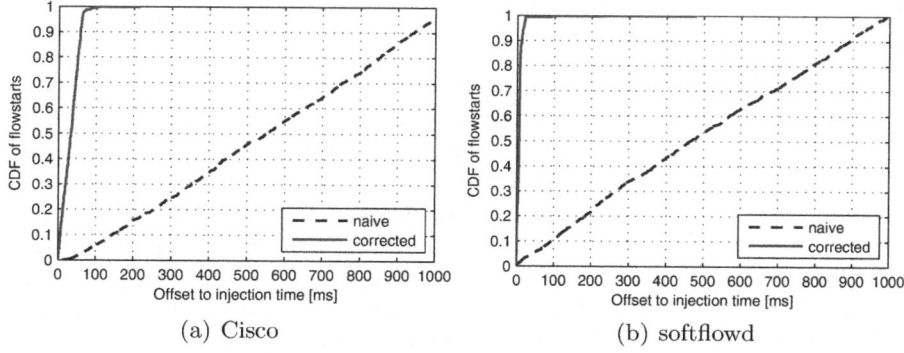

Fig. 4. Corrected and uncorrected flow start times

Here, we see that the flow timestamps calculated from uncorrected basetimes exhibit a uniform deviation to about 1s, caused mainly by the cyclic error in the basetime. If the cyclic error were the only remaining error in the data, we would expect the flow timestamps calculated using the corrected basetimes to exhibit no more than a few milliseconds of error to account for the one-way delay between the source and the router at which the flows were measured.

We see this in the `softflowd` data, as shown in 4(b). This demonstrates that our cyclic error correction method can completely eliminate the timing error introduced by the design of the NetFlow v9 protocol. However, even after applying corrected basetimes, there is an additional source of about 70ms of uniformly distributed error on Cisco routers. Further investigation shows this to be constant across sources and routers, and independent of time, load, or other factors measured in this work. Therefore, we conclude that this error is implementation-specific and an unavoidable property of the packet or flow handling of this specific implementation, either within the metering process or between the metering and exporting processes.

5   Related Work

The question of the fidelity of data used in Internet measurement studies is well-addressed in the literature. The effects of sampling of packets (e.g., as in [4]) as well as flows (e.g., as in [5]) have been widely studied. However, these works tend to be theoretical, focusing more on the mathematical properties of the techniques used and the essential tradeoff between overhead and utility than on the effects of specific implementations or protocols used in the collection of the data used.

Sommer and Feldmann [6] examined the information loss associated with flow measurement as opposed to directly operating on packet data, and find that for one particular application, TCP connection summary generation, flow data suffices "[using] large enough time intervals": an acknowledgement of the impact that flow timeouts and timing in general have on later analysis.

Paxson [7], in establishing a set of best practices for Internet measurement studies, classifies sources of error into precision, accuracy, and misconception. It discusses timing precision and accuracy and discusses the need to consider and calibrate for measurement infrastructure induced error in source data sets. It advocates the export of metadata along with source data for measurement studies, a call we reiterate in our conclusions.

A closer antecedent for the present work is Cunha et. al. [8], which provides a similar study of largely implementation-related artifacts in flow data produced by the Juniper routers which generated commonly-used datasets from Abilene and GEANT. These artifacts were related to timeout and flow cache expiry, and as such have a destructive impact on the distribution of flow duration.

The IETF addressed various design issues with NetFlow v9 in the specification of the IPFIX protocol [9]. Crucially, IPFIX supports flexible timestamps from second to nanosecond resolution, and allows the association of an absolute timestamp with every flow. As it does not mandate the export of potentially inconsistent timestamps in each message, it does not suffer from the cyclic error we present in this work. However, it does not necessarily address other sources of inaccuracy within the implementation of the metering or exporting process.

6   Conclusions

In seeking to maximize the timing precision available from data exported via Cisco NetFlow v9, we discovered and quantified a cyclic source of up to one second of error in flow timestamps, inherent in the design of the protocol. Correcting this cyclic error can improve the accuracy of NetFlow v9 data to millisecond-level. However, inaccuracy remains within the examined Cisco implementation which we do not have sufficient information to correct, limiting our effective correction for our production dataset to one order of magnitude, for about 70ms accuracy.

The set of routers from which we receive NetFlow v9 data represents an admittedly small sample of deployed implementations. However, the cyclic error is a protocol issue. It is therefore implementation-independent, and should affect NetFlow v9 export from any vendor. We note that an implementation built with an awareness of the cyclic error could avoid it, by faking the system uptime and/or export timestamps in order to export real basetimes, but we did not observe this behavior in any examined NetFlow implementation.

In addition, we presume that similarities in NetFlow v9 metering and export process implementations could lead to implementation-specific sources of error similar to those we observed on Cisco devices on implementations from other vendors. These measurements are an area for future work. The guidance to take from our work in any case is this: researchers using NetFlow v9 data sets should not assume better than second-level accuracy unless employing a method for correcting cyclic basetime error such as the one we present here, and should measure the residual error specific to their metering and exporting processes.

In this work, we were able to observe and correct timing error from the Netflow v9 export packet headers which is not apparent from an examination of flow data alone. This leads us to reiterate the call in [7] to export and maintain implementation-specific metadata alongside flow data used for research. Our experience in this work additionally indicates the wisdom of keeping measurement data in as "raw" a form as possible. While all flow data is theoretically the same, and should be freely convertible among formats, this is not the case in practice: as we have shown, implementation matters.

Acknowledgments

The authors would like to acknowledge SWITCH for providing the data used in this study. Thanks as well to the European Commission for its material support of this work through the DEMONS project (FP7-257315).

References

1. Claise, B., Sadasivan, G., Valluri, V., Djernaes, M.: Cisco Systems NetFlow Services Export Version 9. RFC 3954 (Informational) (October 2004)
2. Trammell, B., Boschi, E.: Bidirectional Flow Export Using IP Flow Information Export (IPFIX). RFC 5103 (Proposed Standard) (January 2008)
3. Sadasivan, G., Brownlee, N., Claise, B., Quittek, J.: Architecture for IP Flow Information Export. RFC 5470 (Informational) (March 2009)
4. Brauckhoff, D., Salamatian, K., May, M.: A signal processing view on packet sampling and anomaly detection. In: Proceedings of INFOCOM 2010, San Diego, California, USA, pp. 713–721. IEEE, Los Alamitos (2010)
5. Choi, B.Y., Bhattacharyya, S.: Observations on Cisco sampled NetFlow. SIGMETRICS Perform. Eval. Rev. 33, 18–23 (2005)
6. Sommer, R., Feldmann, A.: Netflow: information loss or win? In: Proceedings of IMW 2002, Marseille, France, pp. 173–174. ACM, New York (2002)
7. Paxson, V.: Strategies for sound internet measurement. In: Proceedings of IMC 2004, Taormina, Sicily, Italy, pp. 263–271. ACM, New York (2004)
8. Cunha, Í., Silveira, F., Oliveira, R., Teixeira, R., Diot, C.: Uncovering artifacts of flow measurement tools. In: Moon, S.B., Teixeira, R., Uhlig, S. (eds.) PAM 2009. LNCS, vol. 5448, pp. 187–196. Springer, Heidelberg (2009)
9. Claise, B.: Specification of the IP Flow Information Export (IPFIX) Protocol for the Exchange of IP Traffic Flow Information. RFC 5101 (Proposed Standard) (January 2008)

Clockscalpel: Understanding Root Causes of Internet Clock Synchronization Inaccuracy

Chi-Yao Hong, Chia-Chi Lin, and Matthew Caesar

University of Illinois at Urbana-Champaign

Abstract. Synchronizing clocks is an integral part of modern network and security architectures. However, the ability to synchronize clocks in modern networks is not well-understood. In this work, we use testbeds equipped with a high-accuracy GPS receiver to acquire ground truth, to study the accuracy of probe-based synchronization techniques to over 1861 public time servers. We find that existing synchronization protocols provide a median error of $2 - 5$ ms, but suffer from a long-tail. We analyze sources of inaccuracy by decoupling and quantifying different network factors. We found that most inaccuracies stem from asymmetry of propagation delay and queueing delay. We discuss possible schemes to compensate these errors to improve synchronization accuracy.

1 Introduction

Probe-based synchronization protocols such as *Network Time Protocol* (NTP) and the *Simple Network Time Protocol* (SNTP) are widely used today. These protocols comprise one of the largest Internet systems, with hundreds of thousands of NTP servers providing service to tens of millions of clients. Understanding the performance of applications that require synchronized time requires understanding the accuracy achievable by these underlying protocols. However, despite the high degree of reliance that many networked systems have on probe-based synchronization protocols, we lack an understanding of how these protocols behave in modern, wide-area networks.

There exists relatively little attention on the performance of probe-based time synchronization in the wide area over the past decade – most recent surveys date back to 1999 [1] and 1990 [2]. Recently, novel frameworks [3,4] are proposed to further improve the synchronization accuracy. While these studies showed that some NTP servers are inaccurate, the underlying cause of inaccuracies remain unclear. However, with the advent of modern network applications that have stringent end-to-end latency requirements on the order of milliseconds or microseconds [5], such as VoIP, interactive video conferencing, automated trading, and high performance computing, understanding *network factors* that affect time synchronization performance becomes increasingly important.

In this work, we take some preliminary steps towards understanding the ability to synchronize time in the wide-area Internet, leading up to potential frameworks that effectively improve synchronization inaccuracy. In particular, we study the

N. Spring and G. Riley (Eds.): PAM 2011, LNCS 6579, pp. 204–213, 2011.

precision of existing time protocols and characterize their performance in terms of the level of synchronization accuracy it provides to hosts. We leverage GPS hardware (which has greatly reduced in cost over the past decade) to provide "ground truth" clock information to parts of our measurement infrastructure. We use this information to directly study the underlying sources of inaccuracies, assess their impact, and evaluate the potential to compensate for or remove these sources.

We have three key findings. First, we find that existing synchronization protocols work well in the common case (with median accuracy of 2-5 ms), but suffer from a long-tail with a few servers/probes incurring high error rates. Second, we found the main sources of this inaccuracy come from propagation delay asymmetry and queueing delay asymmetry in the wide area. Third, although the path delay asymmetry is considered not measurable [3][1], we find that synchronization accuracy is well-correlated with some path properties that can be probed by end-hosts. To address this, we evaluate several heuristics that compensate for this error (by estimating the error and correcting for it).

We hope our results may enable designers of measurement experiments and network applications to better understand effects synchronization protocols may have on their results, and may assist system operators and protocol designers for tuning their configurations and extending synchronization protocols to improve performance.

2   Background

Clock synchronization algorithm works by having the local host periodically probe remote clock sources. The local host acquires (a) the clock value of the remote host when the probe was received and sent (b) an estimate of the RTT to the remote clock source. In particular, client i periodically sends a probe to the server j, and the server replies with a timestamp collected from its local clock. Let the sending times of client i and server j be $t_{i,TX}$ and $t_{j,TX}$, and let their receiving times be $t_{i,RX}$ and $t_{j,RX}$. The round-trip time $RTT_{i,j}$ can be derived by

$$RTT_{i,j} = (t_{i,RX} - t_{i,TX}) - (t_{j,TX} - t_{j,RX}) \tag{1}$$

NTP assumes symmetric delay, allowing it to measure the one-way delay OWD

$$OWD_{i,j} = OWD_{j,i} = RTT_{i,j}/2 \tag{2}$$

The clock offset of the server j relative to client i is then derived as

$$\theta_{i,j} = (t_{j,TX} + OWD_{j,i}) - (t_{i,RX}) = \frac{1}{2}[(t_{j,RX} - t_{i,TX}) + (t_{j,TX} - t_{i,RX})] \tag{3}$$

In reality, the one way delay might not be symmetric, i.e.,

$$OWD_{i,j}^* - OWD_{j,i}^* = \Delta_{i,j} \tag{4}$$

---

[1] A recent study [6] also indicated that router-level asymmetry does not necessarily imply delay asymmetry.

where the difference $\Delta_{i,j}$ is bounded by $\pm RTT_{i,j}$. By (4) and (3), the error of the clock offset θ is equal to $|\Delta|/2$, i.e., *delay asymmetry Δ governs the synchronization accuracy.* Although protocols such as One-Way Active Measurement Protocol (OWAMP) can be used to estimate delay asymmetry on network paths [6], OWAMP requires NTP to synchronize the system clock, which can lead to biased measurements. Since the synchronization inaccuracy is unknown, it can be hard to accurately infer measured properties.

3   Methodology and Data Sets

Ideally, we would like to compare clock values across hosts against an Internet-wide global time. However, this is hard due to lack of "ground truth" on every device. Previous work on studying NTP performance [1,2] focused on computing the difference between the client's clock time and its *estimation* of the NTP server's clock. This metric is useful to indicate how well NTP hosts converge over time, i.e., the value of θ. Unfortunately, this does not give us the actual synchronization error ($|\Delta|/2$), which arguably impossible to derive without the "ground truth" at the client end.

To provide ground truth, we instrumented our local machine with custom hardware to synchronize with GPS time signals. We used a Garmin 18x LVC GPS receiver, which provides a *pulse-per-second* (electrical signal that precisely indicates the start of a second) aligned to within 1 microsecond of UTC time. We then constructed a simple custom circuit to serve as an interface between the GPS receiver and the local machine. The power supply of GPS receiver comes from the PC through a type-B USB connector, while the *GPS signals*, including NMEA sentences and pulse-per-second signal, are transmitted to the local machine over the RS-232 serial port. The GPS receiver is positioned at proper place such that the received SNR is above a certain threshold.

To measure accuracy of clock synchronization, we ran a Linux machine with NTP v4.2.6, and varied the remote server peer that NTP would synchronize with. We modified the NTP source code to print out detailed probe information (e.g., NTP Timestamps). We leveraged ntpdate to send 4 probes at a time (ntpdate's default behavior). To make the pulse-per-second signal accessible to our measurement tools, we then patched the Linux kernel 2.6.32-rc10 with Linux's Pulse Per Second support. In addition, some of our experiments required setting up ntpds using the pulse-per-second signal. To provide additional vantage points to cross-check the results collected in our local testbed, we deployed GPS-instrumented machines in other locations (Table 1). Finally, some of our experiments synchronize our testbed to public NTP servers. To acquire IP addresses of these servers, we start with public NTP time server lists [7], and exploit a spider program [1] which uses xntpdc to crawl the NTP hierarchy, resulting in $67,782$ servers.

We collect three synchronization error data sets of various sizes (Table 2). For the SE-24st1 data set, clients (Table 1) measure the synchronization error to 63 stratum-1 NTP servers with an average interval of 90 seconds between consecutive measurements of the same client/server pair. A more accurate snapshot of

Table 1. GPS-instrumented testbed set

Location name	Location type	Connection type	Upstream network
Cornell Univ., NY	school	1 Gbps LAN	Cornell Univ.
UIUC, IL	school	1 Gbps LAN	Univ. Illinois
Chicago, IL	home	cable modem	Comcast
Green Bay, WI	business	1 Gbps LAN	Road Runner Holding Co.
Taipei, Taiwan	school	100 Mbps LAN	Taiwan Academic Network

Table 2. Synchronization error data set

Data set	#Clients x #Servers	Duration	Starting Date	Interval
SE-24st1	3 x 63 (only stratum-1 servers)	24h	April 18th, 2010	90s
SE-115allsvrs	4 x 1861 (all servers)	115h	May 5th, 2010	90m
SE-403allsvrs	5 x 1861 (all servers)	403h	August 30th, 2010	90m

synchronization error can be collected using smaller timescale. However, it comes with a cost that we can only measure a limited number of servers accurately (63 servers in the first data set). We collect two much larger data set (1861 servers) when the time interval is increased to 90 minutes. For the SE-115allsvrs and SE-403allsvrs data sets, we randomly choose 361 stratum-1 NTP servers and 500 stratum-i NTP servers, $2 \leq i \leq 4$. We ensure that all client-server pairs are measured at least once within a certain interval.

4   Synchronization Accuracy in the Internet

Accuracy across servers: Fig. 1(a) shows the CDF of synchronization error (i.e., $|\Delta/2|$) from our testbeds to 406 NTP stratum-1 servers. As expected, we observed a long-tailed distribution because some stratum-1 servers may have an inaccurate source clock or misconfigured daemon [1,2]. How to choose a right server to synchronize with is important as only $10\% - 20\%$ of servers can provide sub-millisecond accuracy. Fig. 1(b) shows the CDF of "signed" synchronization error (i.e., $\Delta/2$). We observe that the median error is close to zero (< 1 ms). Therefore, this motivates our approach of probing multiple servers to reduce the error as discussed in §6. The distribution in other strata is similar, but the average error is a few milliseconds higher.

Accuracy across time: Fig. 1(c) shows the CDF of standard deviation error. In general, synchronization error is stable over time (i.e., median standard deviation ranges from 0.4 to 2.2 ms), while we observed that some servers have undesirable variation (i.e., the maximal standard deviation is about 120 ms). Fig. 1(d) shows synchronization error from Univ. Illinois to four representative public stratum-1 servers. For server in Univ. Washington (bigben.cac.washington.edu), we observe an average error 0.5 ms, while the error oscillates with a magnitude

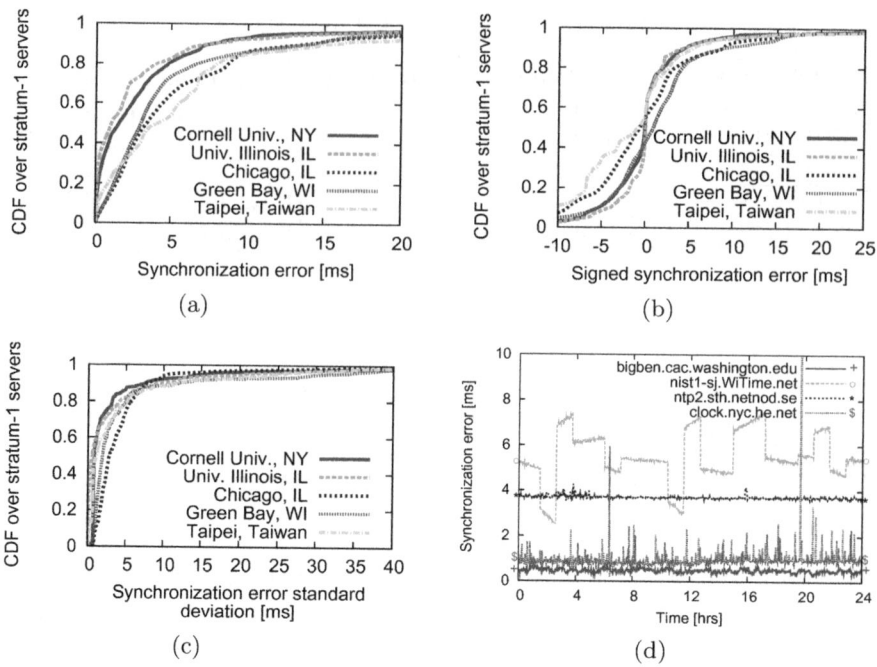

Fig. 1. The CDF of synchronization error for (a) Average error, (b) Average of "signed" error, (c) Standard deviation of "signed" error. (d) The time series of errors from Univ. Illinois to four representative public stratum-1 servers.

of ±0.2 ms. Since a GPS clock is directly attached to this server, the accuracy of the server should be within sub-microsecond, i.e., most of inaccuracies come from network factors. We also synchronize with a public server (nist1-sj.WiTime.net) maintained by National Institute of Standards and Technology (NIST) Internet time services. NIST time servers use dial-up Automated Computer Time Service [8] to synchronize server clock to global time. Again, we observe that the error oscillates in a range of ±0.2 ms. However, the overall error of the NIST server is up to 7 ms, which is significantly more inaccurate than that of GPS-equipped time servers. Also, we notice that the error abruptly changed around every 4000 seconds, as these are intervals between ACTS calibrations (we confirmed this with the NIST Time and Frequency Division). For another GPS-instrumented time server in Stockholm, Sweden (ntp2.sth.netnod.se), the average error over time is about 3.7 ms, which is much higher than that in Univ. Washington. Fig. 1(d) shows the error to a time server (clock.nyc.he.net) in New York City using CDMA signals from cellular networks as time synchronization source. Generally, we found the accuracy of CDMA-based time servers is comparable to GPS-based servers. For CDMA-based and GPS-based time servers, the error is mostly stable over time. However, some sharp spikes happened occasionally are observed. This might come from transient instability of Internet routing (from our testbeds to stratum-1 servers). Other network factors such as

Internet path asymmetry and bandwidth asymmetry are possible root causes to the synchronization errors.

5 Understanding Underlying Factors

Although we observe that the typical synchronization error is around $2-5$ ms, it can undergo very large variations (Fig. 1(a)). Although we observe the characteristics of synchronization error in Fig. 1, the root of inaccuracies is unknown. In this section, we analyze the impact of underlying networking factors that affect the synchronization inaccuracies. As shown in §2 the synchronization error $|\Delta|/2$ is determined by delay asymmetry Δ, which comprises four independent factors. To understand the impacts of these factors, we propose schemes to decouple and measure these factors separately as follows.

5.1 Software Stack Delay Asymmetry

To measure the software stack delay (interrupts, OS, device drivers, NTP software) asymmetry, we conducted an isolated network with only two machines communicating directly through a 1-Gbps Ethernet switch. In this setting, both the transmission delay and propagation delay are perfectly symmetric. The switch is dedicated to this experiment to ensure probes have low queueing delay asymmetry. Under this scenario, we believe the software stack delay asymmetry is the predominant factor of synchronization error. To measure the synchronization error, GPS receivers are attached to the machines as the ground truth as described in §3.

We observed that the software stack delay asymmetry is approximately a uniform distribution with range $(0, 165)$ μs when the CPU utilization is low (Fig. 2(a)). We use a synthetic load generator to inject predictable loads on a server. With heavy system load, we observed a long-tail distribution (Fig. 2(a)) where the maximal error (over $30,000$ trials) is 289.2 μs. We also leverage SystemTap to trace the delay in the Linux kernel, and capture the kernel delay in each directions. The asymmetry of kernel delay is much smaller, with a median of 3.58 ns. This indirectly shows that the software stack delay asymmetry is dominated by the factors that SystemTap missed. For example, SystemTap cannot measure the latency between packets arriving at the system and when the OS interrupt handler is called, which may be the main source of software stack delay asymmetry.

5.2 Queueing Delay Asymmetry

As Internet paths are mostly stable over a few hours [9], their propagation delay and transmission delay are likely to be similar on short time scales. Therefore, if server's clock is accurate, the *variation* of synchronization error (e.g., oscillation in Fig. 1(d)) should come from asymmetries of software stack delay and queueing

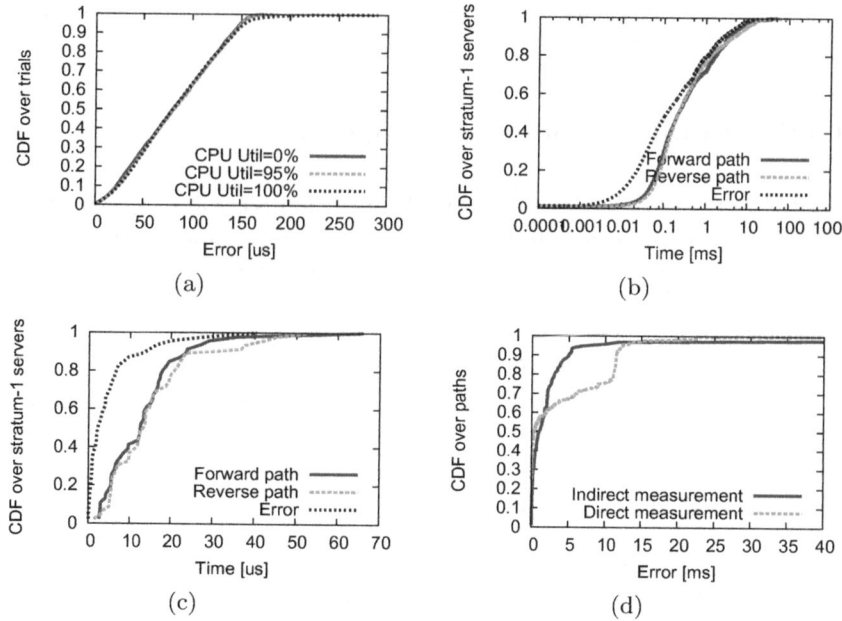

Fig. 2. (a) Synchronization error induced by software stack delay (§5.1) by varying CPU utilization. (b) Queueing delay (§5.2) in both directions, and the induced error for synchronization. Note that the x-axis is log scale. (c) Transmission delay (§5.3) in both directions, and the induced error for synchronization. (d) Comparison between the indirect (§5.4) and the direct (§6) measurement of the error induced by propagation delay asymmetry.

delay. As software stack usually contributes less than 150 μs error, the variation (e.g., spikes in Fig. 1(d)) should be dominated by queueing delay asymmetry.

To quantify the queueing delay asymmetry, we measure the synchronization error from our testbed nodes to GPS-equipped stratum-1 time servers over intervals of 15 minutes. For each measured interval, we assume that the synchronization error derived from probes with *minimal* one-way delay is composed of asymmetries of the propagation and transmission delay. After subtracting the minimal one-way delay in both directions, the remaining synchronization error will be vastly dominated by packet queueing. We observed that the median error is around 150 μs (Fig. 2(b)). However, the last 25% of the path has $\geq$ 1 ms error induced by queueing delay asymmetry. To evaluate this in the larger scale, we conduct the same experiment over paths between 300 lightly loaded PlanetLab nodes, and we obtained a very similar error distribution.

5.3   Transmission Delay Asymmetry

To decouple the transmission delay in the two directions, we send packets with *asymmetric size*. For example, to measure the transmission delay in the forwarding path, we only vary the packet size in the forward direction while the size in the reverse path is fixed. As the transmission delay is exactly proportional to the packet size, we sent probes with different packet sizes to measure the transmission delay. Specifically, to measure the transmission delay of a 76-byte NTP packet (including UDP and IP header size) *in the forward direction*, we send two probes with different sizes, p_1 and $p_2 < p_1$ in bytes in the forward direction, and received the destination reply as equal-size probes in the reverse path. Then the transmission delay of NTP packet is measured by $76 \times (t_1 - t_2)/(p_1 - p_2)$, where t_i represents the RTT of i-th probe.

This measurement scheme assumes that the delay contributed by other factors would remain the same for these two packets, which might hold for propagation delay because Internet paths are stable within a short period. However, software stack delay and queueing delay could vary over consecutive packets. To curtail the variance of queueing delay, we repeat the probes and select the one with minimal delay. The intuition is that the packet with minimal delay would suffer from smaller software stack and queueing asymmetry [4]. We measure the transmission delay asymmetry of NTP packets from our testbed nodes to stratum-1 time servers. We observe the median error is 2.2 μs (Fig. 2(c)). We repeated these experiments on PlanetLab and we got similar results.

5.4   Propagation Delay Asymmetry

Propagation delay asymmetry is hard to acquire accurately without knowing the length of the cables that carried probes. Hence, we determine this information indirectly by simply subtracting the errors induced by other factors from the overall synchronization error. In particular, we use the probes with minimal delay to exclude the synchronization error induced by queueing delay and software stack delay asymmetry. Similarly, as we are able to measure the error induced by transmission delay asymmetry (§5.3), the remaining error after subtraction should come from propagation delay asymmetry. Fig. 2(d) shows that the median error induced by propagation delay asymmetry is 2 ms, while the last 5% paths have error ≥ 10 ms. We are aware that the proposed scheme could be biased by other possible sources of delay, like interrupt coalescence. We will discussed another "direct" scheme to measure propagation delay asymmetry in §6.

Table 3. Error sources and quantity in typical case and worst 5% case. Note the percentage in the worst 5% case column is derived by assuming typical error for the other sources.

Asymmetry source	Typical error (percentage)	worst 5% case (percentage)
Software stack delay	85 μs (1.6%)	150 μs (3.5%)
Queueing delay	150 μs (2.9%)	2 ms (49%)
Transmission delay	2 μs (0.03%)	15 μs (0.7%)
Propagation delay	2 ms (95%)	7 ms (97%)

6   Discussion

For systems and measurements that rely on high degrees of clock accuracy, it may be desirable to reduce inter-host synchronization error over wide-area networks. From our results, several techniques may show promise in reducing these errors.

Pinning network paths: Based on our findings (Table 3), propagation delay asymmetry dominates synchronization error. Because of this, symmetric physical paths may be preferable for clock synchronization. Unfortunately, Internet paths are inherently asymmetric [9,10]. As a result, techniques that can "pin" routes to symmetric paths may provide the largest gains for network synchronization. For example, configuring routing protocols to prefer symmetric paths, or using tunneling protocols [11,12] to assign symmetric paths between devices that need good synchronization (e.g., between NTP servers) may provide benefits. While these techniques require network changes, our results also indicate that gains can be realized by preferring *existing* symmetric paths. To illustrate this, we build a support vector classification model using LIBSVM [13]. By probing a set of NTP servers, end-hosts simply collect multiple network factors such as the maximal and the minimal round-trip time over multiple probes, forwarding and reverse hop counts[2]. Given the sampled instances, the classifier is able to choose the top 5% servers with smallest synchronization error with a cross-validation accuracy of 91.8%. Our model uses the radial basis function (RBF) kernel where the samples are non-linearly mapping to a higher dimensional space.

Compensating at endpoints: Our results indicate that some aspects of delay asymmetry can be estimated. Because of this, it may be possible for end hosts to subtract this estimate to compensate. While we presented an indirect scheme to measure propagation delay asymmetry (§5.4), it requires a GPS receiver in the end host. Instead of using GPS receiver, we could use a geolocation-based service to approximate propagation delay. One could use traceroute (and reverse traceroute [14]) to find IP addresses of intermediate routers in both directions. Then the propagation delay can be estimated based on the geographical distance between intermediate routers, which is given by the IP geolocation services. We implement this by using a commercial IP geolocation service [15]. To reduce inaccuracy, we also inspect DNS names of ISP routers as a hint to infer their geographic location, as done in [16]. We observe that the *round-trip* propagation delay (measured by the geolocation-based service) and actual RTT are correlated with a coefficient of 0.56 (with a p-value $< 10^{-7}$) over PlanetLab nodes. We also compared the error with that measured by indirect measurement (Fig. 2(d)). They are not perfectly matched because the geolocation service may be inaccurate in some cases. The accuracy is likely to be improved by implementing a better IP geolocation optimization model [16].To discard inaccurate results in the indirect scheme, we performed a sanity check to select only paths satisfying $0.9 \leq RTT/(P_f + P_r) \leq 2.5$, where P_f and P_r are the forward and reverse propagation delay as estimated by geolocation-based service. With the limit lookups

---

[2] The reverse hop counts can be derived by guessing the initial TTL of the time server.

of reverse traceroute for security and load reasons, we limit our evaluation to only 8 public time servers, and the average synchronization error is reduced from 2.87 ms to 1.07 ms.

7   Conclusions

In this work we study the ability to synchronize clocks between network devices over the modern Internet. We find that while traditional synchronization protocols have only moderate errors (5 - 10 ms) in the common case, they can suffer from large "bursty" error in some cases. Our work may motivate future work on improving existing synchronization algorithms such as NTP to perform more efficiently in the wide area. Our major next step is to instrument the NTP protocol with our proposed modifications to determine the improvement in synchronization accuracy.

References

1. Minar, N.: A survey of the NTP network (December 1999)
2. Mills, D.L.: On the accuracy and stablility of clocks synchronized by the network time protocol in the Internet system. SIGCOMM Comp. Comm. Rev. (1990)
3. Veitch, D., Ridoux, J., Korada, S.B.: Robust synchronization of absolute and difference clocks over networks. IEEE/ACM Trans. Netw. (2009)
4. Ridoux, J., Veitch, D.: Principles of robust timing over the Internet. Commun. ACM (2010)
5. Kompella, R.R., Levchenko, K., Snoeren, A.C., Varghese, G.: Every microsecond counts: tracking fine-grain latencies with a lossy difference aggregator. In: SIGCOMM (2009)
6. Pathak, A., Pucha, H., Zhang, Y., Hu, Y.C., Mao, Z.M.: A measurement study of internet delay asymmetry. In: Claypool, M., Uhlig, S. (eds.) PAM 2008. LNCS, vol. 4979, pp. 182–191. Springer, Heidelberg (2008)
7. The NTP Public Services Project, http://support.ntp.org/
8. NIST Automated Computer Time Service (ACTS), http://www.nist.gov/physlab/div847/grp40/acts.cfm
9. Paxson, V.: End-to-end routing behavior in the internet. SIGCOMM Comput. Commun. Rev. (2006)
10. He, Y., Faloutsos, M., Krishnamurthy, S., Huffaker, B.: On routing asymmetry in the internet. In: GLOBECOM (2005)
11. Rosen, E., Viswanathan, A., Callon, R.: Multiprotocol Label Switching Architecture. RFC 3031 (January 2001)
12. Hanks, S., Li, T., Farinacci, D., Traina, P.: Generic Routing Encapsulation over IPv4 networks. RFC 1702 (October 1994)
13. Chang, C.-C., Lin, C.-J.: LIBSVM: a library for support vector machines (2001)
14. Katz-Bassett, E., Madhyastha, H., Adhikari, V., Scott, C., Sherry, J., van Wesep, P., Krishnamurthy, A., Anderson, T.: Reverse traceroute. In: NSDI (2010)
15. IPInfoDB, http://www.ipinfodb.com/
16. Katz-Bassett, E., John, J.P., Krishnamurthy, A., Wetherall, D., Anderson, T., Chawathe, Y.: Towards IP geolocation using delay and topology measurements. In: IMC (2006)

FACT: Flow-Based Approach
for Connectivity Tracking

Dominik Schatzmann[1], Simon Leinen[2],
Jochen Kögel[3], and Wolfgang Mühlbauer[1]

[1] ETH Zurich
{schatzmann,muehlbauer}@tik.ee.ethz.ch
[2] SWITCH
simon.leinen@switch.ch
[3] University of Stuttgart
jochen.koegel@ikr.uni-stuttgart.de

Abstract. More than 20 years after the launch of the public Internet, operator forums are still full of reports about temporary unreachability of complete networks. We propose FACT, a system that helps network operators to track connectivity problems with *remote* autonomous systems, networks, and hosts. In contrast to existing solutions, our approach relies solely on *flow-level* information about observed traffic, is capable of *online data processing*, and is *highly efficient* in alerting only about those events that *actually affect* the studied network or its users.

We evaluate FACT based on flow-level traces from a medium-sized ISP. Studying a time period of one week in September 2010, we explain the key principles behind our approach. Ultimately, these can be leveraged to detect connectivity problems and to summarize suspicious events for manual inspection by the network operator. In addition, when replaying archived traces from the past, FACT reliably recognizes reported connectivity problems that were relevant for the studied network.

Keywords: monitoring, connectivity problems, flow-based.

1   Introduction

"Please try to reach my network 194.9.82.0/24 from your networks ... Kindly anyone assist", (NANOG mailing list [1], March 2008). Such e-mails manifest the need of tools that allow to monitor and troubleshoot connectivity and performance problems in the Internet. This particularly holds from the perspective of an individual network and its operators who want to be alerted about disrupted peerings or congested paths before customers complain.

Both researchers [2,3,4,5] and industrial vendors [6,7] have made proposals for detecting and troubleshooting events such as loss of reachability or performance degradation for traffic that they exchange with other external networks, unfortunately with mixed success. Predominantly, such tools rely on active measurements using ping, traceroute, etc. [2,4]. Besides, researchers have suggested

N. Spring and G. Riley (Eds.): PAM 2011, LNCS 6579, pp. 214–223, 2011.

to leverage control plane information such as publicly available BGP feeds [3,8,9], although Bush et al. [10] point out the dangers of relying on control-plane information. Other concerns about existing tools include a high "dark" number of undetected events [8], a narrow evaluation solely in the context of a testbed or small system [5,9], or the time gap between the occurrence of an event and its observation and detection [8].

In this paper we propose FACT, a system that implements a **F**low-based **A**pproach for **C**onnectivity **T**racking. It helps network operators to monitor connectivity with *remote* autonomous systems (ASes), subnets, and hosts. Our approach relies on *flow-level* information about observed traffic (and not on control-plane data), is capable of *online data processing*, and *highly efficient* in alerting only about those events that *actually affect* the monitored network or its users.

In contrast to existing commercial solutions [6,7], we do not consider aggregate traffic volumes per interface or per peering to detect abnormal events, but pinpoint on a *per-flow basis* those cases where external hosts are unresponsive. On the one hand, this requires careful data processing to correctly handle asymmetric routing and to eliminate the impact of noise due to scanning, broken servers, late TCP resets, etc. On the other hand, our flow-based approach allows to compile accurate lists of unresponsive network addresses, which is a requirement for efficient troubleshooting.

To test our system we rely on a one-week flow-level trace from the border routers of a medium-sized ISP [11]. We demonstrate that our approach can be leveraged to detect serious connectivity problems and to summarize suspicious events for manual inspection by the network operator. Importantly, replaying flow traces from the past, FACT also reliably recognizes reported connectivity problems, but only if those are relevant from the perspective of the studied network and its users. Overall, we believe that our approach can be generally applied to small- to medium-sized ISPs, and enterprise networks. In particular networks that (partially) rely on default routes to reach the Internet can strongly benefit from our techniques, since they allow to identify critical events even if these are not visible in the control plane information.

2 Methodology

Our goal is to enable network operators to monitor whether remote hosts and networks are reachable from inside their networks or their customer networks, and to alert about existing connectivity problems. Such issues include cases where either we observe a significant number of unsuccessful connection attempts from inside the studied network(s) to a specific popular remote host, or where many remote hosts within external networks are unresponsive to connection attempts originated by potentially different internal hosts.

To obtain a network-centric view of connectivity, we rely on flow-level data exported by *all* border routers of a network, see Fig. 1. In this regard, our approach is generally applicable to all small- and medium-sized ISPs, and enterprise networks. Monitoring the complete unsampled traffic that crosses the border of our

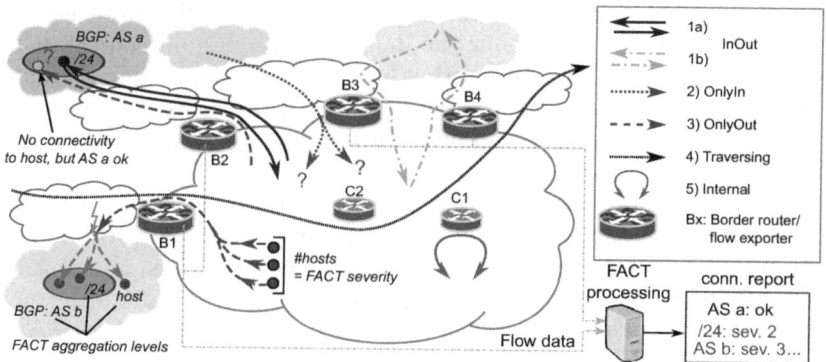

Fig. 1. Measurement infrastructure and flow types

network allows to match outgoing with incoming flows and to check for abnormal changes in the balance between incoming and outgoing flows for external end-points at different *aggregation levels* (hosts or networks). In particular networks that (partially) rely on default routes to reach the Internet can strongly benefit from such an approach, since it allows to identify critical events even if these are not visible in the control plane information.

As shown in Fig. 1, we distinguish between five *flow types*: `Internal` connections never cross the network border, and thus are neither recorded nor studied further in our approach. Since the scope of this paper is limited to cases where remote hosts or networks are unresponsive to connection attempts originated by internal hosts, we ignore flows that traverse our network (`Traversing`) or flows for which we cannot find traffic in the outbound direction (`OnlyIn`), e.g., caused by inbound scanning. If we can associate outgoing flows with incoming flows, we assume that external hosts are reachable (`InOut`) and also take this as a hint that there exists connectivity towards the remote network. Note that the incoming flow can enter the network via the same border router that was used by the outgoing flow to exit the network. Yet, due to the asymmetric nature of Internet paths this is not necessary [9]. Finally, we observe flows that exit the network but we fail to find a corresponding incoming response (`OnlyOut`).

To detect potential connectivity problems, we focus on the latter category `OnlyOut`. Note that we rely on the assumption that our measured flow data is complete, i.e., for any outgoing flow the associated incoming flow is observed by our collection infrastructure provided that there has been a response in reality. Evidently, network operators only want to get informed about critical events that include loss of connectivity towards complete networks or towards popular hosts that a significant share of internal hosts tries to reach. Our approach to achieve this goal is twofold.

First, we heavily rely on data *aggregation* to investigate connectivity towards complete networks. More precisely, we aggregate occurrences of `OnlyOut` flow types across external hosts, /24 networks, or prefixes as observed in public BGP routing tables. For example, only if we observe within a certain time period a considerable number of `OnlyOut` flow types towards different hosts of a specific external network, and no `InOut` types, we conclude that the complete external network is currently not reachable for internal hosts. Hence, our decision is not based on observed connectivity between a single pair of internal and external hosts.

Second, we take into account the number of internal hosts that are affected by connectivity problems towards a host, network, or BGP prefix, i.e., the *severity of an observed event*. For example, loss of connectivity towards an individual external host is interesting for a network operator if a large number of different internal hosts fail to reach such a popular service. Moreover, knowing the number of affected internal hosts is crucial to extract short summaries of candidate events which network operators can check manually in reasonable time.

3   Data Sets

We investigate our approach based on data collected in the SWITCH network [11], a medium-sized ISP in Switzerland connecting approximately 30 Swiss universities, government institutions, and research labs to the Internet. The IP address range contains about 2.2 million internal IP addresses. For our studies we have collected a trace in September 2010 (`OneWeek`) that spans 7 days and contains unsampled NetFlows summarizing all traffic crossing the 6 border routers of the SWITCH network. This results in $14 - 40k$ NetFlow records per second. In addition to `OneWeek` we extract some shorter traces to study selected connectivity problems from the past, see Section 5.

4   Connectivity Analysis

The implementation of FACT includes four major components, see Fig. 2. After `data collection`, a `preprocessing` step removes some flows from the data stream, e.g., blacklisted hosts or information that is not needed to achieve our goals. For a limited time we keep the remaining flows in the `5-tuple cache`, which is continuously updated with the latest flow information. In the following we will provide more details about the implementation of the individual components.

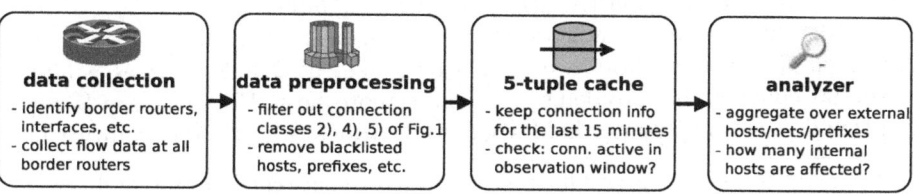

Fig. 2. Architectural components of FACT

4.1   Data Collection and Preprocessing

In addition to standard flow information including IP addresses, port numbers, protocol number, packet counts, byte counts, etc., we store identifiers for the border routers and interfaces over which traffic with external networks is exchanged. Next, we exclude a considerable number of unnecessary flows to save memory and computational resources, but also eliminate flows that have turned out to be harmful for the detection of connectivity problems. Such flows include for example traffic from/to PlanetLab hosts or bogon IP addresses, and multicast. For now, we generate an appropriate blacklist manually, but we plan to automate this process in the future. For reasons already described in the preceding section, we remove in this step also all flows of the class `Traversing` and `Internal`, see Fig. 1.

4.2   5-Tuple Cache

The subsequent data processing respects the fact that the active timeout of our flow collection infrastructure is set to 5 minutes.[1] Therefore, we partition the timeline into intervals of 5 minutes and proceed with our data processing whenever such a time interval has expired. Our goal is to maintain for each interval a hash-like data structure (*5-tuple cache*) that, for observed flows identified by IP addresses, protocol number, and application ports, stores and updates information that is relevant for further analysis. This includes packet counts, byte counts, information about the used border router and the time when the flows were active for the in and out flow. Note that at this point we implicitly merge unidirectional to bidirectional flows (biflows).

After the time interval has expired we extract from the obtained biflows and remaining unidirectional flows two sets: The set `ConnSuccess` includes those biflows of type *InOut* where at least one of the underlying unidirectional flows starts or ends within the currently studied time interval and are initiated by internal hosts[2]. The second set, called `ConnFailed`, includes only those unidirectional flows of type `OnlyOut` where the outgoing flow either starts or ends in the currently studied time interval. To reduce the effect of delayed packets (e.g., TCP resets), we here ignore unidirectional flows if a corresponding reverse flow has been observed during any of the preceding time intervals.[3] All other flows of the *5-tuple cache* that are not in the set `ConnSuccess` or `ConnFailed` are excluded from further consideration for this time interval.

While `ConnSuccess` flows indicate that an internal host in our network can indeed reach the external host, we take occurrences of `ConnFailed` as a hint for potential connectivity problems with the remote host. However, the latter assumption does not necessarily hold when applications (e.g., NTP or multicast)

---

[1] After 5 minutes even still active flows are exported to our central flow repository.

[2] We rely on port numbers to determine who initiates a biflow.

[3] Our hash-like data structure is not deleted after a time period of 5 minutes but continuously updated. Only if a biflow is inactive for more than 900 seconds, it is removed from our hash-like data structure.

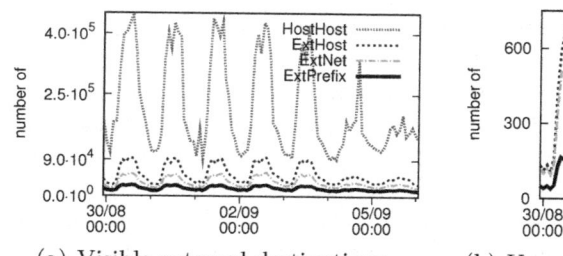

(a) Visible external destinations.

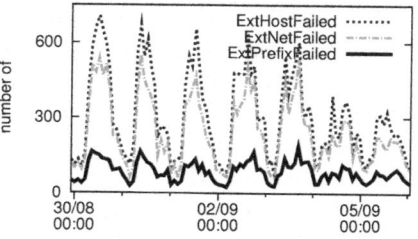

(b) Unresponsive external destinations.

Fig. 3. External hosts, networks, and prefixes

are inherently unidirectional. Hence, we exclusively take into account HTTP traffic using port 80, which is symmetric by nature and due to its popularity visible in any type of network.[4] More marginal fine-tuning of our data processing is required. Yet, given space limitations we refrain from providing more details.

4.3 Analyzer

To study observed connectivity with remote hosts and to detect potential problems, the analyzer component processes the sets `ConnSuccess` and `ConnFailed` every 5 minutes. We aggregate `ConnFailed` and `ConnSuccess` flows for the same pair of internal and external host if we find more than one flow, possibly with different port numbers. The obtained host-host tuples are classified as `HostHostSuccess` if at least one `ConnSuccess` flow has been identified, `HostHostFailed` otherwise. Based on this initial aggregation step, we independently compute three stronger aggregation levels: we group host-host tuples into one tuple if they affect the same external host (`ExtHostSuccess` or `ExtHostFailed`), the same external /24 network (`ExtNetSuccess` or `ExtNetFailed`), and BGP prefixes (`ExtPrefixSuccess` or `ExtPrefixFailed`). With respect to the last granularity, we use publicly available BGP routing tables to determine the corresponding BGP prefix for a given external host. Again, we classify an aggregate class as `Success` if at least one tuple is marked as `HostHostSuccess`.

Fig. 3 displays the number of visible and unresponsive external destinations if the three aggregation granularities are applied to `OneWeek`, see Section 3. According to Fig. 3(a) the absolute number of visible external destinations shows a strong daily and weekly pattern irrespective of the used aggregation level. Aggregating from host-host into `ExtHostFailed` and `ExtHostSuccess`, respectively, reduces the peaks from $525K$ to $90K$ tuples (/24s: $50K$, prefixes: $25K$). This provides evidence for the high visibility that our data has on external networks. However, Fig. 3(b) reveals that generally only a small fraction of external hosts (peaks of 700) are unresponsive and therefore classified as `ExtHostFailed` according to

---

[4] Experiments relying on DNS traffic turned out to work as well.

our methodology. This fraction is significantly smaller for `ExtNetFailed` (peaks of 600) and `ExtPrefixFailed` (peaks of 180), respectively.

However, to cope with daily and weekly fluctuations and to limit the degree to which a single internal host (e.g., a scanning host) can impact our connectivity analysis, we need to take into account the *severity of an observed event* as well. By this we understand the number of internal users that actually fail to establish connectivity with a specific external host, /24 network, or BGP prefix during our 5 minute time intervals. Figure 4(a) displays the number of external /24 networks that are unresponsive to 1, 2, 5, and 10 internal hosts for the time spanned by `OneWeek`. The majority of these `ExtHostFailed` "events", namely 98%, only affect 1 internal host.

Yet, here it is important to study Fig. 4(b). It is also based on `OneWeek` and counts for every external host the number of 5-minute time intervals for which it has been classified as `ExtHostFailed`. This number (x-axis) is plotted against the maximum number of internal hosts (y-axis) that failed to establish connectivity with this external host (`ExtHostFailed`) at *any* 5-minute interval of `OneWeek`. We find that the majority of external hosts (96%) are only unresponsive in less than 10 time intervals of our trace. However, some hosts are unresponsive most of the time, e.g., abandoned ad servers. Data preprocessing as described in Section 4.1 could be refined to automatically blacklist such hosts and possibly their networks. Finally, we observe few external hosts that are unresponsive only during a small number of time intervals, but with a high maximum number of affected internal hosts. Cross-checking with technical forums in the Internet, we find that these events include for example a Facebook outage on August 31, 2010.

We point out that the data processing in FACT is faster than real time for SWITCH, a medium-sized ISP covering an estimated 6% of the Internet traffic in Switzerland and approximately 2.2 million IP addresses: flow data spanning 5 minutes[5] can be processed using a single thread in less than three minutes with a maximum memory consumption of less than 4GB. Aging mechanisms for our data structures[3] ensure that the overall memory consumption does not

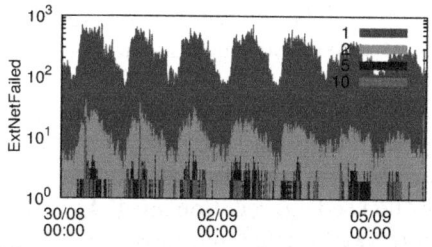
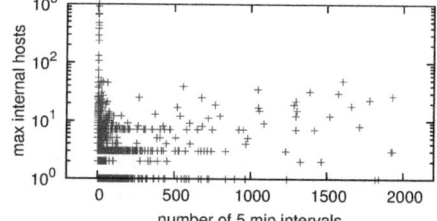
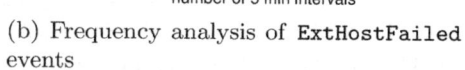

(a) Number of `ExtNetFailed` that are unresponsive to 1, 2, 5, and 10 internal hosts.

(b) Frequency analysis of `ExtHostFailed` events

Fig. 4. Severity of observed events

---

[5] We see up to 200 million flows per hour.

increase during long-term use of our system. Due to hash-like data structures we can access individual flows in our 5-tuple cache in constant time. The total time required for data processing mainly depends on the number of active flows. In principle, it is even possible to parallelize our processing by distributing the reachability analysis for different external networks to different CPU cores or physical machines. Yet, we leave it to future work to study FACT's performance for large tier-1 ISPs and how to make it robust against potentially higher false positive rates if sampled flow data is used.

5 Case Studies

In this section we present a short analysis of three connectivity problems that were either detected by the network operator or publicly documented. To analyze those cases, we rely on data collected as discussed in Section 3.

Black-holing: On May 18, 2010, all services in an external /24 network were not accessible from SWITCH between 08:30 and 08:45. According to the operators of SWITCH, this problem was most likely due to a tier-1 provider that black-holed parts of the reverse traffic towards SWITCH. Yet, at this time the operators could only speculate how many hosts and customers, or even other /24 networks were affected by this problem. Applying FACT we confirm that the reported /24 network is indeed reported as unreachable at around 08:30. Surprisingly, FACT reveals that the overall number of unreachable hosts and /24 networks has doubled compared to the time before 08:30 while the number of unresponsive BGP prefixes is increased by a factor of even 6, see Fig. 5(a). Moreover, the reported /24 network is not even in the top ten list of the most popular unresponsive networks. This suggests that the impact of this event has been more serious than previously believed.

RIPE/Duke event: On August 27, 2010, some parts of the Internet became disconnected for some 30 minutes due to an experiment with new BGP attributes by RIPE and Duke University [12]. FACT reveals that at around 08:45 the number of popular unresponsive /24 networks indeed doubled. According to Fig. 5(b), for some BGP prefixes more than 15 internal hosts failed to establish

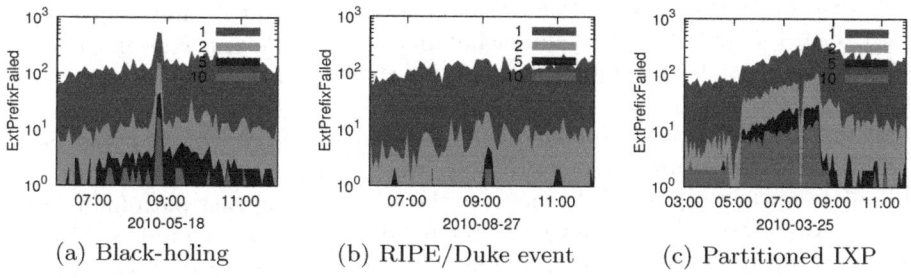

(a) Black-holing   (b) RIPE/Duke event   (c) Partitioned IXP

Fig. 5. Case studies: unresponsive BGP prefixes

connectivity. Yet, overall our analysis reveals that the impact of this incident on SWITCH and its customers was quite limited compared to the public attention that this event obtained.

Partitioned IXP: After scheduled maintenance by AMS-IX, SWITCH's connection to that exchange point came back with only partial connectivity. Some next-hops learned via the route servers weren't reachable, creating black holes. The next morning, several customers complained about external services being unreachable. Overall, it took more than four hours until the problem was finally solved by resetting a port. Fig. 5(c) shows that the number of unresponsive BGP prefixes is almost ten times higher than normal, over a time period of more than four hours. We believe that FACT would have helped to detect such a serious problem much faster and provided valuable hints about the origin of the problem.

6 Related Work

Approaches for detecting and troubleshooting reachability problems can be generally classified into two classes: *active probing* and *control plane based.*

With respect to *active probing*, Paxson et al. [9] are probably the pioneers to use traceroute for studying end-to-end connectivity between a (limited) set of Internet sites. Zhang et al. [2] perform collaborative probing launched from Planetlab hosts to diagnose routing event failures. Commercial solutions such as NetQoS [7] or Peakflow [6] generally rely on *active* measurements using ping, traceroutes, or continuous SNMP queries to network devices. Moreover, they frequently aggregate traffic volumes per interface, peering links, etc. to detect abnormal events, and hence do not base their analysis on a flow-level granularity as our work suggests. In contrast to active probing, the passive monitoring approach of FACT does not impose any traffic overhead and, importantly, only creates alerts for those unreachable hosts/networks that users actually want to access. Finally, FACT avoids an intrinsic problem of active probing techniques such as ping or traceroute, namely the implicit assumption that reachable hosts actually do respond to such tools.

In addition to active probing, a considerable number of research papers, e.g., [8,13] rely almost exclusively on *control-plane information* in the form of BGP routing feeds. However, Bush et al. [10] have clearly pointed out the dangers of such an approach, e.g., the wide-spread existence of default routes. In contrast, FACT is able to detect unreachability at multiple and finer granularities (e.g., on a host basis) than any approach that is purely based on routing data.

Later work including e.g., Hubble [3] and iPlane [4] rely on hybrid approaches combining active measurements with BGP routing information. Feamster et al. [14] adopt such an approach to measure the effects of Internet path faults on reactive routing. Overall, we believe that the passive approach adopted by FACT is very powerful compared to active probing and control-plane based techniques. Yet, we plan to integrate active probing into our system to crosscheck detected reachability problems and to pinpoint the underlying causes.

7   Conclusion

We have proposed FACT, an online data processing system that helps operators to acquire facts about connectivity problems with remote autonomous systems, subnets, and hosts. In contrast to existing solutions, our approach relies solely on flow-level information extracted from traffic crossing the border of the network. We showed, with the help of reported real-world events, that FACT can be used to alert only about those events that actually affect the studied network or its users. Importantly, data processing of FACT is already faster than real time for a medium-sized ISP.

In the future we plan to refine and integrate our techniques into existing tracing tools (e.g., nfdump), to generate alerts based on automatically determined thresholds, and to provide summary reports that allow network operators to quickly troubleshoot connectivity problems. Ultimately, we plan to make our implementation of FACT available for public use.

References

1. Nanog mailing list, website `http://www.nanog.org/mailinglist/`
2. Zhang, Y., Mao, M., Zhang, M.: Effective diagnosis of routing disruptions from end systems. In: Proc. NSDI (2008)
3. Katz-Bassett, E., Madhyastha, H., John, J., Krishnamurthy, A., Wetherall, D., Anderson, T.: Studying black holes in the Internet with Hubble. In: Proc. NSDI (2008)
4. Madhyastha, H., Isdal, T., Piatek, M., Dixon, C., Anderson, T., Krishnamurthy, A., Venkataramani, A.: iPlane: an information plane for distributed services. In: Proc. OSDI (2006)
5. Zhang, M., Zhang, C., Pai, V., Peterson, L., Wang, R.: PlanetSeer: Internet path failure monitoring and characterization in wide-area services. In: Proc. OSDI (2004)
6. Arbor Networks - Peakflow, website `http://www.arbornetworks.com`
7. CA technologies - NetQoS performance center, website `http://www.netperformance.com/`
8. Wu, J., Mao, M., Rexford, J., Wang, J.: Finding a needle in a haystack: Pinpointing significant BGP routing changes in an IP network
9. Paxson, V.: End-to-end routing behavior in the Internet. IEEE/ACM Trans. Networking 5(5) (1997)
10. Bush, R., Maennel, O., Roughan, M., Uhlig, S.: Internet optometry: assessing the broken glasses in Internet reachability. In: Proc. of ACM IMC (2009)
11. The Swiss Education and Research Network (SWITCH), `http://www.switch.ch`
12. RIPE/Duke event, `http://labs.ripe.net/Members/erik/ripe-ncc-and-duke-university-bgp-experiment/`
13. Feldmann, A., Maennel, O., Mao, M., Berger, A., Maggs, B.: Locating Internet routing instabilities. In: Proc. of ACM SIGCOMM (2004)
14. Feamster, N., Anderson, D., Balakrishnan, H., Kaashoek, F.: Measuring the effects of Internet path faults on reactive routing. In: Proc. of ACM SIGMETRICS (2003)

Non-cooperative Diagnosis of Submarine Cable Faults

Edmond W.W. Chan, Xiapu Luo, Waiting W.T. Fok,
Weichao Li, and Rocky K.C. Chang

Department of Computing, The Hong Kong Polytechnic University
{cswwchan,csxluo,cswtfok,csweicli,csrchang}@comp.polyu.edu.hk

Abstract. Submarine cable faults are not uncommon events in the Internet today. However, their impacts on end-to-end path quality have received almost no attention. In this paper, we report path-quality measurement results for a recent SEA-ME-WE 4 cable fault in 2010. Our measurement methodology captures the path-quality degradation due to the cable fault, in terms of delay, asymmetric packet losses, and correlation between loss and delay. We further leverage traceroute data to infer the root causes of the performance degradation.

1 Introduction

Submarine cables are critical elements of the Internet today, because they provide cross-country routes for transoceanic data and voice transmissions. The demand for high-capacity submarine cables has been increasing for the last few years. For instance, the recently deployed Trans-Pacific Unity submarine cable system can transmit data between Japan and the west coast of the United States up to 4.8 Terabits per second (Tbits/s). Dramatic capacity upgrades to the existing Asia-Europe cable systems and the emergence of five new submarine cable systems connecting the Middle East were also reported [11].

Data loss and substantial service interruption as a result of submarine cable faults conceivably entail huge economic cost. Although submarine cable systems are protected by various reliability technologies (e.g., [15,16]), they still appear to be highly vulnerable according to numerous submarine cable faults reported in recent years (e.g., [1,2,3]). The worst one is the incident of massive cable cuts due to the Hengchun earthquake in 2006 [1]. Moreover, a submarine cable fault requires considerable time for tracing the fault location and repairing.

Besides the traffic on the faulty submarine cable, the Internet traffic that is not carried by the faulty cables can also be affected. A common quick-fix strategy for restoring the disrupted communication is to reroute the affected traffic to other submarine/terrestrial/satellite links. However, the side effect of such ad hoc traffic rerouting mechanism is introducing a high volume of traffic, and therefore substantial congestion, to the backup paths. However, the impact of submarine cable faults on the global Internet connectivity has not received attention from the research community. Therefore, very little is known about

N. Spring and G. Riley (Eds.): PAM 2011, LNCS 6579, pp. 224–234, 2011.

the Internet's vulnerability to the faults in terms of path-quality degradation, congestion on the backup paths, and speed of network recovery.

In this paper, we report the impacts of a recent SEA-ME-WE 4 cable fault incident [2] measured from our neighbor-cooperative measurement system [14]. In this system, a number of coordinated measurement nodes persistently monitor the performance of network paths to a set of web servers. The impacts of the cable fault are observed from the degradation in the path quality. To infer the root cause of the degradation, we leverage the forward-path Tcptraceroute gleaned from the measurement nodes to study the IP-level/AS-level route changes. Based on this dataset, we analyze how submarine cable faults affected the routes used by the network paths and the performance of these paths. We also evaluate the effectiveness of network operators' responses to the incident.

The paper is organized as follows. We first introduce our measurement methodology in §2. We then present our measurement findings on the impacts of the SEA-ME-WE 4 cable fault in §3. After discussing the related works in §4, we conclude the paper with future works in §5.

2   Measurement Methodology

2.1   Measurement Setup

We have been conducting end-to-end Internet path measurement from eight Hong Kong universities, labeled by UA–UH, since 1 January 2009. A measurement node is installed just behind the border router of each university to measure network paths to 44 non-cooperative web servers (without requiring software setup on the servers) in Hong Kong, Australia, China, Finland, France, Germany, Japan, Korea, New Zealand, Taiwan, the United Kingdom, and the United States. We use HTTP/OneProbe [17] for data-path quality measurement and Tcptraceroute for forward-path tracing. Our measurement produces 12-GB measurement data daily.

2.2   Measurement Scheduling and Traffic

To obtain comparable results, all the eight measurement nodes measure the same web server around the same time. We employ several measures to avoid congestion introduced by the measurement traffic. In particular, we divide the set of web servers into five groups and measure the groups in a round-robin fashion. The nodes launch HTTP/OneProbe to measure each group for one minute and then perform Tcptraceroute with the default configuration to the same group for another minute. For each path, HTTP/OneProbe dispatches a sequence of Poisson-modulated probe pairs to each web server with a probing frequency of 2 Hz and an IP packet size of 576 bytes, and each probe pair elicits at most two 576-byte response packets from the server. Therefore, the aggregated probe traffic sent to each server is less than 200 Kbits/s. Moreover, we use separate network interfaces for conducting the measurement and receiving the data.

2.3   Metrics

Routing metrics. To evaluate the routing behavior as a consequence of submarine cable faults, we continuously measure both IP routes and the corresponding AS routes (by resolving IP hops into AS numbers) from the measurement nodes to the web servers. To quantify the IP-level route changes, we resort to the IP-level Jaccard distance defined in Eqn. (1) to measure the difference of a route measured at times $i-1$ and i, which are denoted by R_{i-1} and R_i. The Jaccard distance is computed by the number of dissimilar elements divided by the total number of distinct elements in R_{i-1} and R_i. Therefore, the IP-level Jaccard distance is zero for two identical IP routes, and one for two completely different IP routes. We similarly compute an AS-level Jaccard distance for AS routes based on Eqn. (1) to analyze the AS-level route changes.

$$J_\delta(R_{i-1}, R_i) = 1 - \frac{|R_{i-1} \cap R_i|}{|R_{i-1} \cup R_i|}. \tag{1}$$

Using Jaccard distance to characterize route changes is not new. Pathak et al. [18], for example, studied the AS routing asymmetry by computing the Jaccard similarity index between forward-path and reverse-path AS routes. Schwartz et al. [19] used the Levenshtein distance to quantify the difference between the dominant route and other non-dominant routes for a pair of source and destination. Since reordering of elements in the IP/AS routes after route changes is rare in our dataset, we simply use Jaccard distance which does not take into account the order of elements in each route, whereas the Levenshtein distance does.

Path performance metrics. We employ HTTP/OneProbe to measure TCP data-path performance for each path between measurement node and web server. HTTP/OneProbe uses legitimate TCP data probe and response packets to measure RTTs and detect one-way (i.e., forward-path and reverse-path) packet losses. To evaluate the paths' congestion status, we also apply the loss-pair analysis [13] to correlate the one-way packet losses with the RTTs. Moreover, we correlate the route change metrics with the path performance metrics to analyze path-quality degradation due to submarine cable faults.

3   The SEA-ME-WE 4 Cable Fault

The South East Asia-Middle East-Western Europe 4 (SEA-ME-WE 4) submarine cable [8] is a major Internet backbone connecting Southeast Asia, the Indian subcontinent, the Middle East, and Europe. It involves 17 landing points and carries Internet traffic among 15 countries, including Egypt, France, India, Saudi Arabia, and Singapore. The SEA-ME-WE 4 cable has a data rate up to 1.28 Tbits/s [4] and is owned by a consortium of 16 companies, including the Tata Communications (or TATA).

The SEA-ME-WE 4 cable encountered a shunt fault on the segment between Alexandria and Marseille on 14 April 2010 [2,9], but the exact time was not reported. The shunt fault was caused by a short circuit when the submarine cable, whose insulation was damaged, came into contact with the sea water. Since the cable was not severed, it was still operable with limited capacity. The cable fault affected a number of countries whose global connectivity relied on the SEA-ME-WE 4 cable (e.g., [2,12]). The repair was started on 25 April 2010, and it took four days to complete [2]. During the repair, the service for the westbound traffic to Europe was not available.

3.1   Impacts of the Cable Fault

Fig. 1 shows the time series of the average IP-level and AS-level Jaccard distances for the paths from UA–UH to two web servers (BBC and ENG3) in the United Kingdom and one web server (NOKIA) in Finland between 1 April 2010 0:00 and 8 May 2010 0:00 GMT, inclusively. As Fig. 1(a) shows, the IP-level Jaccard distance for the paths overlapped with one another at the beginning and then gradually declined starting from 14 April that coincides with the date of the cable fault incident. The BBC's Jaccard distance dropped to zero with intermittent surges after 16 April 7:30 GMT, whereas the ENG3's and NOKIA's distances fluctuated between 0.05 and 0.22, and experienced another drop on 5 May noon GMT. Moreover, Fig. 1(b) shows some significant AS-level route changes.

To probe deeper into how the paths to BBC, ENG3, and NOKIA evolved after the cable fault, we zoom into an episode e_1 which spans between 13 April 0:00 and 17 April 8:00 GMT in Fig. 1(a). Fig. 2(a) shows that their average IP-level Jaccard distances during e_1 exhibit staircase decreasing patterns, meaning that the paths became more similar after the cable fault. We can also distinguish at

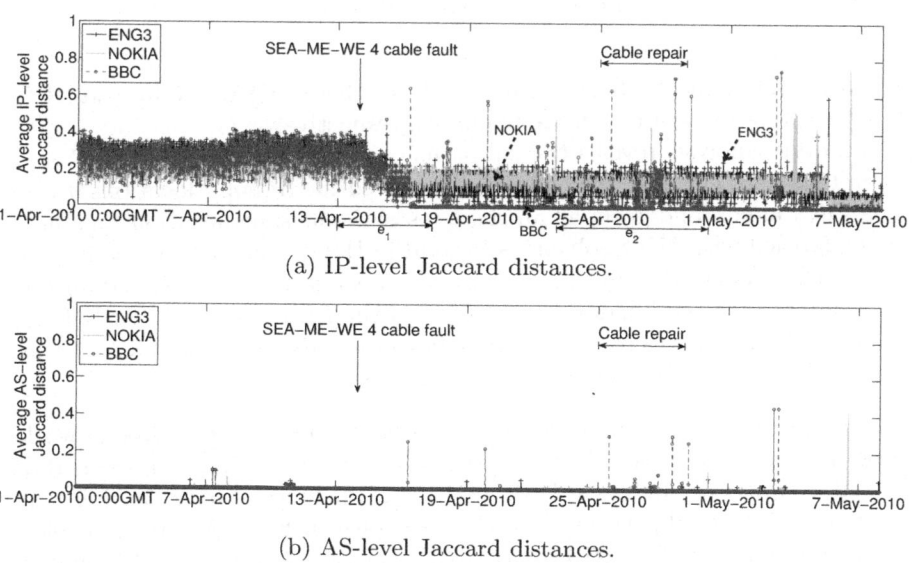

(a) IP-level Jaccard distances.

(b) AS-level Jaccard distances.

Fig. 1. Time series of the average IP-level and AS-level Jaccard distances for the paths to BBC, ENG3, and NOKIA.

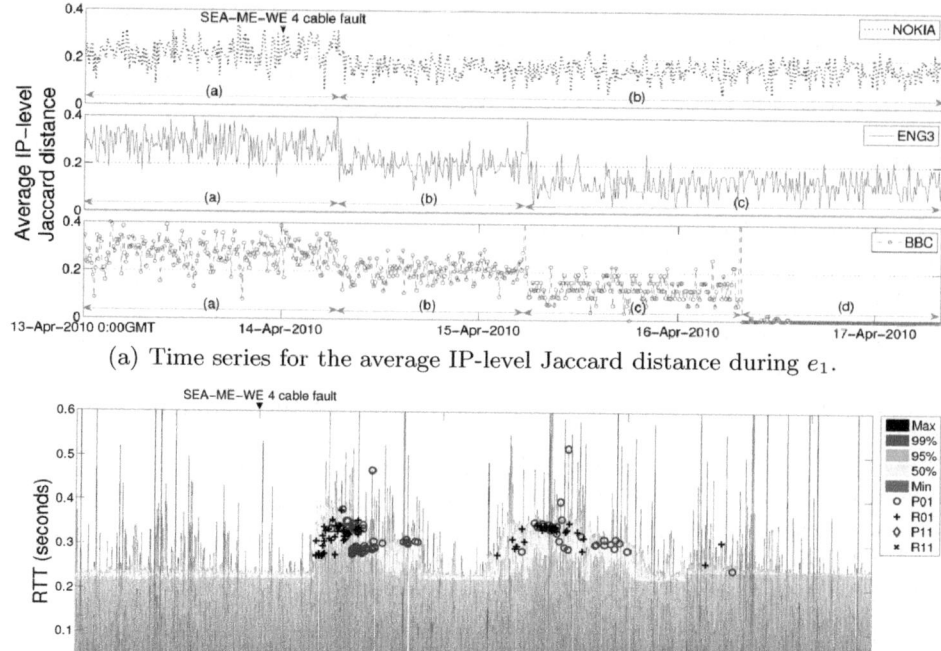

(a) Time series for the average IP-level Jaccard distance during e_1.

(b) RTT time series for the path between UB and BBC during e_1.

Fig. 2. Time series of the average IP-level Jaccard distance for the paths to NOKIA, ENG3, and BBC, and time series of RTT for UB⇌BBC during e_1.

most four distinct phases labeled with (a)–(d) for the NOKIA, ENG3, and BBC paths which have two, three, and four phases, respectively.

A traceroute analysis reveals the subpaths corresponding to the four phases shown in Fig. 3. To generate the figures, we resolved the IP hops' locations based on their DNS names and grouped all the hops with the same location together. The node labeled with "Unresolved" is located in Hong Kong, and we could not resolve its DNS name. Phases (a)-(c) apply to all three web servers, and all the routes went through the London IX (LINX) via the FLAG network (AS15412). On the other hand, phases (d)-(e) apply only to the BBC paths, and TATA was the carrier. We will discuss phase (e) in the next section.

Phases (a) and (b). Fig. 3(a) shows three subpaths inside the FLAG network in phase (a). Upon the onset of phase (b) on 14 April 7:00 GMT (the same day of the reported cable fault), the IP-level Jaccard distance started declining, a result of the missing subpath via Mumbai as shown in Fig. 3(b). We also plot the RTT time series in Fig. 2(b) for the path between UB and BBC (denoted as UB⇌BBC). The figure includes the RTTs obtained from P01s and R01s which are the respective loss pairs on UB → BBC (forward path) and BBC → UB (reverse path). A P01 (R01) is a packet pair in which *only* the first probe

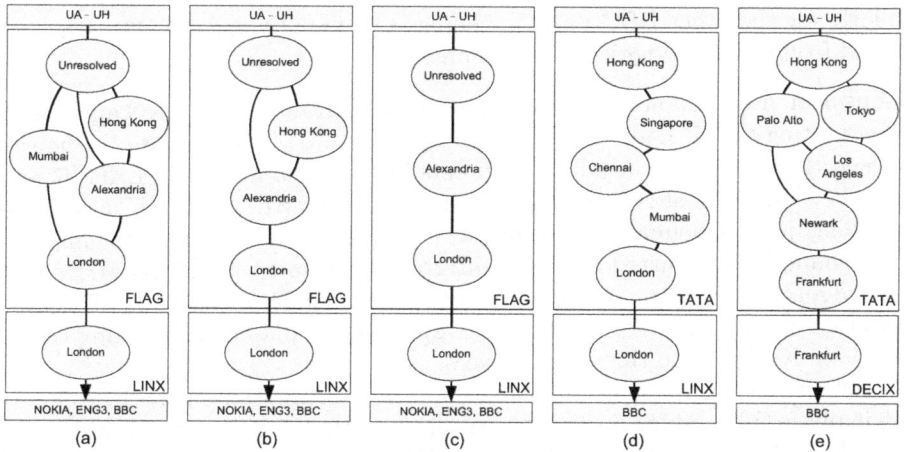

Fig. 3. Five sets of subpaths observed from the NOKIA, ENG3, and BBC paths

(response) packet is received by the destination, and the first packet's RTT can be used to infer a congested router's queueing delay upon packet loss on the forward (reverse) path [13]. Moreover, P11s (R11s) on the x-axis in Fig. 2(b) show the RTTs when *both* packets in a probe (response) pair are lost. We align the x-axes in Figs. 2(a) and 2(b) to facilitate a clear comparison.

Fig. 2(b) shows that UB⇌BBC suffered from significant congestion in phase (b). We also observe similar results for the other BBC paths and the NOKIA and ENG3 paths which are not shown in this paper. Comparing with phase (a), phase (b) exhibits both RTT inflation and more loss pairs with the measured path queueing delay [13] between 34 ms and 228 ms. In many cases, both packets in a probe pair or a response pair were lost. The figure also shows a prolonged congestion period in the forward path, indicated by persistent probe packet losses. However, the path performance improved in the second half of the phase which corresponds to the non-working hours in the United Kingdom.

Phases (c) and (d). Fig. 2(a) shows a further reduction of the IP-level Jaccard distance for the ENG3 and BBC paths on 15 April 5:40 GMT (i.e., the onset of phase (c)), because only the subpath via Alexandria and London was retained in FLAG (as shown in Fig. 3(c)). Moreover, Fig. 2(b) shows more prolonged RTT inflation and packet losses during phase (c), which was probably caused by the reduced alternate routes.

On 16 April 7:30 GMT, the beginning of phase (d), the service provider for UA–UH changed the upstream from FLAG to TATA (AS6453) only for the BBC paths. As a result, the IP-level Jaccard distance shown in Fig. 2(a) dropped to almost zero. We also observe a spike from the AS-level Jaccard distance for the BBC paths at the similar time in Fig. 1(b). Notice that this change significantly improved the performance for the BBC paths. In particular, Fig. 2(b) shows that UB⇌BBC enjoyed relatively stable RTTs and insignificant packet losses (and similarly for the other BBC paths), whereas the NOKIA and ENG3 paths still suffered from severe congestion in this phase.

Discussion. Fig. 4 shows all the submarine cables available to FLAG and TATA for connecting the IP hops' locations in Figs. 3(a)–3(d). We generate the figures by inspecting the cables and landing points in the cable maps of FLAG [6] and TATA [5]. Fig. 4(b) shows that TATA uses only the SEA-ME-WE 4 cable to reach Singapore, Chennai, and Mumbai, but these segments were not affected by the shunt fault occurred in the Mediterranean segment [9]. Moreover, TATA uses different cables between Mumbai and London. On the other hand, Fig. 4(a) shows that FLAG does not use the SEA-ME-WE 4 cable for forwarding traffic from Hong Kong to the three web servers.

Based on Fig. 4, a plausible explanation for the congestion in the FLAG network in phase (b) is taking on rerouted traffic from the SEA-ME-WE 4 cable after the cable fault. Both FEA and SEA-ME-WE 4 (and SEA-ME-WE 3) are the major submarine cables connecting between Europe and Asia. Fig. 4(b) shows that TATA could use FEA to reach BBC when the SEA-ME-WE 4 segment in the Mediterranean region was not available. Therefore, the congestion was introduced as a secondary effect of the cable fault. On the other hand, the path quality for the BBC paths improved after switching to TATA in phase (d). Unlike FLAG, TATA has access to three submarine cables between Suez and Alexandria. There are also two cables between Alexandria and London. Moreover, the reduced path diversity from phase (a) to phase (c) could also be responsible for the congestion in the FLAG network, although the reason for the reduction is unknown to us.

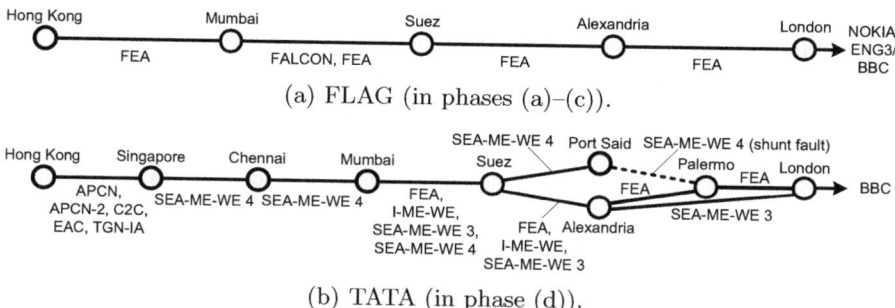

(a) FLAG (in phases (a)–(c)).

(b) TATA (in phase (d)).

Fig. 4. The submarine cables available to FLAG and TATA for connecting the IP hops' locations in Figs. 3(a)–3(d)

3.2   Impacts of the Cable Repair

In this section, we analyze the impact of the four-day (25–28 April 2010) repair of the SEA-ME-WE 4 cable on the routing behavior and path performance. Figs. 5(a) and 5(b) show the respective time series of the average IP-level Jaccard distance (at the top of each figure) for the ENG3 and BBC paths and the RTTs for UB⇌ENG3 and UB⇌BBC between 23–30 April which is labeled as the second episode (e_2) in Fig. 1(a). We do not include the time series for the NOKIA paths, because they are similar to ENG3's. Moreover, the path performance for the other measuring nodes to ENG3 (BBC) also resembles the performance given in Fig. 5(a) (5(b)). To correlate the forward-path routing behavior with the path performance, each figure only shows the loss pairs and both-packet-loss events (i.e., P01 and P11) observed from the forward paths. Note that the ENG3 paths remained in phase (c) during the entire period, whereas the BBC paths switched from phase (d) to phase (e), which involves a significant route change, and then back to phase (d).

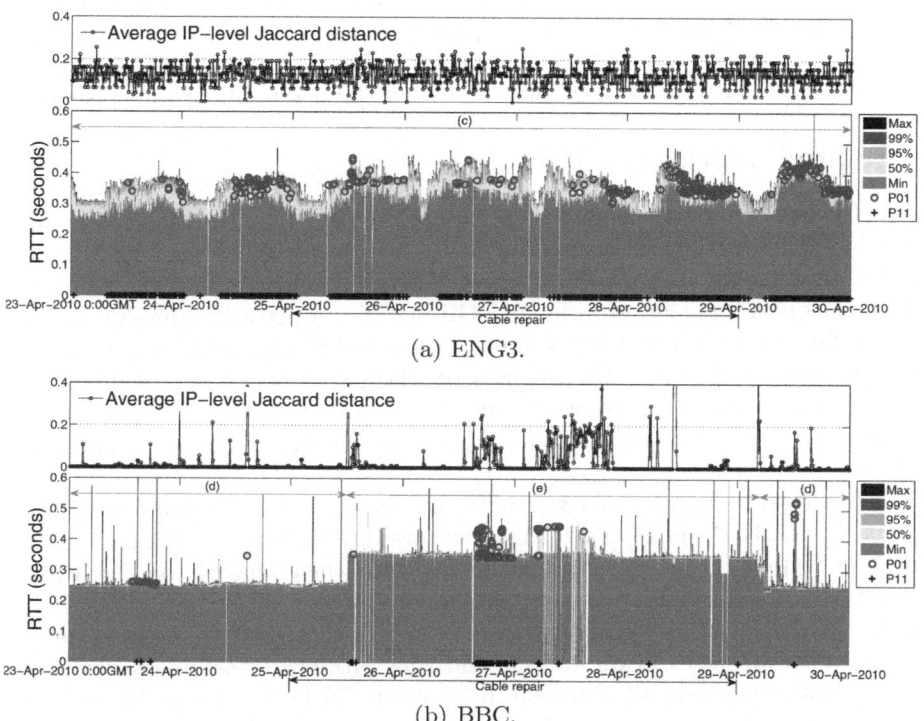

(a) ENG3.

(b) BBC.

Fig. 5. Time series of the average IP-level Jaccard distance for the paths to ENG3 and BBC, and the time series of RTT for UB⇌ENG3 and UB⇌BBC during e_2.

Fig. 5(a) shows that the ENG3 (and also NOKIA) paths suffered from diurnal congestion in e_2. Traceroutes show that the NOKIA and ENG3 paths still went through the FLAG subpaths shown in Fig. 3(b) and 3(c), respectively, for the entire episode. As a result, both the RTT and Jaccard distance time series exhibit similar patterns as in phases (b)–(c) of Fig. 2. The paths also encountered more severe congestion since 25 April when the SEA-ME-WE 4 cable's repair process began. It is thus likely that the FLAG subpaths were further utilized by other affected parties as alternate routes during the repair process. However, FLAG's network operators did not seem to respond to the degraded path performance until they switched to eastbound routes on 5 May noon GMT (which is shown in Fig. 1(a)), and the path performance was subsequently improved.

Fig. 5(b), on the other hand, shows that the BBC paths were quite good during e_2 except for sporadic packet losses and routing instability. In particular, at the beginning of the episode, the paths still went through TATA which routed the BBC traffic via the subpath given in Fig. 3(d). Probably due to the interruption caused by the repair work [2], TATA rerouted the traffic to another set of subpaths with longer RTTs on 25 April 13:30 GMT, and we refer to this period as phase (e). We can also see a positive correlation between fluctuation in the IP-level Jaccard distance and significant forward-path packet losses during phase (e). TATA finally restored the subpath in Fig. 3(d) on 29 April 6:00 GMT (which is close to the completion time of the repair), and therefore the path performance returned to the level observed from the beginning of the episode.

4   Related Work

RIPE NCC [10] reported a longitudinal study of cable cuts in the Mediterranean in 2008 based on its routing information (RIS), test traffic measurements (TTM), and DNS monitoring (DNSMON) services. The study showed that the affected networks involved frequent rerouting in BGP, significant network congestion, and increased latencies. In our study, we mainly use end-to-end path measurement and IP traceroute to study the impacts on the paths under our monitoring. Based on a set of measuring points, we are able to infer that the path congestion was due to the secondary effect of the cable fault, which has not been reported in previous studies.

Renesys [7] also reported a few studies on the impacts of submarine cable faults based on BGP routes and RTTs (measured by traceroute) obtained from its data collection infrastructure. Comparing with their analysis on the same SEA-ME-WE 4 cable fault [12], our methodology uses TCP data packets to measure the data-path performance, instead of ICMP packets that can be processed by different paths in the routers and thus produce biased measurement. Therefore, our measurement observed quite stable RTTs for the paths via the TATA network, whereas Renesys observed significant RTT fluctuation from the TATA network in the similar time period. Besides, our analysis also obtains useful packet loss information that was not considered in their analysis.

5   Conclusion and Future Work

In this paper, we employed non-cooperative path measurement to study the impacts of a recent submarine cable fault on the Internet connectivity and end-to-end path performance. With only eight measurement nodes, we showed that the non-cooperative methods (HTTP/OneProbe and traceroute) could facilitate an in-depth impact analysis of a cable fault occurred thousands miles away. In particular, our analysis revealed that a cable fault could significantly impact on

Internet traffic on other non-faulty paths. Moreover, network operators did not always take immediate action to resolve the performance degradation problem as a result of the cable fault.

As an ongoing work, we will report our impact analysis of other submarine cable faults, such as a SEACOM cable fault in Africa in July 2010. We will also devise new algorithms based on non-cooperative path measurement to promptly identify and respond to path-quality degradation as a result of cable faults.

Acknowledgments

We thank the four reviewers for their comments and Aleksandar Kuzmanovic for shepherding our paper. This work is partially supported by a grant (ref. no. ITS/355/09) from the Innovation Technology Fund in Hong Kong and a grant (ref. no. H-ZL17) from the Joint Universities Computer Centre of Hong Kong.

References

1. Asia communications hit by quake,
   http://news.bbc.co.uk/2/hi/asia-pacific/6211451.stm
2. Beyond the SEACOM network disruptions,
   http://www.seacomblog.com/team-seacom/2010/05/
   beyond-seacom-network-disruptions-april-2010
3. Cable outage (July 5, 2010),
   http://www.seacom.mu/news/news_details.asp?iID=142
4. Fujitsu completes construction of SEA-ME-WE 4 submarine cable network,
   http://www.fujitsu.com/global/news/pr/archives/month/2005/20051213-01.html
5. Global footprint map - Tata Communications,
   http://tatacommunications.com/map/gfp.html
6. Reliance Globalcom,
   http://www.relianceglobalcom.com/RGCOM_CoverageMap.html
7. Renesys - presentations & reports,
   http://www.renesys.com/tech/presentations/
8. SEA-ME-WE 4, http://www.seamewe4.com/
9. SEA-ME-WE 4 maintenance finally over,
   http://sushantwagle.wordpress.com/2010/04/30/se-me-we-4-maintenance-finally-ov
10. Mediterranean fibre cable cut - a RIPE NCC analysis (April 2008),
    http://www.ripe.net/projects/reports/2008cable-cut/index.html
11. Middle East bandwidth pricing report (October 2009),
    http://www.telegeography.com/product-info/pricingdb/download/bpr-2009-10.pdf
12. Bahrain's Internet ecosystem revisited (July 2010),
    http://renesys.com/tech/reports/Renesys-Bahrain-July2010.pdf
13. Chan, E., Luo, X., Li, W., Fok, W., Chang, R.: Measurement of loss pairs in network paths. In: Proc. ACM/USENIX IMC (2010)
14. Chang, R., Fok, W., Li, W., Chan, E., Luo, X.: Neighbor-Cooperative measurement of network path quality. In: Proc. IEEE Globecom (2010)
15. Harasawa, S., Sumitani, M., Ohta, K.: Reliability technology for submarine repeaters. Fujitsu Scientific & Technical Journal (FSTJ): Quality Assurance 44(2), 148–155 (2008)

16. Hodge, K., Vinson, J., Haigh, N., Knight, I.: Reliability of optical fibres: impact on cable design. In: IEE Colloquium on Reliability of Fibre Optic Cable Systems, pp. 1/1 –1/6 (January 1994)
17. Luo, X., Chan, E., Chang, R.: Design and implementation of TCP data probes for reliable and metric-rich network path monitoring. In: Proc. USENIX Annual Tech. Conf. (2009)
18. Pathak, A., Pucha, H., Zhang, Y., Hu, Y., Mao, Z.: A measurement study of internet delay asymmetry. In: Claypool, M., Uhlig, S. (eds.) PAM 2008. LNCS, vol. 4979, pp. 182–191. Springer, Heidelberg (2008)
19. Schwartz, Y., Shavitt, Y., Weinsberg, U.: A measurement study of the origins of end-to-end delay variations. In: Krishnamurthy, A., Plattner, B. (eds.) PAM 2010. LNCS, vol. 6032, pp. 21–30. Springer, Heidelberg (2010)

Measuring and Characterizing End-to-End Route Dynamics in the Presence of Load Balancing

Ítalo Cunha[1,2], Renata Teixeira[2,3], and Christophe Diot[1]

[1] Technicolor
[2] UPMC Sorbonne Universités
[3] CNRS

Abstract. Since Paxson's study over ten years ago, the Internet has changed considerably. In particular, routers often perform load balancing. Disambiguating routing changes from load balancing using traceroute-like probing requires a large number of probes. Our first contribution is *FastMapping*, a probing method that exploits load balancing characteristics to reduce the number of probes needed to measure accurate route dynamics. Our second contribution is to reappraise Paxson's results using datasets with high-frequency route measurements and complete load balancing information. Our analysis shows that, after removing dynamics due to load balancing, Paxson's observations on route prevalence and persistence still hold.

1 Introduction

Our current understanding of end-to-end Internet route dynamics comes mainly from the seminal work of Paxson [11] more than ten years ago. Paxson used traceroute measurements to study routing anomalies, route persistence, and route prevalence in the Internet. Since then, there have been only partial updates to his results [4, 15, 12], even though the Internet has changed significantly and new traffic engineering practices, such as load balancing, multihoming, and tunneling, are now commonplace.

This paper studies the effect of load balancing on the accuracy of measuring route dynamics. While Paxson identified just few examples of routes that oscillated because of load balancing (which he called route fluttering), Augustin et. al. [1] have recently observed that approximately 40% of the source-destination pairs measured in their study were subject to route fluttering because of load balancing.

Load balancing increases the complexity of measuring route dynamics. It introduces route changes that are not due to routing events, but could be misinterpreted as such. Moreover, detecting load balancing requires additional probes [14], which in turn reduces the frequency at which one can measure routes. Current techniques that reduce probing cost and increase the frequency of traceroute measurements [3, 6] are oblivious to load balancing. Sec. 3 quantifies the effect of load balancing on route dynamics using datasets collected with these two extreme approaches: complete load balancing information (at the cost of high probing overhead) and high frequency probing (at the cost misinterpreting load balancing). We show that ignoring load balancers leads to one order of magnitude more observed route changes.

Given the popularity and impact of load balancing, we then analyze the dynamics of routers that perform load balancing (which we name "load balancers"). Our results

N. Spring and G. Riley (Eds.): PAM 2011, LNCS 6579, pp. 235–244, 2011.

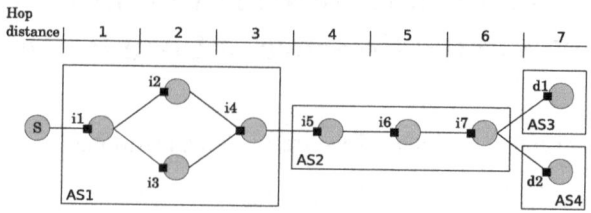

Fig. 1. Multiroutes to d_1 and d_2 at time t_1 traversing a load balancer at i_1

show that only 4% of load balancers need to be remapped more frequently than once a day (Sec. 4). We exploit this property to design a new probing strategy that we call *FastMapping*. FastMapping combines frequent light-weight route probing with daily remapping of load balancers. As a result, it increases the route-probing frequency by a factor of five while maintaining accurate load balancing information.

Last, we confirm Paxson's observations on route prevalence and persistence (Sec. 5). When removing the effects of load balancing, we observe that the properties of Internet routes have not changed in a decade. In summary, many source-destination pairs rarely change routes; most of them have a prevalent route that stays active at least 60% of the time, and suffer from short-lived instability periods 4% of the time.

2   Definitions

This section introduces the notation and explains how we compute route changes.

Routes and virtual paths. We borrow Paxson's terminology [11] and use the term *virtual path* to refer to the connectivity between a monitor and a destination, d, (i.e., the existence of a route between the monitor and d). At any point in time, a virtual path is realized by a *route*, which is the sequence of interfaces from the monitor to d discovered by traceroute. A virtual path changes from one route to another over time as the result of routing changes.

Classic traceroute assumes a single route between a source and a destination. However, load balancing is now common practice [1]. In Fig. 1, the router at i_1 forwards packets to d_1 and d_2 via interfaces i_2 or i_3 to perform load balancing. A traceroute to d_1 or d_2 may infer the route through i_2 and a later traceroute may infer the route through i_3, even though there was no routing change between the two measurements. Routers perform load balancing per packet, per flow or per destination. Per-destination load balancing sends all packets to a given destination on the same route, so only per-packet or per-flow load balancing lead to multiple routes between two end-hosts. We define a load balancer's *divergence* interface as the interface immediately before the multi-interface hops (i_1), and the *convergence* interface as immediately after (i_4).

Instead of assuming a virtual path is realized by a single route at a time, we define a *multiroute* $\mathcal{R}(d, t)$ as the set of all possible routes between the monitor and destination d at time t. We can measure multiple routes between a source and a destination using Paris traceroute's *Multipath Detection Algorithm* (MDA) [14]. We refer to the set of interfaces in the hth hop of a multiroute by $\mathcal{R}(d, t)[h]$, e.g., $\mathcal{R}(d_1, t_1)[2] = \{i_2, i_3\}$. In

Fig. 1, the top ruler shows the hop count h. For simplicity, the rest of this paper uses the term *route* to refer to all simultaneous routes between the monitor and a destination.

Route changes. Given two consecutive routes between a monitor and a destination (say $\mathcal{R}(d, t_1)$ and $\mathcal{R}(d, t_2)$, respectively at time t_1 and t_2), a *route change* represents a contiguous set of interfaces that differs between these two routes. If there are multiple sets of contiguous interfaces that differ between two routes, we consider each as one route change. We say that $\mathcal{R}(d, t_1)[h] = \mathcal{R}(d, t_2)[h]$ if the sets of interfaces at hop h are the same. We match unresponsive routers in our traces (i.e., traceroute "stars") with any interface. This conservative approach avoids detecting route changes due to lost probes or routers that rate-limit traceroutes, but it may miss some route changes. We remove all routes containing repeated interfaces from our analysis in later sections to avoid bias due to measurement errors, as in previous studies [11, 15].

3 Route Dynamics: Fast vs. Complete Measurements

Techniques to measure route dynamics have two conflicting goals. First, the study of fine-grained dynamics requires frequent measurements of a large set of virtual paths. Second, accurate identification of route changes needs information about load balancing, which requires a large number of probes [14]. This section explores this tradeoff using two state-of-the-art route tracing methods: Tracetree [6] and Paris traceroute's Multipath Detection Algorithm [14].

3.1 Measurement Method and Datasets

Fast tracing. Tracetree [6] reduces the overhead to probe all hops in a topology. It starts probing from the set of destinations and decrements the probe TTL. When probes to different destinations discover the same interface, Tracetree keeps probing only one destination. Such backward probing strategy reduces redundant probes close to the monitor.

Complete tracing. Paris traceroute's Multipath Detection Algorithm (MDA) [14] discovers all routes between a source and a destination in the presence of load balancing with high probability. Paris traceroute fixes the flow identifier of probes to ensure all probes follow the same route under per-flow and per-destination load balancing. In addition, MDA varies the flow identifier systematically to enumerate all interfaces in load balancers. However, mapping load balancers requires a large number of probes per hop (at least six probes per hop, but up to hundreds depending on the number of interfaces).

Dataset. We use Tracetree and MDA to measure virtual paths from 23 PlanetLab hosts during seven days starting August 9th, 2010. Monitors collect two topology maps during each measurement round: one with Tracetree and another with MDA. Each measurement round takes 28 minutes on average: the first 25 minutes are used by MDA and the last three by Tracetree. We denote the traces collected with Tracetree as $\mathcal{D}_T$ and those collected with MDA as $\mathcal{D}_1$ and summarize them in Tab. 1.

We also have an earlier dataset collected with MDA and complete load balancer information, denoted $\mathcal{D}_2$. The advantage of $\mathcal{D}_2$ is that it was collected from more

Table 1. Description of datasets

Dataset	Start	Duration	Monitors	Frequency	ASes Covered	Large ASes Covered [10]	Measurement Method
$\mathcal{D}_T$	Aug. 9th, 2010	1 week	23	28 min.	5,043	95%	Tracetree
$\mathcal{D}_1$	Aug. 9th, 2010	1 week	23	28 min.	5,266	95%	Paris' MDA
$\mathcal{D}_2$	Nov. 28th, 2009	13 weeks	122	38 min.	8,692	97%	Paris' MDA

monitors and for a longer period of time. We did not collect Tracetree measurements while collecting $\mathcal{D}_2$, hence we compare MDA and Tracetree using $\mathcal{D}_1$. We use $\mathcal{D}_2$ to study long-term route dynamics.

Except for the measurement method and the parameters in Tab. 1, we collect all our datasets with the same configuration: each monitor selects 1,000 destinations at random from a list of 34,820 randomly chosen reachable destinations, and we use ICMP probes as routers are more likely to respond to ICMP than to TCP or UDP [8]. We complement our datasets with IP-to-AS maps built from Team Cymru[1] and UCLA's IRL [10].

3.2 Analysis

We identify route changes between every pair of consecutive route measurements in $\mathcal{D}_T$ and $\mathcal{D}_1$ as described in Sec. 2. We remove 4.0% of routes from $\mathcal{D}_T$ and 1.8% of routes from $\mathcal{D}_1$ that contain repeated interfaces. Fig. 2 shows the cumulative distribution function of the fraction of virtual paths that change between each pair of consecutive measurement rounds in $\mathcal{D}_T$ and $\mathcal{D}_1$. The $\mathcal{D}_1$ curve shows that the topology is mostly stable: less than 6% of the virtual paths change between 95% of consecutive measurement rounds. Only rarely more than 20% of virtual paths change between maps, and all these instances represent events that happened close to the source.

The difference between $\mathcal{D}_T$ and $\mathcal{D}_1$ is striking. For $\mathcal{D}_T$, there are approximately 76% of consecutive measurements for which more than 20% of virtual paths change. We attribute this difference to the measurement technique itself. MDA detects load balancers explicitly and none of the route changes for $\mathcal{D}_1$ in Fig. 2 are due to load balancing. However, Tracetree is oblivious to load balancing and interprets load balancing as route changes.

We use the load balancer information collected with MDA to filter out all route changes in $\mathcal{D}_T$ due to load balancing ("filtered $\mathcal{D}_T$" line in Fig. 2). We see that load balancers induce most of the dynamics in $\mathcal{D}_T$ (82% of route changes). However, even after filtering, $\mathcal{D}_T$ still has more route changes than $\mathcal{D}_1$. This happens because Tracetree's assumption that the Internet topology is a tree is not always satisfied. For example, routes to multiple destinations may meet at an Internet exchange point (IXP) and still traverse different ASes upstream and downstream this IXP. Whenever the assumption is false, Tracetree infers inexistent links and incorrect routes. Other causes for the difference include *mapping errors*, i.e., when the MDA's probabilistic characterization of load balancers fails to identify all interfaces in a load-balanced hop [14]. Such errors impact our ability to filter dynamics induced by load balancers from $\mathcal{D}_T$.

---

[1] http://www.team-cymru.org/Services/ip-to-asn.html

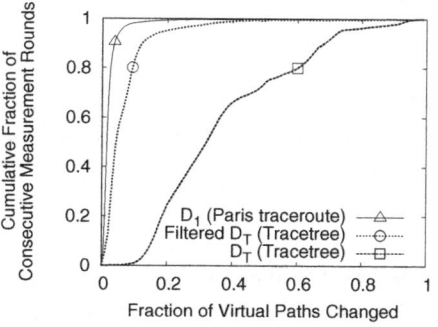

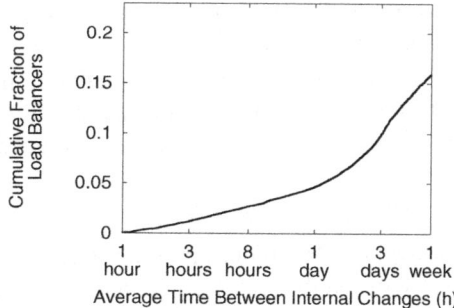

Fig. 2. Virtual path dynamics between two consecutive measurement rounds

Fig. 3. Average time between internal changes in load balancers

4 Measuring Route Dynamics under Load Balancing

Our goal is to reduce the time to perform a measurement round and yet maintain accurate information about load balancers, so that we can distinguish routing changes from load balancer dynamics. We start with an analysis of load balancer dynamics that motivates our probing method.

4.1 Analysis of Load Balancer Dynamics

To maintain an accurate database of load balancers, we need to detect and map load balancers when they first appear in a dataset. After we map all interfaces between the divergence and convergence points of a load balancer, we only need to remap it when it experiences an internal change. We define an *internal change* as a change in the set of interfaces between the divergence and convergence points of a load balancer. Internal changes may represent failures of one of the load-balanced interfaces, load balancer reconfigurations, or mapping errors. Mapping errors are infrequent (4% of MDA runs miss an interface [14]), but show up as internal changes in our analysis. As a result, the internal changes we report next are an upper bound on the real number of internal changes experienced by load balancers during the measurement period.

We use our longer D_2 dataset to study load balancer dynamics. We remove 1.9% of route measurements from D_2 that contain repeated interfaces. D_2 has 535,517 internal changes, which gives an average of one internal change per load balancer every 20 days. Given that D_2 has 85,553,799 MDA measurements with load balancers, the number of internal changes we see is within the MDA's mapping error probability of 4% [14]. In D_2, only 23% of load balancers experience internal changes. Fig. 3 shows the distribution of the average time between internal changes. Very few load balancers experience frequent internal changes. Specifically, only 4.6% of load balancers experience internal changes more frequently than once every day. Among these 4.6% load balancers, 40% span more than 4 hops and 16% perform non-uniform balancing (i.e., split packets unevenly among its next hops). These non-uniform and long load balancers are more likely to suffer from mapping errors [14]. We get similar results from our D_1 dataset: 27% of load balancers experience internal changes and 3.8% experience internal changes more frequently than once every day. If there were no mapping errors, we would see even less internal changes.

These results show that it is possible to maintain an accurate database of load balancers without remapping load balancers frequently and that remapping load balancers once a day is enough to account for internal changes.

4.2 Probing Strategy

We design FastMapping, a probing strategy to measure route dynamics that exploits the observations in the previous section to maintain an accurate database of load balancers with low overhead. FastMapping operates in three main steps:

Create load balancer database. When FastMapping starts, it runs MDA on all monitored virtual paths to populate the load balancer database. For each interface identified with MDA, FastMapping records whether it is the convergence or divergence point of a load balancer, one interface in a multi-interface hop inside a load balancer, or unrelated to load balancing. After building the database of load balancers, FastMapping performs periodic measurement rounds. Each round has two main steps as follows.

Fast route measurements. FastMapping probes all monitored virtual paths periodically to check for route changes. To minimize probing overhead, we turn off MDA and modify Paris traceroute to send a single probe per hop until it reaches the destination. We send one probe per TTL up to TTL 30 spaced by 50ms, and stop as soon as we receive an answer from the destination. We space probes by 50ms instead of waiting for the answer at each hop to reduce the probing time and the probability that a failure or route change will happen while Paris traceroute traces a route. We minimize the number of unresponsive hops by retransmitting timed-out probes up to three times.

Update load balancer database. FastMapping uses the database of load balancers to verify for each observed interface whether it was already seen in past measurements with MDA. If the interface is new (usually few), FastMapping uses MDA to remap the route and update the load balancer database. FastMapping forces periodic updates to the database of load balancers by removing entries older than 24 hours.

This probing strategy guarantees that all probes in a virtual path follow the same route unless there is a route change. The load balancer database allows us to identify cases of per-packet load balancing and disregard them when computing route changes. Finally, any new interface seen in the fast route measurements—due to, e.g., routing changes, new load balancers, or an internal change—triggers an execution of MDA so FastMapping can differentiate between route changes and load balancing.

We compare the route dynamics seen with FastMapping with that observed by MDA using trace-driven simulations. We use $\mathcal{D}_2$ as basis and compute what FastMapping would see. We find 10,013,958 route changes using complete load balancer information from MDA and 9,822,372 route changes using FastMapping, i.e., only 1.9% less changes. This small difference is due to either MDA mapping errors or transient changes. For example, 40% of the missed changes happen in measurement rounds where a load balancer disappears for only one round. FastMapping misses these changes because undetected load balancers are still present in FastMapping's database of load balancers, so FastMapping attributes the differences to load balancing instead of route changes. In this trace-driven comparison, FastMapping can at most detect all route changes seen in $\mathcal{D}_2$. In practice, however, FastMapping probes faster than MDA, so it should detect more transient route changes (as we confirm in Sec. 5).

4.3   Dataset

We use FastMapping to collect a dataset, denoted $\mathcal{D}_3$, from 70 PlanetLab nodes for five weeks starting September 1st, 2010. We use the same destination list and ICMP probes as in $\mathcal{D}_1$ and $\mathcal{D}_2$. Due to FastMapping's probing strategy, $\mathcal{D}_3$ has much higher probing frequency than $\mathcal{D}_1$ and $\mathcal{D}_2$, taking only 4.4 minutes on average to perform a measurement round. We remove 2.1% of route measurements from $\mathcal{D}_3$ that contain repeated interfaces. $\mathcal{D}_3$ traverses 7,842 ASes and 97% of the large ASes [10].

5   Route Prevalence and Persistence

We use $\mathcal{D}_2$ and $\mathcal{D}_3$ to study Internet route dynamics. We reappraise Paxson's previous results on route persistence and prevalence [11] with our recent datasets. $\mathcal{D}_2$ probes 115 times more virtual paths than Paxson's original dataset, and $\mathcal{D}_3$ probes 66 times more virtual paths. In addition, $\mathcal{D}_2$ and $\mathcal{D}_3$ have more frequent route measurements.

Route persistence. Route persistence identifies how long a route remains stable before it changes. The challenge is to know whether a route A measured at times t_1 and t_2 remained stable between t_1 and t_2. If route A changed to B then back to A between t_1 and t_2, then we missed a route change.

Paxson spaced his route measurements using a Poisson process. Although Paxson did not have frequent measurements, the Poisson process enabled him to study route changes at small time scales and compute the probability of missing route changes. In our datasets, we substitute the Poisson probing process with high-frequency periodic measurements that allow the study of persistence at finer time scales. Except for this difference, we follow the same methodology as Paxson: We start by removing very unstable routes from our datasets, and then estimate the probability of missing a route change in the remaining routes. We filter from our dataset virtual paths where we are more likely to miss route changes: We remove 288 (0.4%) virtual paths that change more frequently than once every 20 minutes. Causes for frequent route changes include undetected load balancers, dynamically-allocated IP addresses, and coarse-grained load balancing in server farms. In the remaining virtual paths, the probability of a route changing between two consecutive measurements is small (0.5%). We expect the probability of having two or more route changes between two measurements (and thus missing route changes) to be even less. Moreover, we only report long route durations when the same route is measured repeatedly. These factors give us confidence that long-lived routes are indeed stable.

Fig. 4 shows the cumulative distribution of route durations for every route in $\mathcal{D}_2$ and $\mathcal{D}_3$. We cut the x-axis at 10 hours to focus on the body of the distribution, but some routes last over the entire datasets. We observe that most routes are short-lived, which indicates that virtual paths are rapidly changing routes. Moreover, it shows that measuring virtual paths every 38 minutes is not enough to accurately capture route dynamics: $\mathcal{D}_2$ misses 36% of route changes that last less than 38 minutes when compared to $\mathcal{D}_3$.

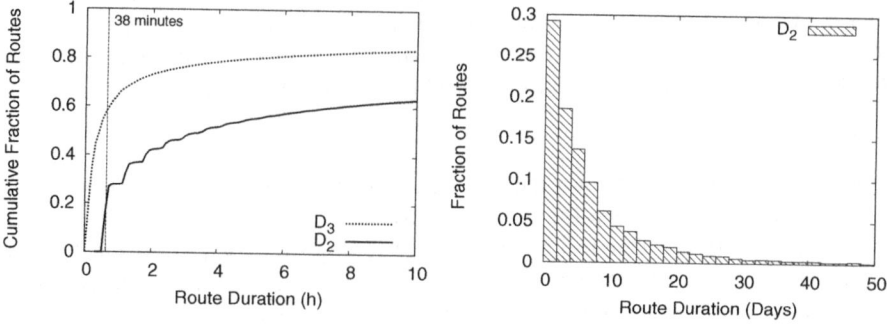

Fig. 4. Persistence of short routes   **Fig. 5.** Persistence of long routes

Although the number of short-lived routes is larger than the number of long-lived routes, the fraction of time virtual paths spend in short-lived routes is small. In $\mathcal{D}_3$, virtual paths spend 96% of the time in routes longer than 6 hours, similar to Paxson's findings [11]. In other words, virtual paths are mostly stable but go through "instability periods" with multiple route changes happening within a short time period. The $\mathcal{D}_3$ line in Fig. 4 shows that 40% of consecutive route changes happen within 15 minutes of each other. Such instability periods with similar characteristics are also reported by Paxson [11] and Feamster et al. [4].

Fig. 5 shows the distribution of route durations longer than 12 hours from our longer $\mathcal{D}_2$ dataset. Results for $\mathcal{D}_3$ (not shown) are similar but skewed towards shorter routes because the dataset lasts only 5 weeks. Our observations are again similar to Paxson's [11], with some differences that we discuss below. Paxson found that long-lived routes could be split in two broad classes: 50% of routes that persist for 1-7 days and 50% that persist for weeks. These two classes were motivated by a sharp knee in his distribution of long-lived route durations at seven days. Our distribution does not have such a sharp knee and it is impossible to identify two classes of stable routes. We believe this difference comes from our larger dataset and higher probing frequency that allows us to detect more route changes. It could also be due to the different set of monitored virtual paths.

Route prevalence. We study the fraction of time a virtual path stays in its *prevalent route*, i.e., the route that most frequently realizes the virtual path. Fig. 6 shows the distribution of the fraction of time a virtual path uses its prevalent route in $\mathcal{D}_3$ ("whole dataset" line). Similar to Paxson [11], we find that 62% of virtual paths have a route that stays active during at least 60% of the time.

Paxson's original definition of prevalence only looked at the route that was prevalent over the whole dataset. We extend Paxson's results and study whether prevalent routes change over time, and for how long they stay prevalent. We study prevalent routes in time windows varying from three days to the whole dataset. Fig. 6 also shows the distribution of the fraction of time a virtual path uses the prevalent route for different time windows (dashed lines). The smaller the time window, the more often virtual paths are in the prevalent route, confirming that prevalent routes change over time. We use $\mathcal{D}_2$, to study the long-term behavior of prevalent routes. We find that for a window of 2 weeks,

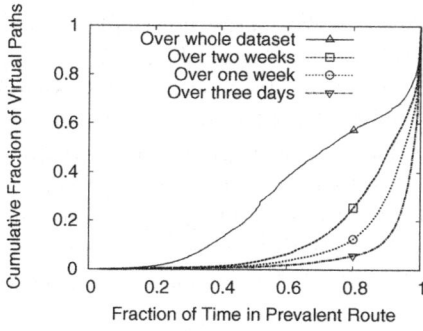

Fig. 6. Route prevalence

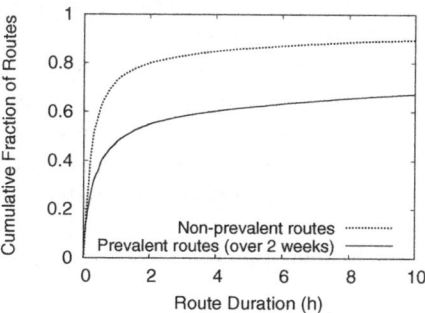

Fig. 7. Persistence of prevalent routes

77% of virtual paths have prevalent routes that stay prevalent for more than one month, and only 14% of paths have a single prevalent route throughout the 13 weeks in $\mathcal{D}_2$.

Fig. 7 shows the distribution of route durations for routes prevalent over a window of two weeks and for non-prevalent routes. It shows that prevalent routes are less likely to have short durations: while 85% of non-prevalent routes have durations shorter than four hours, this fraction is only 60% for prevalent routes. This result suggests that information about whether a route is prevalent is a good indicator of path stability.

6 Related Work

Topology mapping. Techniques such as Tracetree [6] (which we evaluate in Sec. 3), its predecessor DoubleTree [3], and more recently the dynamic destination selection technique of Beverly et. al [2] reduce redundant probes and consequently increase the frequency of topology mapping. None of these techniques explicitly handles load balancers. As a result, they cannot disambiguate routing changes from load balancing as we do with FastMapping. Paris traceroute's MDA explicitly identifies load balancing, but at the cost of large probing overhead [14]. FastMapping represents a tradeoff between these approaches: it achieves fast probing with daily updates of load balancers. FastMapping can be directly applied to large-scale topology mapping projects such as CAIDA's Skitter/Ark [5], DIMES [13], or iPlane [9].

Characterization of route dynamics. Since 1997, few studies have reported some characteristics of the location of route changes [4, 15], but there has been no reappraisal of Paxson's work on end-to-end route dynamics. Most related to our characterization of route dynamics is the recent work by Schwartz et. al [12]. This work uses traceroutes collected by DIMES to study the persistence and prevalence of end-to-end routes, among other properties. Their probing method is oblivious to load balancing, so they cannot differentiate route dynamics from load balancing. For a discussion of BGP dynamics, we refer the reader to the work of Li et. al [7] (and references within).

7 Conclusion

The study of end-to-end Internet route dynamics requires high probing frequency. Unfortunately, the cost of mapping load balancers to disambiguate routing changes from load balancing reduces considerably probing frequency. We address this challenge with FastMapping. Based on the observation that load balancers are stable, FastMapping remaps load balancers when a change is detected and updates them once per day. We use FastMapping to measure route dynamics from PlanetLab for five weeks. The comparison of our observations to Paxson's [11] shows that despite the growth of the Internet and the introduction of new traffic engineering practices, route persistence and prevalence have not changed significantly. Although we use FastMapping to perform high-frequency probing and study route dynamics, FastMapping's probing strategy can also be used to decrease probing overhead while keeping the probing frequency constant.

Acknowledgements. This work was supported by the European Community's 7th Framework Programme (FP7/2007-2013) no. 223850 (NaDa) and the ANR project C'MON.

References

1. Augustin, B., Friedman, T., Teixeira, R.: Measuring Load-balanced Paths in the Internet. In: Proc. IMC (2007)
2. Beverly, R., Berger, A., Xie, G.: Primitives for Active Internet Topology Mapping: Toward High-Frequency Characterization. In: Proc. IMC (2010)
3. Donnet, B., Raoult, P., Friedman, T., Crovella, M.: Efficient Algorithms for Large-scale Topology Discovery. In: Proc. ACM SIGMETRICS (2005)
4. Feamster, N., Andersen, D., Balakrishnan, H., Kaashoek, M.: Measuring the Effects of Internet Path Faults on Reactive Routing. In: Proc. ACM SIGMETRICS (2003)
5. Claffy, K., Hyun, Y., Keys, K., Fomenkov, M., Krioukov, D.: Internet Mapping: from Art to Science. In: Proc. IEEE CATCH (2009)
6. Latapy, M., Magnien, C., Ouédraogo, F.: A Radar for the Internet. In: Proc. First Inter. Workshop on Analysis of Dynamic Networks (2008)
7. Li, J., Guidero, M., Wu, Z., Purpus, E., Ehrenkranz, T.: BGP Routing Dynamics Revisited. SIGCOMM Comput. Commun. Rev. 37(2), 5–16 (2007)
8. Luckie, M., Hyun, Y., Huffaker, B.: Traceroute Probe Method and Forward IP Path Inference. In: Proc. IMC (2008)
9. Madhyastha, H., Isdal, T., Piatek, M., Dixon, C., Anderson, T., Krishnamurthy, A., Venkataramani, A.: iPlane: an Information Plane for Distributed Services. In: Proc. USENIX OSDI (2006)
10. Oliveira, R., Pei, D., Willinger, W., Zhang, B., Zhang, L.: The (in)completeness of the Observed Internet AS-level Structure. IEEE/ACM Trans. Netw. 18(1), 109–122 (2010)
11. Paxson, V.: End-to-end Routing Behavior in the Internet. IEEE/ACM Trans. on Netw. 5(5), 601–615 (1997)
12. Schwartz, Y., Shavitt, Y., Weinsberg, U.: On the Diversity, Stability and Symmetry of End-to-End Internet Routes. In: Proc. of Global Internet (2010)
13. Shavitt, Y., Shir, E.: DIMES: Let the Internet Measure Itself. SIGCOMM Comput. Commun. Rev. 35(5), 71–74 (2005)
14. Veitch, D., Augustin, B., Friedman, T., Teixeira, R.: Failure Control in Multipath Route Tracing. In: Proc. IEEE INFOCOM (2009)
15. Zhang, M., Zhang, C., Pai, V., Peterson, L., Wang, R.: PlanetSeer: Internet Path Failure Monitoring and Characterization in Wide-area Services. In: Proc. USENIX OSDI (2004)

Author Index

GPSR Compliance

The European Union's (EU) General Product Safety Regulation (GPSR)
is a set of rules that requires consumer products to be safe and our
obligations to ensure this.

If you have any concerns about our products, you can contact us on
ProductSafety@springernature.com

In case Publisher is established outside the EU, the EU authorized
representative is:

Springer Nature Customer Service Center GmbH
Europaplatz 3
69115 Heidelberg, Germany

Batch number: 09493398

Printed by Printforce, the Netherlands